D1256624

Critical Essays on
Charlotte Brontë

Critical Essays on
Charlotte Brontë

Barbara Timm Gates

G.K. Hall & Co. • Boston, Massachusetts

Copyright 1990 by Barbara Timm Gates
All rights reserved.

Library of Congress Cataloging in Publication Data

Critical essays on Charlotte Brontë / [compiled by] Barbara Timm
  Gates.
    p. cm. — (Critical essays on British literature)
  Includes Index.
  ISBN 0-8161-8772-X (alk. paper)
  1. Brontë, Charlotte, 1816–1855 — Criticism and interpretation.
I. Gates, Barbara T., 1936–   . II. Series.
PR4169.C75   1989   89-15647
823'.8 — dc20   CIP

This publication is printed on permanent/durable acid-free paper
MANUFACTURED IN THE UNITED STATES OF AMERICA

CRITICAL ESSAYS ON
BRITISH LITERATURE

The Critical Essays on British Literature series provides a variety of approaches to both classical and contemporary writers of Britain and Ireland. The formats of the volumes in the series vary with the thematic designs of individual editors, and with the amount and nature of existing reviews, criticism, and scholarship. In general, the series represents the best in published criticism, augmented, where appropriate, by original essays by recognized authorities. It is hoped that each volume will be unique in developing a new overall perspective on its particular subject.

Barbara Gates has completed the first volume of critical essays on all of Charlotte Brontë's fiction, including her four novels and juvenilia. In her introduction as well as her selection and criticism, Gates traces the shifts of critical perspective from its early preoccupation with biographical affinities between the author and her work, through the formalist critical period, with its emphasis on structure and imagery, to the more recent reemphasis on the social and personal aspects of Brontë's time and background as elucidated by Marxist and feminist critics and contemporary critical theory.

Gates's introduction to the volume provides a clear chart of the main critical paths taken during the last 140 years, with emphasis on individual influential studies and the trends they inspired, and culminates with a perceptive analysis of contemporary feminist critical tendencies.

ZACK BOWEN, GENERAL EDITOR

University of Miami

To the enduring sound of the Bells

CONTENTS

INTRODUCTION

Wiping the dust from over 140 years of criticism involving Charlotte Brontë makes one as aware of the museum of literary criticism as it does of the enduring subtlety of Brontë's work. Since the publication of *Jane Eyre* in 1847, Brontë has never lacked critical attention. Her four novels and, in recent decades, her juvenilia have attracted proponents of every sort of criticism. Like most writers, Brontë has fared better at the hands of some than of others. In general Brontë's critics have reflected the larger, almost circular sweep of critical history. As the nineteenth century with its bias toward biographical criticism closed, the twentieth century saw both the rise and fall of formalist criticism and a proliferation of alternatives to formalism that invalidated the possibility of definitive readings and revalidated the personal viewpoint. The result has been a shift of critical focus from Brontë's life, to her texts, and then to reader responses sometimes as subjective and idiosyncratic as those of Brontë's first critics.

Her first critics were generally kind. Brontë's reputation with her contemporaries was determined by the reception of just three novels: *Jane Eyre* (1847), *Shirley* (1849), and *Villette* (1853). *The Professor* (1857), her first novel, was rejected by six publishers and only published post-humously. But *Jane Eyre* was highly acclaimed for its freshness, vigor, and passion, although the last quality also stimulated a few negative reviews. Early critics reacted to Brontë's first published work with their personal Victorian biases in full view. Elizabeth Rigby's now famous diatribe in the *Quarterly Review* berated *Jane Eyre* for its "vulgarity" and what Rigby perceived to be its "anti-Christian" attitudes, but most critics hailed the new writer. Eagerly awaited after the success of *Jane Eyre*, Brontë's *Shirley* was a disappointment to many. Critics praised it for its characterization and description, but complained about its construction. *Villette*, on the other hand, received a warmer reception, more akin to that of *Jane Eyre*. Brontë's friend, Harriet Martineau, praised *Villette* but also expressed concern over what appeared to be Brontë's anti-Catholic bias and the almost unrelieved misery of the book's central heroine, Lucy Snowe. Her review in the *Daily News* helped end a friendship but not Brontë's already solid reputation as a writer.

Ironically that reputation was more endangered by the hagiography

1

inherent in the long-pervasive biographical approach to Brontë's work. The Brontë lives—especially the relative isolation in Yorkshire, the remarkable talents of the three sisters, Charlotte, Emily, and Anne, the lesser but stormy artistic talent of the brother, Branwell, and the early deaths of all four—were the stuff of novels, as Elizabeth Gaskell demonstrated in the first Brontë biography, *The Life of Charlotte Brontë* (1857). Gaskell in some ways set the tone for criticism to come. In the *Life*, published just two years after Charlotte Brontë's death, she distinguished between the pseudonymous Currer Bell, author, and the real Charlotte Brontë, dutiful daughter, sister, and the heroine of Gaskell's book. Gaskell also discerned and analyzed the internal conflicts in Brontë, tracing them to both nature and nurture. Brontë was Irish on her father's side and Cornish on her mother's, a combination that led to conflicting romantic and pragmatic tendencies. Coupled with the Brontë's Yorkshire environment, this heritage produced a writer of contraries housed in a tiny woman of stature. Subsequent nineteenth- and early twentieth-century critics became preoccupied with Currer Bell/Charlotte Brontë and hunted remorselessly for correspondences between the art and the life. Brontë became the heroine of her own novels as readers and critics stalked the woman behind the text and the text behind the woman. The autobiographer-narrators in Brontë's novels thus became surrogates for the Currer Bell who herself had never pretended to be other than Jane Eyre's editor. By the 1880s, Haworth had become a place of pilgrimage, the spot where one went to pay homage to the mystery of the Brontës' lives, deaths, and art. Enthusiasts formed The Brontë Society in 1883 and acquired the Brontë Parsonage Museum, a shrine where memorabilia and manuscripts are still treasured side by side.

Critics in the late nineteenth century carried the dual interest in life and art into the business of editing. From 1899 to 1903 the Haworth edition of *The Life and Works of Charlotte Brontë and Her Sisters* appeared, with introductions by Mary Augusta Ward. The title is significant for its emphasis on both life and works and for its accentuation of Charlotte Brontë, whose status with critics at this time well exceeded that of her sister Emily. Ward's introductions to Charlotte Brontë's novels offer an insightful novelist's look into another novelist's development and methods. But despite the title of the Haworth edition, its substance prefaced a turn toward Emily Brontë as the more original, and therefore more interesting, of the two famous Brontë sisters and presaged an early twentieth-century revaluation favoring Emily.

Reviewing Clement Shorter's *Charlotte Brontë and Her Circle* (1896), Henry James in *Harper's Weekly* (6 February 1897) cautioned against "confounding" Charlotte Brontë's life and work. As the new century dawned, the biographical approach to Brontë studies certainly did not disappear, but critical emphases did alter. A paucity of new facts about the Brontë lives helped along a new kind of criticism, ready to disengage the work from the life. So did a modernist interest in the form of fiction, which led critics to become more concerned with the interpretation of novelistic structures than with novelists' lives. Formalism, as this new kind of criticism came to be called, favored what seemed the tighter structure and attention to time of Emily Brontë's *Wuthering Heights*, and by the 1930s so influential a critic as Lord David Cecil (*Early Victorian Novelists: Essays in Revaluation*, 1934) would pronounce Emily Brontë the greater novelist of the two sisters, finding Charlotte Brontë's works marred by structural weaknesses and melodramatic improbabilities and barely redeemed through verbal intensity. By the 1940s F. R. Leavis, also scrutinizing the work of both famous Brontës, heaped all the laurels upon the head of the younger sister, dubbing Emily the one Brontë with "genius."[1] Even as late as the 1960s, critics were still seeking failure more than a rationale for Charlotte Brontë's artistic structures. Earl Knies's "Art, Death, and the Composition of *Shirley*" (*Victorian Newsletter* 28 [1968]: 22–24) tied what Knies perceived as Brontë's lack of artistic control to her grief over the loss of the siblings who died one by one as she wrote her book. Similarly, Knies's *The Art of Charlotte Brontë* (1969) championed her first-person narratives at the expense of *Shirley*.

Thus one branch of formalist criticism helped obscure Charlotte Brontë's novelistic structures. Its proponents sought to compare Brontë not only with her sister but with writers as far removed from her as the classical dramatists. They rode through *Shirley* in the wake of Lord David Cecil, who believed that "once fully launched on her surging flood of self-revelation, Charlotte Brontë is far above pausing to attend to so paltry a consideration as artistic unity."[2] At about the same time another branch, New Criticism, discredited authorial intent and scrutinized the language of individual Brontë texts. A generation of critics trained in New Critical analysis of poetry turned to Brontë's novels with amazement. Here was a poet in prose. So began the many studies of image and symbol in *Jane Eyre* and *Villette* that appeared in the 1950s and 1960s. Like lyric poems, the novels of Charlotte Brontë were believed to have controlling images that held the key to their meaning. Fire and ice took on new importance for readers of Brontë in a number of essays centered on the relevance of such imagery to *Jane Eyre*. The main danger of this kind of approach to the novels is, of course, reductivism, implicit in Eric Solomon's statement that these "two images [fire and ice] serve as a sub-structure for the whole novel, the flames of lust and the ice of indifference."[3] Image studies, not surprisingly, eventually burned themselves out. Nonetheless they helped give birth to important broader-based analyses of Charlotte Brontë's language, works like Margot Peters's excellent *Charlotte Brontë: Style in the Novel* (1973) and Cynthia Linder's *Romantic Imagery in the Novels of Charlotte Brontë* (1978), which tied this imagery to narrative voice. And in the hands of their finest practitioners, like Robert B. Heilman in "Charlotte Brontë, Reason, and the Moon" (*Nineteenth-Century Fiction*

14, no. 4 [March 1960]:283–302), image studies linked image to symbol and myth and offered genuinely new insights into the depths of Brontë's imagination.

Most often in the 1950s and 1960s myth was linked to psychology. In some ways this criticism represented a psychosexual update of the earlier biographical approach. Charles Burkhart's 1962 reading of Villette (Explicator 21, no. 1 [September 1962]: entry 8), for example, tied moon imagery to frustrated female sexual love in the novel and related both to Brontë's life. Later, in Charlotte Brontë: A Psychosexual Study of Her Novels (1973), Burkhart related all of Brontë's work to the "unconscious" nature of her writing, suggesting that the mature work was dependent upon an unconscious substratum evident in Brontë's own Angrian myths. Burkhart also focused on the mythic aspects of masculine sexuality in the character of Rochester, a male critical preoccupation dating from Richard Chase's often reprinted 1947 discussion of myth in "The Brontës: A Centennial Observance" (Kenyon Review 9: 487–506). Chase had found in Rochester the embodiment of godlike man symbolically castrated by his fearful female author. Despite a female countermyth put forth by Annette Schreiber in "The Myth in Charlotte Brontë," (Literature and Psychology 17, no. 1 [1968]: 48–67), and despite twenty years of feminist readings of Jane Eyre including Helene Moglen's further revision of Chase in Charlotte Brontë: The Self Conceived (1976) and Diane Sadoff's in Monsters of Affection: Dickens, Eliot, and Brontë on Fatherhood (1982), this male psychosexual reading has often been revived. Harold Bloom's recent introduction to Modern Critical Views: The Brontës (1987) boasts that "it will hardly endear me to feminist critics if I observe that much of the literary power of Jane Eyre results from its authentic sadism in representing the very masculine Rochester as a victim of Charlotte Brontë's will-to-power over the beautiful Lord Byron."[4] Freud and "beautiful Lord Byron" both continue to haunt Brontë studies.

"Myth" is a term used loosely in critical work on Brontë and has been favored by Marxist as well as psychosexual critics. Terry Eagleton called his Marxist study of the Brontës Myths of Power (1975). In this Marxist context, ideology becomes mythology and involves rebellion against or acquiescence toward the economically powerful. Throughout Charlotte Brontë's fiction, rebellion frequently centers upon the heroines' struggles against submission. Although her characters internalize their struggles, Eagleton argues, her heroines nevertheless manifest their powerlessness in the larger socioeconomic structure. Before Eagleton's analysis, Russian critics had expressed similar views. In the introduction to a translation of Jane Eyre (Kiev: Dnipro Press, 1970), Tamara Denysova declared Brontë to be an early champion of the working woman as heroine. Later the Marxist-Feminist Literature Collective's thought-provoking "Women's Writing: Jane Eyre, Shirley, Villette, Aurora Leigh" (Ideology and Consciousness 3 [1978]: 27–48) showed how gender determination and weakened kinship structures force Brontë's female heroes to question or evade confrontation with both patriarchy and capitalism. In general, Marxism and feminism have promoted a revisionist view of self and society in Brontë's novels and helped renew interest in *Shirley*, where history is no longer seen simply as a novelistic backdrop but becomes part of the action, and Brontë is no longer believed to have lost control of her formal structures. Instead discontinuities in self and society are viewed as mirrored in discontinuities in Brontë's text, as in Susan Gubar's 1976 essay, "The Genesis of Hunger, According to *Shirley*" (*Feminist Studies* 3, no. 3/4 [Spring-Summer]: 5–21). According to Gubar, *Shirley* illustrates the deprivation of women and workers and the voracity of the patriarchal system.

The 1970s also witnessed revision in the tradition of Brontë biography. The most influential biography after Gaskell's had been E. F. Benson's *Charlotte Brontë*, which appeared in 1932. Benson overcorrected for Gaskell's heroic view by casting Brontë as brittle and intolerant, thereby preparing the ground for Lord David Cecil's personal "revaluation" two years later. A number of biographers since Benson have tried to correct for both Gaskell's panegyric and Benson's denigration. In 1967, Winifred Gerin's *Charlotte Brontë: The Evolution of Genius* ran to over six hundred pages in an attempt to be thorough and judicious, but in the tradition of earlier Brontë criticism it often failed to separate Brontë's own life from those of her female heroes. Not until Margot Peters's more modest and far more readable *Unquiet Soul: A Biography of Charlotte Brontë* (1975) was there a biography that set Charlotte Brontë squarely in the context of Victorian England, looked clearly and carefully at both her life and works, and discussed her as a woman writer. Peters cleared the way for Tom Winnifrith, whose study *The Brontës* (1978) actually honed in on the differences in Brontë lives and Brontë novels and again sought out the relationship between the books and the society.

Two picture-book studies have also made the Brontës' natural and cultural worlds more accessible. Phyllis Bentley's *The Brontës and Their World* (1969) is not only illustrated with black and white plates showing Brontëana and Brontë places but is artfully written, as were her earlier studies *The Brontës* (1947) and *The Brontë Sisters* (1950). Brian Wilks's *The Brontës* (1976) also concentrates on the milieu and is amply illustrated in color and black and white.

Finally, critical accessibility to Charlotte Brontë has been promoted by two series books intending to give an overview of Brontë's life and works, the Twayne *Charlotte Brontë* (1977) by Margaret Howard Blom and, ten years later, the Macmillan *Charlotte Brontë* (1987) by Pauline Nestor. Nestor's book was preceded by her critical study of *Female Friendships and Communities* (1985), which contains a section on Charlotte Brontë.

In addition to separating Brontë lives from Brontë fictions, Winnifrith has been one of the scholars instrumental in making the early writings of Charlotte Brontë more readily available. His collection, *The Poems of Charlotte Brontë* (1984), reprints all of the poems from the 1846 *Poems by Currer, Ellis and Acton Bell*, which contained the first printed work of the three sisters. So does Victor A. Neufeldt's *The Poems of Charlotte Brontë: A Text and Commentary* (1985), a full and now standard compilation of all of Brontë's poetry. Another valuable contribution to the study of the earlier Charlotte Brontë has come from Christine Alexander. Alexander's tireless work editing and interpreting Brontë's juvenilia is the first such large-scale undertaking since Fannie E. Ratchford drew attention to the juvenilia throughout the 1930s and 1940s, culminating in her well-known study, *The Brontë's Web of Childhood* (1941). Alexander has already traced Brontë's development as an artist in *The Early Writing of Charlotte Brontë* (1983). She has also catalogued all the fragments on Brontë's juvenilia and is currently editing a complete edition of Brontë's unpublished early writing. Placed alongside the now completed Clarendon editions of the four novels of Charlotte Brontë, the new editions of the early work will give students and scholars a full set of authoritative texts.

Other recent criticism has turned in earnest to the narrative voice in Brontë's novels. Partly this has been a response to the separation of the author from her characters that was helped along by formalism. If Brontë was not talking to the reader through the characters, then who was telling the story? In the 1950s and 1960s this question was addressed in criticism like Kathleen Tillotson's discussion of the narrating Jane Eyre in *Novels of the 1840's* (1956). Since the 1970s, the study of narrative has been keenly stimulated by the influence of structural linguistics and its stepchild narratology, which looks at and distinguishes the narration, the narrative, and the narrator of any given text. Readings of *Villette* have been most affected by this critical approach, but there have been discussions of every Brontë novel. An early example of the attention to *Villette*, Jean Franz Blackall's "Point of View in *Villette*" (*Journal of Narrative Technique* 6 [1976]: 14–28), preceded a number of more detailed studies in the 1980s. Notable among them are Mark Kinkead-Weekes's "The Voicing of Fictions," in *Reading the Victorian Novel: Detail into Form*, edited by Ian Gregor (1980), which reveals the structure of *Villette* as determined by Lucy Snowe's voice. Annette Tromly's *The Cover of the Mask: The Autobiographers of Charlotte Brontë's Fiction* (1982) deals with all of Charlotte Brontë's first-person novels, while Rosemary Bodenheimer highlights *Jane Eyre* in her essay on the empowerment of Jane's voice in "Jane Eyre in Search of Her Story" (*Papers in Language and Literature* 16 [1980]: 387–402), recently reprinted in Harold Bloom's collection, *Modern Critical Views: The Brontës* (1987).

Just who Brontë's "Readers" were and are has also become a question frequently discussed by critics of the last decade. Sylvère Monod set forth one of the first responses in "Charlotte Brontë and the Thirty 'Readers' of *Jane Eyre*" (*Jane Eyre*, Norton Critical Edition [1971], 496–507). Monod examined both Jane Eyre and the readers she addressed and decided Jane was a bully, particularly toward male readers. Since Monod's essay, reader-response criticism — an approach valuing the effect of the text on the reader more than any delusively objective meaning or structure discovered in the text — has invited many more such readings. Reader-response has been a branch of criticism highly suited to the novels of Charlotte Brontë precisely because her narrators often do turn to imagined "Readers" and speak directly to them. It is also a form of criticism favored by feminist critics, particularly the earlier feminist critics of the 1970s. In *On Lies, Secrets, and Silence* (1979), Adrienne Rich suggested why women read and interpret literature this way: because we "take the work . . . as a clue to how we live, how we have been living, how we have been led to imagine ourselves, [and] how our language has trapped as well as liberated us."[5] Rich's well-known essay "Jane Eyre: The Temptations of a Motherless Woman" (included in *On Lies, Secrets, and Silence*), is an early and leading example of feminist reader-response criticism. What this essay signaled was a feminist revival of interest in Charlotte Brontë as a woman writing to women. In this revival *Jane Eyre* became the key text and Charlotte Brontë's work again began to draw more attention than her sister Emily's.

During the 1970s each of several major studies of women and literature in nineteenth-century England focused in part upon *Jane Eyre*. These books, now seen as feminist classics, reflected an awakening to the study of women writers as distinct from male writers in their choice of both subject and style. Since Elaine Showalter's valuable coining of the word "gynocritics"[6] to encompass such studies, they can be seen collectively as a specialized contribution to critical discourse. In 1973, the year Adrienne Rich's essay on *Jane Eyre* first appeared in *Ms.* magazine, Elizabeth Hardwick's *Seduction and Betrayal: Women and Literature* cast Jane very clearly as the savior of Rochester. That same year, Carolyn Heilbrun's *Toward a Recognition of Androgyny* found *Jane Eyre*, unlike *Wuthering Heights*, to be a feminist rather than an androgynous novel. In this context, a feminist novel is one in which the reader identifies far more with the female hero than with both female and male characters as she or he would in the case of an androgynous novel. In the following year, Patricia Beer took the title for her book on nineteenth-century women writers from *Jane Eyre* in *Reader I Married Him: A Study of the Women Characters of Jane Austen, Charlotte Brontë, Elizabeth Gaskell, and George Eliot* (1974). Beer viewed Jane as a governess, independent and strong-willed. Preparing the way for her book were two earlier studies, Patricia Thomson's *The Victorian Heroine: A Changing Ideal* (1956), which gave a fine outline of governess heroes, and Inga-Stina Ewbank's *Their Proper Sphere: A Study of the Brontë Sisters* (1966), which distin-

guished Charlotte Brontë from her sisters as female novelists by noting that
the woman question became the "proper sphere" of Charlotte. This same
Woman Question writ large was the subject of Harriet Bjork's *The
Language of Truth: Charlotte Brontë, The Woman Question, and the
Novel* (1971). Bjork felt that Brontë's letters revealed an interest in the
debate on women's place that pervaded her life as well as her novels.

Feminist books of the later 1970s tended to feature *Villette* as well as
Jane Eyre and to discuss the novels of Charlotte and Emily Brontë
alongside one another. This was true of Patricia Spacks's *The Female
Imagination* (1975), which again examined the power struggle between
Charlotte Brontë's male and female heroes, and also of Ellen Moers's
Literary Women (1976), which classified Charlotte Brontë as a feminist
and Emily Brontë as a gothic novelist. Elaine Showalter, in *A Literature of
Their Own: British Women Novelists from Brontë to Lessing* (1977), and
Barbara Hill Rigny, in *Madness and Sexual Politics in the Feminist Novel:
Studies in Brontë, Woolf, Lessing, and Atwood* (1978), refocused the
interest in *Jane Eyre* to include Bertha Mason and reviewed Brontë in the
wider tradition of women novelists. Sandra Gilbert and Susan Gubar, in
their exhaustive and influential *The Madwoman in the Attic: The Woman
Writer and the Nineteenth-Century Literary Imagination* (1979), took
Bertha's madness — not Jane's marriage — for their title and developed
important insights into each of the novels of Charlotte and Emily Brontë.
Gilbert's essay on *Jane Eyre* and Gubar's on *Shirley*, each published
separately before the appearance of *Madwoman*, are included in this
collection.

Feminist criticism, often making use of reader-response criticism and
narratology, has come to dominate Brontë studies in the 1980s. Books like
Rachel Brownstein's *Becoming a Heroine: Reading about Women in
Novels* (1982) and essays like Margaret Kirkham's "Reading the Brontës" in
Women Reading Women's Writing (ed. Sue Roe, 1987) more easily assume
that women readers have always had personal and individual responses to
women's writing. As Kirkham suggests, identification with female characters and their women creators has made "some of the most enjoyable and
stimulating feminist criticism . . . strongly personal, like Adrienne Rich's
essay on *Jane Eyre* or Gilbert and Gubar's chapters on the Brontës in *The
Madwoman in the Attic*."[7] Here is where the full circle of criticism on
Charlotte Brontë becomes most obvious. Feminist readers and feminist
writers, like their often nonfeminist female predecessors in Brontë's day,
have again brought Charlotte Brontë to the forefront, rightly or wrongly
prizing her above her sister Emily, reading her with personal insights, and
presenting her as a voice still very much to be reckoned with, if far from
"vulgar" or "anti-Christian," as Elizabeth Rigby had once believed.

The brief overview of Brontë criticism that I have offered is highly
selective and is intended to serve more as an introduction to the essays to
follow than as a comprehensive study of criticism about Charlotte Brontë

from 1846 to 1988. Comprehensiveness is hardly possible in 1988. R. W. Crump's excellent annotated bibliography, *Charlotte and Emily Brontë: A Reference Guide* (Boston: G. K. Hall, 1982–86), which covers the years 1846–1983, runs to three sizeable volumes and includes more than three thousand entries. Readers of *Critical Essays on Charlotte Brontë* are advised of the usefulness of Crump's work and of three other fine bibliographical studies: Anne Passel's earlier *Charlotte and Emily Brontë: An Annotated Bibliography* (1979); Miriam Allott's introduction to *The Brontës: The Critical Heritage* (London: Routledge and Kegan Paul, 1974), which carefully highlights the critical reception of the Brontë sisters from 1846 to 1900 and briefly examines twentieth-century criticism; and Margot Peters's two-part "Charlotte Brontë: A Critico-Bibliographic Survey, 1945–1974" in the *British Studies Monitor* 6 and 7 (1976–77), which gives a fuller description of many twentieth-century critical trends than is possible in this comparatively brief introduction. This editor is indebted to both Allott and Peters for their review of criticism.

Most but not all of the essays in this volume have appeared since Margot Peters's assessment of the state of criticism on Charlotte Brontë. Part 1 gives an overview of varied approaches that have been brought to bear on one central problem in Brontë study—the divided nature of her heroines. Part 2 offers an essay on the juvenilia and a selection of essays on each of Brontë's four novels. This second part reproduces essays representative of the criticism of the 1970s and 1980s. Selections for each of the four novels have been chosen to create a dialogue centered around an important aspect of recent critical discourse. In addition, in every section of this volume one influential example of the Victorian criticism of Brontë has been included to help show continuities and discontinuities in the evaluation of her reputation.

With a few exceptions, mainly confined to the earlier works of Brontë about which criticism is still sparse, the essays offered here have been printed separately and are not sections from books. Such essays stand well on their own and seem more appropriate for a series book entitled *Critical Essays on Charlotte Brontë*. Although this will be the first collection devoted to all of the novels of Charlotte Brontë, there have been several other selections of criticism dealing with the Brontë family or with Charlotte Brontë's individual novels: Judith O'Neill's *Critics on Charlotte and Emily Brontë* (1968); Anne Passel's edition of *Jane Eyre* (1967), with excerpts from critical opinion; Ian Gregor's *The Brontës: A Collection of Critical Essays* (1971); Richard Dunn's two selections of essays for the Norton Critical Editions of *Jane Eyre* (1971 and 1987); Miriam Allott's *"Jane Eyre" and "Villette": A Casebook* (1973); and Harold Bloom's *Modern Critical Views: The Brontës* (1987). The reader of this volume will find other editorial points of view reflected in these collections.

Of the two parts of the volume, the first was the most editorially challenging. Searching for a topic of common interest to Brontë critics over the last 140 years quickly yielded a preoccupation with dualism in Brontë. But winnowing through the many dozens of essays that dealt with duality and selecting the best for inclusion was far more difficult. Final selections were made from among single essays that discussed more than one of the Brontë novels and clearly represented an important critical trend. Whole books, like Robert Bernard Martin's *The Accents of Persuasion: Charlotte Brontë's Novels* (1966), have been written about the balancing of passion and reason in Brontë's novels, and portions of them might otherwise have been included. So might particularly good essays focusing on just one novel, like Richard Benvenuto's "The Child of Nature, the Child of Grace, and the Unresolved Conflict of *Jane Eyre*" (*ELH* 39 [1972]: 620–38), or on Brontë herself, like Nina Auerbach's "Charlotte Brontë: The Two Countries" (*University of Toronto Quarterly* 42 [1973]: 328–42), which finds that Brontë's own "mind moves always through an unresolved dialectic, which she will continue to translate into the image of a divided country" (328).

Preoccupation with this "divided country" began with the Victorians, as Leslie Stephen's 1877 essay, "Charlotte Brontë," indicates. Possibly the concentration on bifurcation in Brontë studies is traceable to Gaskell's *Life*, with its convenient distinction between "Currer Bell" and Charlotte Brontë; possibly it is inherent in Brontë's writing, or in her era; but certainly it was already firmly in place when Stephen replied to Swinburne's encomium entitled *A Note on Charlotte Brontë*. In an attempt to give Brontë what he thought was a more judicious reading than Swinburne's, Stephen erred on the other side and predicted a waning of Brontë's reputation, not because of the power of her work but because of its limited scope. Stephen felt Brontë was too narrow to appeal to many readers for very long. He was certainly wrong in that judgment, but he helped set the tone of criticism for a hundred years when in the final pages of his essay he focused upon the conflict between passion and duty in Brontë's characters. This he attributed to the lack of a powerful intellect on Brontë's part, seizing negatively upon Swinburne's distinction between genius and intellect and pointing up the inherent inconsistency in Brontë's attraction to both rebelliousness and conventionality.

From Stephen's day on, the passion/reason conflict within Brontë's female heroes and their radical/conservative nature have teased or troubled Brontë's critics, as the remaining essays in part 1 of this volume illustrate. Among the later twentieth-century readings of these internal conflicts is Robert B. Heilman's interpretation of what he calls the dualism of Brontë's moral awareness. Arguing that this dualism was exacerbated for Brontë by her attraction to the irrational, Heilman discusses two-sidedness in terms of a duel between Apollo and the White Goddess in his "Charlotte Brontë, Reason, and the Moon." In a voyage toward light, the female moon becomes a beacon and guide for Brontë's female heroes and serves as their mediatrix—a cool light with whom they, like Brontë, are quite willing to dwell rather than inhabit the sterner sunlit regions of Reason and Apollo. About a decade after Heilman, Terry Eagleton centered on the tension between radical and conservative rather than on the duel between reason and the irrational in Brontë. To Eagleton's mind in his essay "Class, Power and Charlotte Brontë" (*Critical Quarterly* 14, no. 4 [Autumn 1972]: 225–35), Brontë herself opted to "negotiate passionate self-fulfilment on terms which preserve the social and moral conventions intact, and so preserve intact the submissive, enduring everyday self which inheres in them." Thus Brontë's heroines fight for power in sexual struggles marked by both rebellion against and attraction to the world of Brontë's heroes.

Women critics, particularly feminist critics concerned with women writers, as is Carol T. Christ in "Imaginative Constraint, Feminine Duty, and the Form of Charlotte Brontë's Fiction" (*Women's Studies* 6, no. 3 [1979]: 287–96), envision conflict in Brontë quite differently. Christ sees it in terms of Brontë's struggle with the angel in the house, that pervasive creature so eloquently described by Virginia Woolf.[8] According to Christ, Brontë could never quite exorcise the angel that beckoned her on to more conservative female dutifulness but nevertheless exercised the assertiveness which writing requires by maintaining a constant battle with that angel. Christ's essay complements others, not included here primarily because of space, like Carol Ohmann's "Historical Reality and 'Divine Appointment' in Charlotte Brontë's Fiction" (*Signs* 2 [1977]: 757–78). Ohmann examines loss in the Brontë novels as the obverse of fulfillment. The dialectic of loss/fulfillment is, says Ohmann, a manifestation of "resignation and redefinition in . . . woman's consciousness pressing further against its limits of political understanding, exposing contradictions in its own values and commitments, and, unable to resolve them, pulling back from reality, preferring to represent, instead, a world view in which . . . forces outside of society determine who we are and what becomes of us" (778).

Criticism on Charlotte Brontë still awaits a feminist/poststructuralist reading that directly confronts the fuller implications of dualism in Brontë's work. Brontë herself was victim of the binary oppositions described by Jacques Derrida and revisioned from the feminist point of view by Hélène Cixous (*La Jeune*, 1975). The reason/imagination and rebellion/submission dichotomies that seem to have been inherent in Brontë's imaginative constructs were and still are inherent in post-Cartesian Western culture. Head/heart, sun/moon, male/female—such oppositions are part of a patriarchal value system that inhered in Brontë as they have in her Victorian and twentieth-century critics. Much criticism of Brontë has been ideological, partly because the binary oppositions depicted in Brontë's characters have readily allowed critical ideologies to surface. But Brontë could also be viewed as a writer who occasionally collapsed such oppositions, not just finding a moon-like middle ground between reason and intuition, but occasionally absorbing both categories in contradiction. John Kucich's 1985 essay "Passionate Reserve and Reserved Passion in Charlotte Brontë" (*ELH* 52 [Winter 1985]: 913–37) begins to approach such a view. In his psychological reading, Kucich finds that "the oppositional psychic tensions we tend to find so disturbing in Brontë's work are, in fact, unstable oppositions" and discusses the reserved nature of her heroines as representing an autonomy inclusive of oppositions.

Part 2 of the collection refocuses first of all on the recent interest in Brontë's narrators. "The Author's Voice," a selection from Christine Alexander's 1983 book on the juvenilia, *The Early Writings of Charlotte Brontë*, is concerned with the relationship between the voices in Brontë's youthful narrations and those in her later novels. Alexander emphasizes the predominance of male narrators in Brontë's Angrian stories, accounts for this both through the influence of Branwell Brontë and the male tradition in English letters, and compares the "bloodless" voice in Brontë's first novel, *The Professor,* with those of her Angrian heroes. As Mary August Ward's introduction to *The Professor* shows, Victorians, too, were alert to the problems in Brontë's presentation of the hero of her first major work of fiction. "His role," says Ward, "is not particularly manly; and he does not appeal to our pity. The intimate autobiographical note, which makes the spell of *Villette*, is absent." This autobiographical note has come to dominate criticism of all three first-person novels in the 1980s. Annette Tromly's fine reading of the novels from this perspective, *The Cover of the Mask: The Autobiographers in Charlotte Brontë's Fiction* (1982), is represented in this volume by her detailed study of William Crimsworth as hero, narrator, and "central problem" of *The Professor.* Judith Williams's "*The Professor:* Blocked Perceptions," from her book *Perception and Expression in the Novels of Charlotte Brontë* (1988), helps the reader make the quick leap from Brontë's lesser known first work to the power of her most famous novel, begun just two months after completion of *The Professor.*

Without benefit of *The Professor,* the now infamous Elizabeth Rigby appraised *Jane Eyre* as a novel of rebellion, a work that could stimulate unwanted discontent in women and render a disservice to governesses. Rigby is represented in this volume because subsequent criticism of *Jane Eyre* has often included criticism of Rigby. In Brontë study especially, readers like to respond to earlier readers as well as to the texts themselves. Sandra Gilbert's "Plain Jane's Progress" (*Signs: Journal of Women in Culture and Society* 2, no. 4 [1977]: 779–804) opens with a consideration of Rigby and other Victorians before moving on to Jane's Bunyanesque voyaging. That voyaging was itself the subject of readers before Gilbert — of Jane Millgate, for example, in "Jane Eyre's Progress" (*English Studies Anglo-American Supplement* [1969]: xxi–xxix). Gilbert, however, builds a feminist reading that serves as a critical foil to Rigby, revisioning Jane's rebellion for the 1970s. The tendency of women readers/critics to respond to earlier women readers/critics follows throughout the section on *Jane Eyre*. Rich answers Virginia Woolf, Maurianne Adams in *"Jane Eyre: Woman's Estate"* (from *The Authority of Experience: Essays in Feminist Criticism* [1977]), broadens the discourse, and Jean Wyatt, in "A Patriarch of One's Own: *Jane Eyre* and Romantic Love" (*Tulsa Studies in Women's Literature* 4 [1985]: 199–216), tries to account for Rich's and other women's deep personal engagement with the book by focusing on the interaction between *Jane Eyre* and female fantasies.

From the beginning, criticism on *Shirley* has had quite other points of focus. After an opening look at women as writers, George Henry Lewes's early review of Brontë's second published novel settled upon what Lewes thought was *Shirley's* chief defect: its lack of unity. Lewes, like Stephen, led the way for criticism to come. Over a century of ensuing critics have variously accounted for this perceived defect, but in the last twenty years *Shirley's* unity has also had its defenders, two of whom are included here. Arnold Shapiro in "Public Themes and Private Lives: Social Criticism in *Shirley*" (*Papers on Language and Literature* 4, no. 1 [Winter 1968]: 74–84) finds an underlying thematic unifier in the book's concern with selfishness. He answers those who have commented on a disjunction between individual and social strands in *Shirley* by suggesting that Brontë may have intended to show how social changes can hinge upon internal, individual changes. Susan Gubar's feminist reading of *Shirley*, "The Genesis of Hunger, According to *Shirley*," examines theme and structure together. For Gubar, Brontë's artistic problem lay in plotting "a story about characters defined by their inability to initiate action." The importance of Brontë's women, children, and workers is reflected in the disjunctions and unsatisfying ending of Brontë's novel. When seen from Gubar's perspective, *Shirley* emerges with an ironic structure that parallels and parodies the romance plots of historical novels like Scott's. Gubar's is an important essay, precursor to insights like those reached by Rachel Blau Du Plessis in *Writing Beyond the Ending* (1985), who argues that the conclusions of *Jane Eyre* and *Villette* are themselves precursors of what Du Plessis calls in her subtitle, "Narrative Strategies of Twentieth-Century Women Writers."

More than the book's structure, the central female hero of *Villette* has concerned the critics of Brontë's last novel. Although many chose to align themselves with Jane Eyre, few have chosen to identify with Lucy Snowe. Writing in 1853, Harriet Martineau found Lucy Snowe a painful character, too love-obsessed. Well over a hundred years later, Kate Millett featured her in *Sexual Politics* (1969) as being justifiably angry toward a hostile world. For Millett, Lucy is a woman imprisoned by her world and its values. She is also Brontë's most complex and troubling narrator, as Janice Carlisle suggests in "The Face in the Mirror: *Villette* and the Conventions of Autobiography" (*ELH* 46 [Summer 1979]: 262–89). Carlisle's Lucy makes sense of her life by telling its tale to suit herself — even if by so doing she misleads her reader through feints and distortions. Brenda Silver begins where Carlisle leaves off, making Lucy more reliable and the reader more responsible than does Carlisle. In "The Reflecting Reader in *Villette*" (from *The Voyage In: Fictions of Female Development* [1983]), Silver shows how Lucy stimulates reader rebellion on the part of her conventional readers while at the same time she offers collusion to her more rebellious ones. Eventually all readers are wholly engaged with her narrative, and form the community that Lucy otherwise lacks at the end of her story. It is her sense of closeness to this imagined community rather than her deviousness that allows Lucy to include readers in her own misreadings of experience. Reading *Villette* with Silver is rather like participating in psychological transference. Readers and teller swirl round and round in a revolving door. Like other essays in this collection, Silver's alters the perspective on Brontë and then opens the door for critics to come — critics like Karen Lawrence, for example, whose "The Cypher: Disclosure and Reticence in *Villette*" (*Nineteenth-Century Literature* 42, no. 4 [March 1988]: 448–66) takes exception with Silver by seeing Lucy's self-definition as ambiguous more than integrative. Since interpretations of literature change with shifting cultural moments, the dynamic dialogue between the fiction of Charlotte Brontë and the criticism of her readers and even among those readers themselves seems destined to be written and rewritten.

BARBARA TIMM GATES

University of Delaware

Notes

1. F. R. Leavis, *The Great Tradition* (New York: George W. Stewart, 1949), 27.

2. Lord David Cecil, *Early Victorian Novelists* (London: Constable, 1934), 116.

3. Eric Solomon, "*Jane Eyre*: Fire and Water," *College English* 25 (1963):215–17. · Other studies include David Lodge's "Fire and Eyre: Charlotte Brontë's War of Earthly Elements," in *The Language of Fiction* (London: Routledge and Kegan Paul, 1966), 114–43; Janay Dowling's "Fire and Ice Imagery in *Jane Eyre*," *Paunch* 26 (1966): 68–78; and Nina Auerbach's "Charlotte Brontë: The Two Countries," *University of Toronto Quarterly* 42 (1973): 328–42.

4. Harold Bloom, ed., *Modern Critical Views: The Brontës* (New York: Chelsea House, 1978), 3.

5. Adrienne Rich, "When We Dead Awaken: Writing as Re-Vision," *On Lies, Secrets, and Silence* (New York: W. W. Norton, 1979), 35.

6. Elaine Showalter, "Feminist Criticism in the Wilderness," in *Feminist Criticism: Essays on Women, Literature and Theory*, ed. Elaine Showalter (New York: Pantheon Books, 1985), 248.

7. Margaret Kirkham, "Reading the Brontës," in *Women Reading Women's Writing*, ed. Sue Roe (Brighton: Harvester Press, 1987), 61.

8. Virginia Woolf, *The Death of the Moth and Other Essays* (London: Hogarth Press, 1942), 236–37.

CRITICAL PERSPECTIVES ON BRONTË'S DUALISM

Charlotte Brontë
Leslie Stephen*

The well-known phrase as to critics being made of poets who have failed requires to be supplemented. The best critics are often the poets who have succeeded; a truth which has been more than once illustrated by Mr. Swinburne. I shall not ask whether this can be said unreservedly in reference to his recent essay upon Miss Brontë. As usual, he bestows the most enthusiastic and generous praise with a lavish hand, and bestows it upon worthy objects. And, as usual, he seems to be a little too much impressed with the necessary connection between illuminating in honour of a hero and breaking the windows or burning the effigies of the hero's rivals. I do not wish to examine the justice of his assaults, and still less to limp on halting and prosaic feet after his bounding rhetoric. I propose only to follow an inquiry suggested by a part of his argument. After all, though criticism cannot boast of being a science, it ought to aim at something like a scientific basis, or at least to proceed in a scientific spirit. The critic, therefore, before abandoning himself to the oratorical impulse, should endeavour to classify the phenomena with which he is dealing as calmly as if he were ticketing a fossil in a museum. The most glowing eulogy, the most bitter denunciation have their proper place; but they belong to the art of persuasion, and form no part of scientific method. Our literary, if not our religious, creed should rest upon a purely rational ground, and be exposed to logical tests. Our faith in an author must in the first instance be the product of instinctive sympathy, instead of deliberate reason. It may be propagated by the contagion of enthusiasm, and preached with all the fervour of proselytism. But when we are seeking to justify our emotions, we must endeavour to get for the time into the position of an independent spectator, applying with rigid impartiality such methods as are best calculated to free us from the influence of personal bias.

Undoubtedly it is a very difficult task to be alternately witness and judge; to feel strongly, and yet to analyse coolly; to love every feature in a familiar face, and yet to decide calmly upon its intrinsic ugliness or

*Reprinted from *Cornhill Magazine* 36 (November 1877): 723-39.

17

beauty. To be an adequate critic is almost to be a contradiction in terms; to be susceptible to a force, and yet free from its influence; to be moving with the stream, and yet to be standing on the bank. It is especially difficult in the case of writers like Miss Brontë, and of critics who were in the most enthusiastic age when her fame was in its early freshness. It is almost impossible not to have overpowering prejudices in regard to a character so intense, original, and full of special idiosyncrasy. If you did not love her, you must hate her; or, since hatred for so noble a sufferer would imply unreasonable brutality, we may say, feel strongly a hopeless uncongeniality of temperament. The power of exciting such feelings is, indeed, some testimony to an author's intrinsic force; and it may explain the assertion of her latest biographer. If it be true, as he says, that she has been comparatively neglected of late years, that is what may easily happen in the case of writers more remarkable for intensity than comprehensive power. Their real audience must always be the comparatively small number who are in sympathy with their peculiar moods. But their vigour begins by impressing and overawing a large number of persons who do not feel this spontaneous sympathy. They conquer by sheer force minds whom they do not attract by milder methods. In literature, at any rate, violent conquests are generally transitory; and, after a time, those who have obeyed the rule against their natural inclination, fall away and leave an audience composed of those alone who have been swayed by a deeper attraction. Charlotte Brontë, and perhaps her sister Emily in an even higher degree, must have a certain interest for all intelligent observers of character. But only a minority will thoroughly and unreservedly enjoy the writings which embody so peculiar an essence. Some scenery — rich pasturage and abounding rivers and forest-clad hills — appeals more or less to everybody. It is only a few who really love the lonely cairn on a wind-swept moor. An accident may make it the fashion to affect admiration for such peculiar aspects of nature; but, like all affectations, it will die away after a time, and the faithful lovers be reduced to a narrow band.

The comparative eclipse then — if eclipse there be — of Charlotte Brontë's fame does not imply want of power, but want of comprehensiveness. There is a certain *prima facie* presumption against a writer who appeals only to a few, though it may be amply rebutted by showing that the few are also fit. The two problems must go together; why is the charm so powerful, and why is it so limited? Any intense personality has so far a kind of double-edged influence. Shakespeare sympathises with everybody, and therefore every one with him. Swift scorns and loathes a great part of the world, and therefore if people in general read Swift, or said honestly what they felt, most readers would confess to a simple feeling of aversion to his writings. There is, however, a further distinction. One may dislike such a man as Swift, but one cannot set him aside. His amazing intellectual vigour, the power with which he states some of the great problems of life, and the trenchant decision of his answer, give him a right to be heard. We may shudder, but we are forced to listen. If with equal force of character his intellectual power had been less, we should feel the shock without the mysterious attraction. He would be an unpleasant phenomenon, and one which might be simply neglected. It is because he brings his peculiar views to bear upon problems of universal interest that we cannot afford simply to drop him out of mind. The power of grasping general truths is necessary to give a broad base to a writer's fame, though his capacity for tender and deep emotion is that which makes us love or hate him.

Mr. Swinburne takes Miss Brontë to illustrate the distinction between "genius" and "intellect." Genius, he says, as the most potent faculty, can most safely dispense with its ally. If genius be taken to mean the poetic as distinguished from the scientific type of mind — that which sees intuitively, prefers synthesis to analysis, and embodies ideas in concrete symbols instead of proceeding by rule and measure, and constructing diagrams in preference to drawing pictures — the truth is undeniable and important. The reasoner gives us mechanism and constructs automata, where the seer creates living and feeling beings. The contrast used to be illustrated by the cases of Jonson and Shakespeare — by the difference between the imaginative vigour of *Antony and Cleopatra*, and the elaborate construction of *Sejanus*. We must add, however, that the two qualities of mind are not mutually exclusive. The most analytic mind has some spark of creative power, and the great creators are capable of deliberate dissection. Shakespeare could reflect; and Jonson could see. The ideally perfect mind would be capable of applying each method with equal facility in its proper place.

Genius, therefore, manifested in any high degree, must be taken to include intellect, if the words are to be used in this sense. Genius begins where intellect ends; or takes by storm where intellect has to make elaborate approaches according to the rules of scientific strategy. One sees where the other demonstrates, but the same principles are common to both. To say that a writer shows more genius than intellect may mean simply that, as an artist, he proceeds by the true artistic method, and does not put us off with scientific formulae galvanised into an internal semblance of life. But it may mean that his reflective powers are weak, that he has not assimilated the seminal ideas of his time, and is at a loss in the higher regions of philosophic thought. If so, you are setting limits to the sphere of his influence, and show that he is incapable of uttering the loftiest aspirations and the deepest emotions of his fellows. A great religious teacher may prefer a parable to a theory, but the parable is impressive because it gives the most vivid embodiment of a truly philosophical theory.

Miss Brontë, as her warmest admirers would grant, was not and did not in the least affect to be a philosophical thinker. And because a great writer, to whom she has been gratuitously compared, is strong just where she is weak, her friends have an injudicious desire to make out that the matter is of no importance, and that her comparative poverty of thought is no injury to her work. There is no difficulty in following them so far as to admit that her work is none the worse for containing no theological or philosophical disquisitions, or for showing no familiarity with the technicalities of modern science and metaphysics. But the admission by no means follows that her work does not suffer very materially by the comparative narrowness of the circle of ideas in which her mind habitually revolved. Perhaps if she had been familiar with Hegel or Sir W. Hamilton, she would have intruded undigested lumps of metaphysics, and introduced vexatious allusions to the philosophy of identity or to the principle of the excluded middle. But it is possible, also, that her conceptions of life and the world would have been enriched and harmonised, and that, without giving us more scientific dogmas, her characters would have embodied more fully the dominating ideas of the time. There is no province of inquiry — historical, scientific, or philosophical — from which the artist may not derive useful material; the sole question is whether it has been properly assimilated and transformed by the action of the poetic imagination. By attempting to define how far Miss Brontë's powers were in fact thus bounded, we shall approximately decide her place in the great hierarchy of imaginative thinkers. That it was a very high one, I take to be undeniable. Putting aside living writers, the only female novelist whom one can put distinctly above her is George Sand; for Miss Austen, whom some fanatics place upon a still higher level, differs so widely in every way that "comparison" is absurd. It is almost silly to draw a parallel between writers when every great quality in one is "conspicuous by its absence" in the other.

The most obvious of all remarks about Miss Brontë is the close connection between her life and her writings. Nobody ever put so much of themselves into their work. She is the heroine of her two most powerful novels; for Lucy Snowe is avowedly her own likeness, and Lucy Snowe differs only by accidents from Jane Eyre; whilst her sister is the heroine of the third. All the minor characters, with scarcely an exception, are simply portraits, and the more successful in proportion to their fidelity. The scenery and even the incidents are, for the most part, equally direct transcripts from reality. And, as this is almost too palpable a peculiarity to be expressly mentioned, it seems to be an identical proposition that the study of her life is the study of her novels. More or less true of all imaginable writers, this must be pre-eminently true of Miss Brontë. Her experience, we would say, has been scarcely transformed in passing through her mind. She has written down not only her feelings, but the more superficial accidents of her life. She has simply given fictitious names and dates, with a more or less imaginary thread of narrative, to her own experience at school, as a governess, at home and in Brussels. *Shirley* contains a continuous series of photographs of Haworth and its neighbourhood; as *Villette* does of Brussels: and if *Jane Eyre* is not so literal, except in the opening account of the school-life, much of it is almost as strictly autobiographical. It is one of the oddest cases of an author's self-delusion that Miss Brontë should have imagined that she could remain anonymous after the publication of *Shirley*, and the introduction of such whole-length portraits from the life as the Yorke family. She does not appear to have been herself conscious of the closeness of her adherence to facts. "You are not to suppose," she says in a letter given by Mrs. Gaskell, "any of the characters in *Shirley* intended as real portraits. It would not suit the rules of art, nor of my own feelings, to write in that style. We only suffer reality to *suggest*, never to *dictate*." She seems to be thinking chiefly of her "heroes and heroines," and would perhaps have admitted that the minor personages were less idealised. But we must suppose also that she failed to appreciate fully the singularity of characters which, in her seclusion, she had taken for average specimens of the world at large. If I take my village for the world, I cannot distinguish the particular from the universal; and must assume that the most distinctive peculiarities are unnoticeably commonplace. The amazing vividness of her portrait-painting is the quality which more than any other makes her work unique amongst modern fiction. Her realism is something peculiar to herself; and only the crudest of critics could depreciate its merits on the ground of its fidelity to facts. The hardest of all feats is to see what is before our eyes. What is called the creative power of genius is much more the power of insight into commonplace things and characters. The realism of the DeFoe variety produces an illusion, by describing the most obvious aspects of everyday life, and introducing the irrelevant and accidental. A finer kind of realism is that which, like Miss Austen's, combines exquisite powers of minute perception with a skill which can light up the most delicate miniatures with a delicate play of humour. A more impressive kind is that of Balzac, where the most detailed reproduction of realities is used to give additional force to the social tragedies which are being enacted at our doors. The specific peculiarity of Miss Brontë seems to be the power of revealing to us the potentiality of intense passions lurking behind the scenery of everyday life. Except in the most melodramatic— which is also the weakest—part of *Jane Eyre*, we have lives almost as uneventful as those of Miss Austen, and yet charged to the utmost with latent power. A parson at the head of a school-feast somehow shows himself as a "Cromwell, guiltless of his country's blood;" a professor lecturing a governess on composition is revealed as a potential Napoleon; a mischievous schoolboy is obviously capable of developing into a Columbus or a Nelson; even the most commonplace natural objects, such as a row of beds in a dormitory, are associated and naturally associated with the most intense emotions. Miss Austen makes you feel that a tea-party in a country parsonage may be as amusing as the most brilliant meeting of cosmopolitan celebrities; and Miss Brontë that it may display characters capable of shaking empires and discovering new worlds. The whole machinery is in a state of the highest electric tension, though there is no display of thunder and lightning to amaze us.

The power of producing this effect without stepping one hand's-breadth beyond the most literal and unmistakable fidelity to ordinary facts is explicable, one would say, so far as genius is explicable at all, only in one way. A mind of extraordinary activity within a narrow sphere has been brooding constantly upon a small stock of materials, and a sensitive nature has been enforced to an unusual pressure from the hard facts of life. The surroundings must surely have been exceptional, and the receptive faculties impressible even to morbidness, to produce so startling a result, and the key seemed to be given by Mrs. Gaskell's touching biography, which, with certain minor faults, is still one of the most pathetic records of a heroic life in our literature. Charlotte Brontë and her sister, according to this account, resembled the sensitive plant exposed to the cutting breezes of the West Riding moors. Their writings were the cry of pain and of only half-triumphant faith, produced by a life-long martyrdom, tempered by mutual sympathy, but embittered by family sorrows and the trials of a dependent life. It is one more exemplification of the common theory, that great art is produced by taking an exceptionally delicate nature and mangling it slowly under the grinding wheels of the world.

A recent biographer has given us to understand that this is in great part a misconception, and, whilst paying his compliments to Mrs. Gaskell, he virtually accuses her of unintentionally substituting a fiction for a biography. Mr. Wemyss Reid's intention is excellent; and one can well believe that Mrs. Gaskell did in fact err by carrying into the earlier period the gloom of later years. Most certainly one would gladly believe this to be the case. Only when Mr. Reid seems to think that Charlotte Brontë was thoroughly a gay and high-spirited girl, and that the people of Haworth were commonplace, we begin to fear that we are in the presence of one of those well-meant attempts at whitewashing which "do justice" to a marked character by obliterating all its most prominent features. If Boswell had written in such a spirit, Johnson would have been a Chesterfield, and Goldsmith never have blundered in his talk. When we look at them fairly, Mr. Reid's proofs seem to be curiously inadequate for his conclusions, though calculated to correct some very important misconceptions. He quotes, for example, a couple of letters, in one of which Miss Brontë ends a little outburst of Tory politics by saying, "Now, Ellen, laugh heartily at all that rhodomontade!" This sentence, omitted by Mrs. Gaskell, is taken to prove that Charlotte's interest in politics was "not unmingled with the happy levity of youth." Surely, it is just a phrase from the school-girl's Complete Letter Writer. It would be as sensible to quote from an orator the phrase, "but I fear that I am wearying the House," to prove that he was conscious of being an intolerable bore. The next letter is said to illustrate the "infinite variety of moods" of her true character, and its rapid transitions from grave to gay, because, whilst expressing very

strongly some morbid feelings, she admits that they would be contemptible to common sense, and says that she had been "in one of her
sentimental humours." Did anybody ever express a morbid feeling without
some such qualification? And is not "infinite," even in the least mathemati-
cal sense, rather a strong expression for two? A sentimental mood and a
reaction are mentioned in one letter. That scarcely proves much gaiety of
heart or variety of mood. If, indeed, Charlotte had always been at her
worst, she would have been mad: and we need not doubt that she too had
some taste of the gladness as of the sorrows of childhood. The plain truth
is, that Miss Brontë's letters, read without reference to the disputes of rival
biographers, are disappointing. The most striking thing about them is that
they are young-ladyish. Here and there a passage revealing the writer's
literary power shines through the more commonplace matter, but, as a
whole, they give a curious impression of immaturity. The explanation
seems to be, in the first place, that Miss Brontë, with all her genius, was
still a young lady. Her mind, with its exceptional powers in certain
directions, never broke the fetters by which the parson's daughter of the
last generation was restricted. Trifling indications of this are common in
her novels. The idealised portrait of Emily, the daring and unconventional
Shirley, shows her utmost courage by hinting a slight reluctance to repeat
certain clauses in the Athanasian Creed; and the energy with which the
unlucky curates are satirised shows the state of mind to which even a
young clergyman is still invested with more or less superhuman attributes.
The warmth is generated by the previous assumption that a young
gentleman who dons a white neckcloth must, in the normal state of things,
put off the schoolboy and develop a hidden pair of wings. The wrath
excited by their failure to fulfil this expectation strikes one as oddly
disproportionate. And, in the next place, it seems that, even in writing to
her best friends, Miss Brontë habitually dreaded any vivid expression of
feeling, and perhaps observed that her sentiments when spread upon
letter-paper had a morbid appearance. There are many people who can
confide in the public more freely than in the most intimate friends. The
mask of anonymous authorship and fictitious personages has a delusive
appearance of security. The most sacred emotions are for ourselves or for
the invisible public rather than for the intermediate sphere of concrete
spectators. The letters may dissipate some of Mrs. Gaskell's romantic
gloom, but they do not persuade us that the Brontës were ever like their
neighbours. The doctrine that the people of Haworth were really commonplace mortals, may be accepted with a similar reserve. Undoubtedly
every Scotch peasant is not a Davie Deans, nor every Irishman a Captain
Costigan. There are natives of the mining districts who do not throw half-
bricks at every stranger they see; there are Yankees who do not chew
tobacco, and Englishmen who do not eat raw beefsteaks. And so one may
well believe that many inhabitants of Haworth would have passed muster
at Charing Cross; and one may hope and believe that a man like Heathcliff

was an exaggeration even of the most extravagant of the squires in Craven. If there were many such people in any corner of this world, it would be greatly in want of a thorough clearing out. And, therefore, one may understand why the good people of Haworth should be amazed when Mrs. Gaskell set forth as common types the gentleman who fired small shot from his parlour-window at any one who came within convenient range, and the man who chuckled over his luck at dying just after insuring his life.

But, for all this, it is permissible also to suppose that there was a strongly marked provincial character in that region, even if Miss Brontë's life-like portraits were not their own sufficient evidence. All people seem to be commonplace to the commonplace observer. Genius reveals the difference; it does not invent it. In one sense, doubtless, the people were commonplace enough, and in that fact lay part of their offensiveness. Many of the upper classes, one may guess, were hard, crabbed men of business, with even less than the average of English toleration for senti- ment or aesthetic fancies; and their inferiors were sturdy workmen, capable of taking a pride in their own brutality, which would have shocked gentler races. But the precise degree in which these characteristics were manifested must be left to the decision of local observers. We cannot affect to know accurately in what proportion the charge of originality is to be shared between the Brontës and their neighbours; how far the sur- roundings were unusually harsh and the surrounded abnormally tender. In any case, one may assume that Miss Brontë and her sisters were at once even morbidly sensitive and exposed to the contact of persons emphatically intolerant of morbid sentiment. Their ordinary relation to the outside world seems to be indicated by one peculiarity of Miss Brontë's writing. When young Mark [sic] Yorke sees that Moore has been flattered by hear- ing a lady describe him as "not sentimental," that offensive lad gets down a dictionary and endeavours to dash Moore's pleasure by proving that "not sentimental" must mean destitute of ideas. The trait is very probably from life, and is at any rate life-like. There are many amiable people who take a keen pleasure in dashing cold water upon any little manifestation of self- complacency in their neighbours. To find out a man's tenderest corn, and then to bring your heel down upon it with a good rasping scrunch, is somehow gratifying to corrupt human nature. A kindly wit contrives to convey a compliment in affected satire. But the whole aim of a humourist of this variety is to convey the most mortifying truths in the most brutal plain-speaking. Now speeches modelled upon this plan are curiously frequent in Miss Brontë's conversations. Hunsden, the first sketch of the Yorke family in *The Professor*, composes his whole talk of a string of brutal home-truths. The worse characters, like Miss Fanshawe in *Villette*, thor- oughly enjoy telling a friendless governess that she is poor, plain, and sickly. And even her favourites, Rochester and Shirley and Paul Emanuel, have just a leaning to the same trick of speech, though with them it is an occasional bitter to heighten the flavour of their substantial kindness. Miss Brontë has as little sense of humour as Milton or Wordsworth; but her nearest approach to it is in some of those shrewd, bitter sayings which are rather more of a gibe than a compliment. When one remembers that the originals of the Yorkes were amongst her most cherished and cultivated friends, and that they are admittedly painted to the life, one may fancy that she had received a good many of those left-handed compliments which seem to have done duty for pleasant jests in the district.

The soliloquies in which her heroines indulge proceed upon the same plan. Jane Eyre sits in judgment upon herself, and listens to the evidence of Memory and Reason, accusing her of rejecting the real and "rabidly devouring the ideal." And she decides in accordance with her witnesses. "Listen, Jane Eyre, to your sentence; to-morrow place the glass before you and draw in chalk your own picture, faithfully, without softening one defect; omit no harsh line; smooth away no displeasing irregularity: write under it, 'Portrait of a governess, disconnected, poor, and plain!' "

Similar passages occur in *Shirley* and *Villette*, and obviously represent a familiar mood. The original of this portrait was frequently engaged, it would seem, in forcing herself to hear such unpalatable truths. When other people snubbed her, after the fashion of the Yorkes, she might be vexed by their harshness, but her own thoughts echoed their opinion. Lucy Snowe is rather gratified than otherwise when Miss Fanshawe treats her to one of these pleasing fits of frank thinking aloud. She pardons the want of feeling for the sake of the honesty.

Sensitive natures brought into contact with those of coarser grain may relieve themselves in various ways. Some might have been driven into revolt against the proprieties which found so harsh an expression. Poor Branwell Brontë took the unluckily commonplace path of escape from a too frigid code of external morality which leads to the public-house. His sisters followed the more characteristically feminine method. They learnt to be proud of the fetters by which they were bound. Instead of fretting against the stern law of repression, they identified it with the eternal code of duty, and rejoiced in trampling on their own weakness. The current thus restrained ran all the more powerfully in its narrow channel. What might have been bright and genial sentiment was transformed and chastened into a kind of austere enthusiasm. They became recluses in spirit, sternly enforcing a self-imposed rule, though, in their case, the convent walls were invisible and the objects of their devotion not those which dominate the ascetic imagination.

Theorists who trace the inheritance of race-characteristics might be interested in the curious development thus effected. The father of the family was an Irishman, and the mother a Cornish woman; the aunt, who succeeded her in the management of the household, had a persistent dislike for the character of her northern neighbours; even Charlotte herself, we are told, spake in her childhood with a strong Irish accent. And yet, as we find her saying in reference to the troubles of 1848, she has "no sympathy" with French or Irish. She had been spiritually annexed by the people with whom she lived. She was obtrusively and emphatically a Yorkshire woman, though only by adoption; she is never tired of proclaiming or implying her hearty preference of rough Yorkshire people to cockneys, sentimentalists, and that large part of the human race which we describe contemptuously as "foreigners." She is a typical example of the "patriotism of the steeple." She loved with her whole heart the narrowest insular type. She idolised the Duke of Wellington, with his grand contempt for humbug and ideas, terms synonymous — perhaps rightly synonymous — with many people. When she came in contact with the fine foreigners and Papists, it only increased her hearty contempt for forms of character and religion which, one might have fancied à priori, would have had many attractions for her. If at times she felt the aesthetic charm of parts of the Catholic system, she was but the more convinced that it was a poison, dangerous in proportion to its sweetness. The habit of trampling on some of her own impulses had become a religion for her. She had learnt to make a shield of reserve and self-repression, and could not be tempted to lay it aside when gentle persuasion took the place of rougher intimidation. Much is said by her biographers of the heroic force of will of her sister Emily, who presents the same type in an intensified form. Undoubtedly both sisters had powerful wills; but their natures had not less been moulded, and their characters, so to speak, turned inward by the early influence of surrounding circumstances. The force was not of that kind which resists the pressure from without, but of the kind which accepts and intensifies it, and makes a rigid inward law for itself of the law embodied in external conditions.

The sisters, indeed, differed widely, though with a strong resemblance. The iron had not entered so deeply into Charlotte's nature. Emily's naturally subjective mode of thought — to use the unpleasant technical phrase — found its most appropriate utterance in lyrical poetry. She represents, that is, the mood of pure passion, and is rather encumbered than otherwise by the necessity of using the more indirect method of concrete symbols. She feels, rather than observes; whereas Charlotte feels in observing. Charlotte had not that strange self-concentration which made the external world unreal to her sister. Her powers of observation, though restricted by circumstances and narrowed by limitations of her intellect, showed amazing penetration within her proper province. The greatest of all her triumphs in this direction is the character of Paul Emanuel, which has tasked Mr. Swinburne's powers of expressing admiration, and which one feels to be, in its way, inimitable. A more charming hero was never drawn, or one whose reality is more vivid and unmistakable. We know him as we know a familiar friend, or rather as we should know a friend whose character had been explained for us by a common acquaintance of unusual acuteness and opportunity of observation. Perhaps we might venture to add, that it is hardly explicable, except as a portrait dawn by a skilful hand guided by love, and by love intensified by the consciousness of some impassable barrier.

Mr. Swinburne compares this masterpiece of Miss Brontë's art with the famous heroes of fiction, Don Quixote, Uncle Toby, and Colonel Newcome. Don Quixote admittedly stands apart as one of the greatest creations of poetic imagination. Of Colonel Newcome I will not speak; but the comparison with Uncle Toby is enough to suggest what is the great secret both of Miss Brontë's success and its limitations. In one sense Paul Emanuel is superior even to such characters as these. He is more real: he is so real that we feel at once that he must have been drawn from a living model, though we may leave some indefinable margin of idealisation. If the merit of fiction were simply its approach to producing illusion, we might infer that Paul Emanuel was one of the first characters in the world of fiction. But such a test implies an erroneous theory of art; and, in fact, the intense individuality of Paul Emanuel is, in a different sense, the most serious objection to him. He is a real human being who gave lectures at a particular date in a pension at Brussels. We are as much convinced of that fact as we are of the reality of Miss Brontë herself; but the fact is also a presumption that he is not one of those great typical characters, the creation of which is the highest triumph of the dramatist or novelist. There is too much of the temporary and accidental — too little of the permanent and essential.

We all know and love Uncle Toby, but we feel quite sure that no such man ever existed except in Sterne's brain. There may have been some real being who vaguely suggested him; but he is, we assume, the creation of Sterne, and the projection into concrete form of certain ideas which had affected Sterne's imagination. He is not, indeed, nor is any fictitious character, a creation out of nothing. Partly, no doubt, he is Sterne himself, or Sterne in a particular mood; but Uncle Toby's soul, that which makes him live and excite our sympathy and love, is something which might be expressed by the philosopher as a theory, and which has been expressed in an outward symbol by an artist of extraordinary skill. Don Quixote is of perennial interest, because he is the most powerful type ever set forth of the contrast between the ideal and the commonplace, and his figure comes before us whenever we are forced to meditate upon some of the most vital and most melancholy truths about human life. Uncle Toby, in a far less degree, is a great creation, because he is the embodiment of one answer to a profound and enduring problem. He represents, it has been said, the wisdom of love, as Mr. Shandy exemplifies the love of wisdom. More precisely he is an incarnation of the sentimentalism of the eighteenth century. It is a phenomenon which has its bad and its good side, and which may be analysed and explained by historians of the time. Sterne, in describing Uncle Toby, gave a concrete symbol for one of the most important currents of thought of the time, which took religious, moral, and political, as well as artistic, shapes. In many ways the sentiment has lost much of its interest for us; but, though an utterance of an imperfect doctrine, we may infer that Uncle Toby's soul will transmigrate into new shapes, and perhaps develop into higher forms.

When we measure M. Paul Emanuel by this test, we feel instinctively that there is something wanting. The most obvious contrast is that M. Emanuel is no humourist himself, nor even a product of humour. The imperfections, the lovable absurdities, of Uncle Toby are imbedded in the structure of character. His whims and oddities always leave us in the appropriate mood of blended smiles and tears. Many people, especially "earnest" young ladies, will prefer M. Paul Emanuel, who, like his creator, is always in deadly earnest. At bottom he is always (like all ladies' heroes) a true woman, simple, pure, heroic, and loving—a real Joan of Arc, as Mr. Thackeray said of his creator, in the beard and blouse of a French professor. He attaches extravagant importance to trifles, indeed, for his irascible and impetuous temperament is always converting him into an Æolus of the duck-pond. So far there is, we may admit, a kind of pseudo-humorous element in his composition; but the humour, such as it is, lies entirely on the surface. He is perfectly sane and sensible, though a trifle choleric. Give him a larger sphere of action, and his impetuosity will be imposing instead of absurd. It is the mere accident of situation which gives, even for a moment, a ludicrous tinge to his proceedings.

Uncle Toby, on the contrary, would be even more of a humourist as a general on the battle-field than in his mimic sieges on the bowling green. The humour is in his very marrow, not in his surroundings; and the reason is that Sterne feels what every genuine humourist feels, and what, indeed, it is his main function to express—a strong sense of the irony of fate, of the queer mixture of good and bad, of the heroic and the ludicrous, of this world of ours, and of what we may call the perversity of things in general. Whether such a treatment is altogether right and healthy is another question; and most certainly Sterne's view of life is in many respects not only unworthy, but positively base. But it remains true that the deep humourist is finding a voice for one of the most pervading and profound of the sentiments raised in a philosophical observer who is struck by the discords of the universe. Sensitiveness to such discords is one of the marks of a truly reflective intellect, though a humourist suggests one mode of escape from the pain which they cause, whilst a philosophic and religious mind may find another and perhaps a more profound solution.

Now M. Paul Emanuel, admirable and amiable as he is, never carries us into the higher regions of thought. We are told, even ostentatiously, of the narrow prejudices which he shares, though they do not make him harsh and uncharitable. The prejudices were obvious in this case to the creator, because her own happened to be of a different kind. The "Tory and clergyman's daughter" was rather puzzled by finding that a bigoted Papist with a Jesuit education might still be a good man, and points out conscientiously the defects which she ascribes to his early training. But the mere fact of the narrowness, the want of familiarity with a wider sphere of thought, the acceptance of a narrow code of belief and morality, does not strike her as in itself having either a comic or a melancholy side. M. Paul has the wrong set of prejudices, but is not as wrong as prejudiced; and therefore we feel that a Sterne, or, say, a George Sand, whilst doing equal justice to M. Emanuel's excellent qualities, would have had a feeling (which in her was altogether wanting) of his limitation and his incongruity with the great system of the world. Seen from an intellectual point of view, placed in his due relation to the great currents of thought and feeling of the time, we should have been made to feel the pathetic and humorous aspects of M. Emanuel's character, and he might have been equally a living individual and yet a type of some more general idea. The philosopher might ask, for example, what is the exact value of unselfish heroism guided by narrow theories or employed on unworthy tasks; and the philosophic humourist or artist might embody the answer in a portrait of M. Emanuel considered from a cosmic or a cosmopolitan point of view. From the lower standpoint accessible to Miss Brontë he is still most attractive; but we see only his relations to the little scholastic circle, and have no such perception as the greatest writers would give us of his relations to the universe, or, as the next order would give, of his relations to the great world without.

Although the secret of Miss Brontë's power lies, to a great extent, in the singular force with which she can reproduce acute observations of character from without, her most esoteric teaching, the most accurate reflex from her familiar idiosyncrasy, is of course to be found in the characters painted from within. We may infer her personality more or less accurately from the mode in which she contemplates her neighbours, but it is directly manifested in various avatars of her own spirit. Among the characters who are more or less mouthpieces of her peculiar sentiment we may reckon not only Lucy Snowe and Jane Eyre, but, to some extent, Shirley, and, even more decidedly, Rochester. When they speak we are really listening to her own voice, though it is more or less disguised in conformity to dramatic necessity. There are great differences between them; but they are such differences as would exist between members of the same family, or might be explained by change of health or internal circumstances. Jane Eyre has not had such bitter experience as Lucy Snowe; Shirley is generally Jane Eyre in high spirits, and freed from harassing anxiety; and Rochester is really a spirited sister of Shirley's, though he does his very best to be a man, and even an unusually masculine specimen of his sex.

Mr. Rochester, indeed, has imposed upon a good many people; and he is probably responsible in part for some of the muscular heroes who have appeared since his time in the world of fiction. I must, however, admit that, in spite of some opposing authority, he does not appear to me to be a real character at all, except as a reflection of a certain side of his creator. He is in reality the personification of a true woman's longing (may one say it now?) for a strong master. But the knowledge is wanting. He is a very bold but necessarily unsuccessful attempt at an impossibility. The parson's daughter did not really know anything about the class of which he is supposed to be a type, and he remains vague and inconsistent in spite of all his vigour. He is intended to be a person who has surfeited from the fruit of the tree of knowledge, and addresses the inexperienced governess from the height—or depth—of his worldly wisdom. And he really knows just as little of the world as she does. He has to impose upon her by giving an account of his adventures taken from the first novel at hand of the early Bulwer school, or a diluted recollection of Byron. There is not a trace of real cynicism—of the strong nature turned sour by experience—in his whole conversation. He is supposed to be specially simple and masculine, and yet he is as self-conscious as a young lady on her first appearance in society, and can do nothing but discourse about his feelings, and his looks, and his phrenological symptoms, to his admiring hearer. Set him beside any man's character of a man, and one feels at once that he has no real solidity or vitality in him. He has, of course, strong nerves and muscles, but they are articles which can be supplied in unlimited quantities with little expense to the imagination. Nor can one deny that his conduct to Miss Eyre is abominable. If he had proposed to her to ignore the existence of the mad Mrs. Rochester, he would have acted like a rake, but not like a sneak. But the attempt to entrap Jane into a bigamous connection by concealing the wife's existence, is a piece of treachery for which it is hard to forgive him. When he challenges the lawyer and the clergyman to condemn him after putting themselves in his place, their answer is surely obvious. One may take a lenient view of a man who chooses by his own will to annul his marriage to a filthy lunatic; but he was a knave for trying to entrap a defenceless girl by a mock ceremony. He puts himself in a position in which the contemptible Mr. Mason has a moral advantage.

This is by far the worst blot in Miss Brontë's work, and may partly explain, though it cannot justify, the harsh criticisms made at the time. It is easy now to win a cheap reputation for generosity by trampling upon the dead bodies of the luckless critics who blundered so hopelessly. The time for anger is past; and mere oblivion is the fittest doom for such offenders. Inexperience, and consequently inadequate appreciation of the demands of the situation, was Miss Brontë's chief fault in this matter, and most certainly not any want of true purity and moral elevation. But the fact that she, in whom an instinctive nobility of spirit is, perhaps, the most marked characteristic, should have given scandal to the respectable, is suggestive of another inference. What, in fact, is the true significance of this singular strain of thought and feeling, which puts on various and yet closely allied forms in the three remarkable novels we have been considering? It displays itself at one moment in some vivid description, or—for "description" seems too faint a word—some forcible presentation to our mind's eye of a fragment of moorland scenery; at another, it appears as an ardently sympathetic portrayal of some trait of character at once vigorous and tender; then it utters itself in a passionate soliloquy, which establishes the fact that its author possessed the proverbial claim to knowledge of the heavenly powers; or again, it produces one of those singular little prose-poems—such as Shirley's description of Eve—which, with all their force, have just enough flavour of the "devoirs" at M. Heger's establishment to suggest that they are the work of an inspired school-girl. To gather up into a single formula the meaning of such a character as Lucy Snowe, or in other words, of Charlotte Brontë, is, of course, impossible. But at least such utterances always give us the impression of a fiery soul imprisoned in too narrow and too frail a tenement. The fire is pure and intense. It is kindled in a nature intensely emotional, and yet aided by a heroic sense of duty. The imprisonment is not merely that of a feeble body in uncongenial regions, but that of a narrow circle of thought, and consequently of a mind which has never worked itself clear by reflection, or developed a harmonious and consistent view of life. There is a certain feverish disquiet which is marked by the peculiar mannerism of the style. At its best, we have admirable flashes of vivid expression, where the material of language is the incarnation of keen intuitive thought. At its worst, it is strangely contorted, crowded by rather awkward personifications, and degenerates towards a rather unpleasant Ossianesque. More severity of taste would increase the power by restraining the abuse. We feel an aspiration after more than can be accomplished, an unsatisfied yearning for potent excitement, which is sometimes more fretful than forcible.

The symptoms are significant of the pervading flaw in otherwise most effective workmanship. They imply what, in a scientific sense, would be an inconsistent theory, and, in an aesthetic sense, an inharmonious representation of life. One great aim of the writing, explained in the preface to the second edition of *Jane Eyre*, is a protest against convention-ality. But the protest is combined with a most unflinching adherence to the proper conventions of society; and we are left in great doubt as to where the line ought to be drawn. Where does the unlawful pressure of society upon the individual begin, and what are the demands which it may rightfully make upon our respect? At one moment in *Jane Eyre* we seem to be drifting towards the solution that strong passion is the one really good thing in the world, and that all human conventions which oppose it should be disregarded. This was the tendency which shocked the respectable reviewers of the time. Of course they should have seen that the strongest sympathy of the author goes with the heroic self-conquest of the heroine under temptation. She triumphs at the cost of a determined self-sacrifice, and undoubtedly we are meant to sympathise with the martyr. Yet it is also true that we are left with the sense of an unsolved discord. Sheer stoical regard for duty is represented as something repulsive, however imposing, in the figure of St. John Rivers and virtue is rewarded by the arbitrary removal of the obstacles which made it unpleasant. What would Jane Eyre have done, and what would our sympathies have been, had she found that Mrs. Rochester had not been burnt in the fire at Thornfield? That is rather an awkward question. Duty is supreme, seems to be the moral of the story; but duty sometimes involves a strain almost too hard for mortal faculties.

If in the conflict between duty and passion, the good so often borders upon the impracticable, the greatest blessing in the world should be a will powerful enough to be an inflexible law for itself under all pressure of circumstances. Even a will directed to evil purposes has a kind of royal prerogative, and we may rightly do it homage. That seems to be the seminal thought in *Wuthering Heights*, that strange book to which we can hardly find a parallel in our literature, unless in such works as the *Revenger's Tragedy*, and some other crude but startling productions of the Elizabethan dramatists. But Emily Brontë's feeble grasp of external facts makes her book a kind of baseless nightmare, which we read with wonder and with distressing curiosity, but with far more pain than pleasure or profit. Charlotte's mode of conceiving the problem is given most fully in *Villette*, the book of which one can hardly say, with a recent critic, that it represents her "ripest wisdom," but which seems to give her best solution of the great problem of life. Wisdom, in fact, is not the word to apply to a state of mind which seems to be radically inconsistent and tentative. The spontaneous and intense affection of kindred and noble natures is the one really precious thing in life, it seems to say; and, so far, the thought is true or a partial aspect of the truth, and the high feeling undeniable. But then, the author seems to add, such happiness is all but chimerical. It falls to the lot only of a few exceptional people, upon whom fortune or Providence has delighted to shower its gifts. To all others life is either a wretched grovelling business, an affair of making money and gratifying sensuality, or else it is a prolonged martyrdom. Yield to your feelings, and the chances are enormously great that you are trampled upon by the selfish, or that you come into collision with some of those conventions which must be venerated, for they are the only barriers against moral degradation, and which yet somehow seem to make in favour of the cruel and the self-seeking. The only safe plan is that of the lady in the ballad, to "lock your heart in a case of gold, and pin it with a silver pin." Mortify your affections, scourge yourself with rods, and sit in sackcloth and ashes; stamp vigorously upon the cruel thorns that strew your pathway, and learn not to shrink when they lacerate the most tender flesh. Be an ascetic, in brief, and yet without the true aim of the ascetic. For, unlike him, you must admit that these affections are precisely the best part of you, and that the offers of the Church, which proposes to wean you from the world, and reward you by a loftier prize, are a delusion and a snare. They are the lessons of a designing priesthood, and imply a blasphemy against the most divine instincts of human nature.

This is the unhappy discord which runs through Miss Brontë's conceptions of life, and, whilst it gives an indescribable pathos to many pages, leaves us with a sense of something morbid and unsatisfactory. She seems to be turning for relief alternately to different teachers, to the promptings of her own heart, to the precepts of those whom she has been taught to revere, and occasionally, though timidly and tentatively, to alien schools of thought. The attitude of mind is, indeed, best indicated by the story (a true story, like most of her incidents) of her visit to the confessional in Brussels. Had she been a Catholic, or a Positivist, or a rebel against all the creeds, she might have reached some consistency of doctrine, and therefore some harmony of design. As it is, she seems to be under a desire which makes her restless and unhappy, because her best impulses are continually warring against each other. She is between the opposite poles of duty and happiness, and cannot see how to reconcile their claims, or even — for perhaps no one can solve that, or any other great problem exhaustively — how distinctly to state the question at issue. She pursues one path energetically, till she feels her self to be in danger, and then shrinks with a kind of instinctive dread, and resolves not only that life is a mystery, but that happiness must be sought by courting misery. Undoubtedly such a position speaks of a mind diseased, and a more powerful intellect would even under her conditions have worked out some more comprehensible and harmonious solution.

For us, however, it is allowable to interpret her complaints in our own fashion, whatever it may be. We may give our own answer to the dark problem, or at least indicate the path by which an answer must be reached. For a poor soul so grievously beset within and without by troubles in which we all have a share, we can but feel the strongest sympathy. We cannot sit at her feet as a great teacher, nor admit that her view of life is satisfactory or even intelligible. But we feel for her as for a fellow-sufferer who has at least felt with extraordinary keenness the sorrows and disappointments which torture most cruelly the most noble virtues, and has clung throughout her troubles to beliefs which must in some form or other be the guiding lights of all worthy actions. She is not in the highest rank amongst those who have fought their way to a clearer atmosphere, and can help us to clearer conceptions; but she is amongst the first of those who have felt the necessity of consolation, and therefore stimulated to more successful efforts.

Charlotte Brontë, Reason, and the Moon
Robert B. Heilman*

One of Charlotte Brontë's great fears, a biographer has said, was fear of the imagination; entry into the imaginative could actually seem to her to be a guilty self-indulgence. This is not untrue, and yet Charlotte was anything but consistent; one minute she was in the mood of the French-woman who cried out enthusiastically at a party, "J'adore la logique," and then she could turn around and warmly anatomize the defects of reason. The truth is that few artists can have been so beset as she was by the competing claims of the rational and the nonrational upon art and life.

She falls between the counterforces described by Robert Graves in a recent somewhat teasing postscript[1] to his "controversial" *White Goddess* of 1948. "The avowed purpose of science," says Graves, "is to banish all lunar superstitions and bask in the pure light of solar reason." In one mood, Charlotte Brontë would surely subscribe to this purpose. But Graves takes a dim view of this progress, which he says would be fatal to all true poetry; and he foresees historical developments that will include the emergence of a new goddess of "intuition." There is no doubt that among pre-Gravesian devotees of this religion Charlotte would also have to be counted.

We can learn something about Charlotte Brontë's personality and her art by observing how deeply her novels are penetrated by the counterat-tractions of reason and whatever "superstition" or "intuition" or other impulses arise to oppose it. I want to look first at some expository passages, and this will mean risking the catalogue; but the assembling of key statements will make a valuable background against which to see how, at important dramatic crises, the very shape of the action is determined by Charlotte's consciousness of the duel, in Graves's terms, between Apollo and the White Goddess.

Even in *The Professor* and *Shirley*, where Charlotte is consciously restrained, essaying the social-pictorial, and therefore implicitly "Apollo-nian," the struggle appears. In *The Professor* she insists on the "plain and homely," scorns "the idealists, the dreamers," earnestly adjures "novelists . . . never . . . to weary of the study of real life." Her aesthetic is rooted in a rationalistic ethic: ". . . the man of regular life and rational mind never despairs." Crimsworth avers, "Reason was my physician; [and] . . . did me good" and rejoices that in Frances "the more dangerous flame burned safely under the eye of reason," which could "reduce the rebel, and humble its blaze to embers"; with almost doctrinaire insistence he theo-rizes that Reason must secretly justify even those impulses "which control

*©1960 by the Regents of the University of California. Reprinted from *Nineteenth-Century Fiction* 14, no. 4 (March 1960) 283–302 by permission.

us. . . . ." Such maxims are meant to determine the development of both character and plot.

Yet, after all of this, the more sentient and disorderly Brontë emerges — even in the domain of theory. Crimsworth, the apostle of reason, refers to "my darling, my cherished-in-secret, Imagination, the tender and the mighty. . . ." When this "sweet temptress" pictures for him an evening with Frances Henri, he fears that he may not be able "to address her only in the language of Reason and Affection." This is chronologically the introduction to "Imagination," one of Charlotte's two great terms for the nonrational that pulls her strongly. The other is "feeling," and its spokesman in *The Professor* is Frances Henri. Through her the true Charlotte pathos escapes in revolt against the world of rationality which Charlotte formally proclaims as the domain of her first novel. To Yorke Hunsden, Frances retorts, "Better to be without logic than without feeling," and she amplifies the retort into a firm attack on him for "interfering with your own feelings, and those of other people" because "you imagine" them to be "inconsistent with logic."

In *Shirley* there is less direct talk about reason and its counterforces, yet the tendency of both talk and action is toward the validation of the spontaneous. Social order is the rational theme, but the private intuition is where Charlotte repeatedly comes to rest. Caroline Helstone defends "instinct," "the voice we hear in solitude," as the source of trustworthy knowledge. A "strange, excited feeling in my heart" is a clue to stirring events. In the name of "common sense" Mrs. Yorke makes a violent attack upon Caroline for relying upon "impulse" and "*feelings,*" which she says is sentimental and romantic; yet the reader is meant to sympathize with Caroline's earnest credo: "Of course, I should be guided by my feelings: they were given me to that end." Of Shirley, Louis Moore says, "Once I only *saw* her beauty, now I *feel* it." And Charlotte, who constantly wishes to be antiromantic, clearly intends that we accept Caroline's declaration of faith on Shirley's love affair: "It *is* romantic, but it is also right."

Since it is an historical commonplace that Charlotte was imaginatively most free in her second and fourth novels, we might expect to find little play of the "pure light of solar reason" in *Jane Eyre* and *Villette*. Yet, despite a feeling for the "dark" that is of great aesthetic importance, Charlotte is always plagued by the claims of the light. In the fortunetelling scene in *Jane Eyre*, Rochester interprets what Jane's "forehead declares": "Reason sits firm and holds the reins, and she will not let the feelings burst away and hurry her to wild chasms." When Jane thinks that she has let herself love a Rochester who is really in love with Miss Ingram, she reports that "Reason" has told "how I had rejected the real, and rabidly devoured the ideal." It is on this occasion that she tries to "bring back with a strict hand" such "thoughts and feelings" of the heart as "had been straying through imagination's boundless and trackless waste, into the safe fold of common sense." All this might be the burden of an age-of-reason novel —

except that reason is undercut, for imagination's trackless waste turns out to be exactly the route to Jane's well-being. On another occasion reason is almost justified by being given the odd role of aide to feelings. When Rochester ruthlessly pressures Jane to be his mistress, she reports that "my very conscience and reason turned traitors against me, and . . . spoke almost as loud as Feeling: and that clamoured wildly. 'Oh, comply!' it said."

At another time Jane sets forth the basic dualism of Charlotte's moral awareness: "Feeling without judgment is a washy draught indeed; but judgment untempered by feeling is too bitter and husky a morsel for human deglutition." On the whole, the washy draught is the lesser of two dangers; Jane's regular impulse is to say "I feel" this or that, to insist, "I know what I feel." When she splits her inheritance with the Riverses, she calls it "as much a matter of feeling as of conscience: I must indulge my feelings; I so seldom have had an opportunity of doing so." Though feeling may not always be reliable, its dependability appears to grow with the intensity of the crisis; Jane trusts utterly that "feeling . . . as sharp, as strange, as startling" as an electric shock that awakens her to Rochester's telepathic cry. "That wondrous shock of feeling had come like the earthquake which shook the foundations of Paul and Silas's prison; it had opened the doors of the soul's cell, . . ." It saved Jane. And here, surely, Charlotte is writing poetry under the auspices that Robert Graves approves.

After the insistent justification of feeling in *Shirley* and the triumph of the intuitive in *Jane Eyre* we might expect that by the time she came to *Villette* Charlotte would not have to refight the old battle of values. But no such freedom is hers; Lucy Snowe must live through the same conflict in which Crimsworth and Jane Eyre were caught. In religious dispute, of course, Lucy is content to be on the side of Reason (nearly always capitalized in *Villette*), which she is sure condemns Catholicism. On one distressed occasion she feels a "wild longing," but it is "softened into a wish with which Reason could cope: she put it down. . . ." Toward the Brettons, her rescuers, she feels "an importunate gratitude, which I entreated Reason betimes to check"; she approves "these struggles" that help give conduct "that turn which Reason approves, and which Feeling, perhaps, too often opposes. . . ." But the rational virtues are much less attractive in Mme. Beck, who, like other characters that Charlotte does not admire, consults only her "judgment" and is not "led an inch by her feelings," and what is more attributes M. Paul's devotion to Lucy to his "unreliable, imaginative temperament."

Yet as artist Charlotte sees clearly the complex facts of life; she makes Lucy observe that we dislike and avoid some people "though reason confesses that they are good people. . . ." At times Lucy simply cannot stand the "dry, stinting check of Reason" and thinks that she must yield to the "full, liberal impulse of feeling." In *Villette* as a whole Charlotte takes especial pains to justify feelings, almost as if she had to beat down the principles of a too rational world. "Before I *saw*, I *felt* that life was in the great room," says Lucy. "Deep into some of Madame's secrets I had entered — I know not how: by an intuition or an inspiration which came to me — I know not whence." When someone whom she assumes to be a workman opens her door, she "felt a little thrill — a curious sensation, too quick and transient to be analyzed" — and the entrant turns out to be Paul. Lucy recognizes a fellow hypochondriac by facial marks whose meaning "if I did not *know*, at least I *felt*, . . ." Polly Home shares the trust in feeling as a way of knowing: "how strange it is that people seem so slow to feel the truth — not to see, but *feel!*" In these characteristic passages we find not only "intuition," which for Graves denotes a positive value, but three distinct occasions on which "feeling" (repeatedly italicized) is made prior or superior to "knowing" or "seeing" — an implicit rejection of the "pure light of solar reason."

At the apex of the terms in which Charlotte expresses her conflict in impulses and values stands "Imagination." Naturally Lucy is compelled to pit its claims against those of Reason. But against what Reason? A beautiful, Athena-like figure? No, against "This hag, this Reason," with its "withered hand" and "chill blue lips of eld": "Reason might be right; yet no wonder we are glad at times to defy her, to rush from under her rod and give a truant hour to Imagination — *her* soft, bright foe, *our* sweet Help, our divine Hope." But for this defiance Reason, "vindictive as a devil," exacts a "terrible revenge." All the ambiguity of Charlotte's feelings is concentrated in the word "imagination"; it means to her, in one mood, a snare and a delusion; in another mood she could exclaim with Thomas Mann's Felix Krull, "What a glorious gift is imagination, and what satisfaction it affords," and even crave it as a road to safety. Happily Lucy yields to it, or is ravished by it, one summer night after Mme. Beck has given her a sedative:

> Imagination was roused from her rest, and she came forth impetuous and venturous. With scorn she looked on Matter, her mate —
> "Rise!" she said: "Sluggard! this night I will have *my* will; nor shalt thou prevail."
> "Look forth and view the night!" was her cry. . . .

This introduces the most wonderful of Charlotte's nocturnes: the surrealistic park scene that opens the English novel to an extraordinary new perceptiveness and style. The essence of the long passage is the casting of a strange and fascinating veil of illusion over familiar things; through the enchanting veil Lucy makes some errors, and then she rebukes herself — how? "Ah! when imagination once runs riot where do we stop?" And twice she spanks her "Fancy" for leading her astray. But if Lucy thus gives voice to the "rational" element in Charlotte, fortunately the artist in Charlotte lets stand, untouched, the thrilling account of all that Lucy felt and fancied when "Imagination was roused from her rest."

2

The conflict between reason-judgment-common sense and feeling-imagination-intuition, a conflict which lasted through Charlotte's life as an artist, existed not simply as a routine echo of a general human problem but because of the profound attraction which the nonrational had for her. Hence the frequency with which it comes into the words of all her major characters, and, more important, into conflicts between and within characters. But still beyond that, what is at stake is the kind of artist Charlotte is to be; and by that I mean the kind of aesthetic excitement that she is to create when her characters are engaged in crucial actions; that is, in actions in which they must be most freely and wholly themselves. The choice that ends the crux may be "reasonable," but the instrument of decision, the persuasive presence, may be nonrational or suprarational. If the movement in Charlotte's novels—the growth of her protagonists—is toward something that we can call "daylight," the field of significant action is often the dark.

Graves's key phrases are "lunar superstition" and "solar reason." So far we have proceeded as if "superstition" and "reason" encompassed all that is to be inspected, and as if "lunar" and "solar" were not there at all, or were no more than convenient metaphorical tags. But the adjectives are very important to Graves, whose stance is vigorously anti-Apollonian and who attributes "creative power in poetry" to "inspiration," and "inspiration" to "the Lunar Muse." He is almost ostentatious in his salute to the moon, who "moves the tides, influences growth, rules the festal calendar of Judaism, Islam, and Christianity, and possesses other unaccountable magic properties, known to every lover and poet."

Well, if Charlotte Brontë, the anguished devotee of feeling and intuition, had followed Graves in time, it would be difficult not to describe her as under his "influence." Or if a follower of his had set out to establish a lunar cult by fictional propaganda, he could hardly have exploited the moon more fully than she has done. Whether by plan or through an unconscious or semiconscious sense of forces at work in the world, Charlotte tends to make the "White Goddess" a presiding deity, if not over her novels as a whole, at least over moments of crisis.[2]

Even in *The Professor*, that intendedly matter-of-fact tale of plain lovers, Charlotte's attraction to the moon adds a fanciful note. On the night when Crimsworth has a significant interview with disturbing Yorke Hunsden, "there was a crescent curve of moonlight to be seen by the parish church tower. . . ." Later, on a "glorious night," when "an unclouded moon poured her light" down into a beechwood glade, "Hunsden held out under her beam an ivory miniature"—a likeness of an old love in whose face Frances Henri sees signs of a "triumphant effort, to wrest some vigorous and valued faculty from insupportable constraint. . . ." The mild note of revelation in these passages becomes stronger in the episode in which Crimsworth sees Mlle. Zoraïde Reuter, who has been making eyes at him and getting some response from him, carrying on with his employer Pelet: ". . . above me was the clear-obscure of a cloudless night sky— splendid moonlight subdued the tremulous sparkle of the stars—." Later Crimsworth remarks that Pelet was ignorant that "the still hour, a cloudless moon, and an open lattice had revealed to me the secret of his selfish love and false friendship. . . ."

In *Shirley* Charlotte presents a much subtler triangular situation, in a much better-realized scene. It is in the "moonlight beauty" of the estate that Caroline Helstone sees Shirley Keeldar and Robert Moore, whom she wrongly supposes to be in love: "Tree and hall rose peaceful under the night sky and clear full orb; pearly paleness gilded the buildings; mellow brown gloom bosomed it round; shadows of deep green brooded above its oak-wreathed roof. The broad pavement in front shone pale also; it gleamed as if some spell had transformed the dark granite to glistering Parian: on the silvery space slept two sable shadows, thrown sharply defined from two human figures." The word "spell" does not beg the question for Charlotte's art, which here begins to make us respond to the special scenic and tonal vividness to which the moon inspires her.

This is in *Shirley*, where Charlotte is most fully committed to the daylight view of experience. It tells us a great deal about her that even here she is repeatedly drawn to the moonlight, to the shiver of the strange which for her it communicates, and which she communicates by stylistic originality. On a night when Caroline is suffering from her emotional illness we are told not that there is a "full moon" and a "blue sky," but that the sky is "gravely blue" and "full of the moon." Caroline meets fifteen-year-old Martin Yorke, whom she fascinates, under a "pearl-white moon" that "smiles through the green trees." Robert Moore meets a "mad Calvinist" on a "clouded" but "very windy night": ". . . the moon was at the full, and Michael was as near crazed as possible . . ." If this has more of the conventional, we find the special Brontë frisson on the night Robert is shot from ambush, when Mr. Yorke says of the moon that it is "rising into the haze, staring at us wi' a strange red glower. . . . What does she mean by leaning her cheek on Rushedge i' that way, and looking at us wi' a scowl and a menace?"

However, Charlotte lets go most excitingly when the lunar contributes to the kind of task she nearly always performs originally — the exploration of personality. At the end of a hallucinatory period in Caroline's psychosomatic illness, "The moon, lately risen, was gazing full and mild upon her: floating in deep blue space, it watched her unclouded." By this personification, which she uses a number of times, Charlotte edges away from the pictorial toward a concept that can be used thrillingly — the idea of a cosmic sensibility observing mortal actions. This implies a sensitive mortal responsiveness, and with Caroline this sensitivity takes the form of a profound anxiety. She observes, "The moon shines clear," and she imagines grimly that "within the church just now that moonlight shines as softly as in my room. It will fall through the east window full on the Helstone monument. When I close my eyes I seem to see poor papa's epitaph in black letters on the white marble. There is plenty of room for other inscriptions underneath." As often, the moonlight leads to a concreteness that creates the life in the scene.

Or the moon may sponsor a romantic fantasy. Shirley's lover, Louis Moore, who calls himself a "rapt, romantic lunatic," picks a stormy moonlight night to savor waking dreams of Shirley: "the great single cloud . . . tossed buoyant before a continued long-sounding, high-rushing moonlight tempest. The Moon reigns glorious, glad of the gale; as glad as if she gave herself to his fierce caress with love." The erotic shiver, which frequently breaks into Charlotte's fiction, is right enough here, for Louis, insisting, "I *do* dream: I *will* dream," eventually has a vision of Shirley as a Juno replaying the Jupiter-Semele story and becoming, when seen directly, "an insufferable glory burning terribly between the pillars" and destroying a rival lover. The White Goddess admits a destructive hatred into sentimental reverie.

Shirley, who, "her eye full of night and lightning," evades her lover Louis in a cold "moon-lit hall," and who walks at night on "the chance of meeting a fairy," also has nocturnal visions: under a "new throned and glorious" moon she feels a "still, deep, inborn delight."

> This joy gives her experience of a genii-life. Buoyant, by green steps, by glad hills, all verdure and light, she reaches a station scarcely lower than that whence angels looked down on the dreamer of Bethel, and her eye seeks, and her soul possesses, the vision of life as she wishes it. No—not as she wishes it; she has not time to wish: the swift glory spreads out, weeping and kindling, and multiplies its splendours faster than Thought can effect his combinations, faster than Aspiration can utter her longings. Shirley says nothing while the trance is upon her— . . .

Here the lunar muse sets free, for its own sake, a kind of vision fiction had not known since Bunyan.

A virtuoso with the moon, Charlotte uses it to reveal not only "swift glory" but also fascinating horror. Again the vision is Shirley's, and now she tells how a mermaid might appear. Here again the moon is personified, as if it had a mysterious hand in the affair, for Shirley and Caroline are supposedly on the deck of a ship, "watching and being watched by a full harvest moon":

> something is to rise white on the surface of the sea, over which that moon mounts silent, and hangs glorious: the object glitters and sinks. It rises again. I think I hear it cry with an articulate voice: I call you up

from the cabin: I show you an image, fair as alabaster, emerging from the dim wave. We both see the long hair, the lifted and foam-white arm, the oval mirror, brilliant as a star. It glides nearer: a human face is plainly visible; a face . . . paleness does not disfigure . . . I see a preternatural lure in its wily glance: it beckons. Were we men we should spring at the sign, the cold billow would be dared for the sake of the colder enchantress; being women, we stand safe, though not dreadless. She comprehends our unmoved gaze; she feels herself powerless; anger crosses her front; she cannot charm, but she will appal us: she rises high, and glides all revealed, on the dark wave-ridge. Temptress-terror! monstrous likeness of ourselves!

Here once more is the surrealistic toward which Charlotte swings when she is creatively most uninhibited. It is wonderful pictorially, but her adventurous imagination goes beyond stage setting to express a stirring new intuition of reality. The moon visions always partake of the revelatory—of human possibility or human actuality, or of the quality of mind of those who have the visions. When Charlotte wants to make a quick plunge into the rare essence of a character, she instinctively demands the presence of the lunar muse.

3

If one is not prepared for the frequent appearances of the moon in *Shirley,* he would surely expect a Charlotte devoted to the White Goddess to bring her constantly into the kind of book that *Jane Eyre* is. He would be right; in *Jane Eyre* the moon is an aesthetic staple, at times a scenic element inherently charming to the writer, at times almost a character; at its most interesting it reveals an author groping for a cosmic symbolization of reality, or toward a reality beyond the confines of everyday actuality, toward an interplay of private consciousness and mysterious forces in the universe. In a book one of the illustrations that catch Jane's eye is of "cold and ghastly moon glancing through bars of cloud at a wreck just sinking"; in one of her extraordinary surrealistic paintings, the woman "rising into the sky" bears "on the neck . . . a pale reflection like moonlight; the same faint lustre touched the train of thin clouds from which rose and bowed this vision of the Evening Star"; again, when she is "sketching fancy vignettes . . . [from] the ever-shifting kaleidoscope of imagination," Jane draws "the rising moon, and a ship crossing its disk"; she cannot help imagining how "strange" the antique beds on the third floor at Thornfield would have looked "by the pallid gleam of moonlight." Rochester is moonstruck too. Of a past mistress he became jealous on a "moonlit balcony," and he describes one "fiery West Indian night" when, with "black clouds . . . casting up over" the ocean, he listened to his maniac wife shriek curses: ". . . the moon was setting in the waves, broad and red, like a hot cannon-ball—she threw her last bloody glance over a world quivering with the ferment of tempest." The physical universe is in tune with his private agony.

But this is only a start. In Jane's life every crucial event has its special lunar display. To leave Gateshead, she dresses "by light of a half-moon just setting"; at Lowood she and Helen Burns first visit the friendly Miss Temple's room when the "rising wind" swept "some heavy clouds" away and "left the moon bare; and her light, . . . shone full both on us and on . . . Miss Temple"; again, "the light of the unclouded summer moon" aids her on her way to what is to be the death scene of Helen Burns. Always there is the suggestion of a transcendental force mildly at work; but above all, these lunar nocturnes have an air of mystery. Jane meets Rochester by moonlight and accepts his proposal by moonlight; Mrs. Rochester once raids the lower house by moonlight; the moon has a share in the terrors of the night before the abortive wedding, in Jane's decision to leave Thornfield, and finally in her rejection of Rivers and return to Rochester.

On the night Jane meets Rochester she is constantly aware of the moon, which appears on page after page. "On the hill-top above me sat the rising moon; pale yet as a cloud, but brightening momently: she looked over Hay. . . ." Here the moon is detached observer; after Jane meets the fallen rider, "the moon was waxing bright," and she could see him clearly. The moon is protective: ". . . I am not at all afraid of being out late when it is moonlight. . . ." They look at Thornfield Hall, "on which the moon cast a hoary gleam"; Jane observes a willow "rising up still and straight to meet the moonbeams. . . ." The encounter is exciting, particularly because she has been helpful; in this state of mind she hates to return to dull Thornfield and turns instead to the sky: "a blue sea absolved from taint of cloud; the moon ascending it in solemn march: her orb seeming to look up as she left the hill tops, from behind which she had come, far and farther below her, and aspired to the zenith, midnight dark in its fathomless depth and measureless distance. . . ." The lunar being, which can serve as a source of sympathy with an existent mood—here it is a kind of fellow aspirant—can also inspire a fitting mood. One night "when the moon, which was full and bright . . . , came in her course to that space in the sky opposite my casement, and looked in at me through the unveiled panes, her glorious gaze roused me. Awaking in the dead of night, I opened my eyes on her disk—silver-white and crystal-clear. It was beautiful, but too solemn: I half rose, and stretched my arm to draw the curtain." At this moment the house is thrown into terror by mad Mrs. Rochester's attack on Mason.

On the night of Rochester's proposal the lunar symbolization of disorder works somewhat differently. At first the garden is charming in the light of the "now-rising moon"; Rochester's shadow is "thrown long over the garden by the moon not yet risen high," and he urges Jane not to go to bed, "while sunset is thus at meeting with moon-rise"; when he formally proposes, she commands him to "turn to the moonlight," as if for verification. Then: "But what had befallen the night? The moon was not yet set, and we were all in shadow: I could scarcely see my master's face. . . ." It is, I believe, rather easy to overrate the conventional in the scenic details here; this is more likely to happen if we take the episode alone and fail to see it in relation to the whole pattern of lunar imagery. The symbols of the proposal scene — the moon, and the chestnut tree split by lightning — lose whatever they have of an extemporized, melodramatic air when they are carried on into the stormy prewedding night scene and become direct objects of Jane's anxiety-filled contemplation. As she is addressing the two parts of the split chestnut, "the moon appeared momentarily in that part of the sky which filled their fissure; her disk was blood-red, and half-overcast; she seemed to throw on me one bewildered, dreary glance, and buried herself again instantly in the deep drift of cloud."

Through the moon the outer world becomes consonant with Jane's own misgivings. Since it is "moonlight at intervals," Jane looks for Rochester, who is away on business, but he does not come; finally "the moon shut herself wholly within her chamber, and drew close her curtain of dense cloud. . . . rain came driving fast. . . ." Jane gives way to "hypochondriac foreboding," relieved when she finds that "the moon had opened a blue field in the sky, and rode in it watery bright"; she sees Rochester returning. She tells him of a dream of Thornfield Hall in ruins, and herself wandering there "on a moon-light night," looking for him and finally crashing down with a crumbling wall. But he comforts her; the west winds blow the clouds away, and there is a benediction: "The moon shone peacefully."

In *Villette*, as in *Jane Eyre*, the moon comes into its sharpest dramatic role late in the story. But it obsesses Charlotte enough to keep sliding into earlier scenes: Lucy looks at sleeping Polly Home "by the fitful gleam of moonlight," walks on a European street "by a fitful gleam of moonlight," or gazes at "the polar splendour of the new-year moon — an orb white as a world of ice." In this last, the pictorial fact betrays an odd quiver of aesthetic life, as it does, too, when Miss Marchmont tells of her lover's death: "I see the moon of a calm winter night float full, clear, and cold, over the inky mass of shrubbery, and the silvered turf of my grounds": her lover is thrown from his horse, and she asks, "How could I name that thing in the moonlight before me?"

Gradually we become aware that in some vague way that Charlotte has not defined for herself the moon stands for something. This is how Lucy puts her envy of the gay Ginevra Fanshawe: "I too felt those autumn suns and saw those harvest moons, and I almost wished to be covered in with earth and turf, deep out of their influence; for I could not live in their light, nor make them comrades, nor yield them affection." What is significant here is that the sun (the only time it appears in a serious treatment of feeling) and the moon could be felt as "comrades" by and could exert "influence" on a human being. This power to influence is more strongly implied in a later reflection of Lucy's:

> Where, indeed, does the moon not look well? What is the scene, confined or expansive, which her orb does not hallow? Rosy or fiery, she mounted . . . while we watched her flushed ascent, she cleared to gold, and . . . floated up stainless into a now calm sky. Did moonlight soften or sadden Dr. Bretton? Did it touch him with romance?

Such passages prepare us for the series of garden scenes involving the "apparitions" that are important in the story. Lucy's first experience of that frightening event takes place—yes, on a moonlight night: "A moon was in the sky, not a full moon, but a young crescent. I saw her through a space in the boughs overhead. She and the stars, visible beside her, were no strangers where all else was strange: my childhood knew them. I had seen that golden sign with the dark globe in its curve leaning on azure, beside an old thorn at the top of an old field, in Old England. . . ." Now this scene is linked with a subsequent crucial garden scene not only by the moonlight but also by Lucy's association of one lighted night scene with another (a habit which shows that Charlotte's lunar sensibility was regular and stable, not casual and erratic). In the later scene Lucy's moral growth is dramatized by her burial of some letters from Graham and by her refusal to flee from the apparition. "At seven o'clock the moon rose," Lucy notes in the documentary style that often finely supports her non-naturalistic episodes, "The air of the night was very still, but dim with a peculiar mist, which changed the moonlight into a luminous haze. In this air, or this mist, there was some quality—electrical, perhaps—which acted in a strange sort upon me. I felt as I had felt a year ago in England—on a night when the aurora borealis was streaming and sweeping round heaven, . . . I felt, not happy, far otherwise, but strong with reinforced strength." The night Lucy refers to was one on which, returning from a visit, she "should have quailed in the absence of moonlight" but for the "moving mystery—the Aurora Borealis": "Some new power it seemed to bring." On that occasion she resolved to go to London, leaving a desolate life behind her, just as now in the garden she is taking steps to leave a life of fear and psychic dependence behind her; each time it is a nocturnal light from the sky that she identifies as the source of the ability to advance: of power and strength.

In the affair with M. Paul that is the major experience in Lucy's life two key scenes are moonlit—one of them in the same old garden. On this night Paul is distressingly cool and detached: ". . . once again he looked at the moon. . . . In a moment he was gone; the moonlit threshold lay pale and shadowless before the closed front-door." Then he gives her a Catholic pamphlet meant to convert her, one of the moves in the sober dramatic treatment of the important religious theme (to be compared, for instance, with Scott's trivializing of it in *Rob Roy*). The moon presides over a still more serious event, this time in another garden: when Paul gives Lucy a school of her own, "Above the poplars, the laurels, the cypresses, and the roses, looked up a moon so lovely and so halcyon, the heart trembled under her smile. . . ." Although the passage is ambiguous, Lucy appears to be addressing the moon when she apostrophizes: "White Angel! let thy light linger; leave its reflection on succeeding clouds; bequeath its cheer to that time which needs a ray in retrospect." (Paul's surname is Emanuel, and "the assurance of his sleepless interest . . . broke on me like a light from heaven. . . .") The religious implication of the moon imagery is carried further after Paul's proposal: "We walked back to the Rue Fossette by moonlight — such moonlight as fell on Eden — shining through the shades of the Great Garden, and haply gilding a path glorious for a step divine — a Presence nameless." This is the last use of the moon in Charlotte's last novel, and it is the ultimate reach in her interpretation of the moon — the moon that could hallow a scene, be a comrade, exert an influence, supply strength, echo a great myth, and suggest the presence of the divine. Such a range would not be possible if she were idly summoning and manipulating a cliché.

4

Nor would a cliché permit such striking passages as the three to which I finally turn — two in *Jane Eyre* and one in *Villette*. In these what is immediately remarkable is the way in which the moon steps vividly out of the décor to penetrate the dramatic action; and because it penetrates the action, we see the relation of these scenes to the theme which we have been considering in Graves's formulation, and to the underlying, never wholly articulated, meaning which the moon has for Charlotte as artist.

In *Jane Eyre*, we remember, Charlotte assiduously gives "reason" and "judgment" their due but keeps leaning toward "feeling" as the truly desirable and dependable quality in humanity. In fact, when Rochester pleads with Jane to stay with him, her reason all but supports her impulse to give in. But despite this double pressure she leaves. Under what aegis, then? All the forces that make for her departure are summed up in a fortifying dream, and it is right after the dream that she leaves. The dream starts by recalling a childhood terror — a mysterious light moving on an inside wall and seeming to be "a herald of some coming vision from another world." The light pauses "tremblingly" in the center of the ceiling.

> I lifted up my head to look: the roof resolved to clouds, high and dim; the gleam was such as the moon imparts to vapours she is about to sever. I watched her come — watched with the strangest anticipation; as though some word of doom were to be written on her disk. She broke forth as never moon yet burst from cloud: a hand first penetrated the sable folds and waved them away; then, not a moon, but a white human

form shone in the azure, inclining a glorious brow earthward. It gazed
and gazed on me. It spoke to my spirit: immeasurably distant was the
tone, yet so near, it whispered in my heart—
    "My daughter, flee temptation!"
    "Mother, I will."
    So I answered after I had waked from the trance-like dream.

Jane's almost immediate departure can hardly be said to come from
"reason"; in fact, a devotee of reason might well attribute it to what
Graves calls "lunar superstition." For the moon is there, the thrilling center
of a highly original dramatic expression of another "feeling" that effectively counters the feeling (and the reason) that urges her to live with
Rochester. This force is "immeasurably distant" but as "near" as a whisper
in the heart: Charlotte's strong sense of the paradoxical alliance between
the intimately personal and the universal.

Now let us observe the lunar relationship between this scene and the
one in which St. John Rivers almost hypnotizes Jane into marrying him
and she is saved by the telepathic summons from Rochester. The structural
parallel between the scenes is amazingly close: in each, Jane is being
subjected to almost overpowering pressure to accept a man who has some
"reason" on his side and whom she only partly resists. Initially we recall
that she rejects Rivers not for "good reasons" but because of a "sensation"
of "unspeakable strangeness," a "wondrous shock of feeling"; indeed,
Rivers is repeatedly described in a way that might make him a sort of
figure of reason—i.e., by images of cold and ice. By now we can see that
Charlotte would inevitably make a night scene of Rivers's climactic effort
to win Jane, for only in this way can she find the suitable dramatic form
for her notion of how reality becomes known. The long scene starts with
Rivers in the garden watching "the rising of the moon," and his turning
"quite from the moon" to address Jane; then we move indoors and Rivers
reads from the Bible—by a curious propriety from Revelation, for such
scenes are always revelatory; and with great irony, since what is to be
revealed is quite foreign to Rivers's expectations. During the reading "the
May moon [is] shining in through the uncurtained window, and rendering
almost unnecessary the light of the candle on the table." We begin to
suspect an implied, perhaps not wholly conscious, contrast in the "lights"
by which people act, and our suspicion is reinforced by what follows. Jane
almost gives in to Rivers, but she struggles to find a decisive clue to the act
of choice. As she puts it, "I contended with my inward dimness of vision,
before which clouds yet rolled. . . . 'Show me, show me the path!' I
entreated of Heaven." Her entreaty to Heaven is followed by this: "The one
candle was dying out: the room was full of moonlight. My heart beat fast
and thick: I heard its throb. Suddenly it stood still to an inexpressible
feeling that thrilled it through, and passed at once to my head and
extremities." This is the call from Rochester, and what is more, we find
later that at this very time, when Rochester himself, having "supplicated

God," had uttered the call that Jane heard, he "by a vague, luminous haze, knew the presence of a moon." For Jane, the moonlight has put out the candlelight within the minister's house: some larger vision (marriage for love) has transcended a narrow call (marriage for "duty"). The moon is no accident; it is present to two people who have "dimness of vision" and who have called on Heaven; it assists in a discovery which the story presents as utterly right. The lunar light has been present at Jane's two rejections of men, and at her subsequent acceptance of an inexplicable call from one of them. For Charlotte it has become an aesthetic objectification of an "inner light," and yet also a means of relating that inner light to a universal illumination. Charlotte might have described the cosmic imperative by such an abstraction as "Divine Law." That she did otherwise shows the working of a fine aesthetic sensibility: for the simple naming of authority she substitutes a symbolic presence — concrete, pictorially exciting, stimulatingly rich in its undefinedness and in its undeniable suggestion of independent animistic forces and indeed of the pagan. And in the symbolization of an interplay between private feeling and cosmic order, as well as between minds physically far apart, there is an unresolved mystery that takes us far beyond any everyday rationale of things and events.

To some extent in all the lunar scenes, and overwhelmingly in the strongest episodes in *Shirley* and *Jane Eyre,* we respond to that strangely compelling effect which we call "surrealistic." In the most original and stirring scene in *Villette* this rejection of everyday realistic surfaces is not a momentary peek into mystery but is so extended that a whole new atmosphere is created and the effect is one of "enchantment." This is the night when Lucy's "Imagination" takes over, scorning "Matter, her mate," and conducts Lucy, who has had a sedative, on a remarkable midnight tour of the city on a fete day. Our problem is with the artistic means by which the scene is made literally "charming" when Imagination takes over.

> "Look forth and view the night!" was her cry; and when I lifted the heavy blind from the casement close at hand — with her own royal gesture, she showed me a moon supreme, in an element deep and splendid.
>
> To my gasping senses she made the glimmering gloom, the narrow limits, the oppressive heat of the dormitory, intolerable. She lured me to leave this den and follow her forth into dew, coolness, and glory.

Here is the moon again, at this point foremost among the nocturnal beguilements, identified now not with "feeling" as in *Jane Eyre* but with that other challenger of Reason, Imagination. Lucy yearns to enter the "moonlit, midnight park"; she wants to know the hour, and is sure she can read the school clock "by such a moon." Out she glides into the "wanderer-wooing" night: ". . . I see its moon over me; I feel its dew in the air." Continually she pictures her coming to a huge stone basin filled with water; she "longed to come on that circular mirror of crystal, and surprise the moon glassing therein her pearly front." In the park she reaches one wooded spot "aloof even from the lamps," but "with that full, high moon lamps were scarce needed." But this is an urban fete, and there is a wealth of artificial lighting; in one street, "moonlight and heaven are banished . . . ." Or artificial and natural collaborate. Of Madame Walravens's dress: "neither the chasteness of moonlight, nor the distance of the torches, could quite subdue the gorgeous dyes of the drapery." At a moment when a particular assemblage of characters seems to portend a "revelation," the "blaze" of a torch "aided the pale moon in doing justice to the crisis." At this point a very interesting problem comes up: Lucy misinterprets what she sees (she thinks Paul is in love with his goddaughter), and since she is viewing people in a mixed light, it would be easy to read the lunar vision as obscured by man-made lights. But consciously or not, Charlotte does it less simply than that; indeed, Lucy's self-critique is initially puzzling. From a questioning of Imagination itself she goes on to ask, "What winter tree so bare and branchless — what wayside, hedge-munching animal so humble, that Fancy, a passing cloud, and a struggling moonbeam will not clothe it in spirituality, and make of it a phantom?" "Cloud" and "moonbeam" as the source of vital error: it is as if Charlotte is destroying her favorite artistic instruments. And of another occasion when a mere arrangement of clothes had seemed a ghost: "Here again — behold the branchless tree, the unstabled Rosinante; the film of cloud, the flicker of moonshine." But fortunately Charlotte is not declaring for the rational and the literal, and in the end renouncing lunar supersitition, on which she has built so many of her best effects. Rather she is restating in lunar imagery the problem with which she was always concerned — the distinction between an imagination which falsified reality by creating specious comfort or needless fear, and imagination which intuited truth. She rejects moonbeam mirages but never the moon. If she is on guard against quixotic mistakes, it seems to me safe to say that she never rejects the quixotic vision.

In fact, returning from the fete, from the "radiant park and well-lit Haute-Ville," Lucy seems relieved to return to "the dim lower quarter." Then she continues:

> Dim I should not say, for the beauty of the moonlight — forgotten in the park — here once more flowed in upon perception. High she rode, and calm and stainlessly she shone. The music and the mirth of the fête, the fire and bright hues of those lamps had outdone and outshone her for an hour, but now again her glory and her silence triumphed. The rival lamps were dying: she held her course like a white fate. Drum, trumpet, bugle had uttered their clangour, and were forgotten; with pencil-ray she wrote on heaven and on earth records for archives everlasting. She and those stars seemed to me at once the types and witnesses of truth all regnant. The night-sky lit her reign: like its slow-wheeling progress, advanced her victory — that onward movement which has been, and is, and will be from eternity to eternity.

"The rival lamps were dying: she held her course like a white fate." Here is, finally, the antithesis we would expect—the same antithesis that informed the scene in which Rivers's candle was outshone by the moonlight in which Rochester called and was answered. "The "white fate" has made itself felt, in Charlotte's four novels, in a score of crucial actions, of revelations and intuitions; in Louis Moore's dreams; in Caroline Helstone's sufferings and Robert Moore's danger; in Shirley's visions of milennial glories and of harsh human realities; in Jane Eyre's movements and perceptions and saving choices that relieve her from almost shattering pressures; in Lucy Snowe's moments of danger and discoveries of strength, and in the transient bliss that she has earned. "White fate" reminds us of Graves's "White Goddess," and this swings us back to a signal aspect of Charlotte's lunar scenes—the fact that, the more fully they are developed, the more their complex harmonies turn on the note of divinity. But we cannot finally assign an explicit symbolic value to Charlotte's moon. We know it is a "witness of truth"; we know that it represents another realm than that of the "Reason" where she at times aspired to dwell; we know that, in her struggle to find an accommodation between the traditional insight and the private vision, the moon had something of the mediatrix; we know that she wanted to abjure hallucination and the self-indulgent dream and to discover transcendent truth, and that in this struggle her ultimate reliance on feeling recurrently brings the lunar symbol into play.

Definition need not go further than that. In his prose ode to the lunar muse, to the lunar inspiration, Graves ultimately hymns the "muse poetry" that gives readers the shivering spine and the crawling scalp, that is "moon-magical enough to walk off the page." "Moon-magical"—that is the quality of Charlotte's best lunar scenes that we must feel, even though we do not precisely pin their meanings: the quality of those nights when the moon watches serenely from the grave blue, or is glad of the gale; of the mermaid rising from the sea, a temptress-terror; of the glorious gaze that is too solemn, a prelude to evil; of the hand that slides through the sable folds of cloud, preceding a form that speaks; of the far-distant call borne by the moonlit air; of dew, coolness, and glory—the moonlit, midnight park. In these the novel felt a tremor of new life.

Notes

1. "The White Goddess," *New Republic*, CXXXVI (June 24, 1957), 9 ff.

2. For Anne Brontë, too, the moon apparently took on more than pictorial meanings. In the poem "Fluctuations," according to recent biographers, the "moon's re-emergence" symbolizes "divine intervention." See Ada Harrison and Derek Stanford, *Anne Brontë: Her Life and Work* (New York: John Day, 1959), p. 189.

Class, Power and
Charlotte Brontë

Terry Eagleton*

Helen Burns, the saintly schoolgirl of *Jane Eyre*, has an interestingly ambivalent attitude to the execution of Charles the First. Discussing the matter with Jane, she thinks "what a pity it was that, with his integrity and conscientiousness, he could see no farther than the prerogatives of the crown. If he had but been able to look to a distance, and see how what they call the spirit of the age was tending! Still, I like Charles—I respect him—I pity him, poor murdered king! Yes, his enemies were the worst: they shed blood they had no right to shed. How dared they kill him!"

Helen's curious vacillation between a coolly long-headed appreciation of essential reformist change and a spirited Romantic conservatism reflects a recurrent ambiguity in the novels of Charlotte Brontë. It's an ambiguity which shows up to some extent in Helen's own oppressed life at Lowood school: she herself, as a murdered innocent, is partly the martyred Charles, but unlike Charles she is also able to "look to a distance" (although in her case towards heaven rather than future history), and counsel the indignant Jane in the virtues of patience and long-suffering. That patience implies both a "rational" submission to the repressive conventions of Lowood (which she, unlike Jane, does not challenge), and a resigned endurance of life as a burden from which, in the end, will come release.

The problem which the novel faces here is how Helen's kind of self-abnegation is to be distinguished from the patently canting version of it offered by the sadistic Evangelical Brocklehurst, who justifies the eating of burnt porridge by an appeal to the torments of the early Christian martyrs. Submission is good, but only up to a point, and it's that point which Charlotte Brontë's novels explore. Jane's answer to Brocklehurst's enquiry as to how she will avoid hell—"I must keep in good health, and not die"—mixes childish naivety, cheek and seriousness: "*I* had no intention of dying with him," she tells Rochester later. And indeed she doesn't: it is mad Bertha who dies, leaving the way clear for Jane (who has just refused St. John Rivers's offer of premature death in India) to unite with her almost martyred master. Helen Burns is a necessary symbol, but her career is not to be literally followed. When she smiles at the publicly chastised Jane in the Lowood classroom, "It was as if a martyr, a hero, had passed a slave or victim, and imparted strength in the transit." The conjunction of "martyr" and "hero" here is significant: martyrdom is seen as both saintly self-abnegation and heroic self-affirmation, a realization of the self through its surrender, as the name "Burns" can signify both

*Reprinted from *Critical Quarterly* 14, no. 3 (Autumn 1972): 225–35. © T. F. Eagleton, 1972. Reproduced by permission of Manchester University Press.

suffering and passion. But Helen, who fails to keep in good health and dies, symbolises in the end only one aspect of this desirable synthesis, that of passive renunciation. Like Jane, she triumphs in the end over tyrannical convention, but unlike Jane that triumph is achieved through her own death, not through someone else's.

Where Charlotte Brontë differs most from Emily is precisely in this impulse to negotiate passionate self-fulfilment on terms which preserve the social and moral conventions intact, and so preserve intact the submissive, enduring, everyday self which adheres to them. Her protagonists are an extraordinarily contradictory amalgam of smouldering rebelliousness and prim conventionalism, gushing Romantic fantasy and canny hard-headedness, quivering sensitivity and blunt rationality. It is, in fact, a contradiction closely related to their roles as governesses or private tutors. The governess is a servant, trapped within a rigid social function which demands industriousness, subservience and self-sacrifice; but she is also an "upper" servant, and so (unlike, supposedly, other servants) furnished with an imaginative awareness and cultivated sensibility which are precisely her stock-in-trade as a teacher. She lives at that ambiguous point in the social structure at which two worlds — an interior one of emotional hungering, and an external one of harshly mechanical necessity — meet and collide. At least, they do collide if they aren't wedged deliberately apart, locked into their separate spheres to forestall the disaster of mutual invasion. "I seemed to hold two lives," says Lucy Snowe in *Villette*, "the life of thought, and that of reality; and, provided the former was nourished with a sufficiency of the strange necromantic joys of fancy, the privileges of the latter might remain limited to daily bread, hourly work, and a roof of shelter." It is, indeed, with notable reluctance that Lucy is brought to confess the existence of an inner life at all: at the beginning of the novel she tells us, in a suspiciously overemphatic piece of assertion, that "I, Lucy Snowe, plead guiltless of that curse, an overheated and discursive imagination" — and tells us this, moreover, in the context of an awed reference to ghostly haunting. Her response to the "ghost" who flits through Madame Beck's garden is almost comical in its clumsy lurching from romance to realism:

> Her shadow it was that tremblers had feared, through long generations after her poor frame was dust; her black robe and white veil that, for timid eyes, moonlight and shade had mocked, as they fluctuated in the night-wind through the garden-thicket.
>   Independently of romantic rubbish, however, that old garden had its charms. . .

It is a splitting of the self common in Charlotte's novels: Caroline Helstone in *Shirley* feels herself "a dreaming fool," unfitted for "ordinary intercourse with the ordinary world"; and William Crimsworth of *The Professor*, slaving away as an under-paid clerk, finds little chance to prove that he is not "a block, or a piece of furniture, but an acting, thinking, sentient man."

To allow passionate imagination premature rein is to be exposed, vulnerable and ultimately self-defeating: it is to be locked in the red room, enticed into bigamous marriage, ensnared like Caroline Helstone in a hopelessly self-consuming love. Passion springs from the very core of the self and yet is hostile, alien, invasive; the world of internal fantasy must therefore be locked away, as the mad Mrs. Rochester stays locked up on an upper floor of Thornfield, slipping out to infiltrate the "real" world only in a few unaware moments of terrible destructiveness. The inner world must yield of necessity to the practical virtues of caution, tact and observation espoused by William Crimsworth — the wary, vigilant virtues by which the self's lonely integrity can be defended in a spying, predatory society, a society on the watch for the weak spot which will surrender you into its hands. The Romantic self must be persistently re-called to its deliberately narrowed and withered definition of rationality. "Order! No snivel! — no sentiment! — no regret! I will endure only sense and resolution," whispers Jane Eyre to herself, fixing her errant thoughts on the hard fact that her relationship with Rochester is of a purely cash-nexus kind.

In the end, of course, it isn't. With the ambiguous exception of *Villette*, the strategy of the novels is to allow the turbulent inner life satisfying realization without that self-betraying prematureness which would disrupt the self's principled continuity — a continuity defined by its adherence to a system of social and moral convention. The tactic most commonly employed here is the conversion of submissive conventionalism itself from a mode of self-preservation to a mode of conscious or unconscious self-advancement. Mrs. Reed's remark to Jane in the red room — "It is only on condition of perfect submission and stillness that I shall liberate you" — is triumphantly validated by the novel: it is Jane's stoical Quakerish stillness which captivates Rochester. Her refusal to act prematurely for her own ends both satisfies restrictive convention and leads ultimately to a fulfilling transcendence of it. Rochester would not of course find Jane attractive if she were merely dull, but neither would he love her if, like Blanche Ingram, she were consciously after his money. Jane must therefore reveal enough repressed, Blanche-like "spirit" beneath her puritan exterior to stimulate and cajole him, without any suggestion that she is, in Lucy Snowe's revealing words about herself, "bent on success." Jane manages this difficult situation adroitly during their courtship, blending flashes of flirtatious self-assertion with her habitual meek passivity; she sees shrewdly that "a lamb-like submission and turtle-dove sensibility" would end by boring him. She must demonstrate her quietly self-sufficient independence of Rochester as a way of keeping him tied to her, and so, paradoxically, of staying tied to and safely dependent on him. That this involves a good deal of dexterous calculation — calculation which, if pressed too far, would seriously undermine Jane's credibility as a character — should be obvious enough: it isn't, perhaps, wholly insignificant that Rochester's comment to Jane in the original manuscript — "coin one of your wild, shy, provoking smiles" — is misprinted in the first edition as "wild, *sly*, provoking smiles." If Rochester recognises Jane intuitively as a soul-mate, so after all does St. John Rivers, who tells her that his ambition is unlimited, his desire to rise higher insatiable, and his favoured virtues "endurance, perseverance, industry, talent." Rivers must of course be rejected as reason rather than feeling is his guide, and Jane's career can only culminate successfully when "feeling" can be "rationally" released; feeling without judgement, she muses, is "a washy draught indeed," but judgement without feeling is "too bitter and husky a morsel for human deglutition." Even so, there is more than a superficial relationship between Rivers, a rationalist with feverishly repressed impulses, and Jane's own behaviour: in her case, too, "Reason sits firm and holds the reins, and she will not let the feelings burst away and hurry her to wild chasms." Not prematurely, anyway, and certainly not to early death in India.

Rivers's bourgeois values ("endurance, perseverance, industry, talent"), if sinisterly unfeeling in Jane's eyes, are certainly shared by William Crimsworth, whose motto, suitably, is "Hope smiles on effort." Yet Crimsworth is not a middle-class philistine but a feminine, sensitive soul, too delicately genteel to endure the deadeningly oppressive clerical work to which his manufacturing brother Edward sets him. Crimsworth is despised by his brother and jocularly scorned by the radical, sardonic Whig capitalist Hunsden; yet his progress throughout the novel represents an interesting inversion of his original victimised condition. Crimsworth's mother was an aristocrat and his father a manufacturer; but whereas the philistine Edward has inherited, temperamentally, only from his father, Crimsworth has conveniently inherited qualities from both parents, and the combination proves unbeatable. He is superior in imaginative sensibility to both Edward and Hunsden (who hates poetry), and it is this quality which, as with Jane Eyre and Lucy Snowe, brings him at first to suffer isolated torment at the hands of a crassly dominative society. But it is also the quality which, combined with a quietly industrious knack of amassing a little capital through years of "bustle, action, unslacked endeavour," allows him to prosper as a private teacher in Europe and return to England as a gentleman of leisure. Crimsworth is able to make classic bourgeois progress — not, however, on the crudely materialist terms of his brother, but on terms which utilise rather than negate his "genteel" accomplishments. He reproduces the fusion of aristocratic quality and driving bourgeois effort effected in his parents' marriage, and does so in more propitious conditions: his mother had been disowned by her family for marrying beneath her.

To consolidate this progress requires of Crimsworth both a potentially rebellious independence and a prudently conservative wariness, as is evident enough if he is contrasted with Edward on the one hand and

Hunsden on the other. From Edward's conservative standpoint, his brother is a congenital misfit who defiantly throws up a safe job in the name of freedom; from the viewpoint of Hunsden, the Whig reformer and dashing Byronic sceptic, Crimsworth is a pallid, meekly cautious conservative. In fact Crimsworth, like Jane, is both spirited *and* conventional; and like Jane also, although in a considerably more conscious and ruthless way, he learns to turn his protective self-possession to devastating advantage in his relentless power-struggles with Mdlle. Reuter and her unruly girl-pupils. He gains faintly sadistic pleasure from the effects of his own self-defensive impenetrability, enjoying the way Mdlle. Reuter is stung by his coolness, quietly tearing up a pupil's essay before her eyes. Crimsworth the victim becomes Crimsworth the dominator:[1] like Jane, he turns his martyrdom to fruitful profit in this world rather than the next.

Part of what we see happening in these novels, in fact, is a marriage of identifiably bourgeois values with the values of the gentry or aristocracy — a marriage which reflects a real tendency of the "spirit of the age." The Brontës were born at a time when a centuries-old system of cloth-making in the West Riding was coming to an end with the advent of water-power and then steam; they grew up in a context of rapid industrialisation and the growth of a wealthy manufacturing middle-class. It was this phenomenon, as Phyllis Bentley has pointed out, which created the demand for governesses who would give the children of wealthy manufacturers an education equivalent to that of the gentry; and in this sense the sisters were involved in the process of social transition. (As the daughters of an Irish peasant farmer's son who had married into socially superior Cornish stock, they also knew something of social transition in a more direct way). But if the West Riding was undergoing rapid industrialisation, it was also a traditional stronghold of the landed gentry, and among the gentry were men who had gone into manufacturing. Characters like Hunsden, or Yorke in *Shirley*, therefore assume a particular symbolic importance within the novels. They are presented as Carlylean "natural aristocrats": cultivated gentlemen sprung from a long Yorkshire lineage who combine a settled paternalist tradition of "blood" and stubborn native pride with a rebellious, independent spirit of anti-aristocratic radicalism. Hunsden, although a "tradesman," is secretly proud of his ancient lineage and is bidding to repair through trade "the partially decayed fortunes of his house"; he is a hard-headed anti-sentimentalist, but has a library well-stocked with European literature and philosophy. Yorke prides himself on being down-to-earth and speaks a broad Yorkshire dialect when he wants to, but he can also choose to speak very pure English and takes a quiet interest in the fine arts. Both men unite a spirit of wilful, free-wheeling bourgeois independence with the culture and status of the traditional gentry. In this sense they have a peculiar attraction for the cast-off, down-trodden character lower in the social scale, who finds in them at once a "higher" expression of his or her own fiercely repressed defiance, and the embodiment of a respected social tradition to admire or aim at.

Yet the relationship isn't without its conflicts and ambiguities. Crimsworth, who is both bourgeois and "blood" aristocrat, finds Hunsden (bourgeois and "natural" aristocrat) both attractive and repelling: he is attractive in his energy, initiative and independence, but unpleasant and rather dangerous in his sardonic, free-thinking Whig reformism. These characteristics of Hunsden offend those aspects of Crimsworth which are externalised in his dutiful Anglo-Swiss wife Frances: her meek piety and Romantic-conservative patriotism provide an essential foil to Hunsden's racy iconoclasm. The bourgeois values of Crimsworth ally themselves in one direction with the bourgeois radicalism of Hunsden, in opposition to the oppressive and venal society which has forced him into exile; but at the same time Crimsworth clearly can't afford to endorse Hunsden's radicalism to the point where he would risk undermining the very social order into which he has so painfully climbed. Insofar as Hunsden's bourgeois hard-headedness allies him with the hated Edward, Frances is needed as a representative of alternative, Romantic-conservative values, including a respect for "blood" aristocracy; but the two positions are saved from pure mutual antagonism by the fact that Hunsden's personal energy and impeccable pedigree render him impressive in Romantic-conservative eyes. For the progressive bourgeois manufacturer, the traditional social order is merely obstructive and superannuated; for the traditional aristocrat turned prosperous non-manufacturing bourgeois, that order still has its value. The final relationship between Crimsworth and Hunsden, then, is one of antagonistic friendship: on their return to England, Crimsworth and Frances settle, significantly, next to Hunsden's estate, but Frances and Hunsden continue to argue over politics.

Shirley is perhaps the best novel to demonstrate this theme, since the historical incidents it deals with do in fact closely concern the relations between Tory squirearchy and Whig manufacturers in the West Riding in the early years of the nineteenth century. The central dramatic action of the novel — the Luddite attack on Robert Moore's mill — re-creates the assault in 1812 on William Cartwright's mill at Rawfolds in the Spen Valley; and Cartwright's ruthless repulsion of the Luddites signalled, in Edward Thompson's words, "a profound emotional reconciliation between the large mill owners and the authorities"[2] at a time when squire and mill-owner were bitterly hostile to one another over the war and the Orders in Council. That the novel's main thrust is to re-create and celebrate that class-consolidation, achieved as it was by the catalyst of working-class militancy, is obvious enough in the figure of Shirley herself. Shirley is a landowner, but half her income comes from owning a mill; and even though her attitudes to the mill are significantly Romantic (she is "tickled with an agreeable complacency" when she thinks of it), she is adamant that trade is to be respected, and determined to defend her property "like a tigress." "If once the poor gather and rise in the form of the mob," she tells Caroline Helstone, "I shall turn against them as an aristocrat." The novel registers a few feeble liberal protests against this position: Caroline ventures to point out the injustice of including all working people under the term "mob," and elsewhere Shirley (with no sense of inconsistency, and conveniently enough for herself in the circumstances) can denounce all crying up of one class against another. But her "spirited" attitude is in general endorsed, not least because it has behind it the weight of her ancient Yorkshire lineage, with its traditions of paternalist care for the poor. Indeed, because she is a conservative paternalist, Shirley's position can accommodate a fair amount of reformism: she objects to the Church's insolence to the poor and servility to the rich, and believes it to be "in the utmost need of reformation." In this sense Shirley differs from Robert Moore, whose neglect of philanthropy as a manufacturer is implicitly connected with his ill-luck in not having been born a Yorkshireman; but although Moore is critically measured against the robust traditions of Yorkshire paternalism, it is, significantly, Shirley herself who finally comes to the defence of his callousness. He is, she points out, a man who entered the district poor and friendless, with nothing but his own energies to back him; and it's unfair to upbraid him for not having been able to "popularize his naturally grave, quiet manners, all at once." (Moore's original, Cartwright, who defended his property with soldiers, spiked barricades and a tub of vitriol, and is reputed to have refused injured Luddites water or a doctor unless they turned informer, seems less easily excusable on the grounds of shyness.) It is, in other words, the representative of the gentry who comes to the moral rescue of the bourgeois manufacturer; and Moore is in any case defended by the novel by a use of the "split self" image which suggests that a sensitive dreamer lurks behind his "hard dog" social exterior.

As a hybrid of progressive capitalist and traditional landowner, then, Shirley provides an important defence of trade; but her charismatic presence in the novel is also needed to defend Romantic conservatism against bourgeois ideology. She is, for instance, notably hard on the radical manufacturer Yorke, whose doctrinaire Whiggism she sees as unfitting him for true reform; and the novel itself underscores this judgement by its emphasis on Yorke's lack of "veneration." Shirley, in other words, stands to Yorke as Frances Crimsworth stands to Hunsden: both radicals are admired for their verve and fighting Yorkshire blood (qualities on which *Shirley* in particular places tediously chauvinistic emphasis), but their lack of reverence counts heavily against them. It is left to Mrs. Pryor, Caroline's improbably long-lost mother, to deliver the most explicit statement of that reverence, when she tells Caroline that "Implicit submission to authorities, scrupulous deference to our betters (under which term I, of course, include the higher classes of society) are, in my opinion, indispensable to the wellbeing of every community."

Commerce, in the novel's view, represents a genuine threat to such hierarchial harmony: the mercantile classes, Charlotte Brontë remarks, deny chivalrous feeling, disinterestedness and pride of honour in their narrowly unpatriotic scramble for gain. They deny, in fact, the aristocratic, Romantic-conservative virtues: and part of the point of the novel is to validate those neglected virtues without adopting too obviously the bigoted "Church-and-King" posture of Helstone, Caroline's military-parson guardian. This is simple enough, given the novel's structure, since between the formalist Helstone on the one hand and the free-thinking Yorke on the other stands Shirley, paradigm of the desired union between Romanticism and reform, gentry and capitalist, order and progress. By the end of the novel, indeed, the union is literal as well as symbolic: Moore, having recovered his fortunes by the repeal of the Orders in Council, and having been suitably humanised as an employer by Caroline's influence, will add to the income of Shirley (who has married his brother), double the value of her mill-property and build cottages which Shirley will then let to his own workmen. The bond between squire and mill-owner is indissolubly sealed.

The effective *equality* established between Shirley and Robert Moore at the end of the novel is, in fact, only one of the terms on which Charlotte Brontë handles relationships: the others are dominance and submission. The novels dramatise a society in which almost all human relationships are power-struggles, and because "equality" therefore comes to be defined as equality of power, it is an inevitably complex affair. Crimsworth and Hunsden also end up as effectively equal, but within a formal inequality: Hunsden's house, for instance, is a good deal larger than the Professor's. Even Jane Eyre, when stung to righteous anger, is able to claim a fundamentally human equality with Rochester: "Do you think, because I am poor, obscure, plain, and little, I am soulless and heartless?" There are, in fact, reasons other than simple humanitarian ones why Jane and Rochester are not as socially divided as may at first appear. Rochester, the younger son of an avaricious landed gentleman, was denied his share in the estate and had to marry instead into colonial wealth; Jane's colonial uncle dies and leaves her a sizeable legacy, enough for independence. The colonial trade which signified a decline in status for Rochester signifies an advance in status for Jane, so that although they are of course socially and economically unequal, their fortunes spring from the same root. Jane does not, of course, finally claim equality with Rochester: in the end she serves "both for his prop and guide," which is a rather more complex relationship. It suggests subservience, and so perpetuates their previous relationship; but the subservience is also, of course, a kind of leadership. Rochester's blindness inverts the power-relationship between them: it is now he who is the dependent. Whether she likes it or not (and there is no evidence at all that she does), Jane finally comes to have power over Rochester. Her ultimate relation to him is a complex blend of independence (she comes to him on her own terms, financially self-sufficient), deference, and control.

This complex blend is a recurrent feature of relationships in the novels. Charlotte's characters want independence, but they also desire to dominate, and their desire to dominate is matched only by their impulse to submit to a superior will. The primary form which this ambiguity assumes is a sexual one: the need to venerate and revere, but also to exercise power, expresses itself both in a curious rhythm of sexual attraction and antagonism, and in a series of reversals of sexual roles. The maimed and blinded Rochester, for example, is in an odd way even more "masculine" than he was before (he is "brown," shaggy, "metamorphosed into a lion"), but because he is weak he is also "feminine," and Jane, who adopts a traditionally feminine role towards him ("It is time some one undertook to re-humanize you") is also forced into the masculine role of protectiveness. She finds him both attractive and ugly, as he finds her both plain and fascinating. Blanche Ingram is a "beauty," but she also appears as dominatingly masculine beside Jane's subdued femininity; her masculinity leads her to desire a husband who will be a foil to her and not a rival, but it also prompts her to despise effeminate men and admire strong ones. The same applies to Shirley Keeldar, who is decisively independent and believes in sexual equality, but who is also a "masculine" woman holding "a man's position" as landowner. ("Shirley" was the name her parents intended to give to a son.) Physically she is a superior version of Caroline Helstone, whom she resembles; and she thus becomes for Caroline an ideal self-projection to be revered, in a latently sexual relationship. Despite her claims to sexual equality, however, Shirley would be "thrilled" to meet a man she could venerate: she dominates Caroline spiritually but desires to be dominated herself. William Crimsworth, himself a sort of male Jane Eyre, is dominated by the dashing Hunsden, to whom he plays a "feminine" role, but in turn dominates Frances, whose lamb-like devotion to him he smugly savours. Frances continues to call him "Monsieur" after their marriage, and Crimsworth takes a sadistic delight in reproving her; but he is also glad that she (like Jane) isn't all "monotonous meekness," and is thrilled to discover in her flashes of latent defiance which make him "her subject, if not her slave." The relationship recalls that of Lucy Snowe and the fiery Paul Emanuel: Paul enjoys abusing Lucy and tells her that she needs "checking, regulating and keeping down," but he abuses her mainly in order to delight in her anger.

This simultaneity of attraction and antagonism, reverence and dominance, has a relation to the novels' ambiguous feelings about power in its wider senses. It parallels and embodies the conflicting desires of the oppressed outcast for independence, for passive submission to a secure social order, and for avenging self-assertion over that order. Revenge doesn't, in fact, seem too strong a word for what happens at the end of *Jane Eyre*. Jane's repressed indignation at a dominative society, prudently swallowed back throughout the book, is finally released—not by Jane herself, but by the novelist; and the victim is the symbol of that social order, Rochester. Rochester is the novel's sacrificial offering to the social conventions, to Jane's unconscious antagonism and, indeed, to her own puritan guilt; by satisfying all three simultaneously, it allows her to adopt a properly submissive place in society while experiencing a fulfilling love and a taste of power. The outcast bourgeoise achieves more than a humble place at the fireside: she also achieves independence vis-à-vis the upper class, and the right to engage in the process of "taming" it. The worldly Rochester has already been tamed by fire: it is now for Jane to "re-humanize" him.

To put the issue that way is to touch implicitly on the elements of Evangelicalism in *Jane Eyre*, and it is worth adding a final brief comment on this other major image of power in the novels. Insofar as Evangelicalism sets out to crush the Romantic spirit, it is a tangible symbol of social oppression and must be resisted. Jane Eyre rebels against Brocklehurst's cruel cant and St. John Rivers's deathly Calvinism; she also scorns Eliza Reed's decision to enter a Roman Catholic convent, viewing this as a falsely ascetic withdrawal from the world. But she is at the same time "Quakerish" herself, grimly disapproving of worldly libertinism; and in this sense she is torn between a respect for and instinctive dislike of stringent religious discipline, between pious submission and Romantic rebellion. Charlotte Brontë's attitudes to Evangelical discipline are, in short, thoroughly ambiguous, as is obvious enough if the detestable Brocklehurst is placed in the balance against the treatment of spoilt children in *The Professor* and *Villette*, where Evangelical attitudes to childhood strongly emerge. The theme of pampered, perverse children crops up in almost all of the Brontës' novels, and the Evangelical responses involved with it are clearly, in part, class-responses—exasperated reactions to the indolent offspring of the rich as in Lucy Snowe's Nelly Dean-like attitude to Polly Home or Ginevra Fanshawe, or Anne Brontë's talk of the need to crush vicious tendencies in the bud in the Bloomfield family scenes of *Agnes Grey*. Lucy Snowe thinks that Madame Beck's rigid disciplinary system "was by no means bad"; despite the fact that Madame Beck is wholly devoid of feeling, her ruthless efficiency makes her in Lucy's eyes "a very great and very capable woman." It is an Evangelical impulse to avoid the "cowardly indolence" of shrinking from life and sally out instead to put one's soul to the test which motivates Lucy's journey to Villette; it is a similar impulse which brings Caroline Helstone to reject as false, Romish superstition the idea that virtue lies in self-abnegation, and decide instead to become a governess. What Hunsden sees as attractive "spirit" in Crimsworth's son Victor, Crimsworth himself interprets as "the leaven of the offending Adam," and considers that it should be, if not whipped out of him, at least soundly disciplined.

Evangelical discipline, then, is hateful in its sour oppressiveness, but useful in curbing the over-assertive, libertine self; it is to be rejected insofar as, like Rivers's Calvinism, it turns one away from the world, but welcomed as a spur to worldly effort and achievement. The safest solution is a middle way between Dissent and High Church, as in *Agnes Grey*, where the vain, sophisticated Ritualist Hatfield is heavily condemned and the "simple evangelical truth" of the low-church curate Weston deeply admired. The double-edged attitude of *Shirley* to the Church ("God save it . . . God also reform it!") is symptomatic of the compromising middle-ground which Charlotte Brontë's novels attempt to occupy: a middle-ground between reverence and rebellion, land and trade, gentry and bougeoisie, the patiently deferential and the actively affirmative self.

Notes

1. It is of some interest in this context, perhaps, that both Charlotte and Emily had been first pupils, and then pupil-governesses, at the Pensionnat Heger in Brussels; like Crimsworth, they knew the power-relationship from both sides.

2. *The Making of the English Working Class*, Harmondsworth, 1970, p. 613.

Imaginative Constraint, Feminine Duty, and the Form of Charlotte Brontë's Fiction
Carol T. Christ*

The career of Charlotte Brontë offers a striking example of the conflict, common to women writers, between the cultural pressure toward feminine duty and the independence and assertiveness that imaginative writing requires. Before she ever wrote for publication, her letters and the journal that she kept when she was a teacher at Roe Head show a preoccupation with the possible freedoms imagination offers and the constraints a woman's life places upon them. One page of the journal begins:

> I am just going to write because I cannot help it . . . encompassed by bulls (query calves of Bashan) all wondering why I write with my eyes shut—staring, gaping long their astonishment. A C[ook] on one side of me, E L[ister] on the other and Miss W[ooler] in the background, stupidity the atmosphere, school-books the employment, assess the society. What in all this is there to remind me of the divine, silent, unseen land of thought, dim now and indefinite as the dream of a dream, the shadow of a shade. There is a voice, there is an impulse that wakens up that dormant power which in its torpidity I sometimes think dead. That

*Reprinted from *Women's Studies* 6, no. 3 (1979): 287–96. © Gordon and Breach Science Publishers, Inc.

wind pouring in impetuous current through the air, sounding wildly unremittingly from hour to hour, deepening its tone as the night advances, coming not in gusts, but with a rapid gathering stormy swell, that wind I know is heard at this moment far away on the moors at Haworth. . . . O it has wakened a feeling that I cannot satisfy — a thousand wishes rose at its call which must die with me for they will never be fulfilled. now I should be agonised if I had not the dream to repose on — its existences, its forms its scenes to fill a little of the craving vacancy. . .[1]

Driven by the unhappiness of her life at Roe Head, and hoping to make those imaginative satisfactions the source of her livelihood, Charlotte Brontë wrote to Robert Southey, enclosing some of her poems and asking his opinion of their merit. That letter does not survive, but Southey's answer implies that it must have given some indication of the same imaginative cravings that her journal describes. He counsels Charlotte to give up any hope of a literary career because the imagination will raise desires which she cannot satisfy, desires which will provoke discontent with the appropriate duties of a woman's life: "The day dreams in which you habitually indulge are likely to induce a distempered state of mind; and, in proportion as all the ordinary uses of the world seem to you flat and unprofitable, you will be unfitted for them without becoming fitted for anything else. Literature cannot be the business of a woman's life, and it ought not to be. The more she is engaged in her proper duties, the less leisure will she have for it, even as an accomplishment and a recreation."[2] Brontë's answer to Southey shows that she was well aware of the conflict of which he cautioned her.

My father is a clergyman of limited though competent income, and I am the eldest of his children. He expended quite as much in my education as he could afford in justice to the rest. I thought it therefore my duty, when I left school, to become a governess. In that capacity I find enough to occupy my thoughts all day long, and my head and hands, too, without having a moment's time for one dream of the imagination. In the evenings, I confess, I do think, but I never trouble anyone else with my thoughts. I carefully avoid any appearance of preoccupation and eccentricity which might lead those I live amongst to suspect the nature of my pursuits. Following my father's advice — who from my childhood has counselled me, just in the wise and friendly tone of your letter — I have endeavoured not only attentively to observe all the duties a woman ought to fulfill, but to feel deeply interested in them. I don't always succeed, for sometimes when I'm teaching or sewing, I would rather be reading or writing; but I try to deny myself; and my father's approbation amply rewarded me for the privation.[3]

Southey replied praising her self-government and warning her to take care of over-excitement and to endeavor to keep a quiet mind. A month later, on her twenty-first birthday, Brontë sealed both letters in an envelope, inscribing it, "Southey's advice to be kept forever."

Charlotte Brontë did not keep Southey's advice, but the correspondence nevertheless expresses a dilemma central to her attitude toward the imagination. Imagination offers a kind of fulfilment the world denies. It can create a tale, in the words of Jane Eyre, "quickened with all of incident, life, fire, feeling, that I desired and had not in my actual existence."[4] But it provokes a discontent with things as they are, a discontent which an appropriate sense of feminine duty requires one to repress. This discontent afflicted Charlotte with a constant sense of guilt. She wrote to her friend Ellen Nussey: "If you knew my thoughts; the dreams that absorb me; and the fiery imagination that at times eats me up and makes me feel society, as it *is*, wretchedly insipid, you would pity and I dare say despise me."[5]

When Charlotte Brontë began to write for publication, she attempted to resolve the conflict her correspondence with Southey expresses by a moral commitment to what she calls a "plain and homely" realism. She would allow her imagination rein only within the bounds of the possible. But her commitment to realism remains ambivalent. It expresses her sense of the way in which life frustrates desire and the consequent necessity, not originating in morality but comprehended in moral terms, to contain that desire. Because it is based on a resentful conviction of the necessity of self-denial, Brontë has difficulty successfully incorporating it within her fiction. At the same time that her sense of appropriate options for women leads her to inhibit the imagination, she resents the limitations she imposes upon it. This ambivalence toward both the imagination and what she considers necessary realism gives her fiction its characteristic weaknesses and strengths. The two novels in which she self-consciously sets herself a realistic program — *The Professor* and *Shirley* — fail because of the claims of her own aesthetic inhibit her imaginative energy. The greater success of *Jane Eyre* and *Villette* results from her ability to make her aesthetic conflict between the claims of imagination and the claims of realism the propelling conflict of her heroines' personalities.

In the Preface to *The Professor* Brontë explains the commitment to realism which she had determined would control that novel. Asserting that she had overcome any taste she had once had "for ornamented and redundant composition," in preference for "what was plain and homely," she goes on to explain the principles that govern her selection of incident:

> I said to myself that my hero should work his way through life as I had seen real living men work theirs — that he should never get a shilling he had not earned — that no sudden turns should lift him in a moment to wealth and high station; that whatever small competency he might gain, should be won by the sweat of his brow; that, before he could find so much as an arbour to sit down in, he should master at least half the ascent of "the Hill of Difficulty"; that he should not even marry a beautiful girl or a lady of rank. As Adam's son he should share Adam's doom, and drain throughout life a mixed and moderate cup of enjoyment.[6]

Brontë's preface recalls the fear expressed in the correspondence with Southey that imaginative activity creates an unrealistic discontent with things as they are. Realistic principles of plot construction school one to face the bleak facts of experience. Because life permits only moderate fulfillment, one must entertain moderate expectations for one's characters. One can see the peculiar significance of Brontë's sense of realism by comparing her to another Victorian realist, George Eliot. Eliot believes that realism reveals the significance, tragedy, and romance of common life. Like Wordsworth, she tries to make the reader see the marvelous and the pathetic in seemingly insignificant subjects. Brontë, on the other hand, feels the marvelous does not exist save in the world of the imagination and that one must learn to prefer the plain and homely. Her commitment to realism stems not from delight and empathy with the life before her but from a feeling that the world she desires is unattainable and must not be contemplated. Thus her realistic aesthetic is willed and ambivalent, based on a conviction of the necessity of self-abnegation.

The Professor is not a successful book, and the reason lies in Brontë's aesthetic. She creates a hero in William Crimsworth who embodies the values of self-discipline and self-denial that she determined would control her narrative, and the result is a character who is a parody of Protestant virtue. Even at the moment that Crimsworth first kisses his bride-to-be (whom he had conscientiously refrained from visiting until he has secured an economic competency), he must assure himself that Reason approves the act: "There are impulses we can control; but there are others which control us, because they attain us with a tiger-leap, and are our masters ere we have seen them. Perhaps, though, such impulses are seldom altogether bad; perhaps, Reason by a process as brief as quiet, a process that is finished ere felt, has ascertained the sanity of the deed Instinct mediates, and feels justified in remaining passive while it is performed."[7] Because Crimsworth is so self-consciously controlled and because Brontë never takes us beyond the surface of that control, the narrator is both uninteresting and unsympathetic. Brontë's insistence on imaginative control inhibits her own imagination, making her unable to portray the psychology of control in her character with any depth or complexity.

Like *The Professor*, *Shirley* begins with a statement of realistic intention, but unlike *The Professor*, the novel does not consistently maintain the realistic values it initially asserts. It is this divided aesthetic allegiance that is responsible not only for the uncertain narrative tone of the book but also for its inconsistent treatment of its heroine. Brontë begins the novel with a disavowal of the romantic imagination. After setting the scene, she asserts:

> If you think, from this prelude, that anything like a romance is preparing for you, reader, you never were more mistaken. Do you anticipate sentiment, and poetry, and reverie? Do you expect passion, and stimulus, and melodrama? Calm your expectations; reduce them to

a lowly standard. Something real, cool, and solid lies before you; something unromantic as Monday morning, when all who work wake with the consciousness that they must rise and betake themselves thereto.[8]

As in *The Professor*, Brontë's definition of realism emphasizes the necessity of embracing the mundane consciousness of duty the world's frustrations entail. But unlike *The Professor*, *Shirley* does not maintain the realistic standard with which it begins. In a later passage Brontë writes:

. . . who cares for imagination? Who does not think it a rather dangerous, senseless attribute—akin to weakness—perhaps partaking of frenzy—a disease rather than a gift of the mind?

Probably all think it so, but those who possess—or fancy they possess—it. To hear them speak, you would believe that their hearts would be cold if that elixir did not flow about them; that their eyes would dim if that flame did not refine their vision; that they would be lonely if this strange companion abandoned them. You would suppose that it imparted some glad hope to spring, some fine charm to summer, some tranquil joy to autumn, some consolation to winter, which you do not feel. An illusion, of course; but the fanatics cling to their dream, and would not give it for gold.[9]

The passage is curiously ambivalent. The intensity of the images that Brontë uses to describe the imagination suggests that it has her emotional allegiance, but the claims she makes for it are all qualified by the insistence that they may be illusory. Imagination imparts not truth but emotional consolation. The ambivalence of tone is characteristic of the entire novel and qualifies its achievement. Brontë's discomfort with the sources of her own imaginative energy intrudes itself into the narrative voice making the tone of the novel uncertain.

Charlotte Brontë's ambivalence toward her own imaginative energy results in an ambivalence toward the energy of her heroine as well. *Shirley* is a self-conscious examination of the effect of social circumstances upon female character. Shirley's masculine name, title, and fortune foster her extraordinary vitality, while Caroline Helstone's lack of resources seems to create her conventionally feminine meekness of spirit. Shirley's character finds its most forceful expression in her rapturous feminist mythic visions, visions which seem to stem from unimpeded energy.

I saw—I now see—a woman Titan; her robe of blue air spreads to the outskirts of the heath, where yonder flock is grazing; a veil white as an avalanche sweeps from her head to her feet, and arabesques of lightening flame on its borders. Under her breast I see her zone, purple like that horizon; through its blush shines the star of evening. . . . That Eve is Jehovah's daughter, as Adam was His son.[10]

Much as Brontë qualifies the claims of the imagination in her own narrative voice, she subdues Shirley's Titan visions. The novel ends with the double marriage of Shirley and Caroline, a marriage which evades the feminist issue of the plight of the single woman much of the novel has explored. Furthermore, Brontë describes Shirley's marriage as a "taming," and the end of the novel abandons her perspective to tell the story of her courtship through her suitor's eyes. Brontë thus disowns her character's imaginative energy just as she disowns her own. Her ambivalence toward feminine imaginative energy leads her to evasions and inconsistencies which limit the novel's achievement.

Charlotte Brontë's novels are more successful when she can express her conflicted sense of the demands of imagination and realism as her heroine's central dilemma, as she does in *Jane Eyre* and *Villette*. All of the crises of *Jane Eyre* center upon the release or denial of passion — Jane's anger at Mrs. Reed, her lesson in the containment of anger from Helen Burns, her acknowledgement of her passion for Rochester and her flight from it, her acceptance of St. John's denial of self and her rebellion against it. Jane's psychological struggle between the containment and expression of passion parallels Brontë's aesthetic conflict between the claims of imagination and the claims of realism. The romantic elements of the fiction — Bertha Mason, Rochester, Jane's drawings — all express Jane's sense of the claims and dangers of passion. Like Brontë's allegiance to realism, Jane's appeal to reason protects the self from the vulnerability that the claims of imagination and desire entail. The incident, for example, in which Jane contrasts her own realistically drawn portrait with an idealized sketch of Blanche Ingram teaches Jane "to bring back with a strict hand such [thoughts and feelings] as had been straying through imagination's boundless and trackless waste, into the safe fold of common sense."[11] The narrative ultimately satisfies both the claims of desire and the claims of control by giving a more powerful Jane a subdued and disciplined Rochester. The book takes its energy and its coherence from Brontë's ability to express and in some manner resolve her aesthetic conflict through Jane's struggles for self-definition.

In an even more complex way than *Jane Eyre*, *Villette* expresses Charlotte Brontë's aesthetic conflict through the conflicts in the personality of its narrator, Lucy Snowe. The novel alternates two narrative styles which speak for its conflicting psychological and aesthetic claims. Lucy describes external events in a meticulously realistic style in which she attempts to suppress entirely the claims of the self. Here, for example, she describes Polly's running out to meet her father:

> Like a bird or a shaft, or any other swift thing, she was gone from the room. How she got the housedoor open I cannot tell; probably it might be ajar; perhaps Warren was in the way and obeyed her behest, which would be impetuous enough. I — watching calmly from the window — saw her, in her black frock and tiny braided apron (to pinafores she had an antipathy), dart half the length of the street. . .[12]

When Lucy turns from external events to describe her solitary meditations, the style of meticulous description gives way to one that is highly
rhetorical, inditive, fraught with metaphor, allegory, and allusion, in
which the suppressed elements of Lucy's personality struggle to assert
themselves. Here, for example, she describes the conflict within her
between Reason and Imagination:

> This hag, this Reason, would not let me look up, or smile, or hope: she
> could not rest unless I were altogether crushed, cowed, broken-in, and
> broken-down. According to her, I was born only to work for a piece of
> bread, to await the pains of death, and steadily through all life to
> despond. Reason might be right; yet no wonder we are glad at times
> to defy her, to rush from under her rod and give a truant hour to
> Imagination—*her* soft, bright foe, *our* sweet Help, our divine Hope. We
> shall and must break bounds at intervals, despite the terrible revenge
> that awaits our return.[13]

Both modes of narrative are complexly and ambivalently weighted. The
style of passive description protects Lucy from the notice she dreads and
from the acknowledgement of desire that renders her vulnerable, but her
constant self-suppression finally drives her to a nervous breakdown. The
imaginative soliloquies contain the book's poetry and energy, but they
provoke a craving desire in Lucy that leads to rebellion and frustration.

Villette has no resolution, and its lack of an end suggests Brontë's own
inability to resolve her ambivalence. We assume that Paul Emanuel dies at
sea and that Lucy continues to lead a life of emotional privation, but Lucy
will not explicitly acknowledge her fate. Brontë thus gives Lucy neither
gratified desire nor the necessity of contemplating its frustrations and
finally associates herself neither with the romantic nor the realistic
principles conflicting in the novel. Yet the complexity of the portrait of the
warring impulses in Lucy's temperament suggests Brontë's ability to utilize
the energy and to know the outline of her own predicament.

When Lucy describes the performance of the actress Vashti, the
judgment she makes expresses the ambivalence toward the imagination in
Brontë's art.

> It was a marvelous sight; a mighty revelation.
> It was a spectacle low, horrible, immoral.[14]

Spectacle or revelation, a disease or a gift of the mind—the terms of the
conflict show that Brontë herself has not come to a resolution about the
principles of her art. She feels on the one hand a moral and pragmatic
necessity to repress the imagination which leads her to a Calvinistic
realism; she feels on the other hand that imagination gives a kind of joy
and intensity the world denies. It might be argued that Brontë's fiction
shows the common Victorian ambivalence toward the imagination, and
indeed it does. But Brontë's identity as a woman gives that conflict a
peculiar significance. As her correspondence with Southey shows, the

Victorian conception of woman's place did not allow her autonomous imaginative activity. Charlotte Brontë's complex response to that prohibition—anger, guilt, a self-suppression expressed in a commitment to realism—shapes her attitude toward her own art even as she continues to write. On the one hand, she values imaginative energy as a means of achieving satisfying self-expression; on the other hand, her conviction that the world does not permit women such gratification of desire makes her see that energy as vain, self-indulgent, and delusory. She resorts to a quotidien realism to contain imaginative desire, but she resents her self-imposed discipline. Her novels therefore contain an ambivalence both toward the imagination and toward the containment she often espouses.

Virginia Woolf has written that the woman writer must kill the angel in the house—the socially ordained ideal of feminine selflessness—in order to achieve the imaginative freedom necessary for the best writing.[15] Her essay reminds us that sexual and imaginative freedom are closely related, that constraints on the one are felt as constraints on the other. Charlotte Brontë never totally killed the angel. She labored under the conviction that women must suppress desires the world will not fulfill even while she valued those desires as the finest elements of her nature. The resulting conflict between her drive for imaginative expression and her conviction of the necessity of imaginative containment consequently gave her art both its limitations and its strengths.

Notes

1. Quoted by Winifred Gerin, *Charlotte Brontë: The Evolution of Genius* (London, 1967), p. 103.

2. Clement Shorter, *The Brontës: Life and Letters* (New York, 1908), v. 1, p. 128.

3. *Ibid.*, pp. 129–30.

4. Ed., Margaret Smith (London, 1973), p. 110.

5. Shorter, v. 1, p. 119.

6. (London, 1967), p. v.

7. *Ibid.*, p. 212.

8. (London, 1969), p. 1.

9. *Ibid.*, p. 45.

10. *Ibid.*, pp. 319–20.

11. *Jane Eyre*, p. 162.

12. Ed., Geoffrey Tillotson and Donald Hawes (Boston, 1971), p. 12.

13. *Ibid.*, p. 196.

14. *Ibid.*, p. 220.

15. *The Death of the Moth and Other Essays* (New York, 1942), pp. 236–37.

Passionate Reserve and Reserved Passion in the Works of Charlotte Brontë

John Kucich*

"When I first began to write," Charlotte Brontë told George Henry Lewes, "I restrained imagination, eschewed romance, repressed excitement."[1] This pattern of general reserve, a point of self-definition freely avowed both by Brontë as writer and by all of her major characters, is a pattern we have grown accustomed to think of as a tragic psychic compromise, a martyring of creative potential. Such reserve, by which I mean deliberate refusals of self-expression — refusals that ostentatiously dam up passion and desire — appear to us as hopelessly unhealthy, compelled both by outward oppression and deprivation, and by inward paralysis. But our sense of the limitations inherent in Brontë's reserve depends very heavily on neo-Freudian psychology, which tends to equate the pressure of desire toward expression with the more authentic movements of selfhood — an equation our culture too readily accepts as natural and obvious. For Charlotte Brontë, however, desire is engendered by means of reserve rather than despite it. That is to say, desire is not quelled in her constrained characters and narratives; rather, desire articulates itself by collapsing the distinction between expressed passion and reserve, making these gestures parallel, sometimes interchangeable modes of self-extension. The oppositional psychic tensions we tend to find so disturbing in Brontë's work are, in fact, unstable oppositions that, through their very instability, seek to intensify desire and the subjectivity within which desire circulates.

Recently, writers as different ideologically as Michel Foucault, Carl Degler, and Nina Auerbach have argued that forms of Victorian self-control play a more positive, empowering role within subjectivity than we have come to think.[2] Foucault, in particular, has most directly challenged what he calls "the repressive hypothesis" by simply inverting its terms: repression "was not established as a principle of limitation of the pleasures of others by what have traditionally been called the 'ruling classes.' Rather it appears to me that they first tried it on themselves . . . what was involved was not an asceticism, in any case not a renunciation of pleasure or a disqualification of the flesh, but on the contrary an intensification of the body, a problematization of health and its operational terms: it was a question of techniques for maximizing life."[3] For Foucault, Victorian repression becomes an injunction to discover and articulate bodily desire as an infinitely "deep" fund of subjective power:

*Reprinted from *ELH* 52 (Winter 1985): 913–37, by permission of the Johns Hopkins University Press.

"Let us not isolate the restrictions, reticences, evasions, or silences which [Victorian sexuality] may have manifested, in order to refer them to some constitutive taboo, psychical repression, or death instinct. What was formed was . . . an affirmation of self."

Foucault situates repression's expanded subjectivity wholly in relation to multivalent struggles of power (class, familial, individual), and argues that repression can be put to various tactical advantages. This situating of the capacities to reserve the self in relation to struggle is a logical tactic shared by many revisionary discussions of the issue, all of which hope to increase our appreciation for the palpable power mobilized by self-control, and thus to reverse the assumption that repression is a sign of victimization. However, close attention to the writing of a novelist like Charlotte Brontë ultimately overturns the attempt to locate the value of reserve solely in terms of interpersonal struggle. That is to say, because it sees Victorian subjectivity as an object determined and constituted only by "relations of force,"[4] Foucault's work is inadequate to describe the appeal of a certain autonomy generated by Victorian reserve. Brontë, the English novelist who first fully develops a logic of emotional reserve, destabilizes her characters in relation to struggles for power, and in that way promises them a kind of psychic freedom not limited by its relation to "tactical" pressures, a freedom that appears to be more pleasurably undefined and undefinable. The kind of fluid self-extension Brontë can imagine through reserve thus has a readily perceptible affinity with the kinds of self-disruptive, euphoric inwardness that are the legacy of romantic conceptions of the self.

The destabilization of the self's power, which I will take up later in this essay, is made possible in Brontë's novels by the more general unraveling of her opposition between expression and reserve, an unraveling that is at the core of her concept of character. Beginning here, we can trace the various strategies she develops to enhance reserve, which ultimately lead her to empty knowable categories of relationship as determinants of subjectivity. This unraveling of expression and reserve is easiest to see if we examine first the way Brontë describes uninhibited displays of passion. We usually tend to assume that passion means the same thing to Charlotte Brontë that it does to us—that it has a spontaneous connection to desire and interiority and that its primary form is the passion for heterosexual union. But Brontë's passion is, in fact, strangely reserved. The striking thing about expressions of passion in Charlotte Brontë's fiction is that they most often appear as histrionic—as a performance that conceals, rather than reveals, an interior condition of desire. For Brontë, passion implies the existence of an aroused, hypersensitive self that it simultaneously withholds. In her Byronically passionate male characters—and also in her female protagonists, though in more ephemeral ways—passion is a means of distancing the self from others. In effect there is nothing unmediated about the relationship between self and passionate expression as it is imagined in the novels, nothing that might make reserve appear as a falsification by contrast.

This aspect of Brontëan passion is most obvious in her series of benign male tyrants. In *The Professor* Hunsden is a volatile and singularly uncensored egotist, able to indulge every whim of self-expression by virtue of his aristocratic position. Yet Hunsden's willfulness, his "resolution to arrogate to himself a freedom so unlimited that it might often trench on the just liberty of his neighbours,"[5] is presented as the facade concealing a very different, "inner" self that we can never know. His bachelorhood is just one sign of the passional reserve accompanying these moody outbursts. We are also told directly that Hunsden's forwardness hides a mysterious, and far more sensitive being: "he had no English shyness: he had learnt somewhere, somehow, the art of setting himself quite at his ease, and of allowing no insular timidity to intervene as a barrier between him and his convenience or pleasure . . . yet, at times, an indescribable shade passed like an eclipse over his countenance, and seemed to me like the sign of a sudden and strong inward doubt of himself, his words and actions — an energetic discontent at his life or his social position, his future prospects or his mental attainments — I know not which" (*P*, 3). In Hunsden forwardness is indeed "an art" — it is not the direct, unmediated expression of his inward force of character. Instead, that secretive, "energetic discontent," which will later become the unspoken source of Hunsden's power to author the lives of others, defines his personality in terms of a concealed self-conflict: "At that moment one of those momentary eclipses I before alluded to had come over his face, extinguishing his smile, and replacing, by an abstracted and alienated look, the customarily shrewd, bantering glance of his eye. . . . I discerned that there would be contrasts between his inward and outward man; contentions, too" (4). Hunsden's "bantering" public vituperation, which runs counter to his unexpected and elaborately secretive beneficence to William Crimsworth, only attests to the enigma of his doubleness. Through this distancing of himself in the very form taken by his "uninhibited" expressiveness, Hunsden becomes the most mysterious character in the book, powerful in his remoteness — a godlike figure, ubiquitous and autonomous, who acts from behind a mask and certainly can never be understood through self-expression alone. In fact, Hunsden uses histrionic expression in the same strategic, calculating way that Brontëan characters often use reserve — as a point of superior self-control from which he can make others reveal themselves: "There was a tone of despotism in the urgency of the very reproaches by which he aimed at goading the oppressed into rebellion against the oppressor" (4). Crimsworth seems to learn from Hunsden how these seemingly opposite capacities — for histrionic passion and for reserve — can be merged as twin phases of his personality. When the normally self-effacing Crimsworth acquires authority as a teacher, he duplicates Hunsden's distancing, histrionic attitude in relation to that personification of reserve, Frances Henri. Crimsworth treats Frances with "calculated abruptness" (17), and subjects her to an artificial kind of "magisterial" moodiness. This uninhibited presumption on Crimsworth's part is very carefully and consciously adopted—partly, again, as a weapon to force self-revelations from Frances and partly as a means of self-concealment. Even when "mastered" by his desire, Crimsworth's expression of that desire stays well within the catechizing, performative role we have seen him adopt in the course of his teaching—which is one reason he has always struck readers as a peculiarly starchy romantic hero.

The better-known examples of male histrionic passion in Brontë's novels are, of course, Rochester and M. Paul Emanuel. For these two characters as well, passionate displays are calculated both to conceal rather than to reveal the true nature of desire, and to assail the strategic reserve of others. Rochester's roughness is usually transparently facetious. Yet very often the performative nature of Rochester's passion is quite subtle. A skillful actor—he soothes his guests by lying about nightly disturbances; he pretends to be a stranger when he first meets Jane on the road; he disguises himself as a gypsy fortune-teller to provoke a confession of love from her—Rochester's passionate displays are sustained by that very skill for performance. In his bogus parting scene with Jane, for example, Rochester breaks her resistance by robustly pretending to love Blanche Ingram. He manipulates his expressions of passion so as not to reveal himself—always breaking off before completing crucial sentences, allowing innuendoes to stand misunderstood—solely to probe Jane's reserve. When Jane tells him she must leave him because of his future bride, Rochester ambiguously cries:

"My bride! What bride? I have no bride!"
"But you will have."
"Yes—I will!—I will!" he set his teeth.
"Then I must go—you have said it yourself." (JE, 23)

At this point Jane reveals the anguish of her love and jealousy, only to be told that the imminent danger of Rochester's marriage to Blanche had been a trick. Similarly, Rochester's feverish courtship of Jane implies a far different view of their positions than either she or the reader can deduce from his displays of passion—the "strange gleams in [his] eyes" (23), the "signs of bliss in his face" (25) that Jane so obviously misreads. Rochester's extravagant deceit here is matched in more subtle ways in all his expressions of feeling for Jane. Often we can only perceive this deceit in retrospect. Though he confesses to her late in the novel that his curiosity had been piqued at their first meeting, for instance—so much so that he had spied on her the very next morning—we recall that when she was formally presented to him the following evening Rochester had feigned unruly gruffness: "there was something in the forced stiff bow, in the impatient yet formal tone, which seemed further to express, 'What the deuce is it to me whether Miss Eyre be there or not?'" (13).

It is important to recognize that Charlotte Brontë's heroines often display equally histrionic masklike passions. One thinks of Lucy Snowe's carefully orchestrated displays of anger against her students, her discovery that "a very rare flash of raillery did good" (V, 9). Very similar are Lucy's calculated displays of contempt for Ginevra Fanshawe: "An explosion ensued: for I could be passionate, too. . . . Half in earnest, half in seeming, I made it my business to storm down Ginevra" (27). Jane Eyre's eventual proposal to Rochester, expressed in an ironic, tongue-in-cheek manner, is also a flirtatious performance, especially in its coy, calculated insinuations about her relationship to St. John — insinuations that parallel Rochester's earlier insinuations about Blanche. Brontë's female protagonists may have considerably less access to histrionic and manipulative passion than her male protagonists, but they are far from strangers to it. Perhaps the most performative is Shirley Keeldar, who stages a comic humiliation of Mr. Donne and who generally invests herself in rhapsodic but self-obfuscating monologues. Caroline tells her: "Shirley, you chatter so, I can't fasten you: be still" (S, 20). In short, sanctioned expressions of feeling in Charlotte Brontë very often appear as distancing through their very nature as performances. Whenever Brontë exalts and admires passion, what fascinates her is its boldness as a diversion, not some kind of privileged relation to interiority made possible by expression, and denied by reticence.

All this is not to say that there are not sincere expressions of feeling in these characters. Indeed, the novels always feature "breakthrough scenes," in which romantic impulses do find what appears to be simple, direct expression. Certainly Lucy Snowe's "My heart will break!" is one such direct expression of feeling; it is reciprocated by M. Paul's equally direct "Lucy, take my love. One day share my life" (V, 4). But these breakthrough expressions all have an affinity with distance and self-concealment that needs to be recognized. Emotional breakthroughs are always carefully limited by the capacities for reserve they imply; extremes of feeling are never separated from the will to create distance. For example, M. Paul's "one day" significantly qualifies his passion for Lucy and restricts it as a surrender. And Lucy's "heartbreak" is an implicit sign of her longstanding commitment to self-discipline, as well as of her resolution and her ability to endure solitary suffering. Similarly, Jane Eyre's confession of her love for Rochester takes the form of a threat to leave him: "Do you think I can stay to become nothing to you? Do you think I am an automaton? . . . I have as much soul as you — and full as much heart! And if God had gifted me with some beauty and much wealth, I should have made it as hard for you to leave me, as it is now for me to leave you" (JE, 23). Furthermore, breakthrough scenes always consist not of outright declarations and surrenders but of demonstrations of self-conflict. Lucy and Jane reveal their love through tears and emotional struggle. Rochester, at the end of *Jane Eyre*, reveals his through self-accusation. These scenes are also heavily laden with images of mutual conquest that help define an embattled kind of distance between the lovers. The courtship scenes of Louis Moore and Shirley are obvious examples, but even in more sentimental scenes from *Jane Eyre* reconciliation is presented imagistically as a reciprocal contest, a battle of imprisoning wills, rather than as a harmonious merging:

> He groped; I arrested his wandering hand, and prisoned it in both mine.
> "Her very fingers!" he cried. "her small slight fingers! If so, there must be more of her!"
> The muscular hand broke from my custody; my arm was seized, my shoulder, neck, waist—I was entwined and gathered to him.
>
> (*JE*, 381)

Reciprocal combat defines passion as an aggressive opposition to others, rather than as an unguarded relaxing of personal boundaries. Outside of these ambiguous breakthroughs between lovers, the very few spontaneous outbursts of passion by Brontë's heroines—Jane Eyre's verbal conquest of Mrs. Reed, for example—are found to be deeply disturbing in ways that the characters cannot adequately articulate for themselves. In all these ways, expressed passion most often becomes a sign not of the self's unmediated relation to others and to discourse, but of entrance into a complicated fluctuation of disclosures and concealments that obscures individuals (rather than simply fortifying their "self-sufficiency"[6]) even as it brings them into charged contact.

Expression and reserve thus cooperate and enhance each other by being identical in their opposition to direct self-revelation. In numerous instances the two gestures are metaphorically collapsed. Reserve is often read as itself the sign of passion, as an idealized site of energy and fulfillment. Eve Kosofsky Sedgwick has pointed out that the complex of Gothic metaphors Charlotte Brontë draws on makes "depth" and "surface" (or "passion" and "veil") imagery a set of metonymic, interchangeable signs for intense desire.[7] That is to say, in Brontë's novels, characters often focus on reserve itself, rather than on what lies "beneath" it, as the expressive sign of desire's potency. Lucy tells Polly that her new attractiveness to John Graham lies precisely in her enigmatic reserve: "it will increase his pride in you, his love for you, if either be capable of increase" (*V*, 32). Polly's careful letters are meant to represent in their very reserve the presence of her own desire: "with this unconfessed confession, her letters glowed" (37). Elsewhere Polly's reserve is described in oxymoronically sensual terms—as "gentle ice" (37), for instance. And Polly tells Lucy that she is moved most of all by Graham's appearance of stolidity:

"To me he seems now all sacred, his locks are inaccessible, and, Lucy, I feel a sort of fear when I look at his firm, marble chin, at his straight Greek features" (37). Similarly, Louis Moore, after winning Shirley, says: "There is a dearer delight in the reserve with which I am treated, than in all the endearments [Henry] is allowed" (S, 36). In much the same way M. Paul and Lucy's scenes of passion are saturated with images of reserve that become signs of desire. In an especially noteworthy scene M. Paul's inward force appears to Lucy as an odd conjunction of signs for explosiveness and for restraint: "I saw over all M. Paul's face a quick rising light and fire: I can hardly tell how he managed the movement; it did not seem violent; it kept the form of courtesy; he gave his hand; it scarce touched [Mme. Beck], I thought; she ran, she whirled from the room; she was gone and the door shut in one second" (V, 41). The underlying congruence of expression and reserve, as well as their frequently eroticized conjunction, suggest that this opposition is not at all antithetical, but that it generates a series of shifts, or displacements, within a single heterogeneous framework of desire.

This framework of desire, supported by both expression and reserve, has an idiosyncratic structure that bears closer analysis. Brontëan desire can best be defined as a kind of double movement—on the one hand, toward a secretive self-concentration, on the other, toward the continual disruption of this concentrated self by a power greater than selfhood, an impersonal power that shatters self-understanding and psychic stability in the exquisite turbulence of contradictory, unresolvable feeling. This double movement generates and exercises desire in the self through the internal play of concentration and disjunction without ever submitting desire to the stabilizing demands of either intersubjective relationship or self-knowledge. In effect Charlotte Brontë cultivates psychic withdrawal, not simply as a sanctuary, but as the preferred field for a violent kind of emotional extension. I want to look at these two movements of Brontëan desire separately, as a way to show how they are made possible both by expression and by reserve.

The first of these movements, toward self-concentration, is suggested in a number of general ways—for example, by the sketchy, pasteboard nature of characters grouped around Brontë's rich and complex narrators and by the proud independence of Jane, Shirley, Lucy. Brontë's heroines may suffer in their isolation, but their suffering—like all romantic suffering—promises a certain consummation more attractive than the relief of suffering. At its highest pitch, Brontëan desire never seeks to achieve union between two selves or to complete the self in the other. Her characters certainly need others to help instigate and confirm the intensity of their inward feeling, and the indifference of others is intolerable, but the anger and rage this indifference produces often become only another medium of concentrated interiority. In general Brontë's characters use others only as the friction necessary to a heightened inward dynamic of feeling.

The self-concentrating movement of Brontëan desire is clearest in her earliest writing, which has not yet adopted a veil of apparently dreary reserve to obscure insularity's appeal. One of the remarkable things about the juvenilia is that Brontë's characters are all so sharply defined and differentiated; the reason for this is simply that her characters are always passionately out of phase with one another. Each is defined as a discontinuous inward turbulence arbitrarily linked to some object of desire. This arbitrariness is apparent even in characters who do claim something like fusional passion, and whose self-torment seems the consequence of failure to find union. One thinks of Mina Laury, for example, of whom we are told "She had but one idea—Zamorna. Zamorna—! it had grown up with her—become part of her nature . . . she could no more feel alienation from him than she could from herself."[8] But the key to Mina Laury's passion is her ability to transform Zamorna into an abstraction, to make him an "idea" that cannot be separated from her own nature. In fact, Zamorna's existence is singularly irrelevant to Mina Laury's desire: "She did not even repine when he forgot her—any more than the religious Devotee does when his Deity seems to turn away his face for a time and leave him to the ordeal of temporal afflictions—It seemed as if she could have lived on the remembrance of what he had once been to her without asking for anything more." Mina Laury herself tells Lord Hartford: "I know that he even seldom troubles himself to think of what I do, & has never & can never appreciate the unusual feelings of subservience, the total self-sacrifice I offer at his shrine" (FN, 44). The striking feature of Mina Laury's desire is how completely, how obsessively it is concentrated on itself, seeming to be far in excess of her wish for union. Such desire is inherently and defiantly counterdependent in its refusal to accept easy comfort for its pain, comfort usually offered by attractive and even excessively accommodating male surrogates (Hartford, in Mina Laury's case).

There are other characters in the juvenilia who claim fusional desires, but one of the laws of Angria is that such desire can never be fulfilled, and must be transformed into a more self-reflexive form. Refusal of the other comes to be a more frequent narrative situation than seduction: one thinks of Mina Laury's refusal of Hartford, Elizabeth Hasting's of William Percy, Zamorna's of Zenobia Ellrington, or Alexander Percy's of Zamorna. Even Zamorna, who dissipates—but at least expresses and gratifies—his desires endlessly, is ultimately a figure of intensely solitary and self-involved longings. The insufficiency of any single object to Zamorna's desire prevents him from completing any kind of outward consummation. Instead, we frequently see him daydreaming as Charlotte Brontë herself might, generating a wholly inward play of desire: "Long Zamorna lay awake . . . the unslumbering eye wandered over images which the firey imagination pourtrayed upon vacancy" (*FN*, 138). We find him compulsively jealous—that is, perversely focused on rivals rather than on objects of his love. We find that, despite the number of women who are morbidly faithful to him, he takes no comfort from love at all. In these ways, Zamorna typifies the intense loneliness of Brontëan desire. Unrequited love may be the dominant subject of all her fiction, but in a character from the juvenilia like Zamorna, the solitude of desire is clearly less a function of incapacity and exclusion than it is a principle of obsessive inwardness. Far from being a simple fantasy of tyrannical male potency and expression, Zamorna projects in male guise Charlotte Brontë's general interest in self-sustaining and utterly unreciprocated feeling.

In the novels the combative nature of their more domestic sexual passions helps to insure this emotional insularity. A number of readers have been struck by this unrelenting opposition of selves: Terry Eagleton points out that whenever Brontë's protagonists entertain thoughts of "equality," it is always "equality of power," not peaceful union that they have in mind[9]; and according to Karl Kroeber, Brontë conceives all of her characters "as existing, to a considerable degree, only through their antagonism to others and their resistance to external circumstances."[10] Louis Moore and Shirley, for example, find love not in tranquility, but in the tension of continual sparring: "You name me leopardess," Shirley tells him. "Remember the leopardess is tameless" (*S*, 36). As noted earlier, such sparring guarantees the ungraspability of each lover's inward life. And Louis ends his reflections on Shirley, and the penultimate chapter of the novel, at just such a point: "She breathed a murmur, inarticulate yet expressive; darted, or melted, from my arms—and I lost her" (36). But this ungraspability is more than just a fortification of distance; it represents an acute interest in private concentrations of feeling, made available as an effect of love, but pursued for their own sake. As Caroline had advised Shirley earlier, speaking of relationships with men: "Our power of being happy lies a good deal in ourselves, I believe" (12). The complacency with which Brontë dispatches M. Paul or maims Rochester—or with which Jane Eyre agrees to accompany St. John to India while refusing to marry him—is, in part, a reflection of the priority she gives to self-sustaining, inward intensity. Read against the background of Caroline's philosophy, the protracted, combative courtships of M. Paul and Lucy, or Jane and Rochester, can be seen not so much as a means to an end—a struggle Brontë's heroines must endure to discover the safety of real rewards—but as a vivid picture of the kind of unresolved battleground Brontë required of sexual passion. What such characters struggle to attain through combat is the emotional edge of subjective concentration.

The second movement of Brontëan desire, toward self-disruption, is equally important. For to call Brontëan desire self-reflexive is not at all to say that its function is to develop some kind of autonomous psyche as identity and self-presence, or as the object of the desire of others. Instead, for Charlotte Brontë desire begins a radical, potentially euphoric dislocation within the self, a rupture of psychic coherence manifested in anguish, joy, or rage.[11] One obvious phase of this movement is the agony of self-conflict so cherished by her characters. Lucy Snowe envisions the stalemate of her passion for M. Paul—compelled, ironically, by the "Truth" of his love for his ward—as an extravagant, self-rending spectacle: "far from me . . . such paltering and faltering resistance to the Power whose errand is to march conquering and to conquer, such traitor defection from the TRUTH . . . I gathered it to me with a sort of rage of haste, and folded it round me, as the soldier struck on the field folds his colours about his breast" (V, 39). And Vashti, Brontë's emblem of exalted desire, is a precise instance of glorified self-division, the internalization of endless strife: "Scarcely a substance herself, she grapples to conflict with abstractions" (23). Despite their suffering, characters like Lucy or Jane Eyre assure us that the very superiority of their feelings to those of the common herd lies in the painfully exquisite unresolvability of such feelings. Another, less obvious phase of self-disjunction is that Brontëan desire always acquires a certain endless quality—which contributes to the novels' static plot lines—precisely because the equilibrium represented by union with others is antithetical to it. Desire is expressed as a prolonged inward excitation and instability, not as a rhythm of separation and union, yearning and closure. Most obviously in the juvenilia, passion is inexhaustible, insatiable, infinitely renewable—which lends it almost a pornographic quality, as a fantasy of endless and solipsistic arousal. In her famous letter to Hartley Coleridge, Brontë extolled precisely this infinite openness of her characters, calling them "Melchisedecs—without father, without mother, without descent, having neither beginning of days nor end of life."[12] The chief embodiment of this radical, solitary restlessness in the juvenilia is Zamorna himself. With an insatiable appetite for women, for vengeance, for conflict of all kinds, Zamorna's principal virtue is his indomitability—hopelessly defeated and banished from Angria, he returns miraculously in triumph; caught in acts of depravity, he vindicates himself with dauntless eloquence. In a key speech to Alexander Percy, his arch-rival, Zamorna identifies this infinite irrepressibility of his with nature itself: "The Duke was still unquelled—He answered, as he turned & walked slowly through the room, 'In Nature there is no such thing as annihilation—blow me up & I shall live again' " (FN, 358). Zamorna's indomitability makes him fundamentally perverse, unsatisfied by any conventional resolution of desire. And characters like Alexander, Edward, and William Percy—like all of Brontë's later Byronic males—are variations on the same theme of relentlessly instable inward force.

The clearest eruption of this inward force in the novels comes in characters who are ruled by their restlessness. Rochester announces this about himself matter-of-factly. But Jane, too, is identified by St. John as sharing with him that crucial trait: "in your nature is an alloy as detrimental to repose as that in mine" (*JE*, 30). Rochester finds in Jane "a strange perseverance" (28), a description later repeated by St. John: "Well then . . . I yield: if not to your earnestness, to your perseverance: as stone is worn by continual dropping" (33). Throughout the novel Jane repeatedly condemns the tranquility of her life and longs for change—most notably in her wistful attic protest: "it is in vain to say human beings ought to be satisfied with tranquility: they must have action; and they will make it if they cannot find it" (12). In a similar way, Lucy Snowe is sardonic about the periods of tranquility in her life and about her own susceptibility to bland repose. She has great contempt for those who, like Ginevra Fanshawe, "sour in adversity" (*V*, 6). Both Jane and Lucy, by throwing themselves on the world without resources, display a kind of indomitability and preference for risk that even covets the danger of death. Statements like Jane's or Lucy's are usually construed as protests against the denial to women of everyday action in the world; but they can just as easily be interpreted in light of a constant Brontëan dichotomy: the paleness of tranquility and satisfied desire as opposed to the vitality of disruptive change, even if—or precisely because—change brings isolation and "passionate pain." This opposition is made explicit by Rose Yorke's answers to Caroline in *Shirley*:

> "Is change necessary to happiness?"
> "Yes."
> "It is synonymous with it?"
> "I don't know; but I feel monotony and death to be almost the
> same." (23)

This same opposition appears in Lucy Snowe's contempt for the marriage of Polly and John Graham and her preference for her own more difficult—and endlessly self-conflictual—lot.

To turn now to the special aspects of emotional power vested in Charlotte Brontë's reserve: if forms of reserve do dominate the novels, it is only because such reserve has been elaborately adapted to Brontë's framework of desire, with its double movement toward self-concentration and self-disruption. Brontë's very first novel seems a deliberate attempt to create a character who might expend his desire freely within reserve. For William Crimsworth demonstrates far more than just defiance and tactical wisdom through his watchful reticence. William's reserve also becomes the sign of some mysterious and superior inward power. At one point, his brother Edward suspects this might be education, and the social prestige it represents: "he suspected that I kept the padlock of silence on mental wealth in which he was no sharer" (*P*, 4). At another,

Edward suspects it might be a greater industriousness, a sign of worldly competence. But more importantly, William's silence in the face of Edward's harassments and attempted humiliations is a kind of *pot-latch*[13] — a demonstration of one's superior wealth by proof of how much one can afford to destroy, a gesture of destructive luxury. By surrendering all opportunities for self-defense on the vulgar level of Edward's insults — by becoming in effect a voluntary martyr — William demonstrates his superior, if undisplayed, inward wealth of resources. William's forfeiture of self-defense is a continual sign that his abandoning himself to Edward's world of trade has been an extravagant act rather than a mere submission to necessity.[14] His easy submission symbolizes an inexhaustible, continually expended inner strength.

Brontë takes great pains to define for us, if not for Edward, the nature of this mysterious inward strength. For William's *potlatch* is the sign of an inward force which appears to be endless, indomitable, inexhaustible. William tells us that he is able to outlast his brother through the sheer inexhaustibility of his reserve: "Day by day did his malice watch my tact, hoping it would sleep, and prepared to steal snake-like on its slumber; but tact, if it is genuine, never sleeps" (4). "Sleepless-ness" signifies the very quality of inexhaustibility so important to Brontëan desire. And by calling his reserve "genuine," William suggests that reserve's inexhaustibility derives from his own deepest personal qualities, the force of his very being; it is not simply one strategic weapon among many. The superiority of reserve to the fitful, despotic passions of others lies precisely in this apparent inexhaustibility, which seems to manifest an ungraspable, fundamental depth of personal force.

An important development of the later novels consists in their ability to define the nature of reserve's force without recourse to tactical terms. For the power of reserve is often separated from its use as an instrument of mastery and explored instead as a means of purely private self-discovery and self-expansion. This is evident in the way reserve opens up possibilities for histrionic performance, for the luxury of self-dispersion. Jane Eyre, for example, is accused of being "an actress" (2) and "a liar" (4) — accusations that seem unjust and patently false in their context, but that prove suggestive when we consider Jane's alias with the Rivers family; her systematic concealment of her thoughts from other charac-ters; or even her return to Rochester at the end of the novel, when she pretends to be his servant, Mary. In *Villette* Lucy Snowe discovers to her surprise that she, too, has a great talent for acting. Hiding behind her dramatic persona in the vaudeville, she is able to invest her acting with her own spirited desires. And in doing so, she discovers that "a keen relish for dramatic expression had revealed itself as part of my nature" (14). Although Lucy immediately recoils from this capacity, claiming to re-nounce acting, her pretensions to indifference and reserve soon become invested with this same relish for dramatic performance. Her assumption of an indifferent mask before her students, for example, certainly draws on that love of acting. M. Paul often accuses her of being "a mask" (30), and Ginevra Fanshawe accuses her of being an even better actress than Ginevra herself is. This kind of manipulation becomes a source of great inward satisfaction: Lucy tells us, while reflecting on her self-control in the classroom, that she is proud to be "polishing my faculties and whetting them to a keen edge with constant use" (9). The neo-Gothic nun in *Villette* is a subtle sign of this relationship between reserve and performance, since the nun's costume is a theatrical use of "repression" as disguise. As a trick used to negotiate romantic trysts, the nun calls attention to Lucy's own reserve as part of a performative psychological organization.

But this kind of disguised self-performance is still closely related to competition and confrontation, to power over others. After *The Professor*, Charlotte Brontë explores even more purely private dimensions of reserve's power. Reserve becomes simply the sign of a radical self-transcendence, an internal surrender to disruptive, self-destructively expansive power. Reserve comes to define a tremendous and impersonal inward power through its very self-negations. Helen Burns is the first example of this kind of transcendent self-negation, and though her portrait is somewhat crudely drawn, it establishes the main lines of the pattern. Helen's self-sacrifices insist that her desire requires no fusion and no confrontation with others, no object but her own self-expended— and, paradoxically, self-obsessed— power. In this way, Helen's martyrdom turns apparent self-negation into a form of tragic release. Pointedly, then, Helen is described as a day-dreamer—in terms reminiscent of Charlotte Brontë's own image of herself as a visionary writer. The daydream motif suggests not simply a cardboard saintliness on Helen's part, but an experience of euphoric separation from both self and world.

Though Jane Eyre defiantly claims at first that she is "no Helen Burns," she does learn something of this self-transcendence from her. When punished unjustly by Mr. Brocklehurst, she absorbs some of Helen's euphoric relation to suffering from the look Helen gives her: "What a strange light inspired [her eyes]! What an extraordinary sensation that ray sent through me! How the new feeling bore me up! . . . I mastered the rising hysteria, lifted up my head, and took a firm stand on the stool" (*JE*, 7). And when first at Thornfield, Jane succeeds in tapping this infinite but solitary euphoria: she manages "to open my inward ear to a tale that was never ended— a tale my imagination created and narrated continuously" (12). Later, Rochester will be attracted to Jane initially because he sees her as "a dream or a shade" (22), imagery that reminds us of Helen's oblivious otherworldliness. He tells Jane "you have rather the look of another world" (13), and constantly associates her with fairies and elves. When Rochester spies on Jane he is fascinated by her apparently self-sufficient, inward circulation of desire in reverie: "you paced gently on and dreamed. I think those day visions were not dark: there was a pleasurable illumination in your eye occasionally, a soft excitement in your aspect, which told of no bitter, bilious, hypochondriac brooding: your look revealed rather the sweet musings of youth when its spirit follows on willing wings the flight of Hope up and on to an ideal Heaven" (27). When Jane dares death by starvation she completes the parallel with Helen and proves her inward power, which is alternately expended as a solitary self-separation and recuperated as the sign to others of her specialness.

Throughout Charlotte Brontë's fiction we find similar instances of transcendently solitary suffering through self-negation. And although these situations often may protest against certain kinds of oppression and deprivation, they also represent an extravagant elaboration of feeling, of inward strength both tested and exercised through multivalent self-conflictual suffering. Enforced reserve permits Brontë's characters an endless series of turbulent emotional peaks in abnegation, service, and sorrow.[15] When Lucy Snowe buries Dr. John's letters, she cherishes the intense, self-reflexive circulation of feeling she generates, a circulation that compresses subjectivity only to open it to a transcendent pitch:

> I had a dreary something – not pleasure – but a sad, lonely satisfaction
> . . . The air of the night was very still, but dim with a peculiar mist,
> which changed the moonlight into a luminous haze. In this air, or this
> mist, there was some quality – electrical, perhaps – which acted in a
> strange sort upon me. I felt then as I had felt a year ago in England –
> on a night when the aurora borealis was streaming and sweeping round
> heaven, when, belated in lonely fields, I had paused to watch that
> mustering of an army with banners. (V, 26)

Such devotion to a self-conflict more prized than life itself is hardly a conservative or impoverished gesture; it dissolves subjective wholeness in rapture and torment. Only in this way can we understand the various refusals of love that seem so perverse in these characters – sometimes even to themselves.

To claim that reserve bears the same relation to self-concentrating and self-disruptive Brontëan desire as passion does is not, however, to close off the issue. For the pressing question about this fundamental identity of passion and reserve remains: if both gestures share an identical structure as signs of endless and inaccessible force, why are they presented as an opposition at all? Such a stark contrast, the focus of interest for generations of readers, cannot be an arbitrary one. Why is this mercurial difference presented as so central if it can be collapsed into an identity? One answer to this question lies in the very instability and endlessness of the conflict made possible by such a convoluted psychological duality. That is to say, the vacillations of feeling made possible by expression and reserve help sustain insular self-disruption even as they mirror and echo each other, dwelling on their essential sameness. We can trace the infinite play that these twin gestures generate by looking at the oppositional struggle usually defined by predominantly passionate and predominantly reserved characters, the master/slave dynamic so central to Brontë's narratives. For it is here that the supposed vulnerability of reserved characters to figures of authority—the vulnerability we conventionally assume would be remedied by some exercise of passionate resistance—is revealed instead as a kind of necessary, endless cooperation between polarized extremes of power. And it is here that forms of relationship disrupt, rather than constitute, the Brontëan self.

In all of Charlotte Brontë's novels, there is a curious reversibility of these power relations, a reversibility which she seemed increasingly aware of as crucial to her romantic situations. In *The Professor* we see this reversibility drawn in a highly fragmented way, initially in the successive roles played by William Crimsworth. Crimsworth is passive and even deferential in his relations with both Edward and Hunsden early in the novel, but he is metamorphosed into a tyrant when he begins teaching: "a word of impertinence, a movement of disobedience, changed me at once into a despot. I offered them but one alternative—submission and acknowledgement of error, or ignominious expulsion" (7). Similarly Crimsworth undergoes a transformation from underling to master in relation to Mme. Reuter. As Crimsworth's potent reserve early in the novel indicates, it seems important to Charlotte Brontë not only that Crimsworth should openly dominate his opponents, but also that he should be able to play both roles—master and slave—and to turn each to his advantage. Unable to conceive such flexibility within a single relationship as yet, Brontë creates a round-robin situation, in which the two lovers reverse master/slave roles in relation to a third party. In marriage, Crimsworth clearly holds sway over Frances; yet, in relation to Hunsden, Frances reverses this power structure, becoming wonderfully aggressive and intimidating. Repudiating Hunsden's characterization of her Swiss ancestry as "servile," Frances openly mocks Hunsden for his own "British" suppression of feeling and squashes him in argument, which moves Hunsden to warn William about her. After Frances predicts that Hunsden's future, Othello-like wife will some day smother him to death, Hunsden tells William: "I hope yet to hear of a travesty of the Moor and his gentle lady, in which the parts shall be reversed according to the plan just sketched—you, however, being in my nightcap" (24). Brontë refuses to dramatize this reversibility in the romantic couple themselves. Instead, it is only through Hunsden that Crimsworth's own relation to power is made reversible. Early in the novel William defines Hunsden as partially female—"how small, even effeminate, were his lineaments" (4)—and William is able to feel his own strength against him more surely as a result. Yet Hunsden emerges at the end as William's master: not only has Hunsden been William's secret sponsor, but William appears unable to counter Hunsden's presumption and his insults. William declares that Hunsden visits the married couple only "to work me into lunacy by treading on my mental corns" (25). But Frances can respond to Hunsden much more actively, through "revelations of the dragon within her." One of the reasons for this suppleness in Frances's relation to power is Brontë's need to differentiate her humility from the servility of Mme. Reuter. But such modification would not require the oscillation between extremes of domination and deference that we find in this elaborately balanced triangle. Something about the reversal of positions itself seems to interest her.

In *Jane Eyre* the reversibility of power relations is made directly a part of the romantic relationship, without the mediation of a third party. There is, of course, a dramatic change in the relations of dominance between Jane and Rochester at the end of the novel. Yet before concluding that the power is wielded entirely in one direction or the other, we should notice how the rhetoric of the novel stipulates power's reversibility, and how master/pupil relations oscillate even in the conclusion of the novel. Although Jane is, in fact, in a position to "witness the subjection of that vigorous spirit" (37) at the end, she also describes herself metaphorically as more subservient to Rochester—for example, by calling herself a vine which will "lean towards you, and wind round you, because your strength offers [me] so safe a prop." Jane defines Rochester's "subjection" as a very dangerous one, making her extremely cautious about her triumph: he is like "some wronged and fettered wild beast or bird, dangerous to approach in his sullen woe." And of course, Jane continues to call him "master." The narrative makes it clear that Rochester still can control Jane physically: " 'Well, you can leave me, ma'am: but before you go' (and he retained me by a firmer grasp than ever) . . ." (37). His emotional power is more subtly defined, as a continued intensity of inwardness. When they finally agree on marriage, Jane notices immediately that "his old impetuosity was rising": in this key scene, she tries to focus his attention on her own power to guide him (and therefore on his dependence)—"We will go home through the wood: that will be the shadiest way"—but Rochester refuses this diversion, seeming not even to hear her directions, and instead "he pursued his own thoughts without heeding me."

This very unstable alternation of power and dominance at the conclusion only reflects the oscillations between Jane and Rochester throughout the novel. Jane and Rochester's relationship is always constituted as a battleground—but a battleground with power flowing alternately in two directions, thanks in part to the often-neglected power of Jane's reserve. Throughout, the language of mastery flipflops. Jane swears that "he made me love him" (17), and at her first surrender she remarks: "If I had loved him less I should have thought his accent and look of exultation savage" (23). But Rochester continually points out the boldness of Jane's often insulting deference. And at their first reconciliation he says, "I am influenced—conquered; and the influence is sweeter than I can express; and the conquest I undergo has a witchery beyond any triumph I can win" (24), at which Jane smiles with an "inexplicable . . . uncanny turn of countenance" and says: "I was thinking, sir (you will excuse the idea; it was involuntary), I was thinking of Hercules and Samson with their charmers." Over and over we learn of Jane's power with Rochester.[16] Even when she runs away from Thornfield, she is ambiguously aware of the power she has to injure him: "I had injured— wounded—left my master . . . never may you, like me, dread to be the instrument of evil to what you wholly love" (27). The doubleness of the syntax in that final sentence seems eerily appropriate.

Jane herself defines a rationale for this reciprocal exercise of power, a rationale that echoes all the gratifications we have earlier associated with the insularity of Brontëan desire. Taunting Rochester she thinks to herself: "you may fume and fidget as you please: but this is the best plan to pursue with you, I am certain. I like you more than I can say: but I'll not sink into a bathos of sentiment: and with this needle of repartee I'll keep you from the edge of the gulf, too; and moreover, maintain by its pungent aid that distance between you and myself most conducive to our real mutual advantage" (24). This reciprocal combat is precisely what she misses in St. John, who would control her absolutely: "as a man, [St. John] would have wished to coerce me into obedience" (34). The chief focus of this reversibility, however, is not interdependent, but purely private. That is to say, Jane and Rochester's relationship, in its reversible polarities of mastery and slavery, is only the outward manifestation of an inward instability that defines both characters.[17] Rochester seems at first to be all-powerful to Jane, yet she is struck by his sudden transformation at the arrival of the lamblike Mason, who unaccountably terrifies him. Earlier, still thinking Rochester is afraid of Grace Poole, Jane tells us: "It was strange: a bold, vindictive, and haughty gentleman seemed somehow in the power of one of the meanest of his dependents" (16). And Rochester's narration of his own personal history reveals a curious tendency to acquiesce to the power of others. Jane, too, like most of Brontë's narrator/protagonists, is alternately both meek and assertive. Jennifer Gribble has tellingly pointed out, for example, that when Jane studies herself in the red room mirror, she sees a "composite view of the child's insignificance and her power, of her subjection to experience and her control over it."[18] The oscillation of power between Jane and Rochester, then, is not an incongruity that emerges from romantic situations, a prescription for bliss in love. It is primarily a means of heightening an ambiguity in relation to power that is at the heart of each individual character. Both Jane and Rochester define personality itself as a mixture of dominant and submissive impulses—a conjunction of extremes that oddly parallels our earlier conjunction of passion and reserve. The same might be said of Lucy Snowe's alternations between command and subservience, which provoke from Paulina the comment: "Lucy, I wonder if anybody will ever comprehend you altogether?" (V, 27). This instability in relation to power is often overlooked by readers intent on pinpointing the final winner in Brontë's sexual battles.

In the context of the general notions about distance, inexhaustibility, and combativeness developed in this paper, several observations about reversibility of power seem warranted. For one, in Charlotte Brontë's novels master/slave relationships promise distance to both parties equally. In the role reversals of these protagonists, we are made aware that either pole defines the security and the combative freedom of emotional autonomy. The master/slave relation does not limit such autonomy; rather, because it is a relationship without equality, it circumvents emotional sharing and, therefore, fusion.[19] In *The Professor* Crimsworth tells us that his mastering austerity gains him a certain freedom with Frances: by withholding his praise, for example, he is able to continue observing her: "I said nothing of Mdlle. Henri's exercise, and, spectacles on nose, I endeavoured to decipher in her countenance her sentiments at the omission" (16). In less aggressive ways Crimsworth as master is able to transform passion into the responsibilities of duty, guidance, and self-sacrifice; he must, in effect, make himself a model of self-control and self-containment. Crimsworth nurtures Frances from the remote position of his authority: "To speak truth, I watched this change much as a gardener watches the growth of a precious plant" (18). Conversely Frances seems to flourish in the autonomy of her subservient position: "I perceived that in proportion as my manner grew austere and magisterial, hers became easy and self-possessed—an odd contradiction, doubtless, to the ordinary effect in such cases; but so it was" (17). Jane Eyre makes this same dynamic clear in her preference for Rochester's despotism, which releases her from any obligation to expose herself to his scrutiny in some kind of unguarded dialogue between equals. When coupled with the inherent tactical advantages of reserve, this inviolability of the slave produces a feeling of liberty, even as the master is idealized as a figure of superior self-concentration.

The more important consequence of master/slave reversals is that they pluralize and confuse the configurations of power to such a degree that contest—which defines isolation and distance—becomes endless and illimitable, rather than frozen in some kind of permanent structure of relationship. The reversibility of mastery and slavery makes them transient positions of combat—neither one more attractive than the other—that defy permanence within relationship, heightening its instability instead. Though an atmosphere of combat and competition is created as a site of subjective expansion, no one is actually mastered. No one's autonomy and distance is diminished. What we are left with is the expansion of self-concentrated desire itself, without its inhering in any

fixed interpersonal relationship. By being freed from any constant relation to objects, Brontëan desire is made inwardly infinite. At this point it
should be clear that both kinds of conjunction—master/slave, expression/
reserve—have in common a stress on the intensity of a combative struggle
that deprives these relationships of any determining power over individual desire and inwardness. Such reversibility refuses to fix the self, but
instead makes inwardness mercurial and fluid. These oppositions make a
difference in subjective terms because they use interpersonal relationships
and strategies of confrontation to generate intense inward fluctuations.
But rather than being psychically determining oppositions, such oscillations become the fulcrum for inward variation, mutuability, and metamorphosis that make very little difference in outward terms, except to
subsume external relationship wholly within the field of inward emotional concentration and expansion. Thus Brontë manages to locate a
form of experience that seeks to heighten awareness precisely by dissolving stable notions about self, identity, and self-knowledge as they are
formed in relation to others.

To locate the origins of Brontëan desire in double movements of self-
concentration and self-disruption is to suggest that Victorian reserve in
general is a highly ambivalent strategy upon which to found subjectivity,
but nevertheless an attractive—and not simply a defensive or compensatory—maneuver. Reserve's tendencies toward withdrawal and self-efface-
ment, which are absolutely central to the confusingly individualist
anti-individualism of Dickens, or the peculiarly personal "wider sympathy" of George Eliot, tend ultimately—as they do in Charlotte Brontë's
work—to abstract subjectivity completely from relations of interdependence. The great question of the Victorian novel—what does it mean for
individual subjects to be part of a community?—is answered implicitly
by these novelists' promotion of reserve: not much. The romantic self
engendered by reserve, ungraspable and unknown even to itself, is
inherently unsharable and claims an origin outside of relationship.[20] In
this way, attractive forms of Victorian reserve minimize the appeal of
public action, an effect that contributes to political powerlessness and
feelings of anomie. They also border precariously on the more obvious
dangers of exploitative ideologies of self-control with which we are all too
familiar. These are dire consequences from any point of view. But the
self-negating tendencies of reserve also promise to expand emotional life
by concentrating it through an endless play of extreme submission and
extreme exaltation. Reserve appears to be available for the advantage—
one might say even the "fulfillment"—of certain individuals within the
very culture that tries to oppress those individuals by imposing reserve
from without.

A double-edged tool, destructive to individual liberties and the
foundation for them, the effect of reserve depends entirely upon who
controls its significance, not on its inherent psychological properties. The

general Victorian promotion of reserve ought to be seen, then, as a complex alternative to collective sources of satisfaction, and not simply as the invasion of personal life by restrictive communal standards. These satisfactions, as we have seen in Brontë's characters, are meant to extend outside the capabilities of relationship to recuperate the self as an object of knowledge, and, therefore, as an object of social power. In this sense, the reserve of a novelist like Charlotte Brontë is an image of extreme pleasure in autonomy that seeks to oppose and transform the interpersonal coercions of reserve that we too quickly identify as the only — or the dominant — uses Victorian reserve may support.

Notes

1. Letter to Lewes, November 6, 1847, in T. Wise and J. A. Symington, eds., *The Shakespeare Head Brontë: The Life and Letters* (London: The Shakespeare Head Press, 1932), 2:152.

2. I am thinking of Michel Foucault, *The History of Sexuality,* vol. 1, *An Introduction,* trans. Robert Hurley (New York: Random, 1978); Carl N. Degler, *At Odds: Women and the Family in America from the Revolution to the Present* (New York: Oxford Univ. Press, 1980) — which argues that nineteenth-century emphasis on chastity increases the power of female sexuality (see esp. 249–97); and Nina Auerbach, *Women and the Demon: The Life of a Victorian Myth* (New York: Barnes & Noble, 1982).

3. *The History of Sexuality,* 122–23.

4. This is Foucault's term for power in *The History of Sexuality* (93). Though Foucault moderates the tendency of his earlier work to define nineteenty-century subjectivity as "carceral," he nevertheless grounds it in the changing relationship of struggle defined by the culture.

5. *The Professor* (London: Dent, 1969), ch. 4 (hereafter abbreviated as *P*). For Charlotte Brontë's other novels, I have used *Jane Eyre* (Baltimore: Penguin, 1966), abbreviated as *JE*; *Shirley* (Baltimore: Penguin, 1974), abbreviated as *S*; and *Villette* (Baltimore: Penguin, 1979), abbreviated as *V*. All citations refer to chapter numbers.

6. Most readers find the distancing of Brontë's lovers to be only a search for innocent autonomy as a precondition to union-with-independence. See, e.g., Philip Momberger, "Self and World in the Works of Charlotte Brontë," *ELH* 32 (1965): 349–69.

7. "The Character in the Veil: Imagery of the Surface in the Gothic Novel," *PMLA* 96 (1981): 255–70.

8. Charlotte Brontë, *Five Novelettes,* ed. Winifred Gerin (London: Folio Press, 1971), 143. Further references to this edition appear in the text as *FN*.

9. *Myths of Power: A Marxist Study of the Brontës* (London: Macmillan, 1975), 30.

10. *Styles in Fictional Structure* (Princeton: Princeton Univ. Press, 1971), 29.

11. For an interesting meditation on self-disruptive desire in *Wuthering Heights* and in nineteenth-century fiction generally, see Leo Bersani, *A Future for Astyanax: Character and Desire in Literature* (Boston: Little, Brown & Co., 1976). This aspect of Charlotte Brontë's work has been best appreciated by stylistic studies, which tend to focus on the disruptive, seemingly perverse discontinuities of her narrative voice. See esp. Margot Peters, *Charlotte Brontë: Style in the Novel* (Madison: Univ. of Wisconsin Press, 1973). Peters calls Brontë's writing "a prose vitalized by the unresolved battle of its conflicting parts" (156).

12. Quoted by Gerin, 20.

13. See Georges Bataille's work on *potlatch, La part maudite* (Paris: Les Editions de

Minuit, 1967), 107–24; or Marcel Mauss, *The Gift: Forms and Functions of Exchange in Archaic Societies,* trans. I. Cunnison (New York: Norton, 1967).

14. This point is made by Eagleton (35).

15. For many of the ideas in this paragraph I am indebted to my colleague, Martha Vicinus, and to her paper, "Distance and Desire: English Boarding-School Friendships," *Signs* 9 (1984): 600–622, which she shared with me at an earlier, manuscript stage.

16. Robert K. Martin ("*Jane Eyre* and the World of Faery," *Mosaic* 10 [1977]: 85–95) shows how Brontë is able, through the association of Thornfield with the Briar Rose story, "to visualize Jane as the aggressor and Rochester as the enchanted maiden." This pattern is clearly applicable to Caroline Helstone's penetration of Moore's sickroom and other similar role reversals.

17. In a move typical of most commentators, Ruth Bernard Yeazell ("More True than Real: Jane Eyre's 'Mysterious Summons,' " *Nineteenth-century Fiction* 29 [1974]: 127–43) takes a more benign view of such distance, defining it as a wish for union of a cautious kind: "the madness which she fought has at last been destroyed; the passion whose consuming force she resisted has finally been controlled" (142).

18. "Jane Eyre's Imagination," *Nineteenth-century Fiction* 23 (1968): 284. Gribble does not, however, find any causal relation in this composite view.

19. In this paragraph I am indebted to Martha Vicinus's essay.

20. For a provocative discussion of Charlotte Brontë's inwardness in contrast to the yearning for fundamental relationship in Emily's *Wuthering Heights,* see the chapter "Charlotte and Emily Brontë," in Raymond Williams, *The English Novel: From Dickens to Lawrence* (London: Chatto & Windus, 1970), 60–74.

THE FICTION

Juvenilia

The Authorial Voice

Christine Alexander*

All Charlotte's novels except *Shirley* are narrated in the first person. Here again, she has preserved a stylistic convention of the juvenilia. The majority of the early manuscripts are signed with a male pseudonym; and where a signature is missing, the voice of Lord Charles Wellesley, Captain Tree or Charles Townshend can almost always be recognized in the tone of the writing and the attitude of the narrator to his characters.[1] It is worth noting how early Charlotte shows the ability to convey the voice of a particular character.

It is not difficult to see the link between the roles the Brontë children acted in their early impromptu plays and their later habit of writing as characters in their Glass Town Saga. Personal involvement may account for the saga's having continued for so long. Certainly in Charlotte's case her imaginative world became an important source of security: it gave her a sense of "belonging," and took on proportions which threatened to blur different levels of reality in her mind. Well before her emotional crisis at Roe Head, she had considered reality from the point of view of her creations. So real had the world of Glass Town become by August 1830, that she could view with amusement Lord Charles Wellesley's uncertainty "as to whether I am or am not." In a surrealistic dream he senses his symbiotic relationship with his creator:

> It seemed as if I was a non-existent shadow — that I neither spoke, eat, imagined, or lived of myself, but I was the mere idea of some other creature's brain. The Glass Town seemed so likewise. My father, Arthur, and everyone with whom I am acquainted, passed into a state of annihilation; but suddenly I thought again that I and my relatives did exist and yet not us but our minds, and our bodies without ourselves. Then this supposition — the oddest of any — followed the former quickly, namely, that WE without US were shadows; also, but at the end of a long vista, as it were, appeared dimly and indistinctly, beings that really lived in a tangible shape, that were

*Reprinted from *The Early Writings of Charlotte Brontë* (1983), 225–33, with permission of Basil Blackwell Limited.

called by our names and were US from whom WE had been copied by something—I could not tell what.[2]

Like Lemuel Gulliver, he feels himself raised to the ceiling by a hand "wide enough almost to grasp the Tower of all Nations" and stationed opposite two immense sparkling blue globes. Having been returned to the floor again, he sees a huge personification of himself "hundreds of feet high" and is now convinced of his non-existence "except in another corporeal frame which dwelt in the real world, for ours I thought was nothing but idea." An imaginary character's view of reality is a sophisticated concept for a girl of fourteen.

One of the most unusual features of the early manuscripts is their strange amalgam of precocity and naivety. The initial assumption of different voices allowed Charlotte to practise a variety of styles but, as in *Something about Arthur*, the increasing use of the witty satirical narrator (Lord Charles) who must play the role of a child in his own story is often awkward and inappropriate. Because Charlotte fails to observe the limitations of the first person narrator, Lord Charles becomes an implausible character, crouching under tables and behind locked doors in order to be able to overhear and later repeat conversations. He is omniscient and omnipresent, his single viewpoint being used to comment on characters and events. Later, when he becomes Charles Townshend, Charlotte makes an effort to preserve verisimilitude. In the *Duke of Zamorna*, for example, she uses William Percy's letters to Charles to supplement Charles's lack of experience. In *Stancliffe's Hotel*, Charles Townshend again uses William Percy's experience to report on royal events he is now excluded from. But he is always removed from the emotional centre of the stories he tells and he remains an insipid observer.

It was natural that Charlotte should continue the same narrative technique in her first novel: the bloodless hero/narrator of *The Professor* owes much of his pallor and cynicism to Charles Townshend. His narration lacks the emotional intensity of the later Jane Eyre who, unlike Charles Townshend, is the focus of her story. Charlotte is able to identify imaginatively with her because she is female, whereas the preservation of a male narrator in *The Professor* limits her use of experience. In the juvenilia, Charles constantly sympathizes with Zamorna's wives, but nowhere does Charlotte adopt the voice of a female character. When she explores the thoughts of Miss West, Elizabeth Hastings and Caroline Vernon, she remains an outside observer, despite the autobiographical nature of her material.

Why, then, did Charlotte not use a female narrator in the juvenilia, since this would be the most obvious outlet for autobiographical material? Part of the answer must lie in the fact that to the Brontës writing was very much a male domain. It was Branwell who was taught the classics and so gained entry to the male world of knowledge. It was Branwell who was to have a career, to be first a professional writer and then an artist. It was Branwell who was the first of the Brontë children to appear in print[3] and who had the confidence to send work to the editor of *Blackwood's Magazine*. Above all, it was Branwell who initiated the *Young Men's Magazine* and persuaded Charlotte to contribute. It was accepted that if the girls wrote under assumed names and at the dictation of Branwell, they should impersonate men. Besides, there were no females in the early Branwell-dominated games of war and colonization.

Secondly, when women were introduced into the saga, their roles were restricted by their sex. Marian Hume, with her fairy-tale beauty and timid personality, was hardly the ideal persona for a young girl eager to play her part in controlling events. Charlotte automatically identified in her saga with the power and privilege of the male world which allowed her independence of expression. Such freedom and authority enabled her to think out her own unrealized ambitions. Unequal to Branwell in the nineteenth-century world, she could be a strong rival to his control over their dream world.

As she grew older, Charlotte saw that to write as a man allowed her to exercise the same freedom she had wielded as a child. If violence and passion were male prerogatives then she would be identified as "male" since these emotions were the grist of her imaginative mill. The later adoption of a male pseudonym for publication was a natural development of this early bid for independence in writing. "Currer Bell" sought to conceal her identity in an effort to avoid the limitations of the stereotyped "female novelist."

It is not obvious in the juvenilia that the assumption of a male voice was a conscious decision; but about the time that she wrote to Southey, in March 1837, she had clearly been considering her position as a female writer. Southey's simultaneous recognition of the talent she possessed "in no inconsiderable degree"[4] and his strictures that she limit herself to her proper sphere left Charlotte in a dilemma. She replied: "You do not forbid me to write; you do not say that what I write is utterly destitute of merit. You only warn me against the folly of neglecting real duties for the sake of imaginative pleasure; of writing for the love of fame; for the selfish excitement of emulation."[5] Her duties as a Victorian woman were in conflict with her emotional need to express herself. If she persisted in writing, she might be neglecting her duty. She knew her perfervid dreams were unhealthy and now the very act of committing them to paper was to be associated with guilt.

The elements of conflict which complicated Charlotte's attitude towards her writing are worth spelling out clearly, since they affected not only her subject matter but also the style of her narration. The ambiguity of her feelings about her writing had its roots in the fact that she delighted in stories of love and sexual passion, yet she felt moral discomfort over the rakish nature of her material. As a woman and as a

Christian she seems to have felt considerable unease about her favourite subject matter. In addition there was the fear, brought into sharp focus by Southey, that in writing at all she was tending to neglect the duties proper to a woman for a frivolous and unrewarding occupation. And finally there was her intellectual conviction that the head and not the heart should rule, a conviction which many of her juvenile stories seemed designed to overturn.

Charlotte's moral equivocation about her writing helps to explain her reluctance to replace her narrator, Charles Townshend, with a more central character in the Angrian drama. For a time she had written poetry as the romantic pompous young Marquis of Douro, but as his character altered and he developed into the fascinatingly wicked Zamorna, Charlotte preferred to describe his exploits from a respectable distance. The "Roe Head Journal" shows the guilt she felt about her increasing attachment to Zamorna and her "world below"; and Southey's letter had reinforced this. As narrator of Zamorna's deeds, she chose to shelter behind the cynicism of his younger brother. As Lord Charles Wellesley and the later Charles Townshend, she could pretend to disapprove of Zamorna's sinful career.

It is not always easy, however, to judge the moral tone of Charlotte's juvenile writing. Lord Charles's attitude to the central characters is inconsistent and reflects Charlotte's own ambiguous moral attitude to her creations. Lord Charles is not always disapproving: beneath his witty cynicism lurks a vicarious delight in his brother's wicked deeds. His disapproval of Zamorna is rooted in envy. At times in the early stories his cynicism vanishes altogether and Charlotte takes over the narration herself. *Something about Arthur*, for example, begins with a moral maxim. Lord Charles preaches the value of punishment for truancy, but when he begins his exemplum—a tale of one of Zamorna's early peccadilloes—he forgets his intention was critical. None of his usual ridicule is evident in the narration of the romantic part of the story and Zamorna is not criticized for disobeying his father or for his callous treatment of Mina Laury. It is difficult to decide too whether Charlotte is mocking her hero or whether she endorses his exaggerated code of honour. Her tone suggests that she admires his wild posturing and directly contradicts that of her opening chapter.

This ambiguous moral tone is related to her ambivalent attitude to passion. Throughout the juvenilia, so noted for Charlotte's expression of her romantic imagination, there is a distinct theme of anti-romanticism. William Crimsworth's aversion to displays of passion and sentimentality in *The Professor* is clearly anticipated by Charles Townshend. At the beginning of *Stancliffe's Hotel*, for example, Charles deflates Louisa Vernon's romantic reveries of her former elderly husband, the Marquis of Wellesley:

"Charles," said my fair companion in her usual voice, half a whisper, half a murmur. "Charles, what a sweet night, a premature summer night. It only wants the moon to make it perfect, then I could see my villa. These stars are not clear enough to bring out the white front fully from its laurels. And yet I do see a white glittering there. Is it not from my drawing-room window?"

"Probably," was my answer and I said no more. Her ladyship's softness is at times too surfeiting, more especially when she approaches the brink of the sentimental.

"Charles," she pursued, in no wise abashed by my abrupt coolness. "How many fond recollections come on us at such a time as this. Where do you think my thoughts always stray on a summer night? What image do you think 'a cloudless clime and stormy skies' always suggest?"

"Perhaps," said I, "that of the most noble Richard, Marquis of Wellesley as you last saw him reposing in gouty chair and stool, with eyelids gently closed by the influence of the pious libations in claret with which he has concluded the dinner of rice-currie, devilled turkey and guava."[6]

In *Henry Hastings*, Charles Townshend mocks the heroine, Mary Percy, as she displays her displeasure at her husband's philandering and in *Caroline Vernon*, he pillories Zamorna's Byronic pretensions. But it is the mockery of romanticism in the early juvenilia, so pervaded by fairy-tale motif, that is surprising. In the *Young Men's Magazine* for November 1830, Charlotte includes a song by Lord Charles Wellesley in which he jibes at his brother's penchant for lugubrious subjects. The song was suggested by Edward Young's *Night Thoughts on Life, Death and Immortality* which Mr. Brontë owned and which Charlotte had read earlier that year;[7] and it parodies the work of the "graveyard poets":

> Some love Sorrow's dismal howls,
> Write verses on her sighs and scowls
> And rant about her mourning dress,
> Her long black funeral array,
> Her veil which shuts out light and day
>   And love her not the less;
>
> Although She sits with woeful face
> On some old monumental tomb,
> Where yellow skulls and bones have place,
> Where corpses rot in churchyard gloom.
>
> I wish some eve as thus she's weeping,
> While sober men are soundly sleeping,
> Hid [by] the obscurity of night,
> From out its grave a ghost would start
> And make her throat receive her heart
>   And give her sore affright.[8]

Charlotte was taught early that reason was superior to passion. Her early reading reinforced this. In *The Poetaster*, Lord Charles satirizes his brother's adolescent illusions of romantic love. He describes a dream in which he sees the Marquis of Douro's bleeding heart delivered to Marian Hume by Cupid. The smiling Marian then lacerates the heart with very fine scissors, while the Marquis frowns, weeps and sighs pitifully, as Lord Charles suggests he does in his nauseously sentimental rhymes. Charlotte had been reading Jonson's *Poetaster* in which Ovid is criticized for wasting his talents on erotic poems. Charlotte was not slow to learn that the device of a cynical narrator allowed her simultaneously to criticize and to indulge in her romantic fantasies.

Until the end of 1830, her romantic and anti-romantic themes were more or less distinguished by the separate voices of the Marquis of Douro and Lord Charles Wellesley; but when Lord Charles, the anti-romantic, begins to dominate the narration Charlotte's natural preference for romance caused confusion. This is especially marked in the second period of her juvenile writing when she is often carried away by the narration of a love story and, as in *Something about Arthur*, forgets the cynicism of Lord Charles. The two conflicting attitudes run side by side through a single narration. In the later juvenilia, Charlotte became more adept at masking her feelings; but the basic conflict between her attachment to her subject and her critical conscience, expressed by her narrator, extended throughout her writing. Even the outwardly sober Lucy Snowe who protests, "Of an artistic temperament I deny that I am," betrays her nature in every character sketch and literary allusion.

Charlotte gradually learned to confine her view to the limitations of a single character and to use that narrator's personality in her writing. Lord Charles's perversity, for example, allows her to change styles rapidly and to play with the reader. In *Henry Hastings*, he writes with approval of the Verdopolitan Parliament, then immediately undercuts his previous assertion by saying that he wrote it "merely as a specimen of a certain style": "my dear reader, when you are inclined to grow enthusiastic about such things—just recall my image—leaning over the gallery with my hat on & alternately squeezing & sucking a remarkably fine madeira orange—& meantime cocking my eye at the honourable gent on his legs with an expression sufficiently indicative of the absorbing interest I take in his speechifications."[9]

Except in the "Roe Head Journal," "the reader" plays an important part in Charlotte's early writings. Lord Charles's aim is always to please: his literary efforts are likened to a "frail bark" launched on the "boisterous tide of public opinion."[10] The concept of an audience (however imaginary) and the need to communicate, which appear in the earliest of Charlotte's stories, are underlined by her constant reference to the image of a stage, especially at the beginning and end of chapters.[11] The "first scene" of *High Life in Verdopolis*, for example, "is placed in the breakfast-room of Warner Hotel." Chapter 1 concludes when the grand party at Wellesley House moves off-stage to the supper room "through wide-flung folding doors and uplifted draperies, and so for the present (Exeunt Omnes)." The image is even more explicit at the end of chapter 2 when the "voile du théâtre" is dropped by the author and then "raised again" in the following chapter.[12]

Charlotte's role as stage-manager, implicit in her early position as landlord and controlling genie in her stories, is not unlike that of Thackeray or Fielding. Particularly in her later stories, we are conducted through a series of scenes, sometimes with moral judgements but always with the prejudiced comments of Lord Charles Wellesley or Charles Townshend. At the beginning of *The Return of Zamorna*, Charles explains the pictorial nature of his method: "Oh reader what a strange aspect of uncertainty hangs over everything. Do you not now feel in doubt as to what picture the sketchy and airy Townshend will first present to your fancy. I have you by the hand and am your guide, and we are in a long gallery, the paintings of which are all veiled . . . Sit down on that antique chair in the centre and I will pass silently round and draw the curtains one by one."[13]

The self-conscious author is present in Charlotte's earliest productions: in the frequent apostrophes to the reader; in the detailed documentation of the formation of the "plays" and the noting of the exact time that a story took to write: in the title-pages and careful production of her magazines; and in her detailed *Catalogue of my Books*, "with the periods of their completion up to August 3, 1830." The fourteen-year-old Charlotte notes for example in the Preface to *The Adventure's of Mon Edouard de Crack:* "I began this Book on the 22 of February 1830 and finished it on the 23 of February 1830, doing 8 pages on the first day and 11 on the second. On the first day I wrote an hour and a half in the morning and an hour and a half in the evening. On the third day I wrote a quarter of an hour in the morning, 2 hours in the afternoon and a quarter of an hour in the evening, making in the whole 5 hours and a half. CB"[14] Her care in dating and signing almost all her manuscripts also reflects her early awareness of her role as an author. What has been seen as the "suspicious multiplicity"[15] of signatures in some of Charlotte's writings is common in all her volumes of more than one work. In *Corner Dishes*, for example, Charlotte has signed each of the three items and the Preface to the whole volume.

Albion and Marina explicitly "sets up no pretensions" to being a novel; but by the end of the second period of her writing, Charlotte is at pains to include in her stories what she sees as the necessary conventions of a novel: "A novel can scarcely be called a novel unless it ends in a marriage, therefore I herewith tack to, add, and communicate the following *postscriptum*."[16] In *The Spell*, she includes not only this conventional ending but she also experiments with the use of letters and extracts from a journal as part of her text, a possible borrowing from Richardson. It is interesting to compare the opening scenes of *Shirley* with Charlotte's early notion that it is "good policy in an author to make the first pages of his book of a light and miscellaneous character."[17] In the later juvenilia, all her comical and satirical episodes, such as those relating to Methodism, occur in the first chapters of her stories. The author of *High Life In Verdopolis* explains that he opens his narrative with an extract from Captain Tree's "Verdopolitan Magazine" not because he agrees with it, but because "it serves well as an introduction to a book which treats principally of lords, ladies, knights and squires of high degree." In this same manuscript Charlotte prefaces each chapter with an appropriate quotation from Byron's *Childe Harold's Pilgrimage*,[18] a method probably derived from Scott.

Authors hold a high position in Glass Town society. Their ambitions are dramatized in the early rivalries between Captain Tree and Lord Charles Wellesley. The variety of narrative techniques used by Charlotte—the portrait, the allegory, the dream sequence, the tale-within-a-tale,[19] the dialogue, the newspaper review—show an early critical attitude to the art of writing. As this awareness increases, Charlotte's view of the "book-wright's" material changes. We see a gradual progression towards realism. Charlotte becomes more aware of her redundant style: "I keep heaping epithets together and I cannot describe what I mean."[20] Occasionally she reins herself in: "I could have grown poetical. I could have recalled more distant and softer scenes touched with the light of other years, hallowed by higher, because older, associations than the campaign of——33, the rebellion of——36. I might have asked how Sunshine yet became the elms and the turret of Wood-Church, but I restrained myself."[21] Probably with the juvenilia in mind, William Crimsworth refers in *The Professor* to "pictures chequered with vivid contrasts of light and shade."[22] These could be avoided, he states, if novelists never allowed themselves to weary of "the study of real life." We have seen that Charlotte was already attempting to observe this principle in *Henry Hastings* and *Caroline Vernon*.

Notes

1. Mrs Gaskell states that Charlotte occasionally used the pseudonym "Charles Thunder" in letters to her friends, using "her Christian name, and the meaning of her Greek surname," *The Life of Charlotte Brontë*, vol. 1, p. 220. C. W. Hatfield could not recall any extant letters by Charlotte which were signed "Charles Thunder" (*BST*(1940) 10:50:16); and nowhere in her surviving juvenilia does Charlotte use this name.

2. *Strange Events* (in *Young Men's Magazine*), 29 August 1830, *SHCBM*, vol. 1, p. 19.

3. Between August 1841–July 1842, Branwell published six poems in the *Halifax Guardian* (Winifred Gérin, *Branwell Brontë*, p. 186).

4. *SHLL*, vol. 1, p. 155.

5. *Ibid.*, p. 157.

6. Unpublished manuscript (BPM:B114).

7. Charlotte quotes from *Night Thoughts* in *The Poetaster*, vol. 2, *Studies in Romanticism* 20 (Winter 1981), p. 494. Mr Brontë's copy survives in the BPM (526).

8. Unpublished manuscript, "Song" (BPM: 12).

9. Winifred Gérin, ed., *Five Novelettes*, p. 184.

10. Preface to *Corner Dishes*, unpublished manuscript (HL:HM 2577).

11. See p. 105 for a discussion of Charlotte's early fascination with the theatre. Compare also *Villette*, vol. 1, p. 176.

12. Unpublished manuscript (BL: Add. MS. 34255).

13. *SHCBM*, vol. 2, p. 284.

14. Unpublished manuscript (HCL: MS. Lowell I[3]).

15. Tom Winnifrith, *The Brontës and Their Background*, p. 225, n. 43.

16. George Edwin MacLean, ed., *The Spell: An Extravaganza*, p. 143.

17. *SHCBM*, vol. 2, p. 284.

18. Branwell is known to have owned a copy of *Childe Harold's Pilgrimage* (Paris, 1827), which he bought in Liverpool on 30 May 1835 (BPM: 114).

19. Probably derived from the *Arabian Nights' Entertainments*, this is the most common narrative form in Charlotte's early stories.

20. Unpublished manuscript, "Now as I have a little bit of time" (PML).

21. Unpublished manuscript, *Stancliffe's Hotel* (BPM: B114).

22. *The Professor*, p. 166.

The Professor

Introduction to the Haworth Edition of *The Professor*

Mary A. Ward[*]

It is in April 1846 that we discover a first mention of *The Professor* in a letter from Charlotte Brontë to Messrs. Aylott & Jones, the publishers of the little volume of *Poems by Currer, Ellis, and Acton Bell* which made its modest appearance in that year. Miss Brontë consults Messrs. Aylott & Co. "on behalf of C., E. and A. Bell" as to how they can best publish three tales already written by them—whether in three connected volumes or separately. The advice given was no doubt prudent and friendly,—but it did not help *The Professor*. The story went fruitlessly to many publishers. It returned to Charlotte, from one of its later quests, on the very morning of the day on which Mr. Brontë underwent an operation for cataract at Manchester—August 25, 1846. That evening, as we have seen, she began *Jane Eyre*.

After the great success of the first two books, she would have liked to publish *The Professor*. But Mr. Smith and Mr. Williams dissuaded her; and to their dissuasion we owe *Villette*; for if *The Professor* had appeared in 1851, Miss Brontë could have made no such further use of her Brussels materials as she did actually put them to in *Villette*. The story was finally published after the writer's death, and when the strong interest excited by Mrs. Gaskell's *Memoir* led naturally to a demand for all that could yet be given to the public from the hand of Currer Bell.

There is little to add to the writer's own animated preface. As she herself points out, the book is by no means the book of a novice. It was written in the author's thirtieth year, after a long apprenticeship to the art of writing. Those innumerable tales, poems, and essays, composed in childhood and youth, of which Mrs. Gaskell and Mr. Shorter between them give accounts so suggestive and remarkable, were the natural and right foundation for all that followed. *The Professor* shows already a method of composition almost mature, a pronounced manner, and the same power of analysis, within narrower limits, as the other books. What it lacks is colour and movement. Crimsworth as the lonely and struggling

[*]Reprinted from the Haworth Edition of *The Professor* (Harper and Brothers, 1899–1903), xiii–xvii.

101

teacher, is inevitably less interesting—described, at any rate, by a woman—than Lucy Snowe under the same conditions, and in the same surroundings. His role is not particularly manly; and he does not appeal to our pity. The intimate autobiographical note, which makes the spell of *Villette*, is absent; we miss the passionate moods and caprices, all the perennial charm of variable woman, which belongs to the later story. There are besides no vicissitudes in the plot. Crimsworth suffers nothing to speak of; he wins his Frances too easily; and the reader's emotions are left unstirred.

Mademoiselle Reuter is Madame Beck over again, but at once less credible and less complex. Pelet is an extremely clever sketch. And Hunsworth [sic]?

Hunsworth[sic] is really the critical element in the story. If he were other than he is, *The Professor* would have stood higher in the scale. For the conception of him is both ambitious and original. But it breaks down. He puzzles us; and yet he is not mysterious. For that he is not human enough. In the end we find him merely brutal and repellent, and the letter to Crimsworth, which accompanies the gift of the picture, is one of those extravagances which destroy a reader's sense of illusion. Great pains have been taken with him; and when he enters he promises much; but he is never truly living for a single page, and half way through the book he has already become a mere bundle of incredibilities. Let the reader put him beside Mr. Helstone of *Shirley*, beside even Rochester, not to speak of Dr. John or Monsieur Paul, and so realise the difference between imagination working at ease, in happy and vitalising strength, and the same faculty toiling unprofitably and half-heartedly with material which it can neither fuse nor master. There is pungency and power in much of Hunsworth's talk; but it is not a pungency or power that can save him as a creation.

On the other hand Frances Henri, the little lace-mender, is a figure touched at every point with grace, feeling and truth. She is an exquisite sketch—a drawing in pale, pure colour, all delicate animation and soft life. She is only inferior to Caroline Helstone because the range of emotion and incident that her story requires is so much narrower than that which Caroline passes through. One feels her thrown away on *The Professor*. An ampler stage and a warmer air should have been reserved for her; adventures more subtly invented; and a lover less easily victorious. But the scene in which she makes tea for Crimsworth—so at least one thinks as one reads it—could hardly be surpassed for fresh and tender charm; although when the same material is used again for the last scenes of *Villette*, it is not hard to see how the flame and impetus of a great book may still heighten and deepen what was already excellent before.

The Professor indeed is grey and featureless compared with any of Charlotte Brontë's other work. The final impression is that she was working under restraint when writing it, and that her proper gifts were consciously denied full play in it. In the preface of 1851, she says, as an explanation of the sobriety of the story—"In many a crude effort destroyed almost as soon as composed, I had got over any such taste as I might once have had for ornamented and redundant composition, and come to prefer what was plain and homely." In other words, she was putting herself under discipline in *The Professor;* trying to subdue the poetical impulse; to work as a realist and an observer only.

According to her own account of it, the publishers interfered with this process. They would not have *The Professor;* and they welcomed *Jane Eyre* with alacrity. She was therefore thrown back, so to speak, upon her faults; obliged to work in ways more "ornamented" and "redundant"; and thus the promise of realism in her was destroyed. The explanation is one of those which the artist will always supply himself with on occasion. In truth, the method of *The Professor* represents a mere temporary reaction, — an experiment—in Charlotte Brontë's literary development. When she returned to that exuberance of imagination and expression which was her natural utterance, she was not merely writing to please her publishers and the public. Rather it was like Emily's passionate return to the moorland—"I'll walk where my own nature would be leading, / It vexes me to choose another guide." The strong native bent reasserted itself, and with the happiest effects.

But because of what came after, and because the mental history of a great and delightful artist will always appeal to the affectionate curiosity of later generations, *The Professor* will continue to be read both by those who love Charlotte Brontë, and by those who find pleasure in tracking the processes of literature. It needs no apology as a separate entity; but from its relation to *Villette* it gains an interest and importance the world would not otherwise have granted it. It is the first revelation of a genius which from each added throb of happiness or sorrow, from each short after-year of strenuous living, —*per damna, per coedes*—was to gain fresh wealth and steadily advancing power.

The Professor Annette Tromly*

From its earliest reviews onward, critics have accorded *The Professor* the same reception which greeted the return of Milton's Satan to Hell: "a dismal universal hiss." Only one voice has disturbed this reassuring critical certitude; and the dissenting voice has belonged to the person who is apparently least qualified to speak. Charlotte Brontë herself seems not to have faltered in her commitment to her first novel. She tried nine times to

*Reprinted from *The Cover of the Mask: The Autobiographers in Charlotte Brontë's Fiction* (1982), 20–41. Courtesy of English Literary Studies Monograph Series, University of Victoria.

get *The Professor* published (it originally was rejected by six publishers), renewing her effort each time one of her other novels was more sympathetically received.[1] Brontë even attempted to use *Jane Eyre's* popularity as a coat-tail by which her earlier narrative might be introduced to the reading public. Her efforts failed; it was not until after her death that George Smith decided to publish *The Professor* — only because he realized that nothing else was forthcoming.

Brontë described, in the "Biographical Notice of Ellis and Acton Bell," written for the 1850 edition of *Wuthering Heights, Agnes Grey,* and selected poems, her bitter disappointment at the book's reception: "Currer Bell's book found acceptance nowhere, nor any acknowledgement of merit, so that something like the chill of despair began to invade his heart."[2] The consensus that *Jane Eyre* was far superior to *The Professor* she took adamant exception to. The middle and latter portions of *The Professor,* she insisted, contained "more pith, more substance, more reality" than much of *Jane Eyre.*[3] But if Brontë's defence of *The Professor* was fervid, critics' attacks have been equally so. They have either disregarded Brontë's opinions, or, in one telling instance, denounced them. Referring to Brontë's statement about the novel's value, one critic has declared that the author is "in certain ways, as much of a hypocrite as William Crimsworth," the novel's narrator.[4]

Lying behind the animadversions against the book (in varying degrees of explicitness) are assumptions about its relation to Brontë's biography. First, critics have generally seen this maiden, unpublishable novel as a product of Brontë's artistic immaturity, the "work of a beginner."[5] (As a result, the need to make judgments about the novel — to locate signs of Brontë's apprenticeship — has too often taken precedence over the desire to understand it.) More specifically, some critics have seen the author as incompletely detached from her book, compromising its moral vision by her personal entanglements with the characters. Thus they believe that William Crimsworth, a "wholly decent young man,"[6] makes his way in a tough world by voicing directly the opinions of Charlotte Brontë.[7] Even those critics who have attempted to detach Crimsworth from Brontë (and have seen him as an essentially unreliable narrator) have not found credible artistic reasons for his limitations.[8] And similarly, Frances Henri has been seen as an idealized projection of Brontë herself.[9] Inevitably, most critics have fallen back on the shibboleth of Brontë's biography to dismiss what they consider to be *The Professor's* shortcomings. Charlotte must have been, in the last year of correspondence with Heger, exorcising the frustrations of an unrequited love;[10] as a result, she wrote an uncontrolled novel.

No one would want to deny that traces of Charlotte Brontë's private world are present in the novel. In certain sections, particularly the chapters on Belgium, Brontë renders the raw materials of her own experience intensely. But if she appropriated certain materials from her life, she did not do so in any simple way. *The Professor* is not, above all, Brontë's unmediated autobiography. It is, however, William Crimsworth's autobiography. A careful examination of *The Professor* reveals a primary interest in the motives and processes of self-presentation; the book is informed by its exploration of the issue. By means of a thoroughly obtrusive and essentially unreliable narrative voice, Brontë explores the reasons and the ways that an autobiographer presents himself to the world. Decades after Brontë's death, Leslie Stephen observed that "distortions of the truth belong to the values of autobiography and are as revealing as the truth."[11] *The Professor* is a novel about these distortions.

The beginning of *The Professor* has always been an irritant to critics. William Crimsworth's letter to "Charles" — who neither answers the letter nor receives it, and does not appear again in the novel — certainly seems arbitrary and contrived. It is not surprising that one critic has called the letter a "clumsy piece of narrative technique."[12] Yet in being both clumsy and irritating, Crimsworth's letter, sent to nowhere, serves its purpose well. The reader does not get very far into the novel before he is forced to ask questions about the teller of the tale. What kind of person would begin his autobiography by quoting himself at length? Why does he adopt such a self-absorbed and callous tone to his old friend? Why does he write the unsolicited letter in the first place? Why is he clearly more interested in telling his story than in communicating with Charles? Surely Brontë is asking her reader, from the book's first moments, to be aware of the centrality of the narrative voice. William Crimsworth, writing from his study at Daisy Lane, is meant to be an emphatic presence.

Throughout the novel Brontë continues to obtrude Crimsworth onto the reader's attention; the narrator's handling of events continually calls attention to his shaping presence. In a number of instances Crimsworth, by means of brief or oblique allusions, passes over or underplays significant events in his life. Thus toward the end of the book he inserts the birth of his only son as an afterthought. Similarly, he downplays his rescue of Jean Baptiste Vandenhuten (who is introduced only as a means of explaining his progress in the search for employment), and skips completely his own professional experience throughout the years of his marriage. But perhaps the most tantalizing of these manipulations of significant events is his allusion to having once observed a "modern French novel":

> Now, modern French novels are not to my taste, either practically or theoretically. Limited as had yet been my experience of life, I had once had the opportunity of contemplating, near at hand, an example of the results produced by a course of interesting and romantic domestic treachery. No golden halo of fiction was about this example, I saw it bare and real, and it was very loathsome. I saw a mind degraded by the

practice of mean subterfuge, by the habit of perfidious deception, and a
body depraved by the infectious influence of the vice-polluted soul. I
had suffered much from the forced and prolonged view of this spectacle;
those sufferings I did not now regret, for their simple recollection acted
as a most wholesome antidote to temptation.[13]

We hear no more of what must have been a formative experience for
Crimsworth. His reticence about this and other matters points to a mind
which is deliberately shaping its story. The reader is forced to wonder just
what Crimsworth's principles of inclusion are.

If Crimsworth can de-emphasize the important experience, he can
also inflate the unimportant. Under his pen the story of his life often
unfolds as a series of significant inner moments struck into high relief
largely by the force of his narrative determination. After leaving his job in
Bigben Close, for example, he describes his walk into the country. He
designates a fast-flowing river as his symbol-for-the-moment, and takes
pains to impress it on both his memory and ours: ". . . I watched the rapid
rush of its waves. I desired memory to take a clear and permanent
impression of the scene, and treasure it for future years" (194). At other
times the meanings Crimsworth imposes on his experience are more
difficult to achieve. When he thinks he has lost Frances through the
machinations of Zoraïde Reuter, he offers a long disquisition which begins
with the proper sphere of the novelist, passes through the dangers of
sensual indulgence, glances quickly at suffering, and finally alights on the
consolation of Religion to the hopeless man (277–78). And all of this, he
instructs the reader, so that we might infer that — being a reasonable
man — he was able to control his grief. The sheer energy Crimsworth
expends in imposing a rationale on his life suggests that we should be wary
of sharing his perceptions.

Crimsworth's significant moments most often take the form of inner
conflicts between moral abstractions. He regrets having resigned his
teaching job, for example, when he realizes that he is not in a position to
approach the now-employed Frances. But Conscience helpfully inter-
venes:

> "Down, stupid tormentors!" cried she; "the man has done his duty;
> you shall not bait him thus by thoughts of what might have been; he
> relinquished a temporary and contingent good to avoid a permanent
> and certain evil; he did well. Let him reflect now, and when your
> blinding dust and deafening hum subside, he will discover a path." (305)

Shortly afterward, on the night that he longs to give in to his desire to see
Frances, Imagination is the "sweet temptress" which he manages to repel.
There are many such moments in the novel. It is difficult to imagine that,
had *The Professor* been illustrated,[14] Crimsworth would not have been
represented with demons on one shoulder and angels on the other; his
moral universe is thoroughly dichotomized.

Brontë presents her narrator, then, as the central problem of the novel. William Crimsworth the autobiographer is everywhere present, giving shape and emphasis to his story. And Crimsworth's autobiographical manipulations become morally questionable because of his pronounced tendency to self-inflation. The abstractions through which he filters his inner conflicts, for example, impart a self-serving suggestiveness to the events of his life. He elevates his personal significance by means of the patterns he imposes.

If, however, Crimsworth's version of his life gratifies the autobiographer, it suggests something quite different to the reader. What we note in Crimsworth's account — in his omissions, emphases, and interpretations of events — is its decided simplification of complexities. If Crimsworth expands his life's meaning in his own eyes, he contracts it in ours. His act of writing becomes an act of enclosure, an act of imposing a personal mythology upon a life. And through a network of images in the novel, Brontë further undercuts Crimsworth's self-portrait. Images of physical enclosure echo the mental enclosure which lies behind Crimsworth's autobiographical impulse.

Crimsworth: An Israelite in Brobdingnag

Fastidious, hypersensitive William Crimsworth (the name has a Dickensian aural appropriateness) expends a great deal of energy guarding himself against assault: assault by other people, assault by his own impulses, assault by all the untidy circumstances that disrupt a remarkably quotidian existence. Enclosure is his characteristic way of dealing with a world too threatening for his insecure psychic constitution. Crimsworth assumes a defensive self-protectiveness against most of his associates. He finds satisfaction in hiding his real self from his tyrannical brother's gaze: ". . . I felt as secure against his scrutiny as if I had had on a casque with the visor down . . ." (176). Similarly, he handles his students with dispatch: "In less than five minutes they had thus revealed to me their characters, and in less than five minutes I had buckled on a breast-plate of steely indifference, and let down a visor of impassible austerity" (223). When uneasy, Crimsworth seeks places which are small and closed-in; after most events of consequence, he walks in "narrow chambers," or shuts out "intruders" (including, at times, the reader). By shutting himself up, or the world out, then, he manages to maintain a fragile state of equilibrium.

Just how fragile this state is, however, becomes most clear when the intruder is one of his own feelings. The scene mentioned earlier, in which he copes with his grief for the lost (misplaced) Frances, is a good example:

being a steady, reasonable man, I did not allow the resentment, disappointment, and grief, engendered in my mind by this evil chance, to grow there to any monstrous size; nor did I allow them to monopolise the whole space of my heart; I pent them, on the contrary, in one strait and secret nook. In the daytime, too, when I was about my duties, I put them on the silent system; and it was only after I had closed the door of my chamber at night that I somewhat relaxed my severity towards these morose nurslings, and allowed vent to their language of murmurs; then, in revenge, they sat on my pillow, haunted my bed, and kept me awake with their long, midnight cry. (278)

Crimsworth's fear that without his "strait and secret nook" his feelings will grow monstrous is a consequence of his repression; the syndrome has become common coinage in the psychological currency of our day. And as familiar is the ironical result: the sheer act of forceful control defeats its own purpose. The feelings are unearthed in a more painful way— transformed to a morbid state. The strained, hyperbolical, frenzied language in which Crimsworth describes the revenge of his "morose nurslings" is apt. He is clearly so out of touch with his feelings that he can deal with them—and enjoy them—only when they are dressed up in elaborate metaphor. Most of Crimsworth's psychic life can be character- ized in terms of a similar tension: an excessive need for control along with its inevitable opposite.

Other enclosure images emphasize Crimsworth's unwholesome emo- tional obsessions. Sitting "alone near midnight" writing his autobiography at Daisy Lane, he attempts to capture his past. His memories rise before him like ghosts in a graveyard:[15]

Belgium! I repeat the word, now as I sit alone near midnight. It stirs my world of the past like a summons to resurrection; the graves unclose, the dead are raised; thoughts, feelings, memories that slept, are seen by me ascending from the clods—haloed most of them—but while I gaze on their vapoury forms, and strive to ascertain definitely their outline, the sound which wakened them dies, and they sink, each and all, like a light wreath of mist, absorbed in the mould, recalled to urns, resealed in monuments. Farewell, luminous phantoms! (201)

As his griefs are pent in a "strait and secret nook," so his memories have been sealed in urns; both images represent a mind which immures the spacious potential of emotional experience. And in spite of this allusion to sinking phantoms, Crimsworth will never realize how thoroughly unsuc- cessful he is at resurrecting his past. As we shall see, his autobiography does not succeed in liberating his sealed memories; their forms will always remain indistinct to him.

As Crimsworth embalms his memories, so he enshrines his love:

I loved the movement with which she confided her hand to my hand; I loved her as she stood there, penniless and parentless; for a sensualist charmless, for me a treasure—my best object of sympathy on earth, thinking such thoughts as I thought, feeling such feelings as I felt; my ideal of the shrine in which to seal my stores of love. . . . (285)

The woman he chooses is an "object" to contain his love; and he can describe his "ideal" only in terms of the gratifications she will provide for him. Crimsworth's brand of idealism, then, is as constricted as his repressed desires, his love enclosed as tightly as his grief and his memories. As we shall see, this strange person, whose thoughts are avowedly turned heavenward, becomes capable of the grimmest kind of mean-mindedness.

Crimsworth's tendency to enclose is so thoroughgoing that it undermines his perceptions altogether. He perceives his world as a series of pictures; his reliance on the visual arts is the most persistent peculiarity of his language. He consistently represents places (such as Belgium and the river in Grovetown mentioned above) as pictures. And virtually all the people he meets, from an anonymous Flemish housemaid who reminds him of "the female figures in certain Dutch paintings" (202–03) to his good friend Yorke Hunsden, whose "features might have done well on canvas but indifferently in marble" (186) are subjected to the scrutinizing eye of a self-conscious artist. Crimsworth takes great pains when presenting his pictures; they are often overloaded with descriptive minutiae. His efforts at verisimilitude, however, reveal more about the artist than his subjects. Rather than rendering faithful images of the people he describes, Crimsworth avoids or distorts the issue of who they really are. Preoccupation with physical characteristics sometimes permits him to avoid more significant attributes of character. But more serious, perhaps, is his tendency to create simple equations between the outer person and the inner character. His student Eulalie is an example:

> Eulalie was tall, and very finely shaped: she was fair, and her features were those of a Low Country Madonna; many a "figure de Vierge" have I seen in Dutch pictures exactly resembling hers; there were no angles in her shape or in her face, all was curve and roundness — neither thought, sentiment, nor passion disturbed by line or flush the equality of her pale, clear skin; her noble bust heaved with her regular breathing, her eyes moved a little — by these evidences of life alone could I have distinguished her from some large handsome figure moulded in wax. (222)

Crimsworth submits Eulalie to a process of reduction in several ways. First, by associating her with works of art he is able to distance himself from her. Second, in relying on the stock associations of a type of painted figure, he is forcing Eulalie into an easy and pre-existent category. And finally, the blandness of character he attributes to her on the basis of her physical type is predicated on a questionable relation between the inner and the outer person. Interpreting people as works of art enables Crimsworth to categorize his world far too neatly. Once enclosed in frames, his images become easier to control.

Crimsworth depicts himself as well as others. Even as the novel opens, he is speaking (in the letter to Charles) of his own "portrait." And in the most explicit summary he gives us of his past, his life becomes a gallery:

> Three—nay four—pictures line the four-walled cell where are stored for me the records of the past. First, Eton. All in that picture is in far perspective, receding, diminutive; but freshly coloured, green, dewy, with a spring sky, piled with glittering yet showery clouds; for my childhood was not all sunshine—it had its overcast, its cold, its stormy hours. Second, X——, huge, dingy, the canvas cracked and smoked; a yellow sky, sooty clouds; no sun, no azure; the verdure of the suburbs blighted and sullied—a very dreary scene.
>
> Third, Belgium; and I will pause before this landscape. As to the fourth, a curtain covers it, which I may hereafter withdraw, or may not, as suits my convenience and capacity. At any rate, for the present it must hang undisturbed. (200)

In deliberately figuring his past as a gallery of pictures, Crimsworth, characteristically, claims an inflated meaning for his private experience. He presents his past, by analogy, as something that partakes of the heightened significance of paintings. Yet as he inflates, he also deflates. The frames around his past, like the urns that hold his memories, are enclosures. Even the gallery itself is a claustrophobic, four-walled cell. And Crimsworth chooses a curious kind of picture to represent his life. Each painting in the gallery might be titled "A Portrait of the Artist as a Young Landscape"; missing from the canvas is Crimsworth himself. Eulalie, then, is not the only figure who is dehumanized and regarded with detachment; Crimsworth also maintains a disturbing distance from himself. The mysterious fourth, curtained, picture is never alluded to again.[16] But as we shall see, despite Crimsworth's secrecy, it does not hang undisturbed.

From time to time Crimsworth reminds the reader that the pictures he is framing as he tells his story are corrected versions of the inaccurate pictures of his youth. An interesting dynamic develops as Crimsworth the Autobiographer, writing from Daisy Lane, enjoys contemplating his formerly callow perceptions:

> This is Belgium, reader. Look! don't call the picture a flat or a dull one—it was neither flat nor dull to me when I first beheld it. When I left Ostend on a mild February morning, and found myself on the road to Brussels, nothing could look vapid to me. My sense of enjoyment possessed an edge whetted to the finest, untouched, keen, exquisite. I was young; I had good health; pleasure and I had never met. . . . Well! and what did I see? I will tell you faithfully. Green, reedy swamps; fields, fertile but flat, cultivated in patches that made them look like magnified kitchen-gardens; belts of trees, formal as pollard willows, skirting the horizon; narrow canals, gliding slow by the road-side; painted Flemish farmhouses; some very dirty hovels; a gray, dead sky, wet road, wet fields, wet house-tops; not a beautiful, scarcely a

picturesque object met my eye along the whole route; yet to me, all was beautiful, all was more than picturesque. (201–02)

Yet behind Crimsworth's gentle irony against his younger self is a much tougher irony which the narrator fails to see. Brontë would have us note that in correcting the perceptions of his younger self, Crimsworth often encloses himself more tightly into a set of highly inadequate attitudes.

We see these ironies operating in Crimsworth's feelings about the students of Zoraïde Reuter's school. Noticing that the window in his room which opens onto the girls' garden is boarded up (an enclosure image of his young blindness), he feels a strong desire to see behind the boards. He imagines the ground in the garden to be "consecrated," a paradise where angels play. When he is finally hired to teach at the girls' school, he is delighted. " 'I shall now at last see the mysterious garden: I shall gaze both on the angels and their Eden' " (216). All the humour of the delusion is enjoyed by Crimsworth the narrator. He describes his process of disillusionment with the girls:

> Daily, as I continued my attendance at the seminary of Mdlle. Reuter, did I find fresh occasions to compare the ideal with the real. What had I known of female character previously to my arrival at Brussels? Precious little. And what was my notion of it? Something vague, slight, gauzy, glittering; now when I came in contact with it I found it to be a palpable substance enough: very hard too sometimes, and often heavy; there was metal in it, both lead and iron. (231)

But the quasi-objective tone of Crimsworth's voice of experience immediately gives itself the lie. He offers to "open his portfolio" (231) to sketch a few students, and proceeds to reveal his barely suppressed disgust and rage at the girls. His three pictures "from the life" (234) are painted by a vengeful, moralistic hand. One girl he refers to as an "unnatural-looking being," "Gorgon-like," who practises "panther-like deceit" (232). He seems capable of only the crudest kind of adversary relationship with the girls (the way they look at him is their "artillery" [233]), and falls back on his oversimplified moral abstractions in order to place them within his scheme ("Mutiny" and "Hate" are graved on Juanna's brow [234]). When Crimsworth physically confines one of the girls (locks her up in a cabinet), he is only echoing the mental confinement that his descriptions reflect.

What his attitude toward the girls reveals, then, is the constriction of Crimsworth's ostensibly maturing perceptions. Crimsworth approaches his students with naïve idealism; when forced to adjust, he castigates the real rather than tempering the ideal. As we shall see, his ideal remains intact — pent, perhaps, in another strait and secret nook — waiting only for the appropriate woman to be forced into its contracted boundaries.

Before turning to a consideration of the other main characters in the book, it would be useful to note a final pair of images which corroborates the idea of Crimsworth's mental enclosure. As I have noted, the pictures Crimsworth frames of his world are idiosyncratic—a personalized way of imposing a rationale on a perplexing life. Crimsworth is aware of the differences between himself and other people. Early in the novel, he reveals his feelings of separateness to Hunsden with a certain smug satisfaction: " 'I must follow my own devices—I must till the day of my death; because I can neither comprehend, adopt, nor work out those of other people' " (198). Crimsworth's image for himself in the novel's early chapters is as an Israelite in Egypt. Orphaned, confined to drudgery in the counting-house of his unsympathetic brother Edward, he characterizes his work as a "task thankless and bitter as that of the Israelite crawling over the sun-baked fields of Egypt in search of straw and stubble wherewith to accomplish his tale of bricks" (190). The image is apt in several ways. His work is futile; he lives in bondage. But most important, Crimsworth is elevating his separateness into the virtue of a martyr. As an Israelite, he is not only victim, but chosen one. A large part of his self-delusion pertains to a puritanical notion of himself as an anti-sensualist in a world of flesh-pots. Beginning with a reference to his wealthy cousins in the letter to Charles, Crimsworth sets himself apart from women whose attractions he considers himself above. Not for him are the base sexual yearnings of the normal man.[17] (The pronounced element of twisted sexuality in his accounts of his students is an ironic contradiction of his high-mindedness.) But his attitude toward women is only one important element in Crimsworth's Israelite conception of himself. The notion of his own special nature exists in Crimsworth's mind as a means by which to exempt himself, with self-congratulatory glibness, from the humbling exigencies of self-knowledge.

Set off against the Israelite in Crimsworth's mind is a parallel image in the reader's. Brontë very delicately introduces an association between Crimsworth and another literary figure, one not quite so sombre as the Israelite in Egypt. When Crimsworth refers, while observing the Belgian landscape, to a "Brobdignagian [sic] kitchen-garden" (282), we realize that he is not so unlike another fellow-traveller. Associated with Gulliver's innocence, sexual repression, fastidiousness, and, above all, pride, William Crimsworth becomes a figure considerably less elevated than the Israelite. Like Gulliver's, Crimsworth's innocence is not ennobling, but constricting—his pride not a source of dignity, but of self-aggrandizement. The two images coexist, then, as suggestively ironic pieces in the puzzle of Crimsworth's character. Lurking just on the surface is Brontë's suggestion that Crimsworth's idea of his separateness may transform him from his own sublime into the reader's ridiculous. Crimsworth leaves England—his Egypt—in search of the Canaan which he not only feels he deserves but also can use to vindicate his uniqueness. But the reader has discovered that the Israelite's bondage was considerably more than physical.

Hunsden, Reuter, and Frances Henri:
Portrait and Pentimento

Although he enjoys portraying his life as a series of pictures, William Crimsworth remains oblivious to the pentimento which complicates his literary self-portraiture. The personal myth he constructs seems to the reader to be superimposed upon a life which is far less tidy than Crimsworth himself will acknowledge. Presented with the official Crimsworth, we remain constantly aware — though the outlines are never distinct — of the traces of a second image beneath. In the portraits of the other main characters in the novel — Hunsden, Zoraïde Reuter, and Frances Henri — the pentimento is equally pronounced, and equally indistinct. We are presented with their images as seen through the eyes of Crimsworth; yet the shadows of images that Crimsworth does not see flicker always before us.

Although Hunsden Yorke Hunsden is a friend of long standing (he is the only character besides Crimsworth to exist all the way through the novel), Crimsworth's attitude to him is always acrimonious. He presents Hunsden as a presumptuous, eccentric person — a person who seems not to know that he is meant to be of secondary importance in the Crimsworth autobiography. The man who seems irritatingly idiosyncratic to Crimsworth, however, strikes the reader as ironically appropriate. For, viewed in relation to Crimsworth, Hunsden is a running commentary on the protagonist's limitations. Like Crimsworth, he has both the tradesman and the aristocrat in his lineage — but unlike Crimsworth, he is at home in the world. Like Crimsworth, he is a mixture of masculine and feminine characteristics — but unlike Crimsworth, he has the confidence to address aggressively a challenging world. Where Crimsworth is fastidious and constricted, Hunsden is generous and expansive (though the misanthropic directness of Hunsden's speech seems to Crimsworth to be far less kindly than his own minced words). Like Crimsworth, Hunsden has a feminine ideal — but unlike Crimsworth, his ideal coexists with a strong strain of practicality. He can live enthusiastically with the ideal unfulfilled. And finally, like Crimsworth, Hunsden is unique — but whereas Crimsworth's uniqueness exists only in his mind, as a means of separating himself from a tawdry world, Hunsden's uniqueness is palpable. Perhaps that is why he defies even Crimsworth's self-confident descriptive powers: "There is no use in attempting to describe," says Crimsworth, "what is indescribable" (308). The close similarities — and awesome differences — between the two men explain why Crimsworth is so perpetually vulnerable to his friend.

Hunsden is responsible for almost all the good fortune in Crimsworth's career; but he can also be called Crimsworth's nemesis. For reasons which are not quite clear, his early interest in Crimsworth abides throughout the novel. He precipitates the release from Edward's tyranny, makes the crucial referral for a teaching job in Belgium, and buys the only one of Crimsworth's pictures which is ever really important—that of his mother—as an unsolicited gift. But Hunsden's generosity is always resented by Crimsworth. In an interesting juxtaposition of scenes, Brontë demonstrates the ease with which Crimsworth can accept favours from another benefactor, Victor Vandenhuten, as compared with the bitterness that Hunsden's help always elicits. From Crimsworth's description of Vandenhuten, we infer the cause: "in short our characters dovetailed, but my mind having more fire and action than his, instinctively assumed and kept the predominance" (317). With Hunsden, Crimsworth can never keep the predominance; something within him must realize that his friend represents the authentic product of which he is himself only an unconvincing reproduction. The ironic connections between the two men are never completely brought to the consciousness of Crimsworth the narrator—nor, as we shall see, is the implicit threat that Hunsden poses to the autobiographer's happy ending.

Crimsworth's first love, Zoraïde Reuter, is also a victim of his misanthropy. The process of disillusionment which Crimsworth underwent with his students is echoed with Reuter. And echoed as well are the aging Crimsworth's sage amusement at the naïveté of his younger self, and the reader's distance from both narrators. Even at her best, Reuter hardly resembles the Angels in their Eden; she taxes even Crimsworth's ability to idealize. Yet, with great effort, the young man manages to rationalize his love. At their first meeting, he is patronizingly amused by the business talent of a young woman. He must be growing wiser, he feels, since he can admire the "crafty little politician" (226). And if Reuter does not quite fit the "female character as depicted in Poetry and Fiction" (226), she is only a more interesting challenge. When pressed for a rationale by which to justify himself, young Crimsworth is ingenious enough to fall back on religious prejudice: "She has been brought up a Catholic: had she been born an Englishwoman, and reared a Protestant, might she not have added straight integrity to all her other excellences? Supposing she were to marry an English and Protestant husband, would she not, rational, sensible, as she is, quickly acknowledge the superiority of right over expediency, honesty over policy?" (240). The scene in which Crimsworth conveys his strongest moment of infatuation takes place in that touchstone of his romantic imagination, the garden of the Pensionnat:

> In another minute I and the directress were walking side by side
> down the valley bordered with fruit-trees, whose white blossoms were
> then in full blow as well as their tender green leaves. The sky was blue,
> the air still, the May afternoon was full of brightness and fragrance.
> Released from the stifling class, surrounded with flowers and foliage,
> with a pleasing, smiling, affable woman at my side—how did I feel?
> Why, very enviably. It seemed as if the romantic visions my imagination
> had suggested of this garden, while it was yet hidden from me by the

jealous boards, were more than realised; and, when a turn in the alley shut out the view of the house, and some tall shrubs excluded M. Pelet's mansion, and screened us momentarily from the other houses, rising amphitheatre-like round this green spot, I gave my arm to Mdlle. Reuter, and led her to a garden-chair, nestled under some lilacs near. She sat down; I took my place at her side. She went on talking to me with that ease which communicates ease, and, as I listened, a revelation dawned in my mind that I was on the brink of falling in love. (238)

Writing from Daisy Lane, Crimsworth contrives the scene of his young delusion neatly. In retrospect, he sees the garden as the perfect location for the growth of his younger, callow self from innocence to experience.[18] For the reader, however, the garden is yet another enclosure, reflecting ironically upon both the young lover and his wiser, older self. And the author's irony becomes more stringent when, after the inevitable disillusionment, young and old Crimsworth agree in their interpretation of the event.

Appropriately, the disillusionment takes place in the same garden. Crimsworth, dreaming of Reuter at his now unboarded window, hears voices below. It is Reuter and Pelet, talking of their wedding plans, and of him. Neither the old nor the young Crimsworth understands the inadequacy of his response to his disillusionment. The love arose solely from Crimsworth's romantic mind. Yet both Crimsworths view the overheard conversation as an act of treachery, strong enough to extinguish all "faith in love and friendship" (242). The shared vision of old and young Crimsworth is demonstrated through the mixing of past and present tenses:

Not that I nursed vengeance — no; but the sense of insult and treachery lived in me like a kindling, though as yet smothered coal. God knows I am not by nature vindictive: I would not hurt a man because I can no longer trust or like him; but neither my reason nor feelings are of the vacillating order — they are not of that sand-like sort where impressions, if soon made, are as soon effaced. Once convinced that my friend's disposition is incompatible with my own, once assured that he is indelibly stained with certain defects obnoxious to my principles, and I dissolve the connection. (242-43)

Also echoed here are the familiar tones of Crimsworth's moralism: his castigation of whatever fails to live up to his mind-forged ideals, and his claims to a special, exalted nature. As we would expect, he calls on an abstraction — Reason — to be his physician after suffering the blow. Regardless of what his older self may think, Crimsworth has not learned much; his mind remains as sealed off as Mlle. Reuter's "allée défendue."

Thenceforward, Crimsworth's bitterness and distrust regarding Zoraïde Reuter are extreme. Though Reuter continues to be crafty and manipulative, she apparently falls in love with Crimsworth and is treated very cruelly indeed. (The garden again becomes an emblem of

Crimsworth's constricted perceptions.) By the time Reuter fires Frances Henri (probably with at least some justification), Crimsworth's disdain for the directress has turned into loathing. He has successfully reduced a complicated woman to the status of a bad angel.

In Crimsworth's mind, Reuter is an unattractive foil for his heart's desire, Frances. He sees Reuter as fully engaged in her world, Frances as an outsider; Reuter as manipulative, Frances as passive; Reuter as hardened, Frances as tender; Reuter as contrived, Frances as natural; Reuter as self-protective, Frances as vulnerable. Yet the novel suggests that as telling as the differences between the two women are their similarities. First, their careers are parallel: Frances, like Reuter, will become the directress of her own school. But more important, Reuter makes guarded suggestions of deeper similarities between them. " 'Her present position,' " she says, " 'has once been mine, or nearly so; it is then but natural I should sympathise with her . . .' " (254). Within this enigmatic comment, and also within the feelings of animosity between the two women, lurks the possibility, borne out by more direct evidence elsewhere, that Frances Henri is not what Crimsworthy believes her to be.

Although critics have tended to see only Crimsworth's romanticized portraits of Frances, there is ample evidence in *The Professor* that Brontë's portrait, which lurks behind Crimsworth's, is meant to be considerably more subtle, complicated, and ambiguous. First, there are a number of hints that Frances may not always have lived the sheltered, virginal life which Crimsworth complacently assumes she has. Early in their acquaintance, Frances describes her life in Switzerland as being " 'in a circle; I walked the same round every day' " (266). She speaks of knowing something of the " 'bourgeois of Geneva' " and of Brussels (266). And echoing the suggestiveness of these remarks is Reuter's; the older woman says of Frances that she does " 'not like her going out in all weathers' " (276). Later, Frances mentions the frustrations of " 'people who are only in each other's company for amusement' " (328-29). And on several occasions she calmly entertains Crimsworth in her apartment alone.[19]

The evidence for Frances' questionable past is not obtrusive. Rather it is composed of delicately suggestive allusions which only hint at something Crimsworth cannot see. Whether or not she has had a sexual past, though, Frances certainly has had some kind of experience in her life that Crimsworth has not. Both her pronounced independence and her unmistakable emotional separateness from him do not correspond to Crimsworth's portrait of her. The very moment she accepts his proposal of marriage, for example, Frances asks to be allowed to continue teaching (327-28). This hard-headed practicality, as well as her tears on her wedding day (342), indicates that for Frances the choice to marry is far from simple. Although Hunsden may be able to live successfully on his own, Frances does not have the male option of a completely independent life; she must know that spending life alone would mean abandoning her career ambitions. It is clear, then, that Frances' view of the marriage has complications that Crimsworth does not dream of; it is likely that she accepts the marriage proposal as the most attractive of several very limited options open to her.

Frances' "Jane" poem indicates that her need for a "master" — the side of her which Crimsworth emphasizes — is a substantial part of her nature. But as Brontë skilfully demonstrates through suggestive details, the deluded Crimsworth never understands the intricacies of his wife's position. He places her on the conventional pedestal, a pedestal which fits nicely into the myth he is creating of his own "successful" life. Yet Frances knows much more of the world than does her "master." When Crimsworth says of her that "I knew how the more dangerous flame [of passion] burned safely under the eye of reason" (285), he speaks as a puritan; he has no notion of how clearly that eye of reason really sees.

Part of what makes Frances particularly suitable to Crimsworth's autobiographical designs is the fact that she is as homeless as he. Their mutual rootlessness enables Crimsworth to circumvent a certain kind of social definition; it is another means by which Crimsworth can define himself as a man outside — and above — the rest of the world. He delights in Frances' *devoir* about the emigrant and is sensitive to her expressed desire for her own Canaan. The Israelite image which he adopted in the early chapters is appropriately transformed. Crimsworth's Egypt (England) becomes Frances' Canaan, and by means of a letter from Hunsden, the entire notion is ironically reversed. Hunsden imagines Crimsworth as an Israelite in Belgium, not England: " 'sitting like a black-haired, tawny-skinned, long-nosed Israelite by the flesh-pots of Egypt' " (302). The implication is that Crimsworth would be a displaced Israelite wherever he lived; for him, exile is a state of mind. In choosing Frances, Crimsworth can cling to his feelings of being unique, and therefore special. As he speaks of Hunsden's knowledge of him, this need is apparent: "nor could he, keen-sighted as he was, penetrate into my heart, search my brain, and read my peculiar sympathies and antipathies; he had not known me long enough, or well enough, to perceive how long my feelings would ebb under some influences, powerful over most minds; how high, how fast they would flow under other influences, that perhaps acted with the more intense force on me, because they acted on me alone" (312).

If Frances' homelessness is a convenience for Crimsworth, so too is her role as his student. Brontë's frequent use of the teacher-student relationship has prompted many critics to suggest a questionable equivalence between the art and the life. Thus Inga-Stina Ewbank has called the teaching situation "an image of the ideal relationship" for Brontë.[20] In *The Professor*, however, teacher-student relationships are far from ideal: they are based, for the most part, on tyranny. As I have mentioned, Crimsworth relates to his students as an adversary: through his descriptions of the girls in Reuter's school he reveals both his constricted sexual nature and his related need for power. The same kind of problem is a factor in his relationship with Frances. Her status as a social and educational inferior provides easy superiority for Crimsworth; it enables him, through his autobiographical myth, to enclose her emotions into an even smaller nook than his own. There are several scenes when Crimsworth, forcing Frances to speak English with the ostensible purpose of benefiting her language development, becomes almost sadistic in his treatment of her. (And one such scene is the proposal scene.) The kind of dominance over Frances that Crimsworth seems to need is ironically undercut both by the specifics of their relationship and by the echoes of earlier student relationships.

Frances Henri, then, is just what Crimsworth needs. She has — on the surface, at least — precisely those qualities which enable him to impose a gratifying rationale on his life story. She is socially inferior, educationally disadvantaged, and rootless; a difficult life has made her both tractable and desperate for security. But complications arise for Crimsworth. In order to create the picture of his life in the way which gratifies him most, he must do something very earnest, very real: he must take a wife. The shaky foundations of his psychosexual nature catch up with him only moments after he proposes to Frances. His attack of hypochondria is one of Brontë's most interesting ways of revealing the irony of his mental enclosure.

In reading *The Professor* as a straightforward success story, most critics have had difficulty accounting for Crimsworth's bout of hypochondria. Robert Martin, for example, finds it to be "without any apparent relevance," and objects to its coming at a time when "Crimsworth's psychic health has never been better."[21] And Inga-Stina Ewbank reverts to Brontë biography to justify the scene: "Powerful in itself, this passage has no justification in plot or character; there is nothing either before or after to suggest such nervous sensibilities in the very sensible hero. His breakdown here is introduced, it would seem, only to give an excuse for what is a welling-up from the suppressed ego of the author."[22] These critical discussions, however, leave out what seems to me to be Brontë's major effort in the novel. Crimsworth is telling his own story, or, rather, presenting his own myth. While ostensibly creating art which will reflect his life, he is in reality moulding the life to fit the art. But, as Roy Pascal has observed about autobiography, "Consistent misrepresentation of oneself is not easy."[23] Like the other loose ends which Brontë insinuates before us, Crimsworth's attack of hypochondria qualifies his personal mythology. It represents, in Pascal's terms, a "gap" in his self-portrait, or, in James' terms, a "leakage" in his ostensibly watertight scheme. The attack of hypochondria may seem inconsistent to Crimsworth, but for the reader it is part of the pentimento.

Crimsworth's myth about himself, as I have mentioned, is based largely on his feelings of being different from others. An essential part of this difference is his view of himself as an anti-sensualist (a view which the reader has always discredited on the basis of his descriptions of his students). But just after proposing to Frances, he discovers that he is in fact strongly attracted physically to her. As he confesses to the reader: "It appeared then, that I too was a sensualist in my temperate and fastidious way" (329). Crimsworth's acceptance of his own sexual nature is followed immediately by the attack of hypochondria. Apparently his righteous self-delusions do not die easily. It is appropriate that the attack is described as claustrophobic, and as sexual. Crimsworth is imprisoned by hypochondria, who has the bony arms of a death-cold concubine:

> She had been my acquaintance, nay, my guest, once before in boyhood; I had entertained her at bed and board for a year; for that space of time I had her to myself in secret; she lay with me, she ate with me, she walked out with me, showing me nooks in woods, hollows in hills where we could sit together, and where she could drop her drear veil over me, and so hide sky and sun, grass and green tree; taking me entirely to her death-cold bosom, and holding me with arms of bone. . . .
>
> I repulsed her as one would a dreaded and ghastly concubine coming to embitter a husband's heart towards his young bride; in vain; she kept her sway over me for that night and the next day, and eight succeeding days. (330–31)

Crimsworth's amazement that the attack should come at this point in his life – "why did hypochondria accost me now?" (331) – is not shared by the reader. Having abandoned the safety of his clearly-defined self-image, he is bound to suffer greatly. Marriage to Frances (who is surely represented in part by the concubine) will of necessity involve psychic and physical realities which he has never before had to face.

If Crimsworth's pre-marital forebodings are complex, those of his new bride are even more so. During the early descriptions of their relationship, as I have noted, the reader continually senses that Crimsworth is not telling the entire story about Frances. Frances' behaviour strengthens this doubt. Perhaps the height of the reader's wonder about her comes in the remarkable scene when she meets Hunsden. Crimsworth takes a seat on the periphery of the room, thus characteristically removing himself and framing the participants in the spectacle. As he watches in supercilious amusement, his deferential, resigned, often vapid Frances suddenly becomes, as she converses with Hunsden, vital, daring, even sexual.

> Animated by degrees, she began to change, just as a grave night-sky changes at the approach of sunrise: first it seemed as if her forehead cleared, then her eyes glittered, her features relaxed, and became quite mobile; her subdued complexion grew warm and transparent; to me, she now looked pretty; before, she had only looked ladylike.
>
> She had many things to say to the Englishman just fresh from his

island-country, and she urged him with an enthusiasm of curiosity, which ere long thawed Hunsden's reserve as fire thaws a congealed viper. I use this not very flattering comparison because he vividly reminded me of a snake waking from torpor, as he erected his tall form, reared his head, before a little declined, and putting back his hair from his broad Saxon forehead, showed unshaded the gleam of almost savage satire which his interlocutor's tone of eagerness and look of ardour had suffered at once to kindle in his soul and elicit from his eyes: he was himself, as Frances was herself, and in none but his own language would he now address her. (335)

Strangely, Frances' metamorphosis into a person of warmth, relaxation, and beauty does not threaten the complacent Crimsworth. Neither does the vitality of Hunsden who, imaged as a snake who is tempted by Frances, both ironically undercuts the couple's allegedly invulnerable love and also foreshadows their peculiar future. The scene closes with two literary references, both of which serve a purpose similar to that of the passage above. First, a reference to *Othello* reinforces the delicate suggestions of a love (between Frances and Crimsworth) built on a shaky foundation. And second, Hunsden's Byronic farewell, and Frances' positive response to it, emphasize again the potential she has for stepping outside the rigid frame in which Crimsworth has enclosed her.

Throughout the Crimsworths' married life, Brontë continues her intimations that Frances' feelings differ from her husband's. What Crimsworth describes is his pleasure at Frances' continual deference to him, his pride in his own generosity (in allowing Frances to open her school), and his delight at playfully subduing her spirit when he "frequently dosed her with Wordsworth" (348). But though Frances' surface reactions may be just as Crimsworth sees them, they indicate, by now, a great deal more to the reader than they do to Crimsworth. Perhaps the clearest signals Brontë sends to the reader in the novel's final chapters come through the passages about young Victor. When Frances leaves Crimsworth's side to visit her sleeping baby, she "abandons" him. When Victor's dog Yorke is exposed to rabies, Crimsworth coldly shoots it, leaves the body for his young son to find, and then describes the entire scene with sanctimonious relish. As he turns away from Victor's grief, it is Frances who comforts their distraught child. And finally, when Crimsworth discusses his son's treatment at the hands of his gentle mother, we feel the full force of his puritanical rage:

> though Frances will not make a milksop of her son, she will accustom him to a style of treatment, a forbearance, a congenial tenderness, he will meet with from none else. She sees, as I also see, a something in Victor's temper—a kind of electrical ardour and power—which emits, now and then, ominous sparks; Hunsden calls it his spirit, and says it should not be curbed. I call it the leaven of the offending Adam, and consider that it should be, if not *whipped* out of him, at least soundly

disciplined; and that he will be cheap of any amount of either bodily or mental suffering which will ground him radically in the art of self-control. . . . for that cloud on his bony brow — for that compression of his statuesque lips, the lad will some day get blows instead of blandishments — kicks instead of kisses; then for the fit of mute fury which will sicken his body and madden his soul; then for the ordeal of merited and salutary suffering, out of which he will come (I trust) a wiser and a better man. (357–58)

Crimsworth contemplates his son's suffering with chilling complacency. Frances, though she hides it from her husband, clearly has an independent relationship with — and independent opinions on — the boy. Frances seems, then, to have the same wider vision at the end of the novel that she has had throughout. She evidently goes through the motions of living up to Crimsworth's happy ending — but were she to tell the story, we feel certain that her version would be vastly different.

If the relations of the three Crimsworths to each other are ambiguous at the end of the novel, the relations of all of them to Yorke Hunsden are even more so. Hunsden is a strange presence in the Crimsworth family; Hunsden Wood, with its "winding ways," would seem to be a suggestive image of the tangled relations that may exist there. At several points, for instance, Crimsworth refers to the mutual affection between his son and Hunsden. Toward the end of the novel, he observes the two together.

I see him now; he stands by Hunsden, who is seated on the lawn under the beech; Hunsden's hand rests on the boy's collar, and he is instilling God knows what principles into his ear. . . . Victor has a preference for Hunsden, full as strong as I deem desirable, being considerably more potent, decided, and indiscriminating, than any I ever entertained for that personage myself. (358)

As Crimsworth looks on at his son and Hunsden, apparently not deeply threatened when he witnesses their strong bond, we are reminded of the earlier scene in which he observed Hunsden and Frances with a similar complacency as they engaged in animated, almost sexually provocative, conversation. Earlier, Hunsden played the role of lover to Frances; in this scene, he would seem to be acting, at least metaphorically, as father to Victor. Indeed, the reader — accustomed by now to the alternative possibilities which lurk beneath Crimsworth's narrative — might even wonder whether the father-son relationship between Hunsden and Victor is only metaphorical. Perhaps, unbeknownst to Crimsworth, there is another family tree in Hunsden Wood in addition to his own. But whatever the actual relationships among Victor, Frances, and Hunsden may be — and no doubt we are not meant to be certain — Hunsden continues to be a dominant presence for all three members of the Crimsworth family. And, characteristically, Crimsworth continues to be oblivious to the complexities that surround him.

The moral universe of *The Professor* is decidedly postlapsarian. Crimsworth is the innocent of the novel; all the other characters are at home in a world of compromised ideals and limited expectations. Yet — realist that she was — Brontë does not castigate her characters for being less than perfect. It is Crimsworth's brand of innocence, which refuses to recognize the mixed state of humankind and retreats into complacency, that receives the sharpest blows. Only gradually does the reader realize that the novel's moral landscape borrows much of its dark tone from the short-sighted eyes through which it is perceived.

The Fourth Picture: A "Golden Halo of Fiction"

In the novel's final moments, Crimsworth stops framing pictures; instead, he paints one. Although he makes no explicit reference to the fourth picture in the gallery of his life, the final pages in fact represent its unveiling. Crimsworth's fourth picture completes his presentation of his autobiographical myth. He construes an image of his life at Daisy Lane as his final Eden — the family living in an unsullied region, in a "picturesque and not too spacious dwelling" (351), surrounded by roses and ivy. Having discovered, as he thinks, the pitfalls of artificial gardens[24] and the snares of false delusions, he can now envisage his married life as the real paradise. In evoking his ostensible paradise, however, Crimsworth intensifies the dehumanizing natural images he has used throughout the novel's latter sections of his wife and son; they become birds, plants which he tends, or fruit. He had earlier enjoyed characterizing Frances to Hunsden as "an unique fruit, growing wild," tantalizingly natural in contrast to his friend's "hot-house grapes" (313). Now, having transplanted Frances into a rural setting, he revels in the appropriateness of the pastoral life he has created for his "dove," his "butterfly," his "precious plant."

Brontë's ironic manipulation of prelapsarian imagery did not begin with *The Professor*. In one of the earlier novelettes (*Caroline Vernon*, 1839), her unhappy heroine is banished to Eden-Cottage, near Fidena. For Caroline, the cottage becomes a prison; she flees from Eden into the unscrupulous arms of Zamorna.[25] Though not so extreme a torture, Daisy Lane must be for Frances considerably less Edenic than it is for her husband.

The love between Frances and Crimsworth began with the teacher finding his lost student mourning her aunt's death in a cemetery. Leading her from the graveyard, Crimsworth saw himself as effecting a rebirth — a victory over the forces of poverty, death, and an antagonistic world. But after rescuing Frances from the walled-in cemetery, Crimsworth merely substitutes one enclosure — his doubtful Paradise — for another. The thought of Frances and her lifelong partner is unsettling; Brontë might have been describing a Crimsworth when she wrote to Ellen Nussey that "a man with a weak brain, chill affections and a strong will — is merely an intractable fiend—you can have no hold of him—you can never lead him right."[26] With a husband, then, whose illusions require great tact to maintain, a son whose equilibrium is constantly threatened, and the emphatic figure of the serpent-like Hunsden lurking about the "winding ways" of the forest, Frances must find life at Daisy Lane considerably less than spacious.

Such is not the case for Crimsworth. The final enclosure he creates—the pastoral life at Daisy Lane—fulfils his need for an autobiographical rationale as satisfactorily as have all his other techniques for containing experience. Virtually every critic who has written on *The Professor* has commented on Crimsworth's growth during the course of the novel.[27] Yet Crimsworth has not changed essentially since the letter to Charles; only his situation is different. The ironic thrust of Crimsworth's success story is based upon the tension between worldly success and personal delusion. Crimsworth's need to superimpose his mental enclosure onto the world around him has resulted in appalling insensitivity. In the world of *The Professor*, innocence can be considerably darker than experience.

Midway through the novel, in a passage often used to characterize *The Professor*, Crimsworth states his opinion on the kinds of pictures novelists should paint: "Novelists should never allow themselves to weary of the study of real life. If they observed this duty conscientiously, they would give us fewer pictures chequered with vivid contrasts of light and shade . . ." (277). Brontë's success in giving us real life is achieved by means of Crimsworth's failure; in spite of himself, he manages nothing but a "golden halo of fiction" (299). As he ends his story, art appropriately catches up to life, and in fact overtakes it. Crimsworth writes his last page at the moment he lives it; the presence by his side of Frances, who is waiting tea for him, is as pleasant, he says, "as the perfume of the fresh hay and spicy flowers, as the glow of the westering sun, as the repose of the midsummer eve are to my senses" (359). We are not surprised to find Crimsworth so much more engaged in the appearance on his page than in the reality at his elbow. At the penultimate moment, as throughout the tale, art is more real to him than life. "But Hunsden comes." As this familiar intruder forces his presence into the room which frames the family ("disturbing," as Crimsworth writes, "two bees and a butterfly"), we note once again the instability of the autobiographer's smug portrait of blissful domesticity. Crimsworth's hackneyed ending, like all his autobiographical efforts, defeats its own purpose.

Notes

1. See Winnifrith, p. 88.
2. Quoted in Mrs. Gaskell, p. 305.
3. *LFC*, II, 161.
4. Winnifrith, p. 101.

5. W. A. Craik, *The Brontë Novels* (London: Methuen, 1968), p. 48.

6. Martin, p. 34.

7. Martin, p. 41.

8. See, for example, the chapters on the novel in Winnifrith and Dessner.

9. See Margaret Blom, *Charlotte Brontë*, Twayne's English Authors Series (Boston: G. K. Hall, 1977), p. 79.

10. Winifred Gérin advances this argument quite explicitly. See *Charlotte Brontë: The Evolution of Genius* (Oxford: Clarendon, 1967), pp. 316–32.

11. Quoted in Pascal, *Design and Truth in Autobiography*, p. 62.

12. Winnifrith, p. 90.

13. Charlotte Brontë, *The Professor*, ed. Phyllis Bentley (London: Collins, 1954), p. 299; hereafter cited in the text.

14. See *LFC*, II, 161, for Brontë's comments to W. S. Williams about illustrating her novels: ". . . I hope no one will be at the trouble to make portraits of my characters." Considering the intentional ambiguities in Brontë's conception of her characters, it is fortunate that drawings were not done; visual images would necessarily have oversimplified the characters. Smith, Elder and Co. honoured Brontë's wishes in their 1875 edition of the *Life and Works of Charlotte Brontë and her Sisters:* they illustrated only landscapes and houses.

15. The notion of memories sealed in urns has at least two notable historical precedents which may have implications for Brontë's use. Sir Thomas Browne, in his "Urne-Buriall" ("Hydriotaphia," in *Sir Thomas Browne: The Major Works*, ed. C. A. Patrides [Harmondsworth, England: Penguin, 1977], pp. 261–315), emphasized the vanity of earthly memorials and the futility of man's hopes for immortality by means of these memorials. And John Locke, in his *An Essay Concerning Human Understanding* (ed. Raymond Wilburn [London: Dent, 1947]), discussed, using the same image, the fallibility of memory: "Thus the ideas, as well as children, of our youth, often die before us: and our minds represent to us those tombs to which we are approaching; where, though the brass and marble remain, yet the inscriptions are effaced by time, and the imagery moulders away" (p. 56). Brontë's self-deluded autobiographers, all of whom bury and hope to resurrect their pasts, partake of both the vanity which Browne deplores and the faulty recollection of the past which Locke attributes to all men.

16. Robert Martin sees the absence of further reference to the fourth picture as a flaw in the novel: "The author's red herrings succeed only in calling unproductive attention to herself and in distracting the reader from his involvement in the novel" (p. 38).

17. Lawrence Dessner discusses Crimsworth's psychosexual impulses as they are manifested in a number of his relationships (pp. 49–63).

18. Cynthia A. Linder, in her *Romantic Imagery in the Novels of Charlotte Brontë* (London: Macmillan, 1978), discusses Crimsworth's movement from Reuter's artificial garden to Daisy Lane's natural one (pp. 25ff). In my opinion, Linder's discussion of this image and others neglects the novels' ironies. As I attempt to demonstrate, there are often discrepancies between the autobiographers' figurative purposes and the author's.

19. F. T. Flahiff has suggested that the several references in the novel to things that are green (such as the doormat by Frances' flat and her carpet) allude to her possible promiscuity.

20. *Their Proper Sphere: A Study of the Brontë Sisters as Early-Victorian Female Novelists* (London: Edward Arnold, 1966), p. 200.

21. Martin, p. 40.

22. Ewbank, p. 188.

23. Pascal, *Design and Truth in Autobiography*, pp. 189–90.

24. See Linder's discussion of nature imagery in the novel (pp. 29ff.).

25. Charlotte Brontë, *Five Novelettes: Passing Events, Julia, Mina Laury, Captain Henry Hastings, Caroline Vernon*, ed. Winifred Gérin (London: The Folio Press, 1971).

26. *LFC*, II, 136.

27. For example, Tom Winnifrith, whose position on the question of Crimsworth's development is more cautious than most, argues that "Crimsworth is a pitiful creature at the beginning of the novel and is perhaps unduly complacent at the end, but at any rate, *The Professor* traces some pattern of spiritual growth" (p. 96). Elsewhere (p. 51) Winnifrith notes that the Crimsworth of Daisy Lane is much changed from his former self.

The Professor: Blocked Perceptions   Judith Williams*

In *The Professor*, Charlotte Brontë was making a deliberate effort to correct what she considered the imaginative excesses of her Angrian writings, and to create a protagonist the reverse of her Angrian heroes. In the short preface to *The Professor*, written after the appearance of *Shirley*, she explains her reasons for introducing a narrator-protagonist like William Crimsworth: "I said to myself that my hero should work his way through life as I had seen real living men work theirs—that he should never get a shilling he had not earned—that no sudden turns should lift him in a moment to wealth and high station—that whatever small competency he might gain should be won by the sweat of his brow. . . . As Adam's Son he should share Adam's doom—Labour throughout life and a mixed and moderate cup of enjoyment."[1]

Certainly, to a great extent, this aim is achieved: except for the early scenes in X—— and the scenes at the end of the novel, in William and Frances's English country home (a scene which as we shall see bears much examination), the world of *The Professor* is mundane. In William's world, as he describes it about halfway through his narrative, instead of "vivid contrasts of light and shade," "fulness of joy" and "hopeless anguish" (159), extremities neutralize each other, and every evil is balanced by a good—sickness by patience, pain by hope, and death by religion. Paradoxically, having set out to write about the struggles of real life, Charlotte Brontë ends by writing a story in which the hero has very little to struggle with at all. Everything seems to fall into place for him as he moves slowly but surely toward his idyllic country home and family life.[2]

Nor does William seem to be looking back on his experience with the wisdom of later years, though his story bears some superficial resemblances to such an autobiography. Like the later Jane Eyre and Lucy Snowe, William is cast out into the world as a result of family misfortune and, since wealthy relations either cannot or will not help him, must make

*Reprinted from *Perception and Expression in the Novels of Charlotte Brontë* (1988), 7–18, by permission of UMI Press, Ann Arbor, Michigan. © by Judith Williams.

his way alone. William's frequent use of Exodus imagery helps to give his adventure the appearance of a genuine quest: he describes his drudgery in X—— as a "task thankless and bitter as that of the Israelite crawling over the sun-baked fields of Egypt in search of straw and stubble wherewith to accomplish his tale of bricks" (41). And if X—— is Egypt, Brussels is the desert he must struggle through before attaining the promised land of financial independence in England. But the Exodus is, here, simply a metaphor for a mundane experience. William is no quest hero and certainly no Moses. Though the novel is about education, it is certainly not about the education of William Crimsworth: from the beginning he is, in private life if not in public, always in control. His promised land is financial independence, not enlightenment.[3]

WILLIAM AS BARRIER OR CONDUIT

We sense in William a narrator who has been drained of imaginative energy as a result of his author's attempt to discipline her imagination, and we have an unfair tendency to be uneasy with him, even blame him, for being a block or damper on that imagination. We have here a narrator who is trying very hard not to perceive—either to see into his own inner life or to look too thoughtfully and closely at the outer world. His narrative is certainly not an utterance in the sense I use the word. Instead he imposes control on both the inner and the outer realms and keeps them apart. We also begin to feel, about halfway through the novel, that the two sexual poles of male and female are trying to come together and are being blocked by William. These two types of blockage are not unrelated: in all of Charlotte Brontë's novels the movement toward perception and insight is aligned with the bringing together of the outer and inner worlds—with the making of a channel or bridge between them—and the outer and inner are aligned with the male and female, though not in a simple manner.

Before looking at the ways in which William controls himself and his world, it is worth examining the possibility that there may be an ironic viewpoint on him. At the time of writing *The Professor*, Charlotte Brontë was certainly capable of presenting a naïve character in an ironic light: seven years earlier, in 1839, she had written "Caroline Vernon," a story in which an adolescent girl's passion for the Byronic Zamorna is clearly and objectively judged. And indeed, there is in *The Professor* itself a suggestion that Charlotte Brontë may originally have intended to introduce some degree of distance into the portrayal of William Crimsworth. The apparently meaningless machinery of the letter to Charles—machinery abandoned after the first chapter—is one of the most puzzling elements in the novel. The fact that Charlotte Brontë should retain so awkward an introductory device even after having changed her mind about the story's presentation suggests that she sensed the lack of an objective awareness in

The Professor which the letter-to-Charles framework might have supplied. Charles was William's exact antithesis: as a schoolboy he was "a sarcastic, observant, shrewd, cold-blooded creature" (5) who displayed "sardonic coldness" whenever William was moved by "some sentiment of affection, some vague love of an excellent or beautiful object, whether in animate or inanimate nature" (5-6). Thus, there could have been both an older William looking over his past and a sardonic friend whose perceptions and interpretations (especially if his answers to the letters had been included) would have been radically different from the narrator's: there would have been two detached points of view, one in time (the older William) and one in space (the distant Charles). Though nothing further is made of Charles, in this first paragraph we can see embodied in two people the opposing sensibilities, one romantic, the other ironic, which united in one narrator could have provided a clearer perspective on events.[4]

Far more interesting than Charles, as a potential outside observer of William, is Yorke Hunsden. Sardonic, shrewd, and cold-blooded, he functions to some degree as the kind of antithesis to William that Charles might have been; though his role remains sketchy, he is potentially the novel's most interesting and complex character. Hunsden provides an exaggerated and ironic view of William, seeing him from the outside as, for instance, a "fossil" and an "automaton" (36), but since William has no answering ironic view of himself he cannot give us any insight into the justice, or injustice, of Hunsden's accusations. The result is confusion rather than a clarification of the complexities of human psychology. However much we may want to agree with Hunsden, William's controlling point of view as narrator makes his friend's ironic comments seem gratuitous.[5]

Rather than taking a detached viewpoint on his younger self, William dissociates himself completely from most of his background, the materialistic world of, on the one hand, higher-class relatives who try to marry him off to a rich cousin and, on the other, the Mammon-worshipping city of X——. The antipathy between William and his brother serves only to confirm William's good opinion of himself. There is one occasion in the novel — the bout of hypochondria — when William does engage in a struggle with suffering and darkness, but the episode seems gratuitous in its isolation. Everywhere else he withdraws from the field of moral and psychological combat: his only difficulties are practical ones. The enemies with which one expects the protagonist to struggle are projected outward and controlled. William recognizes neither any potential inner darkness in himself, nor any way in which suffering could affect his life: "the man of regular life and rational mind never despairs" (159).

Even throwing himself, a complete stranger, into a foreign city is no great problem for William. We might expect Brussels to be much more than a contrast to X——, to be a literal symbol, a symbol come to life, a place where things have depth as well as surface, and appear first as hieroglyphics that can only gradually be deciphered. Although Brussels in *The Professor* does have some rudiments of this quality — most notably when William reads the characters of his pupils through their physical characteristics — the semi-mythical extension of Brussels in *Villette* is a much fuller development.[6] (In this context it is worth noting that William speaks fluent French, and, unlike Lucy Snowe, has no trouble communicating in the foreign city.) But though William understands the language he is impervious to the complexity of Brussels, where, as in X——, he learns nothing. The foreign element, seen as a symbol of the ambiguous and the complex, is something for William to control rather than to examine and understand. He concludes almost as soon as he arrives that Pelet's school, in which the pupils are stupid and easily dominated, is "merely an epitome of the Belgian Nation" (68). Mdlle. Reuter's female pupils present William with a greater problem, since an undercurrent of sensuality, unrecognized by him, subverts his sentimental and idealistic expectations. Foreignness and sexual license are automatically associated for William as for many other nineteenth-century Englishmen; his curiosity about Mdlle. Reuter's garden — the "green region" (66) he imagines beyond his boarded-up window — amounts almost to voyeurism. But he quickly gets control over the girls, and perhaps over himself as well, by categorizing them as vicious and false; indeed his descriptions make them sound more like monsters than human beings. Beyond admitting his folly in expecting the girls to be "earthly angels and human flowers" (97) — a folly which we assume he sees as being to his credit — William never examines his own feelings. Perhaps the most interesting instance of his inability to deal with both foreignness and (supposed) sexual impropriety occurs when he jumps to the improbable conclusion that old Madame Pelet has invited him to her room for amorous purposes: "Surely she's not going to make love to me. . . . I've heard of old Frenchwomen doing odd things in that line" (71). If William could have seen his own youthful conceit, this scene between himself, Madame Pelet, and Madame Reuter could have been very funny, with its contrast between the two old ladies with their hearty appetites and the priggish and fastidious young man on whom they press food and drink. But as it stands the episode is nothing more than a vignette of foreign life. And though the reader is interested in the foreignness, William does not seem to be: " 'Bien! bien!' interrupted I — for all this chatter and circumlocution began to bore me very much" (75).

The greatest feat of control that William achieves is his mastery over Pelet and Mdlle. Reuter. One might assume that, caught between two older, more sophisticated adults, destined after they marry to enact the plot of a French novel under their roof, the young and inexperienced William would be in some difficulty, if not danger. But he is, from the start, in almost total control of the situation. Standing between Pelet and Mdlle. Reuter, William acts as a sort of catalyst in their relationship, a relationship based not on spiritual or emotional bonds, but on material interest and sensuality. And William is himself by no means untouched by materialism and sensuality; indeed the two older figures can be seen as projections of some of William's own instincts. The "sentiment of exquisite pleasure" (82) he feels in anticipation of teaching at the girls' school is only a more refined version of the emotions behind Pelet's "French, rakish, mocking" laugh (82). William disguises his feeling under sentimental clichés, and though he admits that the clichés are mistaken he never seems to see the link between his sentimentality and Pelet's sensuality. Indeed, the self-deception is necessary for him, since, by projecting the sensuality onto Pelet, William can control and deny it in himself.

If Pelet allows for the displacement of feelings that William cannot or will not acknowledge in himself, then Mdlle. Reuter is the half-recognized object of these feelings: to William she appears at first (in a significant image) like a good apple, "as sound at the core as it is red on the rind" (79). Yet he refuses to see how sensual his feelings really are, though he virtually admits at one point that Mdlle. Reuter's infatuation appeals to what he would see as his baser nature: "strange to say, though my amour-propre was excited not disagreeably by the conquest, my better feelings remained untouched. . . . [H]er presence and manner . . . sealed up all that was good, elicited all that was noxious in my nature; sometimes they enervated my senses, but they always hardened my heart" (183-84). In proportion as Mdlle. Reuter becomes slavish, William becomes tyrannical: "I had ever hated a tyrant, and behold the possession of a slave, self-given, went near to transform me into what I abhorred! . . . When she stole about me with the soft step of a slave—I felt at once barbarous and sensual as a pasha" (184). Though in this part of the novel William's experience is presented more in terms of psychological realism and less in terms of fablelike symbol, William dealing with Pelet and Mdlle. Reuter is exactly like William in X——: a figure of purity untainted by surrounding evil.

THE PROMETHEAN SPARK

Pelet and Mdlle. Reuter are substitutes for the real male and female powers in William's world, since, unlike those real powers, they can be controlled and mastered. Something interesting happens about two-thirds of the way through the novel. Just at the point when Pelet and Mdlle. Reuter exit the scene, Yorke Hunsden reenters.

With his mysterious dark side—"at times, an indescribable shade passed like an eclipse over his countenance"(28) — Hunsden is at the center of what is really going on here. Of all the characters in *The Professor*, only Hunsden has the power to make William nervous: the latter seems always to be struggling to remain detached from his older friend, and from his moral complexity, or rather ambiguity, which William sees in simple terms as diabolical. When he receives the letter announcing Hunsden's arrival,

William says, "were he the Devil himself, instead of being merely very like him, I'd not condescend to get out of his way" (193). But there is another way of seeing this devilishness.

Hunsden presents William with his greatest riddle and most difficult problem. It is certainly not irrelevant that at their first meeting Hunsden reminds William of a "foreigner" (28), for nothing in Brussels is as perplexing as this Englishman, and no other figure has such power over William. They meet first at a party where the socially self-confident Hunsden seeks out the shy and retiring William, and they carry on a conversation in which William takes on a role that is conventionally "feminine": coy and slightly flirtatious. Significantly, they are standing in front of a portrait of William's mother—whom William strongly resembles. The relationship is more complex than simply that of a "masculine" Hunsden and a "feminine" William, however; Hunsden himself combines male and female qualities, having sometimes the "mien of a morose bull" and sometimes that of "an arch and mischievous girl; more frequently the two semblances were blent, and a queer, composite countenance they made" (35). In this powerful androgyny, some of which he confers on William, Hunsden is a contrast to the surroundings of Edward Crimsworth's X——, where the sexual poles are sharply divided and seen in physical, almost animal, terms. Edward and his wife are both perfect physical specimens; Edward is dominating and controlling and drives a "vicious horse" (13), while his wife has "good animal spirits" (12) and is otherwise empty-headed and childlike. Hunsden is the dynamic force in William's life, for it is at Hunsden's instigation and with his help that William leaves X—— and goes to Brussels. Even while William remains trapped in X—— as alien and outcast, Hunsden is associated with the positive imagery of food, warmth, lamplight, comfort, and books. The coldness of William's grate symbolizes the dreariness of his life; but Hunsden has custody of the "Promethean spark" (13), which is the essence of human spirit, imagination, and affection so clearly lacking in people like Edward and his wife, and also the energy of the vital inner center that to William appears diabolical.[7]

Because William takes on a female role vis-à-vis Hunsden, the scenes with Hunsden have more vitality. The energies are flowing back and forth between the poles. Thus "Wilhelmina Crimsworth" (230), as Hunsden refers to William's fiancée, Frances Henri, when he first sees her, exists as a sort of potential heroine partly in William and partly in Frances. But Frances herself is a very important figure. She is the female center in the novel.

When she first appears in William's class, Frances is seen as a figure of spirit, intelligence, and order, in the midst of unthinking material chaos: "I felt assured at first sight that she was not a Belgian, her complexion, her countenance, her lineaments, her figure were all distinct from theirs and evidently the type of another race—of a race less gifted with fulness of flesh and plentitude of blood, less jocund, material, unthinking" (122). Her voice is similarly contrasted with the voices of the other pupils; her "pure and silvery" (126) accent emerges to greater advantage from a background which has consistently been associated with heavy and chaotic matter. "To-day, each in her appropriate key, lisped, stuttered, mumbled and jabbered as usual; about fifteen had racked me in turn, and my auricular nerve was expecting with resignation the discords of the sixteenth, when a full though low voice read out, in clear correct English" (126).

Frances is more than order in the midst of chaos, however. The passage she reads is an oracular utterance, in which a woman is seen as being in possession of, literally, vital truths beyond the reach of even the greatest man: "On his way to Perth, the King was met by a Highland woman calling herself a prophetess; she stood at the side of the ferry by which he was about to travel to the North, and cried with a loud voice, 'My lord the king—if you pass this water you will never return again alive!' " (126). Both Frances and the passage she reads reinforce the idea of the female as the possessor of secrets, decipherer of mysteries, and seer of visions which must be brought together with the male world of outer action.

William's relationships with Frances and Hunsden, the two figures who in a sense are the possessors of his missing personality as well as of the insights and energies he has suppressed, are interestingly patterned, and suggest some dissolving of the boundaries along this male-female spectrum. William's treatment of Frances closely parallels Hunsden's treatment of William: he exercises over her, as Hunsden does over him, the mild sadism that Charlotte Brontë seems always to see as part of masculine love. An interesting and suggestive reinforcement of the parallelism in these relationships has to do with the figure of the mother. William asserts his power over Frances during an English lesson by making a cruel reference to Frances's dead English mother: "you do homage to her memory by forgetting her language? Have the goodness to put French out of your mind so long as I converse with you" (139). But a little later, when Hunsden arrives in Brussels, he tortures William in a not dissimilar way, by belittling the importance of the portrait of William's mother in front of which they originally met in Edward's house: "Oh I know! the thin-faced gentlewoman with a shawl put on like drapery. . . . If you had been rich—you might have bought it—for I remember you said it represented your Mother: you see what it is to be without a sou" (207-8).

Of course, Hunsden has actually bought this portrait—a portrait, one suspects, of the woman William might have been if Charlotte Brontë had used a female narrator-protagonist. Furthermore, Hunsden's interest in such an "androgynous" woman, physically plain but spiritually intriguing, might have been a prefiguration of Rochester's interest in Jane Eyre. And Frances too is in some ways this portrait come to life, though she quickly becomes in her own right a character capable of engaging our sympathies as William never can. Just as Hunsden has the darker qualities we might expect in a protagonist, so Frances has a protagonist's strengths and virtues. Her struggle with poverty, bereavement, and disappointment in love is potentially more moving than William's calm progress, though we can see her only from the outside, and glimpse her suffering only when William eavesdrops or reads her private papers.

Hunsden treats William as William treats Frances, and Frances is a more real and sympathetic female double of William; thus the centers of male and female power in this novel are to be found in Hunsden and Frances respectively — two figures between whom the flat and uninteresting William is a barrier, or perhaps a conduit. This conclusion is borne out in several ways. Hunsden reenters the novel at the significant point when William has just severed his connection with Pelet and Mdlle. Reuter, is looking for another job, and is keeping away from Frances, who is also looking for a job. This hiatus ends when William receives two letters on the same day: one from Frances announcing that she has found work, and one from Hunsden, in a handwriting "neither masculine nor exactly feminine" (192), announcing his imminent arrival in ironically apocalyptic terms, and making fun of William — and thus indirectly reminding us of William's unadmitted sensuality — by picturing him among the "fleshpots of Egypt" (192). Even more interesting is a series of coincidences in the next chapter: Pelet and Mdlle. Reuter are married, William daydreams about Frances, and Hunsden arrives. It is almost as if William's desire for Frances, which he calls "Imagination" (198), has evoked Hunsden — who is after all an embodiment of William's more spontaneous and dangerous self. As the coarsely sensual and materialistic parody lovers — substitutes for the real male and female powers — are united in the background, Hunsden and Frances converge upon William from two directions; when they actually meet, William literally withdraws into the background. During the lively conversation between Hunsden and Frances when they first meet in Frances's rooms — incidentally, the liveliest conversation in the book — William retires "to the window-seat" while Hunsden, "at his hostess's invitation," occupies "a chair near the hearth" (234). It is possible to see behind this novel shadowy lovers, who struggle to get into the narrative sometimes through Hunsden, sometimes through William, and sometimes through Frances. In the later novels, the "William" figure does fade out; all Charlotte Brontë's heroes and heroines can be seen to some extent as developments of Hunsden and Frances. With these later novels in mind, we should note the frequency with which Hunsden and Frances are each associated with hearth fires and food, and that the element of repartee is strong in their conversation. (It is also interesting that the persona in Frances's poem is called "Jane," while the actress Hunsden once loved is called "Lucia.") The figures of Hunsden and Frances reveal much about the creative process in this novel. Just as

William blocks the way between Hunsden and Frances, so, it seems, Charlotte Brontë in her efforts to be realistic—to present a rational and prosaic world—has blocked the flow of her imaginative energies. In the later novels when her imagination is freed, the literary descendants of Hunsden and Frances will come together. Even in *The Professor* it is obvious that Frances and Hunsden are far more passionate and imaginative beings than William, and that both have hidden depths we can only glimpse.[8]

Frances is subdued by marriage to William; or rather, she seems to be split into two women with her energetic self for the most part under William's control. She is in inexplicable "low spirits" (245) on the morning of the wedding, and William tells us that later in their married life her highspiritedness disappears at his touch: when she shows too much raillery and the "wild and witty wickedness that made a perfect white demon of her while it lasted" (253), William grasps her arm and she becomes "a submissive and supplicating little mortal woman" (253). Her strong passion—"the energy of her whole being" (256)—manifests itself only occasionally. Hunsden, however, remains a disturbing figure to the very end.

William and Frances work and save for ten years so that they can retire independent, although it should be noted that their wealth is not all the result of the sweat of their brows; William rather coyly tells us that they had good advice on investments, and the results were "gainful," though "nobody else can be interested in hearing" the details (257). These results are possible because the world of *The Professor* has been a rational, controllable place where people can repay debts, and where irrational forces have little power. Robert Moore, in *Shirley*, will learn that the real world is not like this. But William Crimsworth learns nothing, because the world he inhabits has been, up till now, an exact reflection of his perceptions and expectations. He achieves his goals with only the most mundane and predictable of difficulties, and his and Frances's child, Victor, appears at the end as the inevitable symbol of the harmony and success (victory?) that they have attained.

It is mildly disconcerting that William mentions his son almost as an afterthought and describes him specifically as *Frances's* "own boy" (254). But this is only the beginning of an odd development that occurs late in the novel, after everything has seemed settled: the imagination begins to work only after the exemplary tale is finished. The idealized portrait of married life drawn by William, in which the tamed Frances takes on the role of the perfect wife, mother, and teacher, is subtly undermined not only by Hunsden but by Victor. Hunsden, balked of a relationship with either a female William or Frances herself—or rather, with the potential female protagonist of which William and Frances are manifestations—turns his attention to the offspring of their union.

Like the letter-to-Charles device, the ending of the novel has until fairly recently been oddly neglected by the critics. In fact, it has intriguing implications. William and Frances return to a part of England that is a sort of temporary Eden—"a region whose verdure the smoke of mills has not yet sullied"(257)—but Hunsden lives dangerously close, frequently entertains foreign visitors, "wanders from land to land," and, not yet having found his "ideal" (258), remains unmarried. The relationship between Hunsden and Victor contains in microcosm the world of experience threatening that of innocence; the picture of Hunsden and Frances disputing about the boy's education is emblematic. William and Frances have feared that Hunsden will be a bad influence on their son; Frances feels it is "Better a thousand times he should be a milk-sop than what he—Hunsden, calls 'a fine lad' " (262–63). Finally, at the end of the novel, Hunsden and Frances have stepped into the limelight; William remains back in his study, almost as a mere transcriber of events.

The incident William now relates, where he is forced to shoot Victor's dog, is curious and disconcerting: the dog is a gift from Hunsden (indeed its name is "Yorke") and Victor is strongly attached both to gift and to giver. Victor's first reaction is to cry, "Oh papa! I'll never forgive you! I'll never forgive you! . . . I never believed you could be so cruel—I can love you no more!" (264). This cry gives utterance to a universal human experience (though "papa" is sometimes God or Destiny): it is only through his child that real and universal pain finally enters William's world. The child is, however temporarily, alienated from the father, and experiences—though again only temporarily—the world of suffering in which parents are replaced by tyrants. (The motif of the parent-tyrant as agent of suffering becomes increasingly important in Charlotte Brontë's work, culminating in the motherly yet evil Madame Beck.)

Of course, on the surface of the novel, Victor's suffering is short-lived: William and Frances are good parents who comfort him and explain to him that the dog had to be shot—and, more significantly, that it did not suffer any pain. Reason and order win out, and Victor, "ever accessible" (266) to reason, is soon tranquil again. In the later novels the conflict will not be so easily resolved. And even here there is a troubling undercurrent in William's action. We cannot help seeing his destruction of the dog, which bears Hunsden's name, in the light of what he says about certain aspects of Victor's character. As well as a dispute between William and Frances on the one hand and Hunsden on the other, there seems to be a dispute between Hunsden and Frances on the one hand and William on the other. William and Hunsden seem about to change places. In the child there is "a kind of electrical ardour and power, which emits, now and then, ominous sparks." Hunsden thinks this "spirit" should not be curbed, but William considers it to be "the leaven of the offending Adam," which should be disciplined or even whipped out of the child: "he will be cheap of any amount of either bodily or mental suffering which will ground him radically in the art of self-control" (266). Victor, the living symbol of

William and Frances's wholly reasonable life, still has what William calls the leaven of the old Adam: and this element in the child — this ardour and power — is, unless it is derived from Frances's repressed passionate side, more closely allied to Hunsden than to the parents. Victor has a potential for moral and psychological depth, and a corresponding capacity for suffering, beyond the reach of his father's rational and moralistic mind, and that mind is judging it and condemning it. The spark is no longer "Promethean" but "ominous."

The tableau at the end — the child protected by his parents but obscurely menaced by Hunsden (and by the "Hunsden" part of himself) — is almost an emblem of what has happened to the narrative as a whole: Victor can almost be said to resemble the novel. Like Victor, despite the sober control exercised over its bringing-up, the novel contains, in Hunsden, a leaven of something spontaneous and unpredictable. Charlotte Brontë has tried to keep her imagination in its place ("soundly disciplined"), but Hunsden at the end threatens to bring Angria onto center stage. We sense that there is another novel potential here — a novel in which the Angrian energies would be put to the service of a more mature vision. For instance, in the relationship of Hunsden and Lucia, moral complexity and potential evil present themselves in a far more dramatic and less moralistic light than they have done hitherto in *The Professor*. Lucia, in whom, Hunsden says, "All was real" (261), is an emanation of the imagination in its most unfettered form: William says of Lucia's portrait, "I thought it represented a very handsome and very individual-looking female face with, as he had once said, 'straight and harmonious features' — it was dark; the hair, raven-black, swept not only from the brow, but from the temples — seemed thrust away carelessly as if such beauty dispensed with, nay, despised arrangement" (261). (We should note that it is Frances, not William, who sees beyond Lucia's appearance into her character — and into Hunsden's real attitude toward her.) This reemergence of Angria is not regressive, but rather a step forward: Charlotte Brontë is incorporating Angria into realistic psychology, rather than (as in "Caroline Vernon") incorporating realistic psychology into Angria.

The final paragraphs, in the present tense, lead the reader to wonder what will happen after the last line. Indeed, the act of ending this novel — the narrator's actual act of cutting it off, of stopping writing — bears some examination. William is writing the last words as he waits for Hunsden to arrive for a visit. He has crammed in the description of Victor and the dog under pressure of a very artificial deadline — tea is almost ready! In his haste to cut off his narrative, he almost seems to be inventing a false deadline so as not to have to say too much about Victor — or to look too closely at what is going on. If the novel had started here, it would have been a novel in which the imagination was expressed rather than repressed — a novel much more like *Jane Eyre*. It certainly seems that Charlotte Brontë's vision is about to refocus and readjust itself: Hunsden is about to become a far more sympathetic, or at least interesting, character, while William's rationality is beginning to look somewhat sinister. Though the earlier part of the novel remains two-dimensional, this final scene seems on the point of expanding in many directions. The child is more complex than the father; thus it is appropriate, if not inevitable, that Charlotte Brontë's next novel should begin within the consciousness of a child who is, in the eyes of her guardians, as far from being exemplary as Victor. The crucial difference is that we see — and through the child's eyes this time — a world far more complex than the one William inhabits. Jane Eyre at Lowood is in a situation that echoes and parodies Victor's projected experience at Eton.[9]

Notes

1. Charlotte Brontë, *The Professor*, ed. Margaret Smith and Herbert Rosengarten (Oxford: Clarendon Press, 1987), 3–4. All subsequent references are to this edition and are incorporated within parentheses in the text.

2. Robert Bernard Martin, in *The Accents of Persuasion: Charlotte Brontë's Novels* (London: Faber and Faber, 1966) states that the novel illustrates "the doctrine of self-reliance" (49). But he notes: "*The Professor* is, in part, a repudiation of its preface, for Miss Brontë was unable to avoid showing the necessity of the emotions" (25). For the account of Charlotte Brontë's struggle with Angria — her "murderous expiation of her early romantic extravagances" — see Fannie Elizabeth Ratchford, *The Brontës' Web of Childhood* (New York: Russell and Russell, 1964; reissue of Columbia University Press, 1941), 169–70. Paradoxically, as Ratchford shows, the Crimsworth brothers and Yorke Hunsden have long Angrian pedigrees (190–200).

3. On William as a narrator, see the comments in Helene Moglen, *Charlotte Brontë: The Self Conceived* (New York: Norton, 1976): "Crimsworth's growth is not organic. He achieves complacency rather than wisdom" (85); "Never conscious of his own experience on any but the most immediate level, he is unable to bring to the events he describes a vital complexity of vision" (86). The fact that William learns nothing manifests itself in what Patricia Beer sees as the "adolescent" nature of the novel; see *Reader, I Married Him: A Study of the Women Characters of Jane Austen, Charlotte Brontë, Elizabeth Gaskell, and George Eliot* (London: Macmillan, 1974), 104. Inga-Stina Ewbank, in *Their Proper Sphere: A Study of the Brontë Sisters as Early-Victorian Female Novelists* (London: Arnold, 1966), comments that "the drive to get on is very much seen in economic terms" (157), and sees the novel as "a kind of bourgeois pilgrimage" (169) in which the reader's pleasure derives from "seeing a good man getting on in the world, from a poor and humble start, by his own efforts" (170). Lawrence Jay Dessner, in *The Homely Web of Truth: A Study of Charlotte Brontë's Novels* (The Hague, Paris: Mouton, 1975), has argued that William *is* a deliberate attempt at an unreliable narrator (49–62). John Maynard, in *Charlotte Brontë and Sexuality* (Cambridge: Cambridge University Press, 1984), sees an implied author judging William (76); the narrative is "exploratory" of sexual issues. Annette Tromly, *The Cover of the Mask: The Autobiographers in Charlotte Brontë's Fiction* (Victoria, BC: English Literary Studies, 1982), in an interesting chapter on *The Professor*, also considers William as meant to be an unreliable narrator, and to be seen as not learning much (33). He is the only innocent in a fallen world, but as a complacent innocent is the most blameworthy (39). He is being presented to us by the author as someone we must regard with detached judgment — indeed, as "the central problem of the novel" — a self-server whose "autobiographical manipulations become morally questionable" (23).

4. Charlotte Brontë's sense of the lack of an objective viewpoint on William may be

why she could not bring herself to dispense with the letter device altogether. Many critics remark on its awkwardness. For example, Ewbank sees in the technique only the author's "inexperience" as a novelist (169). Martin says of the opening chapter that "one can hardly avoid irritation" (37); Melvin R. Watson, "Form and Substance in the Brontë Novels," in *From Jane Austen to Joseph Conrad: Essays Collected in Memory of James T. Hillhouse,* ed. Robert C. Rathburn and Martin Steinmann, Jr. (Minneapolis: University of Minnesota Press, 1958), speaks of the "succession of false scents" at the beginning (109). Charles Burkhart, in *Charlotte Brontë: A Psychosexual Study of Her Novels* (London: Gollancz, 1973) calls the letter device "Charlotte's nod to the past, the earlier epistolary style of Richardson" (51) and considers it a throwback to her own juvenilia. See also Tom Winnifrith, *The Brontës* (New York: Macmillan, 1977), 90–93, 95–96. Cynthia A. Linder, in *Romantic Imagery in the Novels of Charlotte Brontë* (London: Macmillan, 1978), considers the letter "a rather clumsy presentation of some background information, which could have been omitted, and the facts incorporated in Chapter II" (7). See Dessner, however, who points out the similarities between Charles and Hunsden (55), and Terry Eagleton, *Myths of Power: A Marxist Study of the Brontës* (London: Macmillan, 1975), who likens the reader's position to Charles's. Tromly sees the letter's importance in another light. In her view, it leads us to ask what kind of self-absorbed narrator this is, who writes an unsolicited letter to someone in whom he doesn't seem interested (21).

There are strong Angrian elements in the letter. Textual evidence suggests that the first chapter may have been written before Charlotte Brontë went to Brussels and thus have originated in Angrian material. See the introduction to the Clarendon edition of *The Professor,* xxx. And "Charles" is, of course, one of the names of Zamorna's ironical younger brother, through whose eyes Zamorna is often seen. See Ratchford, 71, 122, and 193.

5. Hunsden has been the subject of much critical debate. See Ewbank: "Charlotte Brontë tries to avoid priggishness in her hero by having the cynic Hunsden place him, but the total effect is much more of William Crimsworth placing Hunsden" (169). Martin sees Hunsden both as a teacher to William and as part of William's personality, but concentrates on the teacher-pupil theme (30–31). He also takes the view that Hunsden is an "ascetic" (31) whose life remains unfulfilled, and so is a prototype of St. John Rivers, a symbol of the "insufficiency" of reason as a guide to life (32–33). For Burkhart, Hunsden is "the most interesting character in the book and the most unsuccessful. One of his failures is that he has no function" (49). Eagleton, in *Myths,* sees Hunsden as an "idealised" or "higher" form of William and of the bourgeois/aristocratic split within William, and as "a mirror-image of [William's] own covertly dissentient spirit . . . enacted with all the stylish authority of one secure in the worldly success he himself lacks" (37–38); hence William's ambivalent attitude: "To the extent that Hunsden is an *inverted* mirror-image of William, he must clearly be combated" (38). Moglen connects Hunsden with Charlotte Brontë's subversive imagination: "the Hunsden within herself has pushed Brontë to begin, in *The Professor,* a radical line of investigation which must give her future work a new focus" (103). Carol Ohmann, "Historical Reality and 'Divine Appointment' in Charlotte Brontë's Fiction," *Signs,* 2 (1977), 757–78, sees Hunsden as an almost Shelleyan character in possible political or social terms, who though promising goes nowhere. For Sandra M. Gilbert and Susan Gubar, *The Madwoman in the Attic: The Woman Writer and the Nineteenth-Century Literary Imagination* (New Haven and London: Yale University Press, 1979; reprinted 1984), Hunsden is a figure of Charlotte Brontë's rebellion and anger, a manipulator of the plot, and a "narrator-in-disguise" (332–333).

There is textual evidence, indeed, that Hunsden was the most vital and difficult character in terms of the creative process itself; Charlotte Brontë was changing him right up to the end. See the introduction to the Clarendon edition, xxxiv, and M. M. Brammer, "The Manuscript of *The Professor,*" *Review of English Studies,* n.s. 11 (1960), 163.

6. The importance of the exile motif and of foreignness in Romanticism and in Charlotte Brontë is discussed by Enid L. Duthie, *The Foreign Vision of Charlotte Brontë* (London: Macmillan, 1975), 206. As Duthie points out, the cosmopolitan foreign city had

been an important image in Charlotte Brontë's imagination since the invention of Glass Town and Verdopolis. The complex foreign city, both imaginary and real, represented to her a place of "wider mental horizons" (9). Gilbert and Gubar see the "glittering town outside" as the place to which the (usually) female figure, "trapped or buried in the architecture of a patriarchal society," longs to escape (313).

7. The androgyny in this novel has been the subject of much discussion. Ewbank comments that *The Professor* is "the autobiography of a male governess" (112). See Moglen for a discussion of William's feminine qualities, the relation between Hunsden, Frances, and William, and the way Hunsden seems to bring the other two to life (99). For Eagleton, in *Myths*, William is "a male Jane Eyre" to "Hunsden's Rochester" (36). For Gilbert and Gubar, William seems androgynous against the sexually polarized background of X——, though he later becomes more masculine (318–20). For a fuller discussion of androgyny in all of Charlotte Brontë's novels, see F. A. C. Wilson, "The Primrose Wreath: The Heroes of the Brontë Novels," *Nineteenth-Century Fiction*, 29 (1974–75), 40–57. Wilson sees Hunsden as "a concealed focus of erotic interest" and as "transparently androgynous" (47).

8. The fragmented protagonist is discussed by Moglen, who sees Frances, William, and Hunsden as fragments of Charlotte Brontë and versions of one another (87–88). Ewbank feels that there is a blurring of identities, and hints at a certain redundancy or perhaps vacancy when she refers to William and Frances as having "natures and careers so similar as to make them one character distributed over two sexes" (157). Burkhart sees all the characters as aspects of Charlotte Brontë herself; she was unable to identify as completely with any one of them as she could with Jane Eyre and Lucy Snowe.

Frances's greater vitality is emphasized by Rebecca Rodolff, in "From the Ending of *The Professor* to the Conception of *Jane Eyre*," *Philological Quarterly*, 61 (1982), 71–89. This interesting article looks from another angle on the fragmentation of William, seeing a shift in interest to Frances after the proposal scene, anticipation of the Jane-Rochester relation in the Frances-Hunsden relation (80), and even a germ of St. John Rivers in William (85). Tromly has an even more interesting view of Frances: she sees deliberate hints in the novel that Frances may have a "questionable past" of which William is not aware (33–34).

9. It is a measure of the resonances in the ending of this novel that it is susceptible to so many different interpretations. More or less positive views of the ending include, for example, those of Ewbank: "The novel closes quietly with a family tea on the lawn" (168). Martin sees a parallelism between William and Victor, who is "about to undergo the same process that his father has passed through, that of learning self-discipline and a nice adjustment of reason and passion, the education, as Miss Brontë saw it, of the sons and daughters of Adam" (36–37). Burkhart remarks on the "Eden-like" garden at the end, and relates it to the Victorian theme of leisure attained through work; for him, "Daisy Lane" is "a very romantic place" (56). Others, however, see an attempt at the end to keep dangerous elements out. See Eagleton, *Myths:*" For the novel fully to admit the experience of suffering and solitude into its world would be for it to risk collapse; it is only by a constant deflection of those facts that it survives" (78). Robert Keefe, in *Charlotte Brontë's World of Death* (Austin and London: University of Texas Press, 1979), sees Victor as representing a "subtly dangerous threat" (93) and rival to William, reflecting Charlotte Brontë's attitude toward her family's, and especially her mother's, preference for Branwell. Maynard sees the ending as important, but in another way. He sees Charlotte Brontë as hinting that though Frances is happy, William is not, though he won't admit it; he "may have suppressed his complicated interest in Zoraïde for the less sensually compelling relationship with Frances" (91). Thus William's hostility to his son is disguised frustration. Tromly, conversely, sees hints that Hunsden may be Victor's father, especially given the earlier scene where Frances responded to Hunsden in a clearly sexual way (38–39). Certainly her argument is interesting, and the fact that it is as convincing as it is suggests that something is going on here, though I am not sure that Charlotte Brontë was as conscious of it as Tromly thinks. See also Rodolff on the ways the ending is transitional to *Jane Eyre*.

Jane Eyre

Review of *Jane Eyre: An Autobiography*

Elizabeth Rigby*

. . . Jane Eyre is throughout the personification of an unregenerate and undisciplined spirit, the more dangerous to exhibit from that prestige of principle and self-control which is liable to dazzle the eye too much for it to observe the inefficient and unsound foundation on which it rests. It is true Jane does right, and exerts great moral strength, but it is the strength of a mere heathen mind which is a law unto itself. No Christian grace is perceptible upon her. She has inherited in fullest measure the worst sin of our fallen nature—the sin of pride. Jane Eyre is proud, and therefore she is ungrateful too. It pleased God to make her an orphan, friendless, and penniless—yet she thanks nobody, and least of all Him, for the food and raiment, the friends, companions, and instructors of her helpless youth— for the care and education vouchsafed to her till she was capable in mind as fitted in years to provide for herself. On the contrary, she looks upon all that has been done for her not only as her undoubted right, but as falling far short of it. The doctrine of humility is not more foreign to her mind than it is repudiated by her heart. It is by her own talents, virtues, and courage that she is made to attain the summit of human happiness, and, as far as Jane Eyre's own statement is concerned, no one would think that she owed anything either to God above or to man below. She flees from Mr. Rochester, and has not a being to turn to. Why was this? The excellence of the present institution at Casterton, which succeeded that of Cowan Bridge near Kirkby Lonsdale—these being distinctly, as we hear, the original and the reformed Lowoods of the book—is pretty generally known. Jane had lived there for eight years with 110 girls and fifteen teachers. Why had she formed no friendships among them? Other orphans have left the same and similar institutions, furnished with friends for life, and puzzled with homes to choose from. How comes it that Jane had acquired neither? Among that number of associates there were surely some exceptions to what she so presumptuously stigmatises as "the society of inferior minds." Of course it suited the author's end to represent the heroine as utterly destitute of the common means of assistance, in order to

*Reprinted from the *Quarterly Review* 84 (December 1848): 173–76.

exhibit both her trials and her powers of self-support—the whole book rests on this assumption—but it is one which, under the circumstances, is very unnatural and very unjust.

Altogether the auto-biography of Jane Eyre is pre-eminently an anti-Christian composition. There is throughout it a murmuring against the comforts of the rich and against the privations of the poor, which, as far as each individual is concerned, is a murmuring against God's appointment—there is a proud and perpetual assertion of the rights of man, for which we find no authority either in God's word or in God's providence—there is that pervading tone of ungodly discontent which is at once the most prominent and the most subtle evil which the law and the pulpit, which all civilized society in fact has at the present day to contend with. We do not hesitate to say that the tone of mind and thought which has overthrown authority and violated every code human and divine abroad, and fostered Chartism and rebellion at home, is the same which has also written *Jane Eyre*.

Still we say again this is a very remarkable book. We are painfully alive to the moral, religious, and literary deficiencies of the picture, and such passages of beauty and power as we have quoted cannot redeem it, but it is impossible not to be spell-bound with the freedom of the touch. It would be mere hackneyed courtesy to call it "fine writing." It bears no impress of being written at all, but is poured out rather in the heat and hurry of an instinct, which flows ungovernably on to its object, indifferent by what means it reaches it, and unconscious too. As regards the author's chief object, however, it is a failure—that, namely, of making a plain, odd woman, destitute of all the conventional features of feminine attraction, interesting in our sight. We deny that he has succeeded in this. Jane Eyre, in spite of some grand things about her, is a being totally uncongenial to our feelings from beginning to end. We acknowledge her firmness—we respect her determination—we feel for her struggles; but, for all that, and setting aside higher considerations, the impression she leaves on our mind is that of a decidedly vulgar-minded woman—one whom we should not care for as an acquaintance, whom we should not seek as a friend, whom we should not desire for a relation, and whom we should scrupulously avoid for a governess.

There seem to have arisen in the novel-reading world some doubts as to who really wrote this book; and various rumours, more or less romantic, have been current in Mayfair, the metropolis of gossip, as to the authorship. For example, *Jane Eyre* is sentimentally assumed to have proceeded from the pen of Mr. Thackeray's governess, whom he had himself chosen as his model of Becky, and who, in mingled love and revenge, personified him in return as Mr. Rochester. In this case, it is evident that the author of *Vanity Fair*, whose own pencil makes him grey-haired, has had the best of it, though his children may have had the worst, having, at all events, succeeded in hitting that vulnerable point in the

Becky bosom, which it is our firm belief no man born of woman, from her Soho to her Ostend days, had ever so much as grazed. To this ingenious rumour the coincidence of the second edition of *Jane Eyre* being dedicated to Mr. Thackeray has probably given rise. For our parts, we see no great interest in the question at all. The first edition of *Jane Eyre* purports to be edited by Currer Bell, one of a trio of brothers, or sisters, or cousins, by names Currer, Acton, and Ellis Bell, already known as the joint-authors of a volume of poems. The second edition the same — dedicated, however, "by the author," to Mr. Thackeray; and the dedication (itself an indubitable *chip* of *Jane Eyre*) signed Currer Bell. Author and editor therefore are one, and we are as much satisfied to accept this double individual under the name of "Currer Bell," as under any other, more or less euphonious. Whoever it be, it is a person who, with great mental powers, combines a total ignorance of the habits of society, great coarseness of taste, and a heathenish doctrine of religion. And as these characteristics appear more or less in the writings of all three, Currer, Acton, and Ellis alike, for their poems differ less in degree of power than in kind, we are ready to accept the fact of their identity or of their relationship with equal satisfaction. At all events there can be no interest attached to the writer of *Wuthering Heights* — a novel succeeding *Jane Eyre*, and purporting to be written by Ellis Bell — unless it were for the sake of more individual reprobation. For though there is a decided family likeness between the two, yet the aspect of the Jane and Rochester animals in their native state, as Catherine and Heathfield[sic], is too odiously and abominably pagan to be palatable even to the most vitiated class of English readers. With all the unscrupulousness of the French school of novels it combines that repulsive vulgarity in the choice of its vice which supplies its own antidote. The question of authorship, therefore, can deserve a moment's curiosity only as far as *Jane Eyre* is concerned, and though we cannot pronounce that it appertains to a real Mr. Currer Bell and to no other, yet that it appertains to a man, and not, as many assert, to a woman, we are strongly inclined to affirm. Without entering into the question whether the power of the writing be above her, or the vulgarity below her, there are, we believe, minutiae of circumstantial evidence which at once acquit the feminine hand. No woman — a lady friend, whom we are always happy to consult, assures us — makes mistakes in her own *métier* — no woman *trusses game* and garnishes dessert-dishes with the same hands, or talks of so doing in the same breath. Above all, no woman attires another in such fancy dresses as Jane's ladies assume — Miss Ingram coming down, irresistible, "in a *morning* robe of sky-blue crape, a gauze azure scarf twisted in her hair!!" No lady, we understand, when suddenly roused in the night, would think of hurrying on "*a frock.*" They have garments more convenient for such occasions, and more becoming too. This evidence seems incontrovertible. Even granting that these incongruities were purposely assumed, for the sake of disguising the female pen, there is nothing gained; for if we ascribe the book to a woman at all, we have no alternative but to ascribe it to one who has, for some sufficient reason, long forfeited the society of her own sex.

And if by no woman, it is certainly also by no artist. The Thackeray eye has had no part there. There is not more disparity between the art of drawing Jane assumes and her evident total ignorance of its first principles, than between the report she gives of her own character and the conclusions we form for ourselves. Not but what, in another sense, the author may be classed as an artist of very high grade. Let him describe the simplest things in nature—a rainy landscape, a cloudy sky, or a bare moorside, and he shows the hand of a master; but the moment he talks of the art itself, it is obvious that he is a complete ignoramus. . . .

Jane Eyre: The Temptations of a Motherless Woman   Adrienne Rich*

Like Thackeray's daughters, I read *Jane Eyre* in childhood, carried away "as by a whirlwind." Returning to Charlotte Brontë's most famous novel, as I did over and over in adolescence, in my twenties, thirties, now in my forties, I have never lost the sense that it contains, through and beyond the force of its creator's imagination, some nourishment I needed then and still need today. Other novels often ranked greater, such as *Persuasion, Middlemarch, Jude the Obscure, Madame Bovary, Anna Karenina, The Portrait of a Lady*—all offered their contradictory and compelling versions of what it meant to be born a woman. But *Jane Eyre* has for us now a special force and survival value.

Comparing *Jane Eyre* to *Wuthering Heights*, as people tend to do, Virginia Woolf had this to say: "The drawbacks of being Jane Eyre are not far to seek. Always to be a governess and always to be in love is a serious limitation in a world which is full, after all, of people who are neither one nor the other. . . . [Charlotte Brontë] does not attempt to solve the problems of human life; she is even unaware that such problems exist; all her force, which is the more tremendous for being constricted, goes into the assertion, 'I love,' 'I hate,' 'I suffer.' . . ."[1]

She goes on to state that Emily Brontë is a greater poet than Charlotte because "there is no 'I' in *Wuthering Heights*. There are no governesses. There are no employers. There is love, but not the love of men and women." In short, and here I would agree with her, *Wuthering Heights* is

*"Jane Eyre: The Temptations of a Motherless Woman," from *On Lies, Secrets, and Silence, Selected Prose 1966–1978* by Adrienne Rich, is reprinted by permission of W. W. Norton & Company, Inc. © 1979 by W. W. Norton & Company, Inc., and Virago Press, Ltd.

mythic. The bond between Catherine and Heathcliff is the archetypal bond between the split fragments of the psyche, the masculine and feminine elements ripped apart and longing for reunion. But *Jane Eyre* is different from *Wuthering Heights*, and not because Charlotte Brontë lodged her people in a world of governesses and employers, of the love between men and women. *Jane Eyre* is not a novel in the Tolstoyan, the Flaubertian, even the Hardyesque sense. *Jane Eyre* is a tale.

The concern of the tale is not with social mores, though social mores may occur among the risks and challenges encountered by the protagonist. Neither is it an anatomy of the psyche, the fated chemistry of cosmic forces. It takes its place between the two: between the realm of the given, that which is changeable by human activity, and the realm of the fated, that which lies outside human control: between realism and poetry. The world of the tale is above all a "vale of soul-making," and when a novelist finds herself writing a tale, it is likely to be because she is moved by that vibration of experience which underlies the social and political, though it constantly feeds into both of these.

In her essay on *Jane Eyre*, critic Q. D. Leavis perceives the novel's theme as ". . . an exploration of how a woman comes to maturity in the world of the writer's youth."[2] I would suggest that a novel about how a man "comes to maturity in the world of the writer's youth" — *Portrait of the Artist*, for example — would not be dismissed as lacking in range, or, in Woolf's words, a sense of "human problems." I would suggest further, that Charlotte Brontë is writing — not a bildungsroman — but the life story of a woman who is *incapable* of saying *I am Heathcliff* (as the heroine of Emily's novel does) because she feels so unalterably herself. Jane Eyre, motherless and economically powerless, undergoes certain traditional female temptations, and finds that each temptation presents itself along with an alternative — the image of a nurturing or principled or spirited woman on whom she can model herself, or to whom she can look for support.

2

In *Women and Madness* Phyllis Chesler notes that "women are motherless children in patriarchal society." By this she means that women have had neither power nor wealth to hand on to their daughters; they have been dependent on men as children are on women; and the most they can do is teach their daughters the tricks of surviving in the patriarchy by pleasing, and attaching themselves to, powerful or economically viable men.[3] Even the heiress in nineteenth-century fiction is incomplete without a man; her wealth, like Dorothea Brooke's or Isabel Archer's, must be devoted to the support of some masculine talent or dilettantism; economically the heiress is, simply, a "good match" and marriage her only real profession. In nineteenth-century England the poor and genteel woman had one possible source of independence if she did not marry: the profession of governess. But, as I have suggested, Jane Eyre is *not* "always a governess." She addresses us first as a literally motherless, and also fatherless child, under the guardianship of her aunt, Mrs. Reed, who despises and oppresses her. The tale opens with images of coldness, bleakness, banishment. Jane is seated behind the curtains in a window-embrasure, trying to conceal herself from her aunt, her two girl cousins, and her boorish boy cousin John. With the icy coldness of the winter landscape outside on one hand, this chilly family circle on the other, she looks at a book of engravings of Arctic wastes and legendary regions of winter.

3

Moments after the novel begins, John Reed provokes Jane's childish rage by striking her in the face and taunting her with her poverty and dependency. Thus, immediately, the political/social circumstances of Jane's life are established: as a female she is exposed to male physical brutality and whim; as an economically helpless person she is vulnerable in a highly class-conscious society. Her response to John's gratuitous cruelty is to "fly at him" and thereat to be dragged off and locked into the "Red Room," where her uncle had died and which is rumored to be a haunted chamber.

Here begins the ordeal which represents Jane's first temptation. For a powerless little girl in a hostile household, where both psychic and physical violence are used against her, used indeed to punish her very spiritedness and individuality, the temptation of victimization is never far away. To see herself as the sacrificial lamb or scapegoat of this household, and act out that role, or conversely to explode into violent and self-destructive hysterics which can only bring on more punishment and victimization, are alternatives all too ready at hand.

In the Red Room, Jane experiences the bitter isolation of the outsider, the powerlessness of the scapegoat to please, the abjectness of the victim. But above all, she experiences her situation as unnatural: "Unjust — unjust! said my reason, forced by the agonizing stimulus into precocious though transitory power; and Resolve, equally wrought up, instigated some strange expedient to achieve escape from insupportable oppression — as running away, or if that could not be effected, never eating or drinking more, and letting myself die."

I want to recall to you that the person who is going through this illumination — for "dark" and "turbid" as her feelings are, they are illuminating — is a girl of ten, without material means or any known recourse in the outer world, dependent on the household she lives in for physical support and whatever strands of human warmth she can cling to. She is, even so, conscious that it could be otherwise; she imagines alternatives, though desperate ones. It is at this moment that the germ of the person we are finally to know as Jane Eyre is born: a person determined to live, and to choose her life with dignity, integrity, and pride.

Jane's passion in the Red Room comes to its climax; she hallucinates, screams, is thrust back into the dreaded death-chamber, and blacks out. Her ensuing illness, like much female illness, is an acting-out of her powerlessness and need for affection, and a psychic crisis induced by these conditions. During her convalescence from this "fit," she experiences for the first time the decency of the family apothecary and the gentle and caring side of the sharp-tongued young servant Bessie. Bessie is the first woman to show Jane affection; and it is partly the alliance with her that makes it possible for the child Jane to maintain her hope for the future, her will to survive; which prevents her from running away — a self-destructive act under the circumstances — or from relapsing into mere hysteria or depression. It is this, too, which helps her retain the self-respect and the spirit of rebellion in which she finally confronts her aunt:

> Shaking from head to foot, thrilled with ungovernable excitement, I continued —

> "I am glad you are no relation of mine. I will never call you aunt again as long as I live. I will never come to see you when I am grown up; and if anyone asks me how I liked you, and how you treated me, I will say the very thought of you makes me sick, and that you treated me with miserable cruelty."

> . . . Ere I had finished this reply, my soul began to expand, to exult, with the strangest sense of freedom, of triumph, I ever felt. It seemed as if an invisible bond had burst and that I had struggled out into unhoped-for liberty.

This outburst, like much anger of the powerless, leaves Jane only briefly elated. The depressive, self-punishing reaction sets in; she is only pulled out of it by Bessie's appearance and a confirmed sense of Bessie's affection and respect for her. Bessie tells her that she must not act afraid of people, because it will make them dislike her — an odd aslant bit of counsel, yet Jane's precocious courage is able to respond. The next chapter finds Jane on her way to Lowood Institution.

4

Lowood is a charity school for the poor or orphaned genteel female destined to become a governess. It is a school for the poor controlled by the rich, an all-female world presided over by the hollow, Pharisaical male figure of Mr. Brocklehurst. He is the embodiment of class and sexual double-standards and of the hypocrisy of the powerful, using religion, charity, and morality to keep the poor in their place and to repress and humiliate the young women over whom he is set in charge. He is absolute ruler of this little world. However, within it, and in spite of his sadistic public humiliation of her, Jane finds two women unlike any she has ever met: the superintendent Miss Temple, and the older student Helen Burns.

Miss Temple has no power in the world at large, or against Mr. Brocklehurst's edicts; but she has great personal attractiveness, mental and spiritual charm and strength. Unlike the Reeds, she is of gentle birth yet not a snob; unlike Bessie she is not merely sympathetic but admirable. She cannot change the institution she is hired to administer but she does quietly try to make life more bearable for its inmates. She is maternal in a special sense: not simply sheltering and protective, but encouraging of intellectual growth. Of her Jane says later in the novel: ". . . to her instruction, I owed the best part of my acquirements; her friendship and society had been my continual solace; she had stood me in the stead of mother, governess, and latterly, companion."

Helen Burns is strong of will, awkward and blundering in the practical world yet intellectually and spiritually mature beyond her years. Severe, mystical, convinced of the transitory and insignificant nature of earthly life, she still responds to Jane's hunger for contact with a humane and sisterly concern. She is consumptive, soon to die, burning with an other-worldly intensity. Jane experiences Helen's religious asceticism as something impossible for herself, tinged with "an inexpressible sadness"; yet Helen gives her a glimpse of female character without pettiness, hysteria, or self-repudiation; it is Helen who tells her, "If all the world hated you, and believed you wicked, while your own conscience approved you, and absolved you from guilt, you would not be without friends."

Both Miss Temple's self-respect and sympathy, and Helen's transcendent philosophical detachment, are needed by Jane after her early humiliation by Mr. Brocklehurst. For if at Gateshead Hall Jane's temptations were victimization and hysteria, at Lowood, after her public ordeal, they are self-hatred and self-immolation.

Jane is acutely conscious of her need for love: she expresses it passionately to Helen Burns: ". . . to gain some real affection from you, or Miss Temple, or any other whom I truly love, I would willingly submit to have the bone of my arm broken, or to let a bull toss me, or to stand behind a kicking horse, and let it dash its hoof at my chest —." Her need for love is compounded with a female sense that love must be purchased through suffering and self-sacrifice; the images that come to her are images of willing submission to violence, of masochism. Helen calms her, tells her she thinks "too much of the love of human beings," calls on her to think beyond this life to the reward God has prepared for the innocent beyond the grave. Like Simone Weil, like St. Teresa, like Héloïse, Helen Burns substitutes a masculine God for the love of earthly men (or women) — a pattern followed by certain gifted imaginative women in the Christian era.

The discipline of Lowood and the moral and intellectual force of Helen and Miss Temple combine to give the young Jane a sense of her own worth and of ethical choice. Helen dies of consumption with Jane in her arms held like "a little child"; Miss Temple later marries an "excellent clergyman" and leaves Lowood. Thus Jane loses her first real mothers. Yet her separation from these two women enables Jane to move forward into a wider realm of experience.

> My world had for some years been in Lowood: my experience had been of its rules and systems; now I remembered that the real world was wide . . .

> I desired liberty; for liberty I gasped; for liberty I uttered a prayer; it seemed scattered on the wind then faintly blowing. I abandoned it and framed a humbler supplication. For change, stimulus. That petition, too, seemed swept off into vague space. "Then," I cried, half desperate, "grant me at least a new servitude!"

One of the impressive qualities of Charlotte Brontë's heroines, the quality which makes them more valuable to the woman reader than Anna Karenina, Emma Bovary, and Catherine Earnshaw combined, is their determined refusal of the romantic. They are not immune to it: in fact, they are far more tempted by it than are the cooler-headed heroines of Jane Austen; there is far more in their circumstances of orphaned wandering and intellectual eroticism to heat their imaginations — they *have*, in fact, more imagination. Jane Eyre is a passionate girl and woman; but she displays early an inner clarity which helps her to distinguish between intense feelings which can lead to greater fulfillment, and those which can only lead to self-destructiveness. The thrill of masochism is not for her, though it is one of her temptations as we have seen; having tasted a drop of it, she rejects it. In the central episode of the novel, her meeting with Mr. Rochester at Thornfield, Jane, young, inexperienced, and hungry for experience, has to confront the central temptation of the female condition — the temptation of romantic love and surrender.

5

It is interesting that the Thornfield episode is often recalled or referred to as if it *were* the novel *Jane Eyre*. So truncated and abridged, that novel would become the following: A young woman arrives as governess at a large country house inhabited by a small French girl and an older housekeeper. She is told that the child is the ward of the master of the house, who is traveling abroad. Presently the master comes home and the governess falls in love with him, and he with her. Several mysterious and violent incidents occur in the house which seem to center around one of the servants, and which the master tells the governess will all be explained once they are married. On the wedding day, it is revealed that he has a wife still alive, a madwoman who is kept under guard in the upper part of the house and who is the source of the sinister incidents. The governess decides that her only course of action is to leave her lover forever. She steals away from the house and settles in another part of the country. After some time she returns to the manor house to find it has burned to the ground, the madwoman is dead, and her lover, though blinded and maimed by the fire, is free to marry her.

Thus described, the novel becomes a blend of Gothic horror and Victorian morality. That novel might have been written by many a contributor to ladies' magazines, but it is not the novel written by Charlotte Brontë. If the Thornfield episode is central, it is because in it Jane comes to womanhood and to certain definitive choices about what it means to her to be a woman. There are three aspects of this episode: the house, Thornfield itself; Mr. Rochester, the Man; and the madwoman, Jane's alter ego.

Charlotte Brontë gives us an extremely detailed and poetically convincing vision of Thornfield. Jane reaches its door by darkness, after a long journey; she scarcely knows what the house is like till the next day when Mrs. Fairfax, the housekeeper, takes her through it on a tour which ends in the upper regions, on the rooftop. The reader's sense of its luxury, its isolation, and its mysteries is precisely Jane's, seen with the eyes of a young woman just come from the dormitory of a charity school—a young woman of strong sensuality. But it is the upper regions of the house which are of crucial importance—the part of the house Jane lives in least, yet which most affects her life. Here she first hears that laugh—"distinct, formal, mirthless"—which is ascribed to the servant Grace Poole and which she will later hear outside her own bedroom door. Here, too, standing on the roof, or walking up and down in the corridor, close to the very door behind which the madwoman is kept hidden, she gives silent vent to those feelings which are introduced by the telling phrase: "Anybody may blame me who likes . . ."

The phrase introduces a passage which is Charlotte Brontë's feminist manifesto. Written one hundred and twenty-six years ago, it is still having to be written over and over today, in different language but with essentially the same sense that sentiments of this kind are still unacceptable to many, and that in uttering them one lays oneself open to blame and to entrenched resistance:

> It is vain to say human beings ought to be satisfied with tranquility: they must have action; and they will make it if they cannot find it. Millions are condemned to a stiller doom than mine, and millions are in silent revolt against their lot. Nobody knows how many rebellions besides

political rebellions ferment in the masses of life which people earth. Women are supposed to be very calm generally; but women feel just as men feel; they need exercise for their faculties, and a field for their efforts as much as their brothers do; they suffer from too rigid a restraint, too absolute a stagnation, precisely as men would suffer; and it is narrow-minded in their more privileged fellow-creatures to say that they ought to confine themselves to making puddings and knitting stockings, to playing on the piano and embroidering bags. It is thoughtless to condemn them, or laugh at them, if they seek to do more or learn more than custom has pronounced necessary for their sex.

Immediately thereafter we are made to hear again the laugh of the madwoman. I want to remind you of another mad wife who appears in a novel of our own time—the woman Lynda in Doris Lessing's *The Four-Gated City*, who inhabits not the upper story but the cellar, and with whom the heroine Martha (like Jane Eyre an employee and in love with her employer) finally goes to live, experiencing her madness with her.

For Jane Eyre, the upper regions are not what Gaston Bachelard calls in *The Poetics of Space* "the rationality of the roof" as opposed to the unconscious and haunted world of the cellar.[4] Or, the roof is where Jane is visited by an expanding vision, but this vision, this illumination, brings her close to the madwoman captive behind the door. In Lessing's novel the madwoman is herself a source of illumination. Jane has no such contact with Bertha Rochester. Yet Jane's sense of herself as a woman—as equal to and with the same needs as a man—is next-door to insanity in England in the 1840s. Jane never feels herself to be going mad, but there is a madwoman in the house who exists as her opposite, her image horribly distorted in a warped mirror, a threat to her happiness. Just as her instinct for self-preservation saves her from earlier temptations, so it must save her from becoming this woman by curbing her imagination at the limits of what is bearable for a powerless woman in the England of the 1840s.

6

We see little of Bertha Rochester; she is heard and sensed rather than seen. Her presence is revealed by three acts when she escapes into the inhabited part of the house. Two of these are acts of violence against men—the attempted burning of Mr. Rochester in his bed-chamber, and the stabbing of her brother when he visits Thornfield. The third act is the visit to Jane's bedroom on the night before her wedding and the tearing of the wedding veil, the symbol of matrimony. (She does not, interestingly enough, attack Jane.) Only after Bertha's existence is publicly revealed is Jane taken into the madwoman's chamber and sees again, waking, "that purple face—those bloated features." Bertha is described as big, corpulent, virile, with a "grizzled mane" of hair like an animal's; earlier Jane had seen her as resembling "the foul German spectre—the Vampyr." In all this she is the antithesis of Jane, as Mr. Rochester points out: " 'That is *my wife*,' said he. 'Such is the sole conjugal embrace I am ever to know — such are the endearments which are to solace my leisure hours! And *this* is what I wished to have' (laying his hand on my shoulder) 'this young girl, who stands so grave and quiet at the mouth of hell, looking collectedly at the gambols of a demon . . .' "

In his long account of the circumstances of his marriage to Bertha — a marriage arranged for financial reasons by his father, but which he undertook for Bertha's dark sensual beauty — Rochester makes no pretense that he was not acting out of lust. Yet he repeatedly asserts *her* coarseness, "at once intemperate and unchaste," as the central fact of his loathing for her. Once she is pronounced mad, he has her locked up, and goes forth on a life of sexual adventures, one result of which has been the child Adèle, daughter of his French mistress. Rochester's story is part Byronic romance, but it is based on a social and psychological reality: the nineteenth-century loose woman might have sexual feelings, but the nineteenth-century *wife* did not and must not; Rochester's loathing of Bertha is described repeatedly in terms of her physical strength and her violent will — both unacceptable qualities in the nineteenth-century female, raised to the nth degree and embodied in a monster.

7

Mr. Rochester is often seen as the romantic Man of Fate, Byronic, brooding, sexual. But his role in the book is more interesting: he is certainly that which culture sees as Jane's fate, but he is not the fate she has been seeking. When she leaves Lowood for Thornfield, when she stands on the roof of Thornfield or walks across its fields longing for a wider, more expansive life, she is not longing for a man. We do not know what she longs for, she herself does not know; she uses terms like liberty, a new servitude, action. Yet the man appears, romantically and mysteriously, in the dusk, riding his horse — and slips and falls on the ice, so that Jane's first contact with him is with someone in need of help; he has to lean on her to regain his seat on horseback. Again at the novel's end it is she who must lead him, blinded by fire. There is something more working here than the introduction of a stock romantic hero.

Mr. Rochester offers Jane wider horizons than any she has known; travel, riches, brilliant society. Throughout the courtship there is a tension between her growing passion for him and her dislike of and uneasiness with the *style* of his love-making. It is not Rochester's sensuality that brings her up short, but his tendency to make her his object, his creature, to want to dress her up, lavish jewels on her, remake her in another image. She strenuously resists being romanticized as a beauty or a houri; she will, she tells him, be no part of his harem.

In his determination to possess Jane, Rochester is arrogant enough to lie to her three times. During the house party at which Jane, as governess, has to suffer the condescension and contempt of the ladies of the neighborhood, Rochester, disguised as an old Gypsy woman, comes to the door to read fortunes, and he attempts to trick Jane into revealing her feelings for him. It is clear, in this scene, that Rochester is well aware of the strength of Jane's character and is uneasy as to the outcome of his courtship and the kind of marriage he is going to propose to her. In making as if to read Jane's fate in her features, he tells her: ". . . that brow professes to say — 'I can live alone, if self-respect and circumstances require me to do so. I need not sell my soul to buy bliss. I have an inward treasure born with me, which can keep me alive if all the extraneous delights should be withheld, or offered only at a price I cannot afford to give.' " Abruptly at the end of this scene, he reveals himself. But he continues to carry on a flirtation with the heiress Miss Ingram, in order to arouse Jane's jealousy; he pretends to the last possible moment that he intends to marry Miss Ingram, till Jane, in turmoil at the prospect, confesses her grief at having to leave him. Her grief — but also, her anger at the position in which she has been placed:

> "I tell you I must go!" I retorted, roused to something like passion. "Do you think I can stay to become nothing to you? Do you think I am automaton? — a machine without feelings? . . . Do you think because I am poor, obscure, plain, and little, I am soulless and heartless? You think wrong! — I have as much soul as you — and full as much heart! . . . I am not talking to you now through the medium of custom, conventionalities, nor even of mortal flesh: it is my spirit that addresses your spirit; just as if both had passed through the grave and we stood at God's feet, equal — as we are!"

(Always a governess and always in love? Had Virginia Woolf really read this novel?)

8

Jane's parting interview with Mr. Rochester is agonizing; he plays on every chord of her love, her pity and sympathy, her vulnerability. On going to bed, she has a dream. Carried back to the Red Room, the scene of her first temptation, her first ordeal, in the dream, Jane is reminded of the "syncope," or swoon, she underwent there, which became a turning point for her; she is then visited by the moon, symbol of the matriarchal spirit and the "Great Mother of the night sky."[5]

> I watched her come — watched with the strangest anticipation; as though some word of doom were to be written on her disc. She broke forth as moon never yet burst from cloud: a hand first penetrated the sable folds and waved them away; then, not a moon, but a white human form shone in the azure, inclining a glorious brow earthward. It gazed

and gazed on me. It spoke to my spirit: immeasurably distant was the
tone, yet so near, it whispered in my heart—

"My daughter, flee temptation."

"Mother, I will."

Her dream is profoundly, imperiously, archetypal. She is in danger, as she
was in the Red Room; but her own spiritual consciousness is stronger in
womanhood than it was in childhood; she is in touch with the matriarchal
aspect of her psyche which now warns and protects her against that which
threatens her integrity. Bessie, Miss Temple, Helen Burns, even at moments the gentle housekeeper Mrs. Fairfax, have acted as mediators for her
along the way she has come thus far; even, it may be said, the terrible
figure of Bertha has come between Jane and a marriage which was not yet
ripe, which would have made her simply the dependent adjunct of Mr.
Rochester instead of his equal. Individual women have helped Jane Eyre
to the point of her severest trial; at that point she is in relation to the Great
Mother herself. On waking from this dream, she leaves Thornfield, with a
few pieces of clothing and twenty shillings in her purse, to set forth on foot
to an unknown destination.

Jane's rebellion against Rochester's arrogance—for in pleading with
her to stay with him against the laws of her own integrity, he is still
arrogant—forces her to act on her own behalf even if it causes him intense
suffering, even though she still loves him. Like many women in similar
circumstances, she feels that such an act of self-preservation requires her to
pay dearly. She goes out into the world without a future, without money,
without plans—a "poor, obscure, plain, and little" figure of a woman,
risking exposure to the elements, ostracism, starvation. By an act which
one can read as a final unconscious sacrificial gesture, she forgets her purse
with its few shillings in the stagecoach, and thus is absolutely destitute,
forced to beg for the leftovers a farmer's wife is about to feed to her pig. In
this whole portion of the novel, in which Jane moves through the
landscape utterly alone, there is a strong counterpull between female self-
immolation—the temptation of passive suicide—and the will and courage
which are her survival tools.

She is literally saved from death by two sisters, Diana and Mary,
living in a parsonage with their brother, the clergyman St. John Rivers.
Diana and Mary bear the names of the pagan and Christian aspects of the
Great Goddess—Diana or Artemis, the Virgin huntress, and Mary the
Virgin Mother. These women are unmarried bluestockings; they delight in
learning; in their remote parsonage they study German and read poetry
aloud. They live as intellectual equals with their brother; yet with Jane, in
her illness and convalescence, they are maternally tender and sensitive. As
time passes and Jane recovers and begins to teach in the village school,
Diana and Mary become her friends; for the first time since the death of

Helen Burns she has an intellectually sympathetic companionship with young women of her own age.

Once again, a man offers her marriage. St. John has been observing her for his own purposes, and finding her "docile, diligent, disinterested, faithful, constant, and courageous; very gentle, and very heroic" he invites her to accompany him as his fellow-missionary to India, where he intends to live and die in the service of his God. He needs a helpmate to work among Indian women; he offers her marriage without love, a marriage of duty and service to a cause. The cause is of course defined by him; it is the cause of patriarchal religion: self-denying, stern, prideful, and ascetic. In a sense he offers her the destiny of Milton's Eve: "He for God only, she for God in him." What St. John offers Jane is perhaps the deepest lure for a spiritual woman, that of adopting a man's cause or career and making it her own. For more than one woman, still today, the felt energy of her own existence is still diffuse, the possibilities of her life vague; the man who pressures to define it for her may be her most confusing temptation. *He* will give shape to her search for meaning, her desire for service, her feminine urge toward self-abnegation: in short—as Jane becomes soon aware—he will *use* her.

But St. John is offering Jane this "meaning" under the rubric of marriage—and from this "use" of herself she draws back in healthy repulsion.

> Can I receive from him the bridal ring, endure all the forms of love (which I doubt not he would scrupulously observe) and know that the spirit was quite absent? Can I bear the consciousness that every endearment he bestows is a sacrifice made on principle? No: such martyrdom would be monstrous. . . .

> As his curate, his comrade, all would be right: I would cross oceans with him in that capacity; toil under Eastern suns, in Asian deserts with him . . . admire and emulate his courage and devotion . . . smile undisturbed at his ineradicable ambition; discriminate the Christian from the man; profoundly esteem the one, and freely forgive the other. . . . But as his wife—at his side always, and always restrained, and always checked—forced to keep the fire of my nature continually low . . . *this* would be unendurable. . . .

> "If I were to marry you, you would kill me. You are killing me now" [she tells him].

> His lips and cheeks turned white—quite white.

> "*I should kill you—I am killing you?* Your words are such as ought not to be used—they are violent, unfeminine [*sic!*] and untrue . . ."

So she refuses his cause; and so he meets her refusal. In the meantime she has inherited an income; she has become independent; and at this point an extrasensory experience calls her back to Thornfield.

9

"Reader, I married him." These words open the final chapter of *Jane Eyre*. The question is, how and why is this a happy ending? Jane returns to Thornfield to find it "a blackened ruin"; she discovers Rochester, his left hand amputated and his eyes blinded by the fire in which he vainly attempted to save the life of his mad wife. Rochester has paid his dues; a Freudian critic would say he has been symbolically castrated. Discarding this phallic-patriarchal notion of his ordeal, we can then ask, what kind of marriage is possible for a woman like Jane Eyre?

Certainly not marriage with a castrate, psychic or physical. (St. John repels Jane in part because he is *emotionally* castrated.) The wind that blows through this novel is the wind of sexual equality—spiritual and practical. The passion that Jane feels as a girl of twenty or as a wife of thirty is the same passion—that of a strong spirit demanding its counterpart in another. Mr. Rochester needs Jane now—

". . . to bear with my infirmities . . . to overlook my deficiencies."

"Which are none, sir, to me."

She feels, after ten years of marriage, that "I am my husband's life as fully as he is mine." This feeling is not that of romantic love or romantic marriage: "To be together is for us to be at once as free as in solitude, as gay as in company. We talk—I believe, all day long; to talk to each other is but a more animated and an audible thinking."

Coming to her husband in economic independence and by her free choice, Jane can become a wife without sacrificing a grain of her Jane Eyre-ity. Charlotte Brontë sets up the possibility of this relationship in the early passages of the Thornfield episode, the verbal sparring of this couple who so robustly refuse to act out the paradigms of romantic, Gothic fiction. We believe in the erotic and intellectual sympathy of this marriage because it has been prepared by the woman's refusal to accept it under circumstances which were mythic, romantic, or sexually oppressive. The last paragraphs of the novel concern St. John Rivers: whose ambition is that of "the high master-spirit, which aims to a place in the first rank of those who are redeemed from the earth—who stand without fault before the throne of God, who share the last victories of the Lamb, who are called, and chosen, and faithful." We can translate St. John's purism into any of a number of kinds of patriarchal arrogance of our own day, whether political, intellectual, aesthetic, or religious. It is clear that Charlotte Brontë believes that human relations require something quite different: a transaction between people which is "without painful shame or damping humiliation" and in which nobody is made into an object for the use of anybody else.

In telling the tale of Jane Eyre, Charlotte Brontë was quite conscious, as she informed her publisher, that she was not telling a moral tale. Jane is not bound by orthodoxy, though superficially she is a creature of her time and place. As a child, she rejects the sacredness of adult authority; as a woman, she insists on regulating her conduct by the pulse of her own integrity. She will not live with Rochester as his dependent mistress because she knows that relationship would become destructive to her; she would live unmarried with St. John as an independent co-worker; it is he who insists this would be immoral. The beauty and depth of the novel lie in part in its depiction of alternatives — to convention and traditional piety, yes, but also to social and cultural reflexes internalized within the female psyche. In *Jane Eyre*, moreover, we find an alternative to the stereotypical rivalry of women; we see women in real and supportive relationship to each other, not simply as points on a triangle or as temporary substitutes for men. Marriage is the completion of the life of Jane Eyre, as it is for Miss Temple and Diana and Mary Rivers; but for Jane at least it is marriage radically understood for its period, in no sense merely a solution or a goal. It is not patriarchal marriage in the sense of a marriage that stunts and diminishes the woman; but a continuation of this woman's creation of herself.

Notes

An earlier version of this essay was given as a lecture at Brandeis University, 1972; the essay was first published in *Ms.* October 1973.

1. Virginia Woolf, *The Common Reader* (New York: Harcourt Brace, 1948), pp. 221–22. A. R., *1978:* Her *Common Reader* essays, so many of which were on women writers, bear nonetheless the marks of her struggle with masculine ideas of what is important, appropriate, or valid (a struggle eloquently described in her speech before the London National Society for Women's Service, 1931, reprinted with Woolf's own manuscript revisions in *The Pargiters*, Mitchell Leaska, ed. [New York: NYPL/Readex Books, 1977]). So, in 1925, writing of *Jane Eyre*, the future author of *To the Lighthouse* (1927), *A Room of One's Own* (1929), and *Three Guineas* (1938) was able to declare that "Charlotte Brontë does not attempt to solve the problems of human life. She is even unaware that such problems exist." Woolf herself still meets with similar incomprehension today.

2. Q. D. Leavis, Introduction to *Jane Eyre* (Baltimore: Penguin, 1966), p. 11.

3. A. R., *1978:* Ground-breaking as *Women and Madness* (1972) was in its documentation of the antiwoman bias of the psychoanalytic and psychotherapeutic professions, Chesler oversimplified, I believe, the mother-daughter relationship, perceiving it as almost entirely, if tragically, negative. To a large extent she resorts to "blaming the mother" for the daughter's disadvantaged position in patriarchy. The more we learn of actual female history (to take but one example, of the history of black women) the less we can generalize about the failure of mothers to cherish and inspirit daughters in a strong, female tradition.

4. Gaston Bachelard, *The Poetics of Space* (Boston: Beacon, 1967), pp. 17–18.

5. Erich Neumann, *The Great Mother* (Princeton, N. J.: Princeton University, 1972), pp. 55–59.

Plain Jane's Progress

Sandra M. Gilbert*

Her "mind contains nothing but hunger, rebellion, and rage," Matthew Arnold wrote of Charlotte Brontë in 1853.[1] He was referring to *Villette*, but he might as well have been speaking of *Jane Eyre*, for his response to Brontë was typical of the outrage generated in some quarters by her first published novel.[2] "*Jane Eyre* is throughout the personification of an unregenerate and undisciplined spirit," wrote Elizabeth Rigby in the *Quarterly Review* in 1848, and her "autobiography . . . is preeminently an anti-Christian composition. . . . The tone of mind and thought which has overthrown authority . . . abroad, and fostered Chartism and rebellion at home, is the same which has also written *Jane Eyre*."[3] Anne Mozley in 1853 recalled for the *Christian Remembrancer* that "Currer Bell" had seemed on her first appearance an author "soured, coarse, and grumbling; an alien . . . from society and amenable to none of its laws."[4] And Mrs. Oliphant related in 1855 that "ten years ago we professed an orthodox system of novel-making. Our lovers were humble and devoted . . . and the only true love worth having was that . . . chivalrous true love which consecrated all womankind . . . when suddenly *Jane Eyre* stole upon the scene, and the most alarming revolution of modern times has followed the invasion of *Jane Eyre*."[5]

We tend today to think of *Jane Eyre* as moral Gothic, "myth domesticated," *Pamela*'s daughter and *Rebecca*'s aunt, the archetypal scenario for all those mildly thrilling romantic encounters between a scowling Byronic hero (who owns a gloomy mansion) and a trembling heroine (who can't quite figure out the mansion's floor plan). Or, if we're more sophisticated, we concede Brontë's strategic as well as mythic abilities, study the patterns of her imagery, and count the number of times she addresses the reader. But still we overlook the "alarming revolution"—even Mrs. Oliphant's terminology is suggestive—which "followed the invasion of *Jane Eyre*." "Well, obviously *Jane Eyre* is a feminist tract, an argument for the social betterment of governesses and equal rights for women," Richard Chase grudgingly admitted in 1948.[6] But like most other modern critics, he believed that the novel's power arose from its mythologizing of Jane's confrontation with masculine sexuality.

Yet curiously enough, it was not primarily *Jane Eyre*'s sexuality which shocked Victorian reviewers but its "anti-Christian" refusal to accept the forms and customs of society—in short, its rebellious feminism. They were disturbed not so much by the proud, Byronic sexual energy of Rochester as by the Byronic pride and passion of Jane herself, not so much by the asocial sexual vibrations between hero and heroine as by the heroine's refusal to submit to her social destiny. "She has inherited in

*Reprinted from *Signs: Journal of Women in Culture and Society* 2, no. 4 (1977), 779–804, with permission of the University of Chicago Press and of the author.

fullest measure the worst sin of our fallen nature—the sin of pride,"
declared Mrs. Rigby. "Jane Eyre is proud, and therefore she is ungrateful,
too. It pleased God to make her an orphan, friendless, and penniless—yet
she thanks nobody, and least of all Him, for the food and raiment, the
friends, companions, and instructors of her helpless youth. . . . On the
contrary, she looks upon all that has been done for her not only as her
undoubted right, but as falling far short of it."[7] In other words, what
horrified the Victorians was Jane's anger. And perhaps they rather than
more recent critics were correct in their response to the book. For while the
mythologizing of repressed rage may parallel the mythologizing of repressed sexuality, it is far more dangerous to the order of society. The
occasional woman who has a weakness for black-browed Byronic heroes
can be accommodated in novels and even in some drawing rooms; the
woman who yearns to escape entirely from drawing rooms and patriarchal
mansions obviously cannot. And Jane Eyre, as Matthew Arnold, Mrs.
Rigby, Mrs. Mozley, and Mrs. Oliphant suspected, was such a woman.

Her story, providing a pattern for countless others, is a story of
enclosure and escape, a distinctively female bildungsroman in which the
problems encountered by the protagonist as she struggles from the imprisonment of her childhood toward an almost unthinkable goal of mature
freedom are symptomatic of difficulties Everywoman in a patriarchal
society must meet and overcome: oppression (at Gateshead), starvation (at
Lowood), madness (at Thornfield), and coldness (at Marsh End). Most
important, her confrontation not with Rochester but with Rochester's mad
wife, Bertha, is the book's central confrontation, an encounter not with
her own sexuality but with her own imprisoned "hunger, rebellion, and
rage," a secret dialogue of self and soul on whose outcome, as we shall see,
the novel's plot, Rochester's fate, and Jane's coming of age all depend.

Unlike many other Victorian novels, which begin with elaborate
expository paragraphs, *Jane Eyre* begins with a casual, curiously enigmatic remark: "There was no possibility of taking a walk that day." Both
the occasion ("that day") and the excursion (or the impossibility of one) are
significant: the first is the real beginning of Jane's pilgrim's progress
toward maturity; the second is a metaphor for the problems she must solve
in order to attain maturity. "I was glad" not to be able to leave the house,
the narrator continues: ". . . dreadful to me was the coming home in the
raw twilight . . . humbled by the consciousness of my physical
inferiority . . . " (p. 5).[8] As many critics have commented, Charlotte
Brontë consistently uses the opposed properties of fire and ice to characterize Jane's experiences, and her technique is immediately evident in these
opening passages.[9] For while the world outside Gateshead is almost
unbearably wintry, the world within is claustrophobic, fiery, like ten-year-
old Jane's own mind. Excluded from the Reed family group in the drawing
room because *she* is not a "contented, happy, little child"—excluded, that

is, from "normal" society—Jane takes refuge in a scarlet-draped window seat where she alternately stares out at the "drear November day" and reads of polar regions in Bewick's *History of British Birds.* The "death-white realms" of the Arctic fascinate her; she broods upon "the multiplied rigors of extreme cold" as if brooding upon her own dilemma: whether to stay in, behind the oppressively scarlet curtain, or to go out into the cold of a loveless world.

Her decision is made for her. She is found by John Reed, the tyrannical son of the family, who reminds her of her anomalous position in the household, hurls the heavy volume of Bewick at her, and arouses her passionate rage. Like a "bad animal," a "mad cat," she compares him with "Nero, Caligula, etc." and is borne away to the red-room, to be imprisoned literally as well as figuratively. For "the fact is," confesses the grown-up narrator ironically, "I was at that moment a trifle beside myself; or rather *out* of myself, as the French would say . . . like any other rebel slave. I felt resolved . . . to go all lengths" (pp. 8–9).

But if Jane was "out of" herself in her struggle against John Reed, her experience in the red-room, probably the most metaphorically vibrant of all her early experiences, forces her deeply into herself. For the red-room, stately, chilly, swathed in rich crimson, perfectly represents her vision of the society in which she is trapped, an uneasy and elfin dependent. "No jail was ever more secure," she tells us. And no jail, we soon learn, was ever more terrifying, either, because this is the room where Mr. Reed, the only "father" Jane has ever had, "breathed his last." It is, in other words, a kind of patriarchal death chamber; and here Mrs. Reed still keeps "divers parchments, her jewel-casket, and a miniature of her dead husband" in a secret drawer in the wardrobe (p. 11). Is the room haunted? the child wonders. At least, the narrator implies, it is realistically if not Gothically haunting, for the spirit of a society in which Jane has no clear place enlarges the shadows and strengthens the locks on the door.

Panicky, she stares into a "great looking glass" where her own image floats toward her, alien and disturbing. "All looked colder and darker in that visionary hollow than in reality," the adult Jane explains. But a mirror, after all, is also a sort of mysterious chamber in which images of the self are trapped like "divers parchments." So the child Jane, though her older self accuses her of mere superstition, correctly recognizes that she is doubly imprisoned. Frustrated and angry, she meditates on the injustices of her life, and fantasizes "some strange expedient to achieve escape from insupportable oppression—as running away, or, if that could not be effected, never eating or drinking more, and letting myself die" (p. 12).

Escape through flight or escape through starvation: the alternatives will recur throughout *Jane Eyre* and indeed throughout much other nineteenth- and twentieth-century literature by women. In the red-room, however, little Jane chooses (or is chosen by) a third, even more terrifying alternative: escape through madness. Seeing a ghostly, wandering light, as of the moon on the ceiling, she notices that "my heart beat thick, my head grew hot; a sound filled my ears, which I deemed the rushing of wings; something seemed near me; I was oppressed, suffocated; endurance broke down." The child screams and sobs in anguish, and then, adds the narrator coolly, "I suppose I had a species of fit," for her next memory is of waking in the nursery "and seeing before me a terrible red glare crossed with thick black bars" (p. 15) — merely the nursery fire, of course, but to Jane Eyre the child a terrible reminder of the experience she has just had and to Jane Eyre the adult narrator an even more dreadful omen of experiences to come.

For the little drama enacted on "that day" which opens *Jane Eyre* is in itself a paradigm of the larger drama that occupies the entire book: Jane's anomalous, orphaned position in society; her enclosure in stultifying roles and houses; and her attempts to escape through flight, starvation, and — in a sense which will be explained — madness. And that Brontë quite consciously intended the incident of the red-room to serve as a paradigm for the larger plot of her novel is clear not only from its position in the narrative but also from Jane's own recollection of the experience at crucial moments throughout the book: when she is humiliated at Lowood, for instance, and later, on the night she decides to leave Thornfield. In between these moments, moreover, Jane's pilgrimage consists of a series of experiences which are in one way or another variations on the central red-room motif of enclosure and escape.

My allusion to pilgriming is deliberate, for like the protagonist of Bunyan's book, Jane Eyre makes a life journey which is a kind of mythical progress from one significantly named place to another. Her story begins, quite naturally, at *Gateshead*, a starting point where she encounters the uncomfortable givens of her career: a family which is not her real family, a selfish older "brother" who tyrannizes over the household like a substitute patriarch, a foolish and wicked "stepmother," and two unpleasant, selfish "stepsisters." The smallest, weakest, and plainest child in the house, she embarks on her pilgrim's progress as a sullen Cinderella, an angry Ugly Duckling, immorally rebellious against the hierarchy that oppresses her: "I know that had I been a sanguine, brilliant, careless, exacting, handsome, romping child — though equally dependent and friendless, Mrs. Reed would have endured my presence more complacently," she reflects as an adult (p. 12).

But the child Jane cannot, as she well knows, be "sanguine and brilliant." Cinderella never is: nor is the Ugly Duckling, who, for all her swansdown potential, has no great expectations. "Poor, plain, and little," Jane Eyre — her name is of course suggestive — is invisible as air, the heir to nothing, secretly choking with ire. And Bessie, the kind nursemaid who befriends her, sings her a song that no fairy godmother would ever dream of singing, a song that summarizes the plight of all real Victorian Cinderellas:

> My feet they are sore, and my limbs they are weary,
>   Long is the way, and the mountains are wild;
> Soon will the twilight close moonless and dreary
>   Over the path of the poor orphan child. [p. 18]

A hopeless pilgrimage, Jane's seems, like the sad journey of Wordsworth's Lucy Gray, seen this time from the inside, by the child herself rather than by the sagacious poet to whom years have given a philosophic mind. Though she will later watch the maternal moon rise to guide her, now she imagines herself wandering in a moonless twilight that foreshadows her flight across the moors after leaving Thornfield. And the only hope her friend Bessie can offer is, ironically, an image that recalls the patriarchal terrors of the red-room and hints at patriarchal terrors to come—Lowood, Brocklehurst, St. John Rivers.

> Ev'n should I fall o'er the broken bridge passing,
>   Or stray in the marshes, by false lights beguiled,
> Still will my Father, with promise and blessing
>   Take to his bosom the poor orphan child.

It is no wonder that confronting such prospects young Jane finds herself "whispering to myself, over and over again" the words of Bunyan's Christian: " 'What shall I do?—What shall I do?' " (p. 33).[10]

What she does do, in desperation, is to burst her bonds again and again to tell Mrs. Reed what she thinks of her, an extraordinarily self-assertive act of which neither a Victorian child nor a Cinderella was ever supposed to be capable. Interestingly, her first such explosion is intended to remind Mrs. Reed that she, too, is surrounded by patriarchal limits: " 'What would Uncle Reed say to you if he were alive?' " Jane demands, commenting. "It seemed as if my tongue pronounced words without my will consenting to their utterance: something spoke out of me over which I had no control" (p. 23). And indeed even imperious Mrs. Reed appears astonished by these words. The explanation, "Something spoke out of me," is as frightening as the arrogance, suggesting the dangerous double consciousness that brought on the fit in the red-room. And when with a real sense that "an invisible bond had burst, and that I had struggled out into unhoped-for liberty," Jane tells Mrs. Reed that " 'I am glad you are no relation of mine' " (p. 31), the adult narrator remarks that "a ridge of lighted heath, alive, glancing, devouring, would have been a meet emblem of my mind"—as the nursery fire was, flaring behind its black gates, and -as the flames consuming Thornfield also will be.

Significantly, the event that inspires little Jane's final fiery words to Mrs. Reed is her first encounter with that merciless patriarch Mr.

Brocklehurst, who appears now to conduct her on the next stage of her pilgrimage. As many readers have noticed, this personification of the Victorian superego is — like St. John Rivers, his counterpart in the last third of the book — consistently described in phallic terms: he is a "black pillar" with a "grim face at the top . . . like a carved mask," almost as if he were a funereal and oddly Freudian piece of furniture (p. 26). But he is also rather like the wolf in "Little Red Riding Hood." "What a face he had . . . what a great nose! . . . And what large prominent teeth!" Jane Eyre exclaims, recollecting that terror of the adult male animal which must have wrung the heart of every female child in a period when men were defined as "beasts." Simultaneously, then, a pillar of society and a large bad wolf, Mr. Brocklehurst has come with news of hell to remove Jane to *Lowood*, the aptly named school of life where orphan girls are starved and frozen into proper Christian submission. Where else would a beast take a child but into a wood? Where else would a column of spirituality take a homeless orphan but to a sanctuary where there is neither food nor warmth? Yet "with all its privations," Lowood offers Jane a valley of refuge from "the ridge of lighted heath," a chance to learn to govern her anger while learning to become a governess in the company of a few women she admires.

Foremost among those Jane admires are noble Miss Temple and pathetic Helen Burns. And again, their names are significant. Miss Temple, for instance, with her marble pallor, is a sort of shrine of ladylike virtues: magnanimity, cultivation, courtesy — and repression. As if invented by Mrs. Sara Ellis, that indefatigable writer of conduct books for Victorian girls, she dispenses food to the hungry, visits the sick, encourages the worthy, and averts her glance from the unworthy. Yet it is clear enough that she has repressed her own share of madness and rage. Though she is angered by Mr. Brocklehurst's sanctimonious stinginess, for example, she listens to his sermonizing in ladylike silence, with her mouth "closed as if it would have required a sculptor's chisel to open it . . ." (p. 55). Certainly she will never allow "something" to speak through her, no wings will rush in her head, no fantasies of fiery heath disturb her equanimity.

Nevertheless, repressed as she is, Miss Temple is closer to a fairy godmother than anyone else Jane has met. By the fire in her pretty room, she feeds her starving pupils tea and emblematic seedcake, nourishing body and soul together. "We feasted," says Jane, "as on nectar and ambrosia." But still, she adds, Miss Temple always had "something . . . of state in her mien, of refined propriety in her language, which precluded deviation into the ardent . . ." (p. 63). Rather awful as well as very "awesome," Miss Temple embodies that impossible Victorian ideal, the woman-as-angel-in-the-house. Indeed, to the extent that her name defines her, she is even more house than angel, a beautiful set of marble columns designed to balance that bad pillar, Mr. Brocklehurst. And dispossessed Jane, who is not only poor, plain, and little but also fiery and ferocious, realizes that she can no more become such a woman than fleshly Cinderella can become her own fairy godmother.

Helen Burns, Miss Temple's other disciple, presents a different but equally impossible ideal to Jane: the ideal of self-renunciation, of all-consuming (and consumptive) spirituality. Like Jane "a poor orphan child," Helen longs alternately for her old home in Northumberland and for the true home which she believes awaits her in heaven. As if echoing the last stanzas of Bessie's song, "God is my father, God is my friend," she tells Jane; and one's duty, she declares, is to submit to the injustices of this life, in expectation of the ultimate justice of the next: " 'It is weak and silly to say you *cannot bear* what it is your fate to be required to bear' " (p. 48). Yet significantly Helen does no more than bear her fate. " 'I make no effort to be good, in Lowood's terms,' " she confesses, " 'I follow as inclination guides me' " (p. 49). Labeled a slattern for failing to keep her drawers in ladylike order, she meditates on Charles I, as if commenting on all inadequate fathers, and studies *Rasselas*, perhaps comparing Dr. Johnson's Happy Valley with the unhappy one in which she herself is immured. Clearly, despite her outward submissiveness, there is a vein of concealed resentment in Helen Burns, just as there is in Miss Temple. And like Miss Temple's, her name is important. Burning with spiritual passion, she also burns with anger, leaves her things "in shameful disorder," and dreams of freedom in eternity: " 'By dying young, I shall escape great sufferings' " (p. 71), she declares; and when the "fog-bred pestilence" of typhus decimates Lowood, she is carried off by her own fever for liberty, as if her body, like Jane's mind, were a "ridge of lighted heath . . . devouring" the dank valley in which she has been caged.

This is not to say, however, that Miss Temple and Helen Burns do nothing to help Jane come to terms with her fate. Both are in some sense mothers for Jane, as Adrienne Rich has pointed out,[11] comforting her, counseling her, feeding her, embracing her. And from Miss Temple in particular the girl learns to achieve "more harmonious thoughts. . . . I appeared a disciplined and subdued character" (p. 73). Yet because Jane is an Angrian Cinderella, a Byronic heroine, she can no more be "subdued" by conventional Christian wisdom than Manfred or Childe Harold could. Thus, when Miss Temple leaves Lowood, Jane tells us, "I was left in my natural element." Gazing out a window as she had on "that day" which opened her story, she gasps for liberty: "For liberty I uttered a prayer." Her way of confronting the world is still the Promethean way of fiery rebellion, not Miss Temple's way of ladylike repression, not Helen Burns's way of saintly renunciation. What she has learned from her two mothers is, at least superficially, to compromise. If pure liberty is impossible, she exclaims, "then . . . grant me at least a new servitude" (p. 74).

It is of course her eagerness for a new servitude that brings Jane to the painful experience that is at the center of her pilgrimage, the experience of

Thornfield, where, biblically, she is to be crowned with thorns, she is to be cast out into a desolate field, and most important, she is to confront the demon of rage who has haunted her since her afternoon in the red-room. Before the appearance of Rochester, however, and the intrusion of Bertha, she — and her readers — must explore Thornfield itself. This gloomy mansion is often seen as just another Gothic trapping introduced by Brontë to make her novel salable. Yet not only is Thornfield more realistically drawn than, say, Otranto or Udolpho; it is more metaphorically radiant than most Gothic mansions: it is the house of Jane's life, its floors and walls the architecture of her experience.

Beyond the "long cold gallery" where the portraits of alien ancestors hang the way the specter of Mr. Reed hovered in the red-room, Jane sleeps in a small, pretty chamber, as harmoniously furnished as Miss Temple's training has supposedly furnished her own mind. Youthfully optimistic, she notices that her "couch had no thorns in it" and trusts that with the help of welcoming Mrs. Fairfax "a fairer era of life was beginning for me, one that was to have its flowers and pleasures, as wells as its thorns and toils" (pp. 85–86). Christian, entering the Palace Beautiful, might have hoped as much.

Thornfield's third story is, however, even more obviously emblematic than the ambiguously pleasant room of her own which Jane finally receives. Here, amid the furniture of the past, down a narrow passage with "two rows of small black doors, all shut, like a corridor in some Bluebeard's castle" (p. 93), Jane first hears the "distinct formal mirthless laugh" of mad Bertha, Rochester's secret wife and in a sense her own secret self. And just above this sinister corridor, leaning against the picturesque battlements and looking out over the world like Bluebeard's bride's sister Anne, Jane is to long again for freedom, for "all of incident, life, fire, feeling that I . . . had not in my actual existence" (p. 96). These upper regions, in other words, symbolically miniaturize one crucial aspect of the world in which she finds herself: enigmatic ancestral relics wall her in; locked rooms guard a secret which may have something to do with *her*; distant vistas promise an inaccessible but enviable life.

Even more important, Thornfield's attic soon becomes a complex focal point where Jane's own rationality (what she has learned from Miss Temple) and her irrationality (her "hunger, rebellion, and rage") inter-sect.[12] She never, for instance, articulates her rational desire for liberty so well as when she stands on the battlements of Thornfield, looking out over the world. However offensive these thoughts may have been to Mrs. Rigby, the sequence of ideas expressed in the famous passage beginning "Anybody may blame me who likes" is as logical as anything in an essay by, say, Wollstonecraft or Mill. What is somewhat irrational, however, is the restlessness and passion — the pacing "backwards and forwards" — which as it were italicize Jane's little meditation on freedom. And even more irrational is the experience which accompanies her pacing: "When thus alone, I not unfrequently heard Grace Poole's laugh: the same peal, the same low, slow ha! ha! which, when first heard, had thrilled me: I heard, too, her eccentric murmurs; stranger than her laugh" (p. 96). Eccentric murmurs that uncannily echo the murmurs of Jane's imagination, and a low, slow ha! ha! which is a bitter refrain to the tale Jane's imagination creates. Despite Miss Temple's training, the "bad animal" who was first locked up in the red-room is, we sense, still lurking somewhere, behind a dark door, waiting for a chance to get free. That early consciousness of "something near me" has not yet been exorcised. Rather, it has intensified.

Many of Jane's problems, particularly those which find symbolic expression in her experiences in the third story, can be traced to her ambiguous status as a governess at Thornfield. As M. Jeanne Peterson has pointed out, every Victorian governess received strikingly conflicting messages (she was and was not a member of the family, was and was not a servant).[13] But Jane's difficulties arise also from her constitutional *ire*, and interestingly none of the women she meets at Thornfield has anything like that last problem, though all suffer from equivalent ambiguities of status. Aside from Mrs. Fairfax, the three most important of these women are little Adèle Varens, Blanche Ingram, and Grace Poole. All are important negative role models for Jane, and all suggest problems she must overcome before she can reach the independent maturity that is the goal of her pilgrimage.

The first, Adèle, though hardly a woman, is already a doll-like "little woman," evidently the natural daughter of Edward Rochester's dissipated youth. Accordingly, she longs for fashionable gowns rather than for freedom and sings and dances for her supper the way Céline, her mother, did, as if she were a clockwork temptress invented by E. T. A. Hoffmann. Where Miss Temple's was the way of the lady and Helen's that of the saint, Adèle's and her mother's are the ways of Vanity Fair, ways which have troubled Jane since her days at Gateshead. For how is a poor, plain governess to contend with a society that rewards beauty and style? May not Adèle, the daughter of a "fallen woman," be a model female in a world of prostitutes?

Blanche Ingram, also a denizen of Vanity Fair, presents Jane with a slightly different female image. Tall, handsome, and well born, she is worldly but, unlike Adèle and Céline, has a respectable place in the world: she is the daughter of "Baroness Ingram of Ingram Park" and — along with Georgiana and Eliza Reed — Jane's classically wicked stepsister. But while Georgiana and Eliza are dismissed to stereotypical fates, Blanche's history teaches Jane ominous lessons. First, the charade of "Bridewell" in which she and Rochester participate relays a secret message: conventional marriage is not only, as the attic implies, a "well" of mystery, it is a Bridewell, a prison, like the Bluebeard's corridor of the third story. Second, the charade of courtship in which Rochester engages her suggests a grim question: Is not the game of the marriage "market" a game even scheming women are doomed to lose?

Finally, Grace Poole, the most enigmatic of the women Jane meets at Thornfield, is obviously associated with Bertha, almost as if, with her pint of porter, her "staid and taciturn" demeanor, she were the madwoman's public representative. "Only one hour in the twenty four did she pass with her fellow servants below," Jane notes, attempting to fathom the dark "pool" of the woman's behavior; "all the rest of her time . . . she sat and sewed . . . as companionless as a prisoner in her dungeon" (p. 144). And that Grace is as companionless as, for instance, Bertha or Jane herself is undeniably true. Women in Jane's world, acting as agents for men, may be the keepers of other women. But both keepers and prisoners are bound by the same chains. In a sense, then, the "mystery of mysteries" which Grace Poole suggests to Jane is the mystery of Jane's own life, so that to question Grace's position is to question her own. Interestingly, Jane at one point speculates that Mr. Rochester may formerly have entertained "tender feelings" for the woman, and when thoughts of Grace's "uncomeliness" seem to refute this possibility, she cements her bond with Bertha's keeper by reminding herself that, after all, "*you* are not beautiful either, and perhaps Mr. Rochester approves you" (p. 137). Can appearances be trusted? Who is the slave, the master or the servant, the prince or Cinderella? What, in other words, are the real relationships between the master of Thornfield and all these women whose lives revolve around his? None of these questions can of course be answered without reference to the central character of the Thornfield episode, Edward Fairfax Rochester.

Jane's first meeting with Rochester is a fairy-tale meeting. Brontë deliberately stresses mythic elements: an icy twilight setting out of Coleridge or Fuseli, a rising moon, a great "lion-like" dog gliding through the shadows like "a North-of-England spirit, called a 'Gytrash' . . . [which] sometimes came upon belated travellers," followed by "a tall steed, and on its back a rider." Certainly the romanticized images seem to suggest that universe of male sexuality with which Richard Chase thought the Brontës were obsessed.[14] And Rochester, with "stern features and a heavy brow," himself appears the very essence of patriarchal energy, Cinderella's prince as a middle-aged warrior (pp. 98–99). Yet what are we to think of the fact that the prince's first action is to fall on the ice, together with his horse, and exclaim prosaically, " 'What the deuce is to do now?' " Clearly the master's mastery is not universal. Jane offers help, and Rochester, leaning on her shoulder, admits that " 'necessity compels me to make you useful.' " Later, remembering the scene, he confesses that he too had seen the meeting as a mythic one, though from a perspective entirely other than Jane's. " 'When you came on me in Hay Lane last night, I . . . had half a mind to demand whether you had bewitched my horse . . .' " (p. 107). His playful remark acknowledges *her* powers just as much as (if not more than) her vision of the Gytrash acknowledged his. Thus, though in one sense Jane and Rochester begin their relationship as master and servant, prince and Cinderella, Mr. B. and Pamela, in another way they begin as spiritual equals.

As the episode unfolds, their equality is emphasized in other scenes as well. For instance, though Rochester imperiously orders Jane to "resume your seat, and answer my questions" while he looks at her drawings, his response to the pictures reveals not only his own Byronic broodings but also his consciousness of hers: " 'Those eyes in the Evening Star you must have seen in a dream. . . . And who taught you to paint wind? . . . Where did you see Latmos?' " (p. 111). Though such talk would bewilder Rochester's other dependents, it is a breath of life to Jane, who begins to fall in love with him not because he is her master but in spite of the fact that he is, not because he is princely in manner but because, being in some sense her equal, he is the only qualified critic of her art and soul.

Their subsequent encounters develop their equality in even more complex ways. Rudely urged to entertain Rochester, Jane smiles "not a very complacent or submissive smile," obliging her employer to explain that " 'the fact is, once and for all, I don't wish to treat you like an inferior. . . . I claim only such superiority as must result from twenty years differences in age and a century's advance in experience' " (p. 117). Moreover, his long account of his adventure with Céline — an account which incidentally struck many Victorian readers as totally improper, coming from a dissipated older man to a virginal young governess[15] — emphasizes, at least superficially, not his superiority to Jane but his sense of equality with her. Both Jane and Brontë correctly recognize this point, which subverts those Victorian charges of impropriety. "The ease of his manner," Jane comments, "freed me from painful restraint. . . . I felt at these times as if he were my relation rather than my master" (p. 129). For of course, despite critical suspicions that Rochester is seducing Jane in these scenes, he is, on the contrary, solacing himself with her unseduceable independence in a world of self-marketing Célines and Blanches.

His need for her solace, strength, and parity is made clearer soon enough — on, for instance, the occasion when she rescues him from his burning bed (an almost fatally symbolic plight) and later on the occasion when she helps him rescue Richard Mason from the wounds inflicted by "Grace Poole." And that all these rescues are facilitated by Jane's and Rochester's mutual sense of equality is made clearest of all in the scene in which Jane, and only Jane of all the "young ladies" at Thornfield, fails to be deceived by Rochester in his gypsy costume; " 'With the ladies you must have managed well,' " she comments, but " 'you did not act the character of a gypsy with me' " (pp. 177–78). The implication is that he did not — or could not — because he respects "the resolute, wild, free thinking looking out of Jane's eyes as much as she herself does and understands that, just as he can see beyond her everyday disguise as plain Jane the governess, she can see beyond his temporary disguise as a gypsy fortune-teller — or his daily disguise as Rochester the master of Thornfield.

This last point is made again, most explicitly, by the passionate avowals of their first betrothal scene. Beginning with similar attempts at disguise and deception on Rochester's part (" 'One can't have too much of such a very excellent thing as my beautiful Blanche . . .' "), that encounter causes Jane in a moment of despair and ire to strip away her own disguises in her most famous assertion of her integrity:

> "Do you think, because I am poor, obscure, plain, and little, I am soulless and heartless? You think wrong! — I have as much soul as you, — and full as much heart! And if God had gifted me with some beauty, and much wealth, I should have made it as hard for you to leave me, as it is now for me to leave you. I am not talking to you now through the medium of custom, conventionalities, or even of mortal flesh: — it is my spirit that addresses your spirit: just as if both had passed through the grave, and we stood at God's feet equal, — as we are!" [p. 222]

Rochester's response is another casting away of disguises, a confession that he has deceived her about Blanche and an acknowledgement of their parity and similarity: " 'My bride is here,' " he admits, " 'because my *equal* is here, and my *likeness*.' " The energy informing both speeches is significantly not so much sexual as spiritual; the impropriety of its formulation is, as Mrs. Rigby saw, not moral but political, for Brontë appears here to have imagined a world in which the prince and Cinderella are democratically equal. Pamela is just as good as Mr. B., master and servant are profoundly alike. And to the marriage of true minds, it seems, no man or woman can admit impediment.

But of course, as we know, there is an impediment, and that impediment paradoxically preexists in both Rochester and Jane, despite their avowals of equality. Though Rochester, for instance, appears in both the gypsy sequence and the betrothal scene to have cast away the disguises that gave him mastery, it is obviously of some importance that those disguises were necessary in the first place. Why, Jane herself wonders, does Rochester have to trick people, especially women? What secrets are concealed behind the character he enacts? One answer is surely that he himself senses that his trickery is a source of power and therefore, in Jane's case at least, an evasion of that equality in which he claims to believe. Beyond this, however, it is clear that the secrets he is concealing or disguising throughout much of the book are themselves in Jane's — and Brontë's — view secrets of inequality.

The first of these is suggested both by his name, apparently an allusion to the dissolute Earl of Rochester, and by Jane's own reference to the Bluebeard's corridor of the third story: it is the secret of masculine potency, the secret of male sexual guilt. For like those pre-Byronic heroes the real Restoration Rochester and the mythic Bluebeard (indeed, in relation to Jane, like any experienced adult male), Rochester has "guilty" sexual knowledge which makes him in some sense her "superior." Though this may seem to contradict the point made earlier about his frankness to Jane, it really should not. Rochester's apparently improper recounting of his sexual adventures *is* an acknowledgment of Jane's equality with him. His possession of the hidden details of sexuality, however — his knowledge, that is, of the *secret* of sex, symbolized both by his doll-like daughter Adèle and by the locked doors of the third story behind which mad Bertha crouches like an animal — qualifies and undermines that equality. And though his puzzling transvestism, his attempt to impersonate a *female* gypsy, may be seen as a semiconscious attempt to reduce the sexual advantage his masculinity gives him (by putting on a woman's clothes, he puts on a woman's weakness), both he and Jane obviously recognize the hollowness of such a ruse. The prince is inevitably Cinderella's superior, Brontë saw, not because his rank is higher than hers but because it is *he* who will initiate *her* into the mysteries of the flesh.

That both Jane and Rochester are in some part of themselves conscious of the barrier which Rochester's sexual knowledge poses to their equality is further indicated by the tensions that develop in their relationship after their betrothal. Rochester, having secured Jane's love, almost reflexively begins to treat her as an inferior, a plaything, a virginal possession — for she has now become his initiate, his "mustard-seed," his " 'little sunny-faced . . . girl-bride' ": " '. . . It is your time now, little tyrant,' " he declares, " 'but it will be mine presently' " (p. 238). She, sensing his new sense of power, resolves to keep him "in reasonable check": "I can never bear being dressed like a doll by Mr. Rochester," she remarks, and more significantly, " 'I'll not stand you an inch in the stead of a seraglio. . . . I'll prepare myself to go out as a missionary to preach liberty to them that are enslaved' " (pp. 236–37). While such assertions have seemed to some critics merely the consequence of Jane's (and Brontë's) sexual panic, it should be clear from their context that they are, as is usual with Jane, political rather than sexual statements, attempts at finding emotional strength rather than expressions of weakness.

Finally, Rochester's ultimate secret, the secret that is revealed together with the existence of Bertha, the literal impediment to his marriage with Jane, is another and perhaps most surprising secret of inequality: but this time the hidden facts suggest the master's inferiority rather than his superiority. Rochester, Jane learns after the aborted wedding ceremony, had married Bertha Mason for status, for sex, for money, for everything but love and equality. " 'Oh, I have no respect for myself when I think of that act!' " he confesses. " 'An agony of inward contempt masters me' " (p. 264). And his statement reminds us of Jane's earlier assertion of her own superiority: " 'I would scorn such a union as the loveless one he hints he will enter into with Blanche: therefore I am better than you' " (p. 222). In a sense, then, the most serious crime Rochester has to expiate is not even the crime of exploiting others but the sin of self-exploitation, the sin of Céline and Blanche, to which he at least has seemed completely immune.[16]

That Rochester's character and life pose in themselves such substantial impediments to his marriage with Jane does not mean, however, that Jane herself generates none. For one thing, "akin" as she is to Rochester, she suspects him of harboring all the secrets we know he does harbor and raises defenses against them, manipulating her "master" so as to keep him "in reasonable check." In a larger way, moreover, all the charades and masquerades—the secret messages—of patriarchy have had their effect upon her. Though she loves Rochester the man, Jane has doubts about Rochester the husband even before she learns about Bertha. In her world, she senses, even the equality of love between true minds leads to the minor despotisms of marriage. " 'For a little while,' " she says cynically to Rochester, " 'you will perhaps be as you are now but . . . I suppose your love will effervesce in six months, or less. I have observed in books written by men, that period assigned as the farthest to which a husband's ardor extends' " (p. 228). He of course vigorously repudiates this prediction, but his argument—" '. . . You master me because you seem to submit' "—implies a kind of Lawrentian sexual tension and only makes things worse. For when he asks, " 'What does that inexplicable . . . turn of countenance mean?' " Jane's ironic smile, reminiscent of Bertha's mirthless laugh, signals a subtly hostile thought of "Hercules and Samson with their charmers." And that hostility becomes overt at the silk warehouse, where she notes that "the more he bought me, the more my cheek burned with a sense of annoyance and degradation . . ." (p. 236).

Jane's whole life pilgrimage has of course prepared her to be angry in this way at Rochester's—and society's—concept of marriage. Rochester's loving tyranny recalls John Reed's unloving despotism, and the erratic nature of his favors ("In my secret soul I knew that his great kindness to me was balanced by unjust severity to many others" [p. 129]) recalls Brocklehurst's hypocrisy. It is no wonder, then, that as her anger and fear intensify Jane begins to be symbolically drawn back into her own past and specifically to reexperience the dangerous sense of doubleness that began in the red-room. The first sign that this is happening is the powerfully depicted recurrent dream of a child she begins to have as she drifts into a romance with her master.

Significantly, Jane tells us that she "was awakened from companionship with this baby-phantom" on the night Bertha attacked Richard Mason, and "on the afternoon of the day following" she is actually called back into her past, back to Gateshead to see dying Mrs. Reed, who will remind her again of what she once was and potentially still is: " 'Are you Jane Eyre? . . . I declare she talked to me once like something mad, or like a fiend' " (p. 203). Even more significantly, the phantom child reappears in two dramatic dreams Jane has on the night before her wedding eve, during which she experiences "a strange, regretful consciousness of some barrier" dividing her from Rochester. In the first, "burdened" with the small, wailing creature, she is "following the windings of an unknown road" in cold, rainy weather, straining to catch up with her future husband but unable to reach him. In the second, she is walking among the ruins of Thornfield, still carrying "the unknown little child" and still following Rochester; as he disappears around "an angle in the road," she tells him, "I bend forward to take a last look; the wall crumbled; I was shaken; the child rolled from my knee, I lost my balance, fell, and woke" (pp. 247–49).

What are we to make of these strange dreams or — as Jane would call them — these "presentiments"? To begin with, it seems clear that the wailing child who appears in all of them corresponds to the "poor orphan child" of Bessie's song at Gateshead and therefore to the child Jane herself. That child's complaint — "My feet they are sore, and my limbs they are weary: / Long is the way, and the mountains are wild" — is still Jane's or at least the complaint of that part of her which resists a marriage of inequality. And though consciously Jane wishes to be rid of the heavy problem her orphan self presents, "I might not lay it down anywhere, however tired were my arms, however much its weight impeded my progress." In other words, until she reaches the goal of her pilgrimage — maturity, independence, true equality with Rochester (and therefore in a sense with the rest of the world) — she is doomed to carry her orphaned alter ego everywhere. The burden of the past cannot be sloughed off so easily — not, for instance, by glamorous love making, silk dresses, jewelry, a new name. Jane's "strange regretful consciousness of a barrier" dividing her from Rochester is thus a keen though disguised intuition of a problem she herself will pose.

Almost more interesting than the nature of the child image, however, is the *predictive* aspect of the last of the child dreams, the one about the ruin of Thornfield. As Jane correctly foresees, Thornfield *will* within a year become "a dreary ruin, the retreat of bats and owls." Have her own subtle and not so subtle hostilities to its master any connection with the catastrophe that is to befall the house? Is her clairvoyant dream in some sense a vision of wish fulfillment? And why specifically is she freed of the burden of the wailing child at the moment *she* falls from Thornfield's ruined wall?

The answer to all these questions is closely related to events which follow upon the child dream. For the apparition of a child in these crucial weeks preceding her marriage is only one symptom of a dissolution of personality which Jane seems to be experiencing at this time, a fragmentation of the self comparable to her "syncope" in the red-room. Another symptom appears early in the chapter that begins, anxiously, ". . . There was no putting off the day that advanced — the bridal day" (p. 241). It is her witty but nervous speculation about the nature of "one Jane Rochester, a person whom as yet I knew not," though "in yonder closet . . . garments said to be hers had already displaced [mine]: *for not to me appertained that . . . strange wraith-like apparel*" (p. 242; italics mine). Again, a third symptom appears on the morning of her wedding: she turns toward the mirror and sees "a robed and veiled figure, so unlike my usual self that it seemed almost the image of a stranger" (p. 252), reminding us of the moment in the red-room when all had "seemed colder and darker in that visionary hollow" of the looking glass "than in reality." In view of this frightening series of separations within the self — Jane Eyre splitting off from Jane Rochester, the child Jane splitting off from the adult Jane, and the image of Jane weirdly separating from the body of Jane — it is not surprising that another and most mysterious specter, a sort of "vampyre," should appear in the middle of the night to rend and trample the wedding veil of that unknown person Jane Rochester.

Literally, of course, the nighttime specter is none other than Bertha Mason Rochester. But on a figurative and psychological level, it seems suspiciously clear that the specter of Bertha is still another — indeed the most threatening — avatar of Jane. What Bertha now does, for instance, is what Jane wants to do. Disliking the "vapoury veil" of Jane Rochester, Jane Eyre secretly wants to tear the garment up. Bertha does it for her. Fearing the inexorable "bridal day," Jane would like to put it off. Bertha does that for her too. Resenting the new mastery of Rochester, whom she sees as "*dread* but adored" (italics mine), she wishes to be his equal in size and strength, so that she can battle him in the contest of their marriage. Bertha, "a big woman, in stature almost equalling her husband," has the necessary "virile force" (p. 258). Bertha, in other words, is Jane's truest and darkest double: the angry aspect of the orphan child, the ferocious secret self Jane has been trying to repress ever since her days at Gateshead. For, as Claire Rosenfeld has pointed out, "the novelist who consciously or unconsciously exploits psychological Doubles" frequently juxtaposes "two characters, the one representing the socially acceptable or conventional personality, the other externalizing the free, uninhibited, often criminal self."[17]

It is only fitting, then, that the existence of this criminal self imprisoned in Thornfield's attic is the ultimate legal impediment to Jane and Rochester's marriage and that its existence is paradoxically an impediment raised by Jane as well as by Rochester. For it now begins to appear, if it did not earlier, that Bertha has functioned as Jane's dark double throughout the governess' stay at Thornfield. Specifically, every one of Bertha's appearances — or more accurately her manifestations — has been associated with an experience (or repression) of anger on Jane's part. Jane's feelings of "hunger, rebellion, and rage" on the battlements, for instance, were accompanied by Bertha's "eccentric murmurs." Jane's apparently secure response to Rochester's apparently egalitarian sexual confidences was followed by Bertha's attempt to incinerate the master in his bed. Jane's unexpressed resentment of Rochester's manipulative gypsy masquerade found expression in Bertha's terrible shriek and her even more terrible attack on Richard Mason. Jane's anxieties about her marriage and in particular her fears of her own alien "robed and veiled" bridal image were objectified by the image of Bertha in a "white and straight" dress, "whether gown, sheet, or shroud I cannot tell." Jane's profound desire to destroy Thornfield, the symbol of Rochester's mastery and of her own servitude, will be acted out by Bertha, who burns down the house and destroys *herself* in the process, as if she were an agent of Jane's desire as well as her own. And finally, Jane's disguised hostility to Rochester, summarized in her terrifying prediction to herself that "you shall, yourself, pluck out your right eye; yourself cut off your right hand" (p. 261), comes strangely true through the intervention of Bertha, whose melodramatic death causes Rochester to lose both eye and hand.

These parallels between Jane and Bertha may at first seem somewhat strained. Jane, after all, is poor, plain, little, pale, neat, and quiet; while Bertha is rich, large, florid, sensual, and extravagant; indeed, she was once even beautiful, somewhat, Rochester notes, " 'in the style of Blanche Ingram.' " Is she not, then, as many critics have suggested, a monitory image rather than a double for Jane? "May not Bertha, Jane seems to ask herself," says Richard Chase, "be a living example of what happens to the woman who [tries] to be the fleshly vessel of the [masculine] élan?' "[18] Nevertheless, it is disturbingly clear from recurrent images in the novel that Bertha not only acts *for* Jane; she also acts *like* Jane. The imprisoned Bertha, running "backwards and forwards" on all fours, for instance, recalls not only Jane the governess, whose sole relief from mental pain was to pace "backwards and forwards" in the third story, but also that "bad animal" who was ten-year-old Jane, imprisoned in the red-room, howling and mad. Bertha's "goblin-appearance" — " 'half dream, half reality,' " says Rochester — recalls the lover's epithets for Jane: "malicious elf," "sprite," "changeling," etc. as well as his playful accusation that she had magically downed his horse at their first meeting. Rochester's description of Bertha as a "monster" (" 'A fearful voyage I had with such a monster in the vessel' " [p. 272]) ironically echoes Jane's own fear of being a monster ("Am I a monster? . . . Is it impossible that Mr. Rochester should have a sincere affection for me?" [p. 233]). Bertha's fiendish madness recalls Mrs. Reed's remark about Jane (" 'She talked to me once like something mad or like a fiend' ") as well as Jane's own estimate of her mental state ("I will hold to the principles received by me when I was sane, and not mad — as I am now" [p. 279]). And most dramatic of all, Bertha's incendiary tendencies recall Jane's early flaming rages at Lowood and at Gateshead as well as that "ridge of lighted heath" which she herself saw as emblematizing her mind in its rebellion against her position in society.

For despite all the habits of harmony she gained in her years at

Lowood, we must finally recognize, with Jane herself, that on her arrival at Thornfield she only "*appeared* a disciplined and subdued character" (italics mine). Crowned with thorns, finding that she is, in Emily Dickinson's words, "the wife without the sign," she represses her rage behind a subdued facade, but her soul's impulse to "dance like a bomb abroad," to quote Dickinson again,[19] will not be exorcised until the literal and symbolic death of Bertha frees her from the furies that torment her and makes possible a marriage of equality—makes possible, that is, wholeness within herself. At that point, significantly, when the Bertha in Jane falls from the ruined wall of Thornfield and is destroyed, the orphan child too, as her dream predicts, will roll from her knee—the burden of her past will be lifted—and she will wake. In the meantime, as Rochester says, " 'Never was anything at once so frail and so indomitable. . . . Consider the resolute wild free thing looking out of Jane's eye. . . . Whatever I do with its cage, I cannot get at it—the savage, beautiful creature' " (p. 280).

That the pilgrimage of this "savage, beautiful creature" must now necessarily lead her away from Thornfield is signaled, like many other events in the novel, by the rising of the moon, which accompanies a reminiscent dream of the red-room. Unjustly imprisoned now, as she was then, in one of the traps a patriarchal society provides for outcast Cinderellas, Jane realizes that this time she must escape through deliberation rather than through madness. The maternal moon, admonishing her (" 'My daughter, flee temptation!' ") appears to be "a white human form . . . inclining a glorious brow," a strengthening image, as Adrienne Rich suggests, of the Great Mother.[20] Yet this figure has its ambiguities, just as Jane's own personality does, for the last night on which she watched such a moon rise was the night Bertha attacked Richard Mason; and the juxtaposition of the two events on that occasion was almost shockingly suggestive: "The moon's glorious gaze roused me. . . . I half rose, and stretched my arm to draw the curtain. Good God! What a cry!" (p. 181). Now, as Jane herself recognizes, the moon has elicited from her an act as violent and self-assertive as Bertha's. "What was I?" she thinks, as she steals away from Thornfield. "I had injured—wounded—left my master. I was hateful in my own eyes" (p. 283). Yet though her flight may be as morally ambiguous as the moon's message, it is necessary for her own self-preservation. And soon, like Bertha, she is "crawling forwards on my hands and knees, and then again raised to my feet—as eager and determined as ever to reach the road."

Her wanderings on that road are a symbolic summary of those wanderings of the poor orphan child which constitute her entire life's pilgrimage. For like Jane's dreams, Bessie's song was an uncannily accurate prediction of things to come. "Why did they send me so far and lonely, / Up where the moors spread and grey rocks are piled?" Far and lonely indeed Jane wanders, starving, freezing, stumbling, abandoning her few possessions, her name, and even her self-respect in her search for a new home. For "men are hardhearted, and kind angels only / Watch'd o'er the steps of a poor orphan child." And like the starved wanderings of Hetty Sorrel in *Adam Bede*, her terrible journey across the moors suggests the essential homelessness of women in a patriarchal society. Yet because, unlike Hetty, Jane has an inner strength which her pilgrimage seeks to develop, "kind angels" finally do bring her to what is in a sense her true home, the house significantly called *Marsh End* (or Moor House) which is to represent the end of her march toward selfhood. Here she encounters Diana, Mary, and St. John Rivers, the "good" relatives who will help free her angry memories of that wicked step-family, the Reeds. And that the Riverses prove to be literally her relatives is not, in psychological terms, the strained coincidence some readers have suggested. For having left Rochester, having torn off the crown of thorns he offered and repudiated the unequal charade of marriage he proposed, Jane has now gained the strength to begin to discover her real place in the world. St. John helps her find a job in a school, and once again she reviews the choices she has had: "Is it better, I ask, to be a slave in a fool's paradise at Marseilles . . . or to be a village schoolmistress, free and honest . . . ?" (p. 316). Her unequivocal conclusion that "I was right when I adhered to principle and law" is one toward which the whole novel seems to have tended.

The qualifying word "seems" is, however, a necessary one. For though in one sense Jane's discovery of her family at Marsh End does represent the end of her pilgrimage, her progress toward selfhood will not be complete until she learns that "principle and law" in the abstract do not always coincide with the deepest principles and laws of her own being. Her early sense that Miss Temple's teachings had merely been superimposed on her native "hunger, rebellion, and rage" had already begun to suggest this to her. But it is through her encounter with St. John Rivers that she assimilates this lesson most thoroughly. As a number of critics have noticed, all three members of the Rivers family have resonant, almost allegorical names. The names of Jane's true "sisters," Diana and Mary, notes Adrienne Rich, recall the Great Mother in her dual aspects of Diana the huntress and Mary the virgin mother;[21] in this way as well as through their independent, learned, benevolent personalities, they suggest the ideal of female strength for which Jane has been searching. St. John, on the other hand, has an almost blatantly patriarchal name, one which recalls both the masculine abstraction of the gospel according to Saint John ("In the beginning was the Word") and the misogyny of Saint John the Baptist, whose patristic and evangelical contempt for the flesh manifested itself most powerfully in contempt for the female. Like Salome, whose rebellion against such misogyny Oscar Wilde was also to associate with the rising moon of female power, Jane must symbolically, if not literally, behead the abstract principles of this man before she can finally achieve her true independence.

At first, however, it seems that St. John is offering Jane a viable alternative to the way of life proposed by Rochester. For where Rochester, like his dissolute namesake, ended up appearing to offer a life of pleasure, a path of roses (albeit with concealed thorns), and a marriage of passion, St. John seems to propose a life of principle, a path of thorns (with no concealed roses), and a marriage of spirituality. His self-abnegating rejection of the worldly beauty Rosamund Oliver—another character with a strikingly resonant name—is disconcerting to the passionate and Byronic part of Jane; but at least it shows that, unlike hypocritical Brocklehurst, he practices what he preaches. And what he preaches is the Carlylean sermon of self-actualization through work: "Work while it is called today, for the night cometh wherein no man can work."[22] If she follows him, Jane realizes, she will substitute a divine Master for the master she served at Thornfield and replace love with labor—for " 'you are formed for labour, not for love,' " St. John tells her. Yet when, long ago at Lowood, she asked for "a new servitude," was not some such solution half in her mind? When pacing the battlements at Thornfield she insisted that "women need a field for their efforts as much as their brothers do" (p. 96), did she not long for some such practical "exercise"? "Still will my Father, with promise and blessing, / Take to his bosom the poor orphan child," Bessie's song had predicted. Is not Marsh End, then, the promised end and St. John's way the way to His bosom?

Jane's early repudiation of the spiritual harmonies offered by Helen Burns and Miss Temple is the first hint that, while St. John's way will tempt her, she must resist it. That, like Rochester, he is "akin" to her is clear. But where Rochester represents the fire of her nature, her cousin represents the ice. And while for some women ice may "suffice," for Jane, who has struggled all her life, like a sane version of Bertha, against the polar cold of a loveless world, it clearly will not. As she falls more deeply under St. John's "freezing spell," she realizes increasingly that to please him "I must disown half my nature." In fact, as St. John's wife she will be entering into a union even more unequal than that proposed by Rochester, a marriage reflecting once again her absolute exclusion from the life of wholeness toward which her pilgrimage has been directed. For despite the integrity of principle that distinguished him from Brocklehurst, despite his likeness to "the warrior Greatheart, who guards his pilgrim convoy from the onslaught of Apollyon" (p. 398). St. John is finally, as Brocklehurst was, a pillar of patriarchy, "a cold, cumbrous column" (p. 346). But where Brocklehurst had removed Jane from the imprisonment of Gateshead only to immure her in a dank valley of starvation and even Rochester had tried to make her the "slave of passion," St. John wants to imprison the "resolute wild free thing" that is her soul in the ultimate cell, the "iron shroud" of principle (p. 355).

Though in many ways St. John's attempt to "imprison" Jane may seem the most irresistible of all, coming as it does at a time when she is congratulating herself on just that adherence to "principle and law" which he recommends, she escapes from his fetters more easily than she had escaped from either Brocklehurst or Rochester. Figuratively speaking, this is a measure of how far she has traveled in her pilgrimage toward maturity. Literally, however, her escape is facilitated by two events. First, having found what is, despite all its ambiguities, her true family, Jane has at last come into her inheritance. Jane Eyre is now the heir of that uncle in Madeira whose first intervention in her life had been, appropriately, to define the legal impediment to her marriage with Rochester; now, literally as well as figuratively, she is an independent woman, free to go her own way and follow her own will. But her freedom is also signaled by a second event; the death of Bertha.

Her first "presentiment" of that event comes dramatically, as an answer to a prayer for guidance. St. John is pressing her to reach a decision about his proposal of marriage. Believing that "I had now put love out of the question, and thought only of duty," she "entreats Heaven" to "show me, show me the path." As always at major moments in Jane's life, the room is filled with moonlight, as if to remind her that powerful forces are still at work both without and within her. And now, because such forces are operating, she at last hears — she is receptive to — the bodiless cry of Rochester: "Jane! Jane! Jane!" Her response is an immediate act of self-assertion. "I broke from St. John . . . It was *my* time to assume ascendancy. *My* powers were in play and in force" (pp. 369–70). But her sudden forcefulness, like her "presentiment" itself, is the climax of all that has gone before. Her new and apparently telepathic communion with Rochester, which many critics have seen as needlessly melodramatic, has been made possible by her new independence and Rochester's new humility. The plot device of the cry is merely a sign that the relationship for which both lovers have always longed is now possible, a sign that Jane's metaphoric speech of the first betrothal scene has been translated into reality: "My spirit . . . addresses your spirit, just as if both had passed through the grave, and we stood at God's feet, equal — as we are!" For to the marriage of Jane's and Rochester's true minds there is now, as Jane unconsciously guesses, no impediment.

Jane's return to Thornfield, her discovery of Bertha's death and of the ruin her dream had predicted, her reunion at Ferndean with the maimed and blinded Rochester, and their subsequent marriage form an essential epilogue to that pilgrimage toward selfhood which had in other ways concluded at Marsh End with Jane's realization that she could not marry St. John. At that moment, "The wondrous shock of feeling had opened the doors of the soul's cell, and wakened it out of its sleep" (p. 371). For at that moment she had been irrevocably freed from the burden of her past — freed both from the raging specter of Bertha (which had already fallen in fact from the ruined wall of Thornfield) and from the self-pitying specter of the orphan child (which had symbolically, as in her dream, rolled from her knee). And at that moment, again as in her dream, she had *wakened* to her own self, her own needs. Similarly Rochester, "caged eagle" that he seems (p. 379), has been freed from what was for him the burden of Thornfield, though at the same time he appears to have been fettered by the injuries he received in attempting to rescue Jane's mad double from the flames devouring his house. That his "fetters" pose no impediment to a new marriage, that he and Jane are now, in reality, equals, is the thesis of the Ferndean section.

Many critics, starting with Richard Chase, have seen Rochester's injuries as "a symbolic castration," a punishment for his early profligacy and a sign that Brontë (as well as Jane herself), fearing male sexual power, could only imagine marriage as a union with a diminished Samson. "The tempo and energy of the universe can be quelled, we see, by a patient, practical woman," notes Chase ironically.[23] And there is an element of truth in this idea. The angry Bertha in Jane *had* wanted to punish Rochester, to burn him in his bed, destroy his house, cut off his hand, and pluck out his overmastering "full falcon eye." It had not been her goal, however, to quell the "energy of the universe" but simply to make herself an equal of the world Rochester represents. And surely another important symbolic point is implied by the lovers' reunion at Ferndean: when both were physically whole they could not in a sense *see* each other because of the social disguises — master/servant, prince/Cinderella — blinding them; but now that those disguises have been shed, now that they are equals, they can (though one is blind) see and speak even beyond the medium of the flesh. Apparently sightless, Rochester — in the tradition of blinded Gloucester — now sees more clearly than he did when as a "mole-eyed blockhead" he married Bertha Mason (p. 269). Apparently mutilated, he is paradoxically stronger than he was when he ruled Thornfield; for now, like Jane, he draws his powers from within himself rather than from inequity, disguise, deception. Then, at Thornfield, he was "no better than the old lightning-struck chestnut tree in the orchard," whose ruin foreshadowed the catastrophe of his relationship with Jane. Now, as Jane tells him, he is " 'green and vigorous. Plants will grow about your roots whether you ask them or not' " (p. 391). And now, being equals, he and Jane can afford to depend upon each other with no fear of one exploiting the other.

Nevertheless, despite the optimistic portrait of an egalitarian relationship that Brontë seems to be drawing here, there is, as Robert Bernard Martin points out, "a quiet autumnal quality" about the scenes at Ferndean.[24] The house itself, set deep in a dark forest, is old and decaying: Rochester had not even thought it suitable for the loathsome Bertha, and its valley-of-the-shadow quality makes it seem rather like a Lowood, a school of life where Rochester must learn those lessons Jane herself absorbed so early. As a dramatic setting, moreover, Ferndean is notably stripped and asocial, so that the physical isolation of the lovers suggests their spiritual isolation in a world where such marriages as theirs are rare, if not impossible. True minds, Brontë seems to be saying, must withdraw into a remote forest, even a wilderness, in order to circumvent the strictures of society.

Does Brontë's rebellious feminism, that "irreligious" dissatisfaction with the social order noted by Victorian Mrs. Rigby, compromise itself in this withdrawal? Has Jane exorcised the rage of orphanhood only to retreat from the responsibilities her own principles implied? Tentative answers to these questions can be derived more easily from *The Professor, Shirley,* and *Villette* than from *Jane Eyre;* for the qualified and even (as in *Villette*) indecisive endings of Brontë's other novels suggest that she herself was unable clearly to envision viable solutions to the problem of patriarchal oppression. In all her books, writing in a sort of trance,[25] she was able to act out that passionate drive toward freedom which offended agents of the status quo, but in none was she able consciously to define the full meaning of achieved freedom—perhaps because no one, not even Wollstonecraft or Mill, could adequately describe a society so drastically altered that the matured Jane and Rochester could really live in it.

What Brontë could not logically define, however, she could embody in tenuous but suggestive imagery and in her last, perhaps most significant redefinitions of Bunyan. Nature in the largest sense seems to be now on the side of Jane and Rochester. *Ferndean,* as its name implies, is without artifice—"no flowers, no garden-beds"—but it is as green as Jane tells Rochester he will be, green and ferny and fertilized by soft rains. Here, isolated from society but flourishing in a natural order of their own making, Jane and Rochester will become physically "bone of [each other's] bone, flesh of [each other's] flesh" (p. 397); and here the healing powers of nature will eventually restore the sight of one of Rochester's eyes. Here, in other words, nature, unleashed from social restrictions, will do "no miracle—but her best" (p. 370). For not the Celestial City but a natural paradise, the country of Beulah "upon the borders of heaven," where "the contract between bride and bridegroom [is] renewed," has all along been, as we now realize, the goal of Jane's pilgrimage.[26]

As for the Celestial City itself, that goal, Brontë implies here (though she will later have second thoughts), is the dream of those who accept inequities on earth, one of the many tools used by patriarchy to keep, say, governesses in their "place." Because she believes this so deeply, she quite consciously concludes *Jane Eyre* with an allusion to *Pilgrim's Progress* and a half-ironic apostrophe to that apostle of celestial transcendence, that shadow of "the warrior Greatheart," St. John Rivers. "His," she tells us, "is the exaction of the apostle, who speaks but for Christ when he says— 'Whosoever will come after me, let him deny himself and take up his cross and follow me' " (p. 398). For it was finally to repudiate such a crucifying denial of the self that Brontë's "hunger, rebellion, and rage" led her to write *Jane Eyre* in the first place and to make it an "irreligious" redefinition—almost a parody—of John Bunyan's vision.[27] And the astounding progress toward equality of plain Jane Eyre, whom Mrs. Rigby correctly saw as "the personification of an unregenerate and undisciplined spirit," answers by its outcome the better question Emily Dickinson was to ask fifteen years later: " 'My Husband'—women say— / Stroking the Melody— / Is *this*—the way?' "[28] No, Jane declares in her flight from Thornfield, *that* is not the way. *This*, she says—this marriage of true minds at Ferndean—this is the way. Qualified and isolated as her way may be, it is at least an emblem of hope. Certainly Brontë was never again to indulge in quite such an optimistic imagining.

Notes

This essay is part of a two-volume study of nineteenth- and twentieth-century literature by women, entitled *The Madwoman in the Attic*, which I am at present writing in collaboration with Susan Gubar of Indiana University. A number of the major points in the piece therefore are as much Susan's as my own, although any inadequacies in their formulation here are entirely mine. I should note, in addition, that Ellen Moers's *Literary Women* and Helene Moglen's perceptive new biographical study of Charlotte Brontë, with their fresh evaluation of *Jane Eyre*, both appeared too late for me to make reference to them in my work; but their approaches are similar to mine, and I am gratified to think that, working independently, we have all reached compatible conclusions.

1. Matthew Arnold, *Letters of Matthew Arnold*, ed. George W. E. Russell (New York and London: Macmillan Co., 1896), 1:34.

2. It should be noted, however, that *Jane Eyre* (like *Villette*) was warmly praised by many reviewers, usually for what George Henry Lewes, writing in *Fraser's Magazine* (36 [December 1847]: 690–93), called its "deep, significant reality."

3. *Quarterly Review* 84 (December 1848): 173–74.

4. *Christian Remembrancer* 25 (June 1853): 423–43.

5. *Blackwood's Magazine* 77 (May 1855): 554–68.

6. Richard Chase, "The Brontës, or Myth Domesticated," in *Jane Eyre*, ed. Richard J. Dunn (New York: W. W. Norton & Co., 1971), pp. 468, 464 (first published in *Forms of Modern Fiction*, ed. William V. O'Connor [Minneapolis: University of Minnesota Press, 1948]).

7. *Quarterly Review* 84 (December 1848): 173–74. That Charlotte Brontë was herself quite conscious of the "revolutionary" nature of many of her ideas is clearly indicated by the fact that she puts some of Mrs. Rigby's words into the mouth of the unpleasant Miss Hardman in *Shirley*.

8. All page references to *Jane Eyre* are to the Norton Critical Edition, ed. Richard J. Dunn (New York: W. W. Norton & Co., 1971).

9. See, e.g., David Lodge, "Fire and Eyre: Charlotte Brontë's War of Earthly Elements," in *The Brontës*, ed. Ian Gregor (Englewood Cliffs, N.J.: Prentice-Hall, Inc. 1970), pp. 110–36.

10. See *The Pilgrim's Progress*: ". . . Behold I saw a man clothed with rags . . . he brake out with a lamentable cry, saying, 'What shall I do?' " (New York: Airmont Library,

1969; the quotation is on p. 17). Brontë made even more extensive references to *The Pilgrim's Progress* in *Villette*, but in her use of Bunyan she was typical of many nineteenth-century novelists who—from Thackeray to Louisa May Alcott—relied on his allegory to give point and structure to their own fiction. For comments on Brontë's allusions to *The Pilgrim's Progress* in *Villette*, see Q. D. Leavis, introduction to *Villette* (New York: Harper & Row, 1972), pp. vii–xli.

11. Adrienne Rich, "Jane Eyre: The Temptations of a Motherless Woman," *Ms.* 2, no. 4 (October 1973): 69–70.

12. In *The Poetics of Space* (Boston: Beacon Press, 1969), Gaston Bachelard speaks of "the rationality of the roof" as opposed to "the irrationality of the cellar."

13. See M. Jeanne Peterson, "The Victorian Governess: Status Incongruence in Family and Society," in *Suffer and Be Still: Women in the Victorian Age*, ed. Martha Vicinus (Bloomington: Indiana University Press, 1972).

14. Chase, n. 6 above.

15. See, e.g., Mrs. Oliphant, "The Sisters Brontë," in *Women Novelists of Queen Victoria's Reign* (London: Hurst & Blackett, 1897), p. 19.

16. In a sense, Rochester's "contemptible" prearranged marriage to Bertha Mason is also a consequence of patriarchy or at least of the patriarchal custom of primogeniture. A younger son, he was encouraged by his father to marry for money and status because sure provisions for his future could be made in no other way.

17. Claire Rosenfeld, "The Shadow Within: The Conscious and Unconscious Use of the Double," in *Stories of the Double*, ed. Albert J. Guerard (Philadelphia: J. B. Lippincott Co., 1967), p. 314. Rosenfeld also notes that, "when the passionate uninhibited self is a woman, she more often than not is dark. . . ." Bertha, of course, is a Creole—swarthy, "livid," etc.

18. Chase, p. 467.

19. See Emily Dickinson, #J. 1072, "Title divine—is mine! / The Wife—without the Sign!" and #J. 512, "The Soul has Bandaged Moments," in *The Complete Poems of Emily Dickinson*, ed. Thomas J. Johnson (Boston: Little, Brown & Co., 1955).

20. Rich, p. 106.

21. Ibid.

22. Thomas Carlyle, *Sartor Resartus*, chap. 9.

23. Chase, p. 467.

24. Robert Bernard Martin, *The Accents of Persuasion: Charlotte Brontë's Novels* (New York: W. W. Norton & Co., 1966), p. 90.

25. For a discussion of Brontë's "trance-writing"—her habit, e.g., of literally writing with her eyes shut—see the excerpts from her Roe Head journal quoted by Winifred Gérin in *Charlotte Brontë: The Evolution of Genius* (Oxford: Oxford University Press, 1967) and in Charlotte Brontë, *Five Novelettes*, ed. Winifred Gérin (London, 1971).

26. See *The Pilgrim's Progress*, pp. 140–41.

27. Brontë's use of *The Pilgrim's Progress* in *Villette* is much more conventional. Lucy Snowe seems to feel that she will only find true bliss after death, when she literally enters the Celestial City.

28. See Dickinson, #J. 1072, "Title divine—is mine!"

Jane Eyre: Woman's Estate

Maurianne Adams*

The experience of rereading *Jane Eyre* as an adult is unnerving, to say the least. This is not the novel we were engrossed by in our teens or preteens, when we saw in Jane's dreadful childhood the image of our own fantasies of feeling unloved and forever unloveable, and of fearing that we were "unpromising" girlchildren, whose lack of beauty and unpredictable tempers cut us off from an imaginable and acceptable future. Perhaps I am writing too personally, but I suspect we share, if only in transient fantasy, an attachment to several girlhood books — *Jane Eyre, The Secret Garden, Sara Crewe,* and the many versions of Cinderella's story — and an attachment to the portrait they convey of the unhappy and mostly secret underside of girlhood. I do not mean to overdarken our early readings of Jane's saga, for the other side of that coin, which we latched onto with equal fervor and which also fed our fantasies, was the happy ending, the relief we felt when this homely and stubborn Cinderella also made good, reunited finally with her loving and understanding Edward Rochester.

The reexperiencing and rethinking of this most important novel unnerves the adult reader, I think, because the elements we retain from earlier memories of Jane interact with our more mature understanding of the enormous complications that beset her difficult, strongly willed and ambivalent development from child to woman. Jane *is* (what most of us "merely" fantasize ourselves to be) an extreme case: she is an unloved, unlovely, unpleasant, poor and dependent orphan child, without prospects, and without a hopeful future. It is this daily and daytime nightmare of childhood burdensomeness and of unwelcome and unrelieved dependence — personal, familial, social, and economic — that haunts Jane's slumbers right up to the eve of her marriage to Rochester. Driving her from Thornfield, it is exorcized only by a full replication of her childhood, through a process that takes her to the breast of "the universal mother" (Jane's words, not mine) on the hard ground at Whitcross, and then to a welcomed and beloved recuperation at Moor House, where she grows from the surrogate younger sister into the financial resource of an entire family of equals — a family, mirabile dictu, that turns out to be her true family.

To adapt a Wordsworthian and Freudian adage to literal interpretive purposes, the child Jane is mother to the woman. Her hopes and dreams of a happy adulthood, fed by the generous love of Rochester and the perfect fit of his nature to hers, are nonetheless undermined by her conscious recognition of the disparity in their position and her inevitable reliance upon him for everything — money, status, and family. Her anticipation of her situation as Rochester's wife reactivates an unconscious fear that her

*Reprinted from *The Authority of Experience: Essays in Feminist Criticism*, ed. Arlyn Diamond and Lee R. Edwards (Amherst: University of Massachusetts Press, 1977), 137–59. © 1977 by the University of Massachusetts Press.

childhood experience might now be perpetuated into adult life. The recurrent burdensome children who haunt Jane's nightmares on the evenings preceding the intended nuptials, come, with some comment on her own part as to their portentousness if not their literal application, as a warning from within herself, that this marriage, in these terms, simply will not do. "Gentlemen in his station are not accustomed to marry their governesses," warns Mrs. Fairfax. Accordingly, the sudden emergence of Bertha Mason Rochester from her attic hideaway confirms and verifies what Jane had already feared, that as Rochester's wife she would be but his mistress, a kept woman, without any independent social status. Thus, even without foreseeing Bertha, the careful reader of Chapters 24 and 25 will find that the spectre of unrelieved dependency, however beloved and welcome Jane may feel in her lover's arms, gives urgency to her procrastinations and her efforts to find some other way out. She postpones the inevitable wedding day until she can do so no longer, she looks at her wedding dress and the packed trunks labelled with her new name with fear and trepidation, she feels degraded by Rochester's lavish gifts of jewels and satins, and she writes to her Uncle John in Madeira to track down the unexpected hint of her inheritance: "if I had a prospect of one day bringing Mr. Rochester an accession of fortune, I could better endure to be kept by him now."[1]

Not only does the revelation of Bertha's existence verify Jane's fears, that as a dependent wife she would be little better than a mistress; it also reactivates her fears that as a dependent she might with time become burdensome once again, the tiresome successor of Céline, Giacinta, and Clara, of whom Rochester freely admits, "Hiring a mistress is the next worst thing to buying a slave: both are often by nature, and always by position, inferior: and to live familiarly with inferiors is degrading" (p. 274).

Quite simply stated, Jane Eyre's childhood and her efforts to achieve adult womanhood are characterized by two needs, at times in competition with one another: the one to love and be loved, and the other to be somebody in her own right, a woman of achievement and integrity, with an outlet in the world for her passions and her energies.

The major theme is, I believe, the first of these two, the romantic theme, and the novel concludes in romantic terms, although I might note the forested-in, stagnant and physically oppressive atmosphere at Ferndean. (It was too unhealthy to send Bertha there!) I think that the hemmed-in and darkened visual quality at Ferndean indicates the price exacted by domestic romance, the impossibility of reconciling Jane's desperate need to be loved, to be useful, with her less urgent venturesomeness and independent curiosity.

Necessarily, these two major themes have further complications in Jane's narrative, just as they do often enough for women in real life. The first of these, the romantic theme, has interlocking elements I have commented on already — (1) Jane's need to *be* loved (this, I believe, is a more clearly and urgently articulated force in the novel than her direct experience of loving) as it competes with fears of a life without love and is fed by childhood starvation for love; (2) her causal linking of lovelessness and rejection with the continued experience of economic, social, and personal dependence; (3) her alienation from the social and domestic world around her (Reeds, Brocklehursts, Ingrams, and Eshtons) and her fears that they constitute the *only* world, that she will remain alienated by her lack of beauty and unfeminine traits (4) her uncontrollable outbursts of mutiny and rage which might afford momentary relief to her integrity and sense of outraged justice but which scarcely endear her to the social superiors whose love and approval she craves; and (5) her explicit differentiation of her "real" family (Reeds are all she knows, until her fortuitous encounter with the Rivers) from her "spiritual" kin (first Helen Burns, later Edward Rochester), a split perpetuated until the happy Moor House resolution of the familial elements — blood, spiritual affinity, economic inheritance and interdependence, even religious persuasion and social status.

The second theme, the desire to *be* somebody, complicates integrity with a drive toward upward mobility. This second theme as it emerges in the novel is uneven and inconsistent, characterized by the sporadic outbursts of mutiny and rage mentioned above, but in every instance undermined by regret, loneliness, and an over-eagerness to serve others as a means of earning their approval and love.

Jane Eyre, like other novels about women, traces the competing and possibly irreconcilable needs for perpetual love and perpetual autonomy. Jane's brief stint as a teacher at Morton constitutes her single experiment in autonomy and independence, but even it is marred by loneliness, and by a sense of personal waste in the rural countryside. Clearly, *Jane Eyre* is a developmental novel, a female bildungsroman as it were, and necessarily the interactions of personal and social roles and dilemmas differ from those of a male developmental novel, as they differ in life experience. *Jane Eyre* presents a girl emerging into womanhood, and it does so in essentially domestic contexts, contexts which nonetheless make severe demands upon Jane's person, integrity, status, family, and financial position.

Rereading *Jane Eyre* I am led inevitably to feminist issues, by which I mean the status and economics of female dependence in marriage, the limited options available to Jane as an outlet for her education and energies, her need to love and to be loved, to be of service and to be needed. These aspirations, the ambivalence expressed by the narrator toward them, and the conflicts among them, are all issues raised by the novel itself and not superimposed upon it by an ideological or doctrinaire reader. Now that the burden of trying to pretend to a totally objective and value-free perspective has finally been lifted from our shoulders, we can all admit, in the simplest possible terms, that our literary insights and perceptions come, in part at least, from our sensitivity to the nuances of our own lives and our observations of other people's lives. Every time we rethink and reassimilate *Jane Eyre,* we bring to it a new orientation. For women critics, this orientation is likely not to focus particular attention upon the dilemmas of the male, to whom male critics have already shown themselves understandably sensitive, but rather to Jane herself and her particular circumstances.

We begin, then, with a nine-year-old child at Gateshead. She sits withdrawn into a window-seat, cut off by a red moreen curtain from the Reed family clustered around the drawing-room hearth. The curtain is a barrier which serves to protect Jane, to isolate her, and to reinforce her identification both with interior space (she daydreams over her book) and with the barren landscape on the other side of the uncurtained window-pane. Only momentarily is she secure in her retreat, where her fantasies take an inward journey through the storm-tossed icy landscapes of Bewick's *History of British Birds* and an outward journey into the wet lawn and storm-blasted shrubbery of the wintry afternoon. This is a paradigmatic situation and is recalled later, when the same details of crimson curtain, window-seat, and book separate Jane at Thornfield from the drawing-room society of Ingrams and Eshtons. Again she is a solitary dependent in a great house, and through an apparent paradox, associates her inner resources with her defenses against the humiliations of social class and estrangement from family life.

Jane's continuing dependence, as a child, a poor relation, a charity schoolgirl, and a governess, is primary and it is explicit: "My first recollections of existence included . . . this reproach of dependence" (p. 10). Her alternatives are retreat and rage. Symptomatically, Jane's outburst of mutinous fury in the opening pages of the book is triggered by John Reed's violation of her sole remaining sanctuary. Jane's protective withdrawal thus is not to be confused with total acquiescence. As she notes subsequently in her narrative: "I know no medium: I never in my life have known any medium in my dealings with positive, hard characters, antagonistic to my own, between absolute submission and determined revolt. I have always faithfully observed the one, up to the very moment of bursting, sometimes with volcanic vehemence, into the other" (p. 342).

It does not require great psychological insight to understand Jane's coping devices and their image-equivalents in the inner and outer landscapes of Jane's fantasy and social worlds. Jane's estrangement from social and familial life is imaged by her protective isolation from domestic interiors, while her spirit is constantly vigilant to search out spiritual affiliation in the outer landscape—she meets both Helen Burns and Edward Rochester outdoors. Both interior and exterior landscapes afford important interpretive clues, and the psychic demarcation of the Gateshead drawing room (where Jane is unwelcome) from the fantasy/natural icy landscapes (with which Jane feels at one) is repeated with careful attention to nuance and detail at Thornfield, where Jane meets with Rochester as kin and equal, beyond the orchard well, screened in by beech trees and sunken fences. This sequestered world, equivalent in some ways to the earlier window-seat retreat, is now mutually shared. Rochester in these early scenes of awakening love, brings together themes which will drive them temporarily asunder: on the one hand he identifies directly with Jane's alienation from the social world and is seen by her as her spiritual kin, on the other hand he is her vicarious means of access to a status far beyond her own grasp.

The recurrent clues afforded by domestic interiors and external landscapes as to Jane's estrangement or her affinities, serve a further visual purpose. They image in the world of society a retreat and alienation from the adults from whose hands Jane must take her daily bread; this, in personal and psychological terms, has consequences for a far more profound and dangerous dissociation of spirit from flesh. This split is revealed in the recurrent references to Jane as a caged bird, an image by which Jane is seen as simultaneously fettered (to her flesh and to her social position) and free (to her inward fantasy and spiritual space). It is in connection with this dissociation or alienation of Jane's psyche from her position in social space that plain Jane, and symbolic Eyre have special interpretive value.[2] Surely one test of Rochester's affinity is his recognition of Jane's duality, in that he sees her as "a curious sort of bird [seen] through the close-set bars of a cage; . . . were it but free, it would soar cloud-high. . . . If I tear, if I rend the slight prison, my outrage will only let the captive loose. Conqueror I might be of the house; but the inmate would escape to heaven before I could call myself possessor of its clay dwelling-place" (pp. 122 and 280).

The images suggest that Jane's interaction with Rochester in the initial Thornfield phase of their relationship is in spirit only, dissociated from the alternative examples of social womanhood that surround her, those large and fleshly creatures, her Aunt Reed, Rochester's wife, and his presumptive bride-to-be, Blanche Ingram.

It is significant for later developments in the novel to understand the psychogenesis of the ethereal Jane by tracing it back to her early trauma of extreme ostracism, her incarceration in the Red Room, an episode in which her outburst against John Reed's taunts is followed by solitary confinement and an even more extreme psychic withdrawal. It is as if the sole protective retreat available is her inner and non-corporeal self. The terror haunting the Red Room is not the ghost of her dead uncle, nor the shadows in the garden outside, but the image of Jane's self etherealized in the darkened mirror: "All looked colder and darker in that visionary hollow than in reality: and the strange, little figure there gazing at me, with a white face and arms specking the gloom, and glittering eyes of fear moving where all else was still, had *the effect of a real spirit:* I thought it like *one of the tiny phantoms, half fairy, half imp . . ."* (p. 11, emphasis mine).

There is an important psychological process implicit in this mirror image, which is related to the relative absence of overt and explicit sexuality in Jane's relationship with Rochester. Jane has pulled inward, and withdrawn from a physical self occupying social and familial space at Gateshead, into a "placeless" or status- and space-free spiritual and moral identity, occupying thin air. Jane withdraws into her imagination and her spiritual integrity, a process by which ego is reduced to its irreducible and invulnerable inner core. Withdrawal, however, is not to be understood as simply negative. Although the elfin and visionary mirror image also presents to Jane an image of terrifying supernaturalism, this effect is the pagan antecedent for Helen Burns's mystic and Christian anticipation of that happy day when the spirit would be freed from the fetters of the flesh. Under the influence of Helen's "doctrine of equality of disembodied souls" (p. 208), Jane's terrifying vision of herself is eventually transmuted by the coeval claims of Christian supernaturalism and human justice. Jane can in the same utterance deny both flesh and the social world defined by the flesh, and thus claim Rochester as her equal, as if she were spirit addressing spirit: "I am not talking to you now through the medium of custom, conventionalities, nor even of mortal flesh—it is my spirit that addresses your spirit; just as if we have both passed through the grave, and we stood at God's feet, equal, —as we are!" (p. 222). If the early vision of herself in the Red Room mirror prepares for a spiritualized or elfin Jane born of the cast-off Jane, it also produces a Jane capable of "charming" Rochester beyond the capacities of a mere Blanche Ingram. Indeed, the inception of their love is perceived through a mutual recognition of spiritual affinity that takes us back to the imagery of the Red Room: Rochester emerges before Jane's astonished gaze as a phantom figure, the "gytrash" of Bessie's evening stories whom Jane had *seen* in the Red Room mirror, while she in turn reminds Rochester "unaccountably of fairy tales" (p. 107). Their early love is characterized in the language of fantasy and folk-tale, and the negative and dispossessed qualities associated with Jane's elfin-self are temporarily driven away by Rochester's fond endearments— she is his "malicious elf," his "sprite" and "changeling," "a fairy, and comes from Elf-land . . . to make me happy; and I must go with it out of the common world to a lonely place—such as the moon, for instance" (p. 235).

In the "both/and" manner Jane's narrative has of pursuing a personal and economic dilemma simultaneously, using the psychic mode of fantasy interchangeably with the social mode of realism, Rochester had indeed fortuitously emerged as a spirit-being intimately associated with Jane's most traumatic childhood experience of psychological withdrawal. He is thus Jane's spirit-mate in the sense that Jane appears supernatural to him. The mutual identification and recognition of each in the other suggests a modality of love as fusion.

But the spiritual kinship which is an important dimension of Jane's and Rochester's love—and indeed, an affiliation leading directly to their reunion at the end of the novel, brought together by that otherwise inexplicable spiritual call—is balanced by Rochester's solidity for Jane as a social presence in the outside world. Rochester is introduced into Thornfield mere paragraphs after we read of Jane restlessly pacing the Thornfield battlements, wearied by her passive life, aching for a wider field of activity and for more various experience. This is an important occasion in the novel, for it defines the single moment of understanding that might be called feminist ("women feel just as men feel; they need exercise for their faculties and a field for their efforts as much as their brothers do") and I shall return to it shortly. The point here is that Rochester's entrance to Thornfield at this very juncture affords Jane a domestic and romantic rather than independent and autonomous field for activity, a person to whom she manages to prove useful (note the three-fold repetition of Rochester's request to "lean" on Jane) and who reciprocally serves as a vicarious channel for Jane's yearning for the greater world beyond Thornfield's gates.

The emphasis thus far has been upon Jane's preservation of an irreducible core of personal integrity in the face of social alienation and ostracism. Although her outrage at injustice becomes more explicit as she grows older, only on one occasion are the upheavals of Jane's passionate integrity identified with an overt feminist understanding. What seems to me most significant about her extended pyschic explosion on Thornfield's battlements is not so much the fact of its existence within a novel that takes autonomy and action in the real world as at least one of its themes, but rather the various subterfuges by which it is quickly undermined. The recurrent apologies that attend it suggest Jane's uneasiness with her feminist awareness. Further, the passage is actually the second occasion upon which Jane wishes to be up and out in the active world of towns, and to burst through the constraints of domestic service in other people's households. This theme, the wish for an autonomous outlet for her talents, education and energies, her longing, that is, to move out of the confines of her status and place, to the larger and more exciting world "out there," will be treated subsequently. The feminist outburst is in keeping with Jane's earlier mutinies, like them regretted after the fact, and like them undermined by her desperate need to be loved and accepted. It is no accident that this long passage occurs immediately prior to Rochester's emergence on the scene, following which Jane's feminism per se is not heard from again, although the issues of independence and integrity, insofar as they too are feminist, of course remain.

This passage, taken as a whole, repeats the early Gateshead outburst in the light of a more analytic understanding. "Children can feel, but they cannot analyse their feelings; and if the analysis is partially effected in thought, they know not how to express the result of the process in words" (p. 19). The new element in the Thornfield passage is Jane's consciously expressed aspiration "for a power of vision which might overpass that limit" (p. 95). This aspiration pursues a double course within the novel. As vision, it becomes internalized into Jane's dreamlife, her surreal paintings, and the tales her imagination creates and narrates continuously. But as a longing for direct action, it belongs to the sequence of thwarted impulses toward "the regions full of life" which Jane experiences for the first time at Lowood following the loss of Maria Temple through marriage. On both occasions, this longing is immediately undermined, first by the humbler aspiration toward a new servitude reinforced by the Lowood dinner gong, and later by Bertha Mason's demonic laughter and eccentric murmurs. Bertha's subhuman voice resonates in Jane's apologies which relentlessly punctuate the Thornfield outburst ("Anybody may blame me who likes," "Whom blames me? Many, no doubt").

Bertha's role in undercutting Jane's feminist outrage is not without purpose in that Bertha characterizes the dangers of ungoverned passion and rage, forced into demonic intensity. She is like Jane in the Red Room, a hidden and ostracized figure, locked into solitary confinement and thereby presenting a monstrous equivalent to Jane's "deep ire and desperate revolt." Jane calls our attention to the anxiety that attends her awareness of her own fluctuations between repression and rage. But she does not note what the pattern of her narrative implies, that the rage, indignation and rebelliousness characteristic of Jane the child finds a feminist voice in Jane the woman, and in her longing "for a power of vision that might overpass that limit; which might reach the busy world" (p. 95).

Jane's consciousness of her possible participation in a world beyond her social barriers occurs first at Lowood, where Jane sees in the horizon a space more objective, substantial and inviting than the interiorized and icy wasteland imaged in Bewick. The Lowood landscape is presented in a series of concentric half-circles, with Jane at its center, "the high and spike-guarded" Lowood walls encircled in turn by summits and further encircled by the great dome of the horizon (p. 66). Looking out, Jane longs to explore as far as her eye can see, but firmly represses her desire (at the last moment) "in a manner suiting [the] prospects" (p. 29) toward which her entire Lowood training has been directed. The oscillation in this episode between longing and repression makes the apologies and Bertha's laughter, both of which undercut Jane's more conscious feminism at Thornfield, appear both characteristic and inevitable in retrospect.

> I went to the window, opened it, and looked out. There were the two
> wings of the building . . . the skirts of Lowood; there was the hilly

horizon. My eye passed all other objects to rest on those most remote, the blue peaks: it was those I longed to surmount, all within their boundary of rock and heath seemed prison-ground, exile limits. I traced the white road winding round the base of one mountain, and vanishing in a gorge between two: how I longed to follow it further! . . . I tired of the routine of eight years in one afternoon. I desired liberty; for liberty I gasped; for liberty I uttered a prayer; it seemed scattered on the wind then faintly blowing. I abandoned it and framed a humbler supplication; for change, stimulus: that petition, too, seemed swept off into vague space: "Then," I cried, half desperate, "grant me at least a new servitude!" (p. 74)

Compared with this, the Thornfield scene suggests a final and fully-fledged burst of consciousness—Jane's vision strained yet again along the "dim sky-line" in a last-ditch effort to "overpass that limit" and reach the busy world, towns, "regions full of life I had heard of but never seen . . . more of intercourse *with my kind*" (p. 95, emphasis mine). In each instance Jane is dramatically situated within barriers (spiked walls, battlements) that define her "place," and each time the impulse to reach the horizon and move beyond is vitiated by both inner checks ("a new servitude," "Anybody may blame me who likes") and outer mockery.

Yet it is worth noting that Jane's aspirations are also displaced in their pure form to the other major male character in her narrative. St. John is the male embodiment of Jane's ambitions. Representing the conscience uncomplicated by feelings, and "the ambition of the high master-spirit" (p. 398), he is the type of heroic wanderer which Jane had at moments longed to be and earns the closing paragraph in a tale which presumes to be Jane's narrative of her own life.

The nature and limits upon Jane's capacity for exploration and autonomy are tested at Morton, where she is economically independent, engaged in worthwhile and serviceable work, but bereft of emotional sustenance. Jane's refusal of a loveless marriage, even though it would allow her to fulfill the aspiring and ambitious side of her nature through missionary work, is a further test of her venturesomeness. Although the alleged social impossibility of her accompanying St. John as a co-worker but not wife is an impediment obviously not of her making, it does appear that Jane's feminism is ambivalent at best, and her drive toward autonomy and an independent working life is undermined by her need for a sustaining and nurturing love. Sides of her nature are presented as polar opposites, without an alternative posed by which they might be fused. Jane's life is posed in terms of contrasting locales, opposing imageries, irreconcilable life choices.

But Jane's integrity is quite another matter. She consistently bridles at efforts to exploit her dependent status, whether the motives be sadistic (John Reed), possessive (Rochester), or egocentric (St. John). She will not marry St. John because she is afraid to lose her independence. As his comrade "my heart and mind would be free," and "there would be recesses in my mind which would be only mine, to which he never came . . . *but as his wife — at his side always, and always restrained, and always checked* — forced to keep the fire of my nature continually low, to compel it to burn inwardly and never utter a cry, though the imprisoned flame consumed vital after vital — this would be unendurable" (pp. 358–359, emphasis mine).

Even the relation with Rochester is characterized by a pervasive word-play on "master" and "governess" in what appears to be, in part at least, Jane's struggle for self-mastery and self-governance at Thornfield. The more unrelenting and competitive struggle between two strong wills and similar temperaments in Jane's parallel conflict with St. John, is expressed with far stronger reference to the "fetters" and "ascendancy" of the male and the "thralldom" of the female, perceptions which carry the reader back to the petty tyrannies of John Reed (whose name and initials St. John Rivers echoes): "as a man, [St. John] would have wished to coerce me into obedience" (p. 360).

Prior to her flight from Thornfield and experience at Moor House, Jane's efforts to maintain both independence and integrity are rendered untenable. Acceptance of her social and economic dependence on the whims of others proves emotionally intolerable. Even the small sanctuaries to which she retreats are violated time and again. The avenues open for making her own way in the world impose restrictions upon her nature, whether as governess for Rochester's ward, as teacher among the poor children at Morton village, or as St. John's missionary wife or co-worker. No alternative provided by the first two-thirds of this novel enables her to integrate the dislocated aspects of her nature.

The plot of *Jane Eyre* follows psychic necessity in a way we have come to expect of dream-work. One characteristic of Jane's narrative is her inordinate attentiveness to the details of her dream life. Similarly, the plot, understood as the manipulation of the world to conform to desired and inner necessity, is complicated by the censorship exercised by Jane's reason, even while her dreams and fantasies serve as psychological and interpretive clues to the reader. Jane's imagination is constantly at work creating a tale independent of any source other than its own creative and compensatory power, "a tale that was never ended — a tale my imagination created. . . . quickened with all of the incident, life, fire, feeling, that I desired and had not in my actual existence" (p. 96). Strengthened by reason, it also serves the purpose of admonition. To master her feelings for her master, Jane draws the exaggerated portraits of "a Governess, disconnected, poor, and plain" as contrasted to "Blanche, an accomplished lady of rank," with her round arm, diamond ring and gold bracelet — and these form the pictorial equivalents for "Reason having come forward and told in her own quiet way, a plain, unvarnished tale" (pp. 140–141). Similarly, Jane's triptych, painted at Lowood but displayed at Thornfield, images the ambivalence that accompanies her great expectations in a series of psychological landscapes which repeat the elemental language of the novel (air and water, in one case iced over), with much of the scene submerged below the waterline or horizon in a suggestion of the relationship of Jane's conscious and unconscious life.[3] The first of the series shows a swollen sea claiming all but a partially submerged mast, a golden bracelet, and the arm from which the bracelet has been washed or torn. This symbolic association with Blanche Ingram's jewels and Rochester's lavish wedding gifts prefigures and reinforces the submerged fears expressed in Jane's dream of buoyant but unquiet seas, driving her back from the sweet shores of Beulah: "I could not reach it, even in fancy" (p. 133). The second painting images a female form which Rochester interprets as evening star and wind, an etherealized cluster that anticipates the moon, not moon "but a white human form" prefigurative of the white apparition that warns Jane to flee Thornfield, as well as the wind on which Jane's initial supplications for liberty are lost, but which subsequently carry Rochester's entreaties to her at Moor House at the moment of their greatest crisis and triumph. The third panel depicts the ice-bound landscape of Jane's despair. The triptych's symbolic relevance to Jane's emotional and religious crises at Thornfield and later, suggests a technique of illuminating through pictorial and dream montage many of the implicit personal themes.

Jane's compulsively active dreamlife is further characterized by recurrent, anxiety-ridden, and regressive nightmares, with images of barriers, closed doors and phantom-children. The Thornfield nightmares focus upon the psychic as well as the social obstacles to Jane's imminent marriage, through a recapitulation of Jane's obsessive anxiety over her humiliating childhood and perpetual homelessness. Jane's dreamlife is the dark underside of her rational self-control. Rochester arouses her with talk of their natural affinity and Jane dreams of billows of trouble under surges of joy.

Dreams portending death and still-birth are the grotesque accompaniments of Jane's efforts to envision herself a married woman. Debarred from "the new life which was to commence to-morrow" (p. 241) by internal inhibitions, small wonder at her otherwise inexplicable procrastination until there could be no more "putting off the day that advanced — the bridal day" (p. 241). The dreams explain Jane's procrastination, which is never accounted for directly, beyond the tacit equation of her rebirth as a married woman with a new identity and a new name — Jane Eyre transformed into Jane Rochester. This transformation is in itself traumatic, a "newborn agony — a deformed thing which I could not persuade myself to own and rear" (p. 214).

Jane's anxiety dreams on the eve of the wedding express her premonitions of rebirth as a deformed adult. Jane's nightmares find symbolic reinforcement in a landscape of separation and division, represented by a chestnut-tree riven to its roots, apples divided (the ripe from the unripe), drawing-room curtain pulled down, moon eclipsed by curtains of dense clouds. The dream motifs are mutually reinforcing: a consciousness of some barrier dividing her from her husband-to-be; the burdensome child; the strain to overtake Rochester, despite fettered movements; then a second dream of Thornfield in ruin, the child still in Jane's arms, impeding her progress, nearly strangling her in its terror while Rochester disappears like a speck on a white track. Two nightmares dramatize a single although complex perception. Associating the adult woman Jane Rochester with the abandoned and alien child Jane Eyre of her earliest memories, they identify the abandoned child with the anticipated yet feared prospect of awakening a "young Mrs. Rochester — Fairfax Rochester's girl bride."

But worse is yet to come. Two nightmares prepare for a third, the nightmare into which Jane in fact awakens to see the apparition of Bertha Rochester looming over the bedstead. Bertha's appearance further confirms Jane's fears of the still-birth of her marriage, for Bertha *is* the real Mrs. Rochester and Jane's hopes now in fact lie dead, "cursed like the first-born out of the land of Egypt," and "my love: that feeling which was my master's . . . shivered in my heart, like a suffering child in a cold cradle" (p. 260). The grotesque connection of Jane's nuptials with Bertha's marriage is reinforced by Bertha's face seen by Jane in her mirror, an image which serves as the maniacal opposite of the elf seen earlier in the Red Room mirror.[4] The two mirror images render, by polarized extremes, the terms of Jane's spiritual and physical dissociation, on the one hand the asexual self who is spiritually akin to Rochester but cannot be his wife; on the other a passionate and sex-crazed creature, a woman of satin and jewels who tries on (and then destroys) the extravagant veil which (as a symbol of wealth) Jane had reluctantly accepted. Once again, psychic and economic issues overlap. By destroying this symbol of Rochester's wealth and pride, Bertha ironically paves the way for Jane's ultimate reunion with a humbled Rochester in a smaller estate.

But here, in this recognition scene, Bertha and Jane are merged for a single awful moment. The fusion is more than Jane can bear, and her collapse here repeats her collapse in the Red Room under equally severe psychic pressure. The episode concludes in the regressive mode, Jane asleep in Adèle's crib as she had once slept in the dead Helen's arms, the child "so tranquil, so passionless, so innocent. . . . She seemed the emblem of my past life; and he, I was not to array myself to meet, the dread, but adored type of my unknown future day" (p. 252).

It is clear that marriage at this point in the novel is not a smooth developmental transition so much as a rupture, raising a host of questions which the work, to its credit, does address. There is the question of identity: Who, and what, is a "Mrs. Rochester"? There is the question of continuity: Can one imagine an equal and independent adulthood as female and wife, given the background of one's daily humiliations as someone else's dependent throughout childhood and adolescence? And there is the question of integrity and power: Is there an imaginable mutuality that does not perpetuate the master/subordinate economics of Jane's status at Thornfield?

Jane reaches the threshold of marriage three times in the novel. She cannot cross it until she can meet her "master" as his partner and equal, his equal by virtue of her inheritance and family solidarity, his partner by virtue of their interdependence. Before she leaves Thornfield, Jane's visions of herself as an adult are simultaneously regressive and parental. Her blighted hopes leave "Jane Eyre, who had been an ardent expectant woman — almost a bride . . . a cold, solitary girl again" (p. 260). Now, the hope of mature love, a feeling "which was my master's — which he had created" is thwarted. Jane's articulation of her disappointment points to an aspect of her dependence on Rochester not noted earlier — *he makes of her a woman;* she is not a woman in her own right. Without him, she is once again a child, with all the terrors of her situation as a child reactivated. Rochester is not unaware of Jane's fear of, and her resistance to, adult love and its attendant sexuality. Although her resistance is handled playfully for the most part, Rochester does comment upon her "fear in the presence of a man and a brother — or father, or master, or what you will" (p. 122), and the presence in this catalogue of familial rather than sexual bonds between male and female is noteworthy. Subsequently, in what cannot be ignored as role reversal, Jane's nurturing custodianship of the blinded and maimed Rochester is again parental rather than sexual. The sole distinguishing feature of the child born of their marriage (the dailiness of marital life is scarcely commented on at the end of the novel) is that he is a child-Rochester, his father in miniature.

By now, it is apparent that family harmony, a sense of belonging somewhere and to someone, is identified by Jane with her own psychic "kind" or kindred, and with sympathetic understanding and shared feelings and tastes. Looking out from the Thornfield window-seat at Rochester among his own social set, for example, Jane discovers that she loves Rochester because she finally perceives that "he is not of their kind. I believe he is of mine . . . I feel akin to him . . ." (p. 156). This is a woman's narrative in which blood runs thick, but psychic kinship is deeper and more sustaining, so that Rochester can be seen as "my relation, rather than my master. . . . So happy, so gratified did I become with this new interest added to life, that I ceased to pine after kindred" (p. 129). Similarly, on Rochester's side, the cord of "natural sympathy" which he admits binds him to her, also has subtle umbilical nuances: "a string somewhere under my left ribs, tightly and inextricably knotted to a similar string situated in the corresponding quarter of your little frame . . . I am afraid that cord of communion will be snapt; and then I've a nervous notion I should take to bleeding inwardly" (p. 221).

Rochester does in fact offer Jane a home after what must have seemed endless wanderings. "A little, roving, solitary thing" to Bessie, a "little castaway," and "interloper and alien" to Brocklehurst, Jane moves from one temporary refuge to another. Rochester recognizes Jane for the "poor orphan child" that she is, for he, like Jane, is also a homeless wanderer, and welcomes her into his heart and hearth as if she were the prodigal returning: "here, come in, bonny wanderer" (pp. 120–121), to which she responds in kind, "I was now at last in safe haven" (p. 85), "wherever you are is my home—my only home" (p. 216).

Rochester's protective and paternal role is particularly apparent in a scene which recalls the earlier domestic grouping at Gateshead which had visually consolidated Jane's isolation; but the Gateshead scene is recalled in this Thornfield instance for the purposes of total reversal. This time around, Jane sits by Mrs. Fairfax's side, with Adèle nearby, in a complex of interrelationships in which Jane is simultaneously daughter to Mrs. Fairfax and mother to Adèle, with Rochester looking on as lord protector and bemused pater-familias to them all. It is important to separate the two elements, the paternal and protective support provided by Rochester as head of the household, and the internal sharing of kinship and support of the essentially fluid motherly-sisterly-daughterly roles and relations among the three Thornfield women, and even more dramatically among the other beneficent and triadic mother/daughter/sisterhoods of the novel: Maria Temple/Helen Burns/Jane Eyre, and Diana Rivers/Mary Rivers/Jane Eyre. In these last two positive "sisterhoods" the paternal figure is absent. His protective role is shared among women, although what is omitted, and what Jane Eyre misses, is, of course, the romance.

We all know, having read *Jane Eyre* many times over, that in the end she seems to have it both ways, or indeed, *all* the ways that the novel presents as worth having. Jane regains her lover, stumbles upon her real family, discovers her status and is showered by an inheritance that gives her far more money than she can possibly use, thus turning her into the protector and head-of-household at Moor House that Rochester had been at Thornfield. All this, with no loss of integrity, and only a slight softening around the edges of her north-of-England orneryness. The "happy" ending, which resolves some issues but sweeps others under the carpet, is presented, as suggested early on in this discussion, in the Cinderella mode, although with important differences. The bare outlines of the plot suggest that Jane *is* Cinderella, supplanting bad foster-parents and sisters with good (from Reeds to Rochester/Rivers) and winning a chastened Prince Charming as well. Cinderella is an essentially girlhood fantasy (although Dickens' *Great Expectations* imagines aspects of the fable along male lines), the fable of a young girl beautiful but exploited, rewarded for her patience, goodness, submission and beauty by the miraculous appearance of Prince Charming to lift her forever out of her misery. This fable, as received along traditional lines, is clearly inappropriate to our Jane, who so passionately values her conscience and her independence, who tends toward action rather than passivity, and who intermittently aspires toward her own life in the larger world. Rather we have in Jane a Cinderella reimagined, unsubmissive and unrelenting on the issues of paying her own way and of being loved for her better moral and personal qualities. No passive capitulation into the arms of Prince Charming for her, but continued governess pay at thirty pounds per annum, even after the ringing of the wedding bells. For this impoverished young woman, once again, the social and economic dilemmas of status cannot be severed from the marital and sexual dilemmas of role. Perpetual degradation in poverty keeps Jane from her spiritual kin and kind, while the degradation of a dependent marriage to a social superior would alienate Jane from her better self.

The Cinderella paradigm will carry us a long way in understanding the interaction of personal and social motifs in both Jane's romantic and worldly aspirations. The significance of the Moor House episode rests in the fact that the Cinderella dilemmas are resolved within the family structure in which they initially occur. They are resolved, that is, through the discovery of a nurturant and self-supporting sisterhood. Prince Rochester does *not* lift Cinderjane out of her misery. Looked at in this way, and focussing upon the characterizing domestic and interior housescapes that are the major "landscape" of this novel, cruel stepsisters crop up like the recurrent bad dreams they in fact embody, the perpetual reinforcers of Jane's dispossession at Gateshead, Lowood, and Thornfield. And as if to insist upon this Cinderella equation, the cruel stepsisters turn up wealthy and favored by nature, with a cruel mama in tow, evil female mother/daughter triads of Reeds, Brocklehursts and Ingrams, fortune's darlings, all of them marriageable and promising in the accepted terms of the day and of the novel. But these figures are exorcized by the Rivers sisters, whose fostering sisterhood is anticipated in the earlier triads of Maria Temple, Helen Burns, and Jane Eyre. And as if to further the emerging equation of sisterhood with spiritual kinship, and of sisterhood and kinship with equivalent social status, there is the fact that both pairs of "good" foster-sisters are themselves impoverished governesses, earning their keep while trying to maintain their integrity.

From this analysis, it follows that Jane's transition from poor orphan into secure woman could not possibly be achieved through marriage to Rochester at Thornfield. Instead, at Moor House she reenacts an emotional and psychic equivalent to the experiences of infancy and childhood, moves quickly through the maturational process — becoming a younger, then an older sister, and, finally, an heiress, the cause of her family's reunification, independence, and status in the larger world. As in the way of folktale and fantasy, the evil stepmother is exposed and punished, and the stepsisters who had lorded it over the orphan are cast down; accordingly, the Reeds are destroyed one by one and the Brocklehursts and Ingrams evaporate from the scene, their psychic function now complete.

Despite the careful paralleling of psychic and status motifs in the presentation of Jane's situation, there is a clear primacy established of the personal over the social/economic issue, however much the second might prove a necessary precondition for independence in the first. Jane's inheritance, when it finally comes to her, seems at first only another painful reminder of her isolation. Far more satisfying is the discovery that she is indeed part of a family, a family whom she might now assist. Her joy has all the poignancy of remembered isolation, as she reminds St. John, who, insensitive to the warmth provided by nurturing family love, believes she is throwing her money away: " 'And you,' I interrupted, 'cannot at all imagine the craving I have for fraternal and sisterly love. I never had a home, I never had brothers or sisters; I must and will have them now . . . I want my kindred: those with whom I have full fellow-feeling' " (p. 341). The language here is redolent of the familial and kinship aspects of Jane's attachment to Rochester. Money is related to independence, making possible the relative equality and strength which underpins the rather more forced reallocation of dependence and status at Ferndean: "Are you an independent woman? A rich woman?" (p. 382), with the not surprising rejoinder, "I love you better now, when I can really be useful to you, than I did in your state of proud independence, when you disdained every part but that of the giver and protector" (p. 392).

One can imagine alternative endings to the one offered by this novel. The themes traced out in the Rochester-romance, an aspect of Jane's narrative that receives more than its fair share of critical attention, are in fact resolved at Moor House in a familial scene that provides warmth, kinship, status and shared wealth. A twentieth-century novel might well have ended on this note, with cousins marrying or not as they wish, and with Jane continuing at Morton or finding some larger arena for her energies, her commitments, her education and skill. Some women's lives have always pursued this course, likely enough with similar sacrifice, in Brontë's time and earlier; Charlotte Brontë is herself an instance, in her life, if not in her fiction.

There are, however, determinant characteristics of this novel that make a non-romantic resolution of the personal and social themes out of the question. First, there is considerable ambivalence expressed toward the aspiration to be truly free, to live out as fully as possible one's ambitions and aspirations. Second, Jane's energies are transformed into a form more socially acceptable for a woman, in her desire to serve and be of use. Early on at Lowood, Jane abandons her spontaneous cry for liberty, replacing it with the humbler supplication, "Grant me at least a new servitude!" (p. 74). Service at Thornfield is her new servitude, to Rochester especially, who leans on her time and again, encouraged by her offer, "Can I help you, sir? — I'd give my life to serve you" (p. 179).

But finally, and I think most importantly, questions of estate and position, status, integrity and equality are resolved in the romantic mode, in what is undeniably a romantic novel, which is to say one characterized by fortuitous interventions which enable events and the world to conform to the shape of wish and desire. *Jane Eyre* is marked by the fantasy that love is a fusion of souls, a conception of love out of which it is difficult to imagine an ongoing, humdrum daily adult life. "I am my husband's life as fully as he is mine. No woman was ever nearer to her mate than I am; ever more absolutely bone of his bone and flesh of his flesh" (pp. 396–397). A comparable twentieth-century instance, dealing with similar issues of love and autonomy, sexual passion and sisterhood, is Doris Lessing's *Golden Notebook*, in which the world is far less tractable and more resistant to resolutions between life issues which may, after all, prove to be irreconcilable. But in *Jane Eyre* love and autonomy are at odds, and only "romance" makes some modicum of equality available in so extreme a case.

The Jane/Rochester symbiosis at Ferndean has been commented on in print, with predictable sympathy to Rochester's diminution. At the risk of seeming heartless, it seems important to say that Rochester is not so central to Jane's own story as an easy reading might suggest, and as the neglect of the Moor House episodes in the interpretive and critical literature on this novel appears to confirm. Clearly Rochester's possessive mastery is purged (literal fire putting out symbolic fire) at the same point in the narrative chronology at which Jane is exorcizing the icy wastelands of her moral conscience. Similarly, the decline in Rochester's status is a precondition of their marriage, but it is difficult to determine whether his physical maiming is to be read as the harsh biblical punishment for adultery and pride, or whether its very harshness draws our attention to Jane's extreme, perhaps excessive, need to be needed, as yet another requisite for their married interdependence. The gap between them during the early days at Thornfield loomed very large indeed; thus the measures necessarily taken to close that gap might seem excessive to twentieth-century eyes.

What does seem clear is that to marry prior to Moor House would mean an exchange of childhood for adult dependence, bound this time by diamond fetters. Jane's suspicion, that as his wife she would be his mistress, and as his mistress his slave, is given substance by the unexpected Gothic twist to the plot. What is important is not Jane's moral scruple, but the certain inference that psychic kinship and spiritual equality cannot transcend the social degradation of a dependent relationship.

The novel can imaginatively suggest the necessary adjustments between psychic energy and social limits, but cannot enact them in Jane's status-ridden world except by a fortuitous inheritance and family reunification. With Jane's great expectations and fervent aspirations toward the active life displaced onto the cold figure of St. John Rivers, her prayers for liberty subdued into the search for a new servitude, and her early withdrawal redeemed by the kinship patterns in the novel, there is nothing left for her to do but marry. But to marry both she and Rochester must change—she in her objective circumstances, he in his social pride. To look to marriage merely as an easy escape out of a child's isolation and the fulfillment of girlish dreams would be an emotional lie, an alternative that Jane explores in fantasy but whose complications overwhelm her rational consciousness. To look to a man's world of heroic activity is forbidden and Jane's aspirations subside. Jane will relinquish liberty for new servitudes; she will relinquish the great world for vicarious and useful experience in the small. But she will not accept the degradation of continued dependence, the condition of hireling, slave, or kept woman by which the associational language of this narrative defines the position of a wife with no estate to call her own.

Notes

1. Charlotte Brontë, *Jane Eyre*, ed. Richard Dunn (New York: Norton, 1971), p. 236. All further references to the text will be taken from the Norton Edition and identified with parentheses.

2. Multiple puns revolve around Jane's surname, with the obvious allusion to *air* (for which *eyre* is an archaic spelling) and the French *aire* that Adèle calls attention to ("Aire? Bah! I cannot say it" [p. 89]), which means nesting place (for a bird of prey) as well as area or space. Interpretively, both puns are of value, the one with its obvious elemental and spiritual associations, the other with its reference to Jane's various retreats (window-seat, Thornfield arbor, the recesses of her own mind). There is further obsolete and archaic reference to *eyre* meaning the itinerant medieval circuit judges (Jane's peripatetic movements?). The primary pun on *air* reinforces the elemental imagery of other place-names (Marsh End, Moor House, Lowood, Thornfield, Ferndean) and of surnames (Burns, Rivers—the uncertain status of Reed seems interconnected peripherally with Rivers in an appropriately familial manner). On the elemental imagery in its own right, useful interpretations can be found in David Lodge, "Fire and Eyre: Charlotte Brontë's War of Earthly Elements," in *The Language of Fiction* (London: Routledge, 1966), pp. 114–143, and in Eric Solomon, "*Jane Eyre*: Fire and Water," *College English*, 25 (1963), 215–217. Jane's given name (plain Jane—how far back does the cliché go?) carries us to the class and status theme in the novel, contrasting markedly with the fancy foreign names of well-born women of "place" (Blanche, Eliza, Georgiana, Diana, Rosamond) as well as with the designation of foreign women of uncertain status (Céline and Adèle). Much is in a name and the name change required by marital status, Jane Eyre becoming Jane Rochester, invokes critical issues of identity and of status.

3. See Jane Millgate, "Narrative Distance in *Jane Eyre*: The Relevance of the Pictures," *Modern Language Review*, 63 (1968), 315–319, where all of the paintings, not merely the triptych shown at Thornfield, are discussed; and Thomas Langford, "The Three Pictures in *Jane Eyre*," *Victorian Newsletter*, 31 (1967), 47–48, the triptych here interpreted, wrongly I think, with reference to the structural divisions of Gateshead, Thornfield, and Marsh End. See also Jennifer Gribble, "Jane Eyre's Imagination," *Nineteenth Century Fiction*, 23 (1968–69).

4. Reminders of the psychic connection between Jane and Bertha recur in Jane's third-floor restless pacing and Bertha's maniacal grovelling; Jane's confinement after the outburst at John Reed and Bertha's after flying at Mason; Jane, like Bertha, is compelled to sleep "in a

small closet by myself" (22); Jane fears she is "insane—quite insane" (279) in her temptation to stay with Rochester, the temptation characterized by "my veins running fire," "his flaming glance" (279), "terrible moment: full of struggle, blackness, burning" (278). On the other hand, as elemental opposites, Bertha applies fire and Jane water to Rochester's bedchamber, and the two are compared by him (in an implicit parallel to the Blanche/Jane contrasting portraits) as good angel to hideous demon (277).

A Patriarch of One's Own: *Jane Eyre* and Romantic Love

Jean Wyatt*

Jane Eyre has been a focus for feminist literary analysis from the first: early texts that have subsequently become models of feminist criticism, like Elaine Showalter's *A Literature of Their Own*, Ellen Moers' *Literary Women*, Patricia Spacks' *The Female Imagination*, and Sandra M. Gilbert and Susan Gubar's *A Madwoman in the Attic*, all give *Jane Eyre* a central place. Gilbert and Gubar take their title from *Jane Eyre* because of its psychological relevance: they rightly point out that its imagery of enclosure and escape and its doubling of the female self into the good girl Jane and the criminally passionate Bertha reflect the experiences and corresponding psychic patterns of women living under patriarchy.[1] The note of self-recognition in many women's emotional responses to *Jane Eyre* seems to corroborate the critics' sense of its psychological significance. Harriet Martineau said, in her autobiography published in 1877, "I was convinced that it was by some friend of my own, who had portions of my childish experience in his or her mind."[2] A century later, Adrienne Rich reported she was "carried away as by a whirlwind" when she read *Jane Eyre* as a child; she returned to it in her twenties, her thirties, and again in her forties, drawn by "some nourishment I needed and still need today."[3] Jane Lazarre found in "that adored book of my childhood, *Jane Eyre*," self-validation, an affirmation of her own rebel identity; like Rich she reread it twenty years later to find a new perspective on her own problems.[4] These women echo voices from my own experience: students in Women in Literature classes, as well as female colleagues a generation older, respond to *Jane Eyre* passionately, feel it has something important to say about their own lives.

I want to explore the interaction between novels and female fantasy patterns by asking two related questions about reader response to *Jane Eyre*. First, how can we explain that women widely separate in time and nationality share psychic patterns that make them recognize in *Jane Eyre* hidden truths about their own inner lives? Second, since girls often read *Jane Eyre* at a formative time in their lives, what fantasies does it offer

*Reprinted from *Tulsa Studies in Women's Literature* 4 (1985): 199–216.

them? Does it reinforce fantasy patterns acquired from growing up female in the Western nuclear family, or does its appeal come from the pattern of resistance to patriarchal forms that attracts Rich and Lazarre? In fact, *Jane Eyre* is rich in fantasies addressed to the frustrations of growing up female in a white middle-class family structure skewed by the unequal distribution of power and mobility along gender lines: fantasies of a young girl's defiant autonomy, fantasies of a good mother (Miss Temple) and a bad mother (Mrs. Reed), and fantasies of revenge on bullying brothers and prettier sisters (the Reed children). Perhaps most appealing, at least to a female reader with a strong, dominant father who fits the patriarchal model, Rochester offers Jane the excitement combined with frustration and enigma that characterize father-daughter interactions.[5] By showing how the extraordinarily complicated sexual politics between Jane Eyre and Rochester reflect the convolutions of father-daughter relations in a nuclear family where the mother is largely responsible for childcare, the father for work outside the home, I hope to make the broader point that some structural features of romantic love are grounded in traditional patterns of relationship between fathers and daughters. Against the pull of its patriarchal love fantasy, *Jane Eyre* presents an equally passionate protest against patriarchal authority. The contradiction, I claim, mirrors a female reader's ambivalence toward her father. Part of *Jane Eyre*'s appeal lies in the way it allows girls (and women) to work out fantasies of desire and rage against fathers that stem from the power and inaccessibility of a father in a traditional Western family structure and his ambiguous position in regard to his daughter's sexuality.

Jane Eyre exerts a powerful attraction on female readers partly because it combines unconscious fantasies centering on Bertha Mason — fantasies that appeal directly to the unconscious quirks of a woman brought up in this culture — with political analysis directed by Jane at the reader's conscious mind. While Jane reasons out the causes and effects of women's domestic oppression, Bertha burns down the imprisoning house. This combination of revenge fantasy with conscious political analysis raises the question: can a novel release the energy stored in a reader's unconscious fantasies of rage against patriarchal family structures and rechannel it into a desire for social change?

The question is important, bearing on the relation between reading and fantasy. Norman Holland, in *The Dynamics of Literary Response*, says that a fictional pattern attracts us because it corresponds to an unconscious fantasy we already possess. Our fantasy structures — which govern our desires — reflect early family configurations. By the time we reach the age of reading, Holland maintains, our personality structure is firmly established, our repertoire of fantasies already set: books cannot influence us in any long-lasting way, they can only provide new details to embellish old fantasies.[6] According to Holland's model we are all stuck: if reading can cut only the same channels that early family configurations stencilled into the unconscious, then the potentially creative energy of desire is bound to old routes, doomed to recreate the family structures in which we first experienced satisfaction—or frustration. If, for example, *Jane Eyre* attaches female readers primarily because Jane's passion for Rochester follows the lines of a girl's love for her father, then reading *Jane Eyre* can only reinforce readers' tendencies to recreate in their adult lives the asymmetrical power structures of the patriarchal family—structures that, by distributing power and opportunity unequally along gender lines, have severely limited female development.

If, however, *Jane Eyre* manages to combine infantile fantasy with new vision—if it follows the destruction of the patriarchal mansion with the vision of a different domestic structure organized according to more egalitarian principles—then perhaps reading the novel with the intense identification that the underlying fantasy structures compel can allow a reader's imagination, thus heated and heightened, to infuse a new fantasy vehicle with desire, take it in, and make it her own. Perhaps novels that involve readers on the passionate level of their own most cherished fantasies do not merely allow them to revel in infantile fantasies, but afford them the extra pleasure of releasing the energy buried in old restrictive fantasy patterns and rechanneling it into new, potentially liberating ones.

Fantasies are important because they set before us objects of desire. If we are unable to change our minds, as Holland's model of reading implies, if we are unable to imagine something fundamentally new, we can only repeat. But readers like Rich and Lazarre report having become attached to *Jane Eyre* because they found there something not provided by family and culture, an alternative female scenario: the pattern of a girl continuously, defiantly asserting her right to be herself. They give us the hope that young readers can find in novels alternative plots that meet their needs better than family stories and that they can, by rereading them, make the new patterns of living their own. According to such a theory of reading, we would be freer to adopt alternatives to the structures we have grown up in. If women are to change how they live, they must change what they want, so that the energy of desire can be mobilized in the fight for a better life.

Because romantic love fantasies exert a pull toward traditional feminine passivity and dependence by promising happiness to her who sits and waits for the right man to sweep her away to the heights of passion, they arouse the scorn and anger of feminists dedicated to ideals of female autonomy and self-realization. But because their appeal is so powerful (*The New Yorker* reports that the Harlequin Romances sell two hundred million copies annually)[7] and because their message is so reactionary, directing women's desire exclusively toward love and marriage, it seems important to explore the source of their attraction.[8] My thesis is that the fantasy of romantic love is both powerful and regressive because it repeats

structural features of a daughter's relationship to her father in a patriarchal nuclear family organization and so channels desire back into recreat-
ing the patterns of female subordination and dependency on a man that
characterize the Western family.

Romantic love in the Western world, as Denis de Rougemont has
shown, has at its heart a desire for desire. A lover's self-definition depends
on the intensity of his or her feelings. Since possession takes the edge off
passion, brings it down to the level of everyday experience, what the lovers
need is not so much one another's presence as one another's absence.[9]
Freud concurs: "The value the mind sets on erotic needs instantly sinks as
soon as satisfaction becomes readily obtainable. Some obstacle is needed to
swell the tide of the libido to its height."[10] Where do we get such delight in
frustration? Little boys cannot have their mothers, little girls cannot have
their fathers: one's first heterosexual erotic object is unattainable. A little
girl's oedipal wish is to have her father all to herself forever, yet insuper-
able barriers prevent his being hers. The irreconcilable tension between
the dream of union and the reality of separation in this first love provides a
blueprint for maintaining intact the intensity of desire.

Inaccessibility, of course, allows the lover's imagination boundless
scope, since the reality of the beloved is not there to check idealizing
embellishments. Again, the romantic love tradition imitates a feature of
the post-industrial family organization that gives women primary responsibility for child care, men financial responsibility for the family. Since her
father works outside the home, in a mysterious world a child can only
imagine, her love for him is less embedded in actual contact than her
feelings for her mother and is therefore likely to involve fantasy and
idealization. In fact, a girl's relation to her father trains her to idealize a
distant and mysterious figure whose absences she can fill with glamorous
projections.

The romantic myth, as retold by Simone de Beauvoir, repeats the
roles allocated to women and men in the nuclear family: "Woman is the
Sleeping Beauty, Cinderella, Snow White, she who receives and submits.
In song and story the young man . . . slays the dragon, he battles giants:
she is locked in a tower, a palace, a garden, a cave, she is chained to a
rock, a captive, sound asleep: she waits."[11] And when he enters, of course,
"real life" begins. The romantic pattern recapitulates the distribution of
power and mobility to father and daughter: he comes and goes as he likes,
she remains cooped up in the house, awaiting his return. His arrival injects
some of the glamor of the outside world into the domestic round, so that at
the moment of his homecoming life seems intensified.[12]

Rochester slips right into the slot prepared for him in the reader's
unconscious: "I am old enough to be your father," he reminds Jane at
intervals.[13] "I have . . . roamed over half the globe, while you have lived
quietly with one set of people in one house" (137).[14] Mastery of the wide
world, freedom, autonomy are his. Jane remains enclosed in *his* home,

subordinate to him and subject to his orders, in a position parallel to a girl's in her father's household. Far above Jane in rank and power, Rochester seems inaccessible; his mysterious absences and even more mysterious broodings over his hidden inner life endow him with the glamor of the unknown and make him a target for idealization.[15]

Further, the stages of Jane's relationship with Rochester recapitulate structural features of father-daughter relations: waiting, flirting, and the oedipal triangle.

First, waiting. Although Adrienne Rich rightly corrects those readers who remember from *Jane Eyre* only the love episodes, pointing out that the novel stretches over Jane's whole life, Brontë contributes to the effect of isolating the love story in her readers' minds by setting it off as if she were beginning anew. She wipes out all Jane's previous experience and concerns to make her simply a woman waiting, stripping both the scene and Jane's consciousness to create a frame of emptiness waiting to be filled by the man:

> The ground was hard, the air was still, my road was lonely. . . . the charm of the hour lay in its approaching dimness. . . . I was . . . in a lane noted for wild roses in summer, for nuts and blackberries in autumn . . . but whose best winter delight lay in its utter solitude and leafless repose. If a breath of air stirred, it made no sound here; for there was not a holly, not an evergreen to rustle, and the stripped hawthorn and hazel bushes were as still as the white, worn stones. . . . Far and wide, on each side, there were only fields, where no cattle now browsed. . . . in the absolute hush I could hear . . . thin murmurs of life [from the distant village of Hay]. . . . A rude noise broke on these fine ripplings and whisperings . . . a positive tramp, tramp; a metallic clatter, which effaced the soft wave-wanderings. (114–15)

This description elaborates what isn't there: no roses, no nuts, no black-berries, no holly, no evergreen, no leaves on the hawthorn and holly bushes, not even a rustle of sound — and, framing this picture of nothing, vacant fields where no cattle browse. Jane's mind is equally empty of present concerns, focused on what is about to happen ("the approaching dimness"). The "absolute hush" is the hush of expectancy, and into the empty center of Jane's life rides, on cue, the man. He brings the distant promise of the world into the foreground, transforming the aerial whisperings of Jane's imagination into the concrete noise of life. Building on a girl's daily experience of the excitement injected into domestic routine by the return of her father from the glamorous outside world, this sequence of life suspended followed by life intensified upon the entrance of the hero encourages female readers to think of their time alone as mere prelude, perhaps even a necessary prelude: if they wait long enough, the right man will enter so life can begin. This waiting robs women's time alone of meaning, save that of preparation and expectation.

Rochester's bizarre behavior toward Jane — compounded of ambiguity, disguise, and deception—imitates a peculiarity of father-daughter interactions. The psychoanalytic account of female development stresses the importance of the father's role in directing his daughter's erotic impulses, first oriented toward her mother, into heterosexual channels. The taboo on incest, though, prevents a father from following through. As Nancy Chodorow says, "The father's role is to shape his daughter's sexuality (without getting too involved in it)"; he is "supposed to make himself available (while not making himself available) to his daughter" as her first heterosexual object of desire (139, 118). A father walking this tightrope of sexual flirtation is bound to give his daughter contradictory signals, and she is bound to be confused. Rochester enacts the same baffling behavior, again and again signalling his attraction to Jane only to put her off by insisting he means to marry Blanche Ingram—his equal in a social hierarchy that, echoing the oedipal configuration, enthrones the legitimate couple on a level beyond Jane's reach. The hidden promise of Rochester's seductive behavior toward Jane fills Jane with the excitement mixed with bewilderment and resentment of a girl encountering again and again a mysterious promise she can't read, a promise continuously deferred: "To speak truth, sir, I don't understand you at all" (140); I don't understand enigmas" (199); "[his] discourse was all darkness to me" (141). In response to Rochester's ambiguous come-ons, Jane alternates between fantasies of desire and strict self-inhibition. The oscillation between hope and guilt, between the illusion of intimacy and the irremediability of distance, puts the female reader identifying with Jane into a familiar bind. Indeed, if the reader weren't familiar with the prolongation, over years, of such teasing behavior, the cruelty of Rochester's vacillation between attraction and withdrawal, lasting 180 pages as it does, would undermine his attractiveness.

A girl feels uneasy inveigling her father, partly because the attention he gives her seems to be stolen from her mother. Bertha Mason is Rochester's legal wife, and her physical power and rage make her a satisfyingly ferocious mother avenger. Her presence also keeps the oedipal dream of marrying one's father from coming too true. As Norman Holland and Fredric Jameson point out, we can tolerate watching our primitive desires played out in art only if they are contained within strictly symbolic structures.[16] Otherwise, the dread and guilt attached to archaic desires would overwhelm us. As Jane's wedding day approaches, her increasing anxiety and fragmentation reflect a female reader's malaise at the imminence, on the level of unconscious fantasy, of marriage with the father. On the night before the wedding, Jane's fears explode from nightmare into reality as Bertha invades her room to tear up her wedding veil. The next day this symbolic prevention of marriage becomes actual as the discovery of Bertha's existence stops the wedding. Bertha's presence thus prevents oedipal desire from passing the point of safety, ensures its containment within the purely symbolic structure of a white wedding.

Rochester embeds the acknowledgment of his wife's existence in a flattering comparison: "With a fierce cry . . . the clothed hyena rose up. . . . the maniac bellowed. . . . I recognized that purple face—those bloated features. . . . "That is *my wife*," said [Rochester]. . . . "and *this* is what I wished to have . . . this young girl. . . . Compare these clear eyes with the red balls yonder—this face with that mask—this form with that bulk" (295–96). "This young girl," or the reader identifying with her, can rest secure with this unambiguous declaration of preference: the desired father considers *her* a fresh pure radiance, his wife a monster. Rochester wants to keep Jane innocent, "wants to find in her the very opposite of that aggressive sexuality, that uncontrollable passionate will that has its form in Bertha," as Helene Moglen says (127). So he defines her femininity as elfin—that is, confined to a world of fantasy that excludes sexuality—or childlike: "a little sunny-faced girl with . . . dimpled cheeks and rosy lips" (260), "this one little English girl" (271). He thus underlines, continuously, his attraction to a childlike Jane, reinforcing the parallel with a father's flattering attentions to his female child. Oedipal fantasy has it both ways, as usual in *Jane Eyre*: the father figure makes a clear statement of undivided love for his girl; yet the existence of Bertha prohibits his acting it out.

How does Charlotte Brontë manage a reader's oedipal anxiety in the end, then, when—Bertha dead—Jane returns to marry Rochester? Jane's adventures alone, after the discovery of Bertha, follow the plan of a child leaving the parental home to establish his/her own place in the world. Jane leaves the patriarchal mansion governed by Rochester to find work and establish a family of her own. But, unlike a girl who has to leave an adored father behind forever, Jane unexpectedly discovers that her new family (Diane, Mary, and St. John Rivers) are actually blood relations—cousins, or, as she affectionately calls them, "brother and sisters." Brontë thus turns the newly established family unit into Jane's original one, which Jane must now leave to marry an exagomous lover—Rochester after all. By thus manipulating the blood-lines of Jane's kinship chart Brontë effectively disguises what is after all the fulfillment of the oedipal dream, eternal and exclusive union with the father figure.

Illusion in various guises—Rochester's deception and ambiguity, her year-long separation from him—sustains Jane's love for Rochester at the height of intensity. If, as I maintain, romantic love derives some of its features from father-daughter relations, it is no wonder that many of its excitements are based on illusion. A daughter's erotic love must remain a fantasy because of the taboo on incest—but the attentions of a father responsible for guiding his daughter's erotic feelings into heterosexual channels continually feed the fantasy. If we think of the features of female romantic love that prolong its intensity—the glamor it gives to a distant or absent lover; the desire which hope and uncertainty impart to waiting for his call or his return; the attraction of alternatingly seductive and rejecting behavior; the increment of desire that a love triangle adds — all the fevered excitements of elusive love have their source in the shadow-play of love between father and daughter. Romantic love is debilitating, then, not only because it encourages women to reproduce the male-dominant structure of their first heterosexual love, but because it encourages them to find again the excitement of desire in games that manipulate illusion based on a man who is in important ways not there. We would be better off if our first relationship were with a man who *was* there, with a father who bore as much responsibility for parenting as his wife, so that our model of heterosexual relationship would be embedded in concrete daily interaction rather than in a distance that fosters idealization.

Jane Eyre provides a satisfying fantasy vehicle for the other side of a girl's feelings toward her father, as well: the anger that must accompany her disappointment in not getting what she wants from him. According to Nancy Chodorow's retelling of the female developmental story, a girl turns toward her father for reasons beyond the need to find a heterosexual love object: feeling hemmed in by the primary relationship with her mother that seems overwhelmingly close, "she looks for a symbol of her own autonomy and independence, and a relationship which will help her to get this." By allying herself with her father, she hopes to share in his power, mobility, and independence: but she is disappointed on all counts. Fathers are more apt to gender-type their daughters than are mothers, according to the studies Chodorow cites, discouraging "masculine" assertiveness and rewarding their daughters for stereotypical feminine qualities such as coyness, submissiveness, and docility (124, 118–19, 138–39). Brontë's insistent imagery of female containment must appeal to female readers' angry memories of bumping up against the walls of parental sex role definitions. And Jane's repeated, and repeatedly thwarted, attempts to gain autonomy must call up the anger associated with her female readers' similarly frustrated declarations of independence. Whenever Jane claims the right to her own identity, the patriarchy inevitably puts her in her place: being locked into the Reeds' Red Room is only the most forcible of her confinements to the gender compartments of the patriarchal family. Jane's angry response to all attempts to define her as a subordinate is one of defiant autonomy: "I am not an angel . . . I will be myself" (262). Jane's repeated refusals to be contained within gender categories can inspire her reader with a similar determination to make the fantasy of autonomy a reality in her own life.

If Jane's verbal defiance of patriarchal restrictions presents the reader with an appealingly noble image of herself as brave resistance fighter, Bertha satisfies the reader's anger against patriarchal constraints on a more primitive level.[17] Bertha raging in triumph on the battlements of the burning house, Rochester pinned beneath by its falling pillars, must gratify a female reader's repressed rage against her father and the whole patriarchal family structure that limits female aspiration.

This combination of Jane's verbal protest with Bertha's vivid action is only one example of the way Brontë uses Bertha and Jane to lodge a powerful protest against women's oppression at all levels of her reader's psyche. Bertha, appropriately preverbal (she groans, screams, mutters, and laughs, but never speaks) addresses the quirks of a female unconscious through images of painful incarceration and fiery revenge. Jane appeals to the reader's intellect with a social analysis of how confinement in domestic structures damages women. While Bertha demonstrates, Jane articulates the causes of her madness. Brontë thus manages to appeal to the reader's unconscious fantasies of revenge while analyzing the social oppressions that cause them.[18]

A fairly simple example of their collaboration occurs when Jane makes her famous third-story speech against the confinement of women to domestic tasks; as she finishes elaborating the damages that can result from "too rigid a constraint, too absolute a stagnation," Bertha's mad laughter rings out in confirmation (112–13).

Jane's long enumeration of the ills she would suffer as St. John's wife is a more complex example of how Jane's commentary reflects on Bertha's ordeal. Brontë's hold on the reader's imagination comes, at least in part, from the cumulative effect of varying the same fantasy, now in Jane's experience, now in Bertha's. The dumb show of Bertha lays down the basic fantasy structure: being locked up in a patriarchal system and burning it down in revenge. Jane's impassioned rhetoric — addressed to St. John, who wants her to be his wife — adds a layer of elaboration, a coherently argued articulation of the oppressions of wifehood inherent in Bertha's images:

> I . . . fancied myself in idea *his wife*. Oh! it would never do! As his curate, his comrade. . . . my heart and mind would be free. I should still have my unblighted self to turn to: my natural unenslaved feelings with which to communicate in moments of loneliness. There would be recesses in my mind which would be only mine, to which he never came; and sentiments growing there fresh and sheltered, which his austerity could never blight . . . but as his wife — at his side always, and always restrained, and always checked — forced to keep the fire of my nature continually low, to compel it to burn inwardly and never utter a cry, though the imprisoned flame consumed vital after vital — *this* would be unendurable. (410)

It is as if Bertha's fire had found a voice to explain the suffering that passion turned inward by patriarchal prohibition inflicts on wives. When Jane imagines how her own fire would destroy her if confined by her husband's disapproval, she makes Bertha less a monster, more an emblem of *wife* (the italicized word recalls Rochester's term for Bertha, loaded with all the sarcasm of his bitterness). Jane's picture of physical annexation — "at his side always" — and radical constraint — "always restrained, and always checked" — similarly glosses Bertha's immobilization, presenting wifehood as the utter loss of freedom and mobility. Not even Virginia Woolf's Mrs. Dalloway could conjure up a more frightening vision of patriarchal domination invading every room of the soul.

Part of the constriction Jane (and, one supposes, Bertha) feels comes from the readiness of patriarchal authority both to define female propriety and to punish infractions of it. Just as Rochester banned Bertha for being "intemperate and unchaste," St. John unhesitatingly brands Jane's words "violent and unfeminine" (309, 415), punishing her with a spiritual isolation that is the counterpart of Bertha's solitary confinement. But allowing St. John to impose his definition of female virtue on her—"you are docile, diligent, disinterested, faithful, constant and courageous; very gentle, and very heroic"—makes Jane feel threatened, too. Her desires, vague and diffuse before, "assumed a definite form under his shaping hand . . . my iron shroud contracted around me" (406). The metaphor extends the constraint of Bertha's prison cell to an image of deadly spiritual constriction. Jane's repetition of death images implies that both succumbing to patriarchal definitions and braving them imperil her survival as an individual:

> "If I were to marry you, you would kill me. You are killing me now." (415)
> All this was torture to me—refined, lingering torture. It kept up a slow fire of indignation, and a trembling trouble of grief, which harrassed and crushed me altogether. I felt how—if I were his wife, this good man . . . could soon kill me. (413)

Jane brings out the full emotional weight of pain and indignation implicit in the image of Bertha's "slow fire." Bertha's death borrows meaning retrospectively from Jane's images of violent annihilation. Jane feels not only "banished," but "banned" (414) by St. John—deleted like Bertha from the rolls of patriarchy for transgressing patriarchal limits on female behavior.

By thus building up, through Jane's elaboration of Bertha's primitive images, several layers of fantasy based on the common female experience of confinement and repression, Brontë must draw out her reader's resentment at being hemmed in by patriarchal strictures and structures. Two interrelated question arise. If a novel attaches a reader, as Holland says, by reflecting his or her infantile fantasies, does that mean that the novel simply reinforces existing unconscious fantasies, or can awakening the repressed emotion attached to old wounds make it available for investment in the new patterns the novel suggests? Does a reader simply revel in burning down Thornfield, or does destroying the patriarchal household clear a space in the reader's imagination, as in the novel, for the construction of a more egalitarian domestic structure? The second question has to do with what fantasy patterns *Jane Eyre* actually offers readers, what finally attaches them so powerfully to the novel. After the novel's imagery of wifehood as "iron shroud" has focused a reader's anger at the cramp of growing up female in a patriarchal family, does the novel channel that energy into a vision of alternative living arrangements that would offer women more room for development and self-expression? Is reading *Jane Eyre* an imaginative experience that leads to change, or does it simply reinforce old patterns?

Jane Eyre does present an alternative living structure in Moor House, a family based on sisterly solidarity that opens up paths for Jane's intellectual and emotional growth rather than closing down female development like the patriarchal family Brontë impugns. But the sequence in which Brontë offers alternatives determines their relative impact on a reader's imagination. Just as at Thornfield Jane gave up her fantasy, newly articulated, of exploring the wide world and claiming a larger field for her endeavors when Rochester rode into the picture, she gives up the community at Moor House, which includes everything but romance, to return to Rochester and the fulfillments of passionate love.[19]

After inheriting a fortune from her uncle, Jane becomes the mistress of her own house, which she delights in making comfortable for her cousins, Mary and Diana. Her new family is utterly satisfying to her in its combination of support and intellectual challenge: "What they enjoyed, delighted me; what they approved, I reverenced. . . . Thought fitted thought; opinion met opinion: we coincided, in short, perfectly" (351–52). Yet dreams of Rochester haunt her — "dreams where, amidst unusual scenes, charged with adventure . . . I still again and again met Mr. Rochester, always at some exciting crisis; and then the sense of being in his arms, hearing his voice, meeting his eye, touching his hand and cheek, loving him, being loved by him — the hope of passing a lifetime at his side, would be renewed, with all its first force and fire" (369). The Moor House episode is marked by Jane's joy in daily tasks — cleaning and refurbishing her home for the family she loves — but the new note of domestic realism cannot compete with the excitements of the old romantic dream. When Rochester calls, Jane returns to him without a backward glance. Passion infuses Brontë's celebration of permanent and exclusive union with the beloved, making female intellectual community seem but a pale substitute. Mary and Diana marry in the end, too, reinforcing the message of Jane's final felicity: what makes a woman *really* happy is love and marriage. To introduce the possibility of a community of women based on shared intellectual pleasures and mutual affection, only to reject it without question for a man, does not so much suggest an alternative to convention as reinforce the cultural myth: time spent with other women is merely a prelude to marriage.

In the next to last chapter, Jane returns to Rochester a new woman — that is, rich and independent. Since Bertha has burned down Thornfield, Jane and Rochester are free to build a new domestic structure from the ground up. At first they seem emotionally free, too, to imagine new ways of living together. In a bantering review of alternative structures, Rochester suggests — yet again! — that they could be father and daughter to each other, or nurse and patient (439). Jane boasts of her new independence: "I can build a house of my own close up to your door" (438). As an alternative to the hierarchy of a patriarchal household, the model of houses side by side embodies a notion of marriage as "parallel lives," in Phyllis Rose's phrase: together, yet with a margin of separation, husband and wife would be equally powerful and autonomous, equally masters of their own houses.[20]

This vision of a separate and equal love is but the creation of a moment's imaginative freedom, though, swept away almost immediately by the ideology of love that floods the last chapter. It begins with a cry of triumph: "Reader, I married him!" (453).[21] Brontë forgets her own powerful argument against the constraints of being a *wife* to embrace the happy ending of romantic fantasy:

> I have now been married ten years. I know what it is to live entirely for and with what I love best on earth. I hold myself supremely blest — blest beyond what language can express: because I am my husband's life as fully as he is mine. No woman was ever nearer to her mate than I am; ever more absolutely bone of his bone, and flesh of his flesh. I know no weariness of my Edward's society: he knows none of mine, any more than we each do of the pulsation of the heart that beats in our separate bosoms; consequently, we are ever together. To be together is for us to be at once as free as in solitude, as gay as in company. We talk, I believe, all day long: to talk to each other is but a more animated and an audible thinking. All my confidence is bestowed on him, all his confidence is devoted to me; we are precisely suited in character — perfect concord is the result. (454)

I have quoted the passage at length because the tone is important. Karen Rowe claims that by the time Jane marries, Brontë has found the fairytale paradigm of romantic love wanting and developed in its place a broader concept of romance based on Shakespearean and Miltonic models: "the domestic realism of the reconciliation scene testifies to Jane's mature concept of romance."[22] But Jane's rhapsodic tone powerfully reinforces the fairytale message of the romantic ending: if you marry the right man, you will live happily ever after. Jane has lived out this static happiness for ten years without a wrinkle in her bliss. Janice Radway's *Reading the Romance* posits that what satisfies female readers of romance is not so much the heroine's acquisition of a strong, virile man as the vicarious recovery of a maternal nurturing figure via the hero's unexpected tenderness.[23] Although Rochester can never be mistaken for a maternal nurturer, Radway's insight can perhaps illuminate one aspect of the passage's appeal to female readers. Out of the frustration of not having the father, oedipal fantasy spins a dream of plenitude: the father figure fills Jane's life, leaving no aspiration or need unfulfilled. But the content of this oedipal dream, complete fusion — "bone of his bone, and flesh of his flesh" — can't be found in the ambivalence and distance between father and daughter: it must come from the remembered symbiosis of a girl's first relationship, with a mother whom the infant does not distinguish from herself. Freud describes this first sense of a self fused with the mother in *Civilization and Its Discontents;* Chodorow points out that in female development mother-daughter symbiosis commonly lasts long past infancy because of mothers' unconscious tendency to regard their daughters as extensions of themselves. So Jane's celebration of marital fusion probably engages readers not only on the level of desire for the father figure, but also as a recovery of the bliss, comfort, and unity of that initial boundary-free connection with another. As Freud says in "Female Sexuality," the object of desire changes — from mother to father — in the oedipal stage, but the form of relationship remains the same.[24]

Jane and, vicariously, her reader, get it all then — except autonomy. Merged with Rochester, "literally the apple of his eye" (454), his vision, and his right hand, she cannot move away to pursue any autonomous activity whatever: even childcare must be shelved, Adèle packed off to boarding school because "my husband needed all my [time and care]" (453). Brontë's effusions here seem like a lesson in the power of unconscious fantasy to overthrow intellectual and political commitment: the argument against the domestic bondage of wives is wiped out by Brontë's passionate endorsement of that most confining of all female spaces, the shared bubble of bliss promised by romantic love and the oedipal fantasy beneath it.

Adrienne Rich insists that the tone of the above passage is not that of "romantic love or romantic marriage," pointing to the terms of equality that Jane's economic independence and freedom of choice impose on her marriage to Rochester (107).[25] Indeed, Brontë's acute awareness of social and economic issues makes her resolution more complicated than a simple fairytale ending. Jane has acquired a fortune that makes her the economic equal of a Rochester diminished by the destruction of Thornfield; and Rochester's loss of hand and eye leaves no doubt that he needs Jane as much as she needs him. She is Rochester's "guide" as well as his "prop," "leading" him as well as "waiting on" him (451, 448): Brontë articulates precisely the degree of control in Jane's help that distinguishes it from her former service to her "master."[26] The balance of power has shifted so that their relationship no longer recapitulates, on the political surface, the asymmetries of a father-daughter relationship; yet on the personal level Rochester still embodies the patriarchal strength a girl can depend on: "His form was of the same strong and stalwart contour as ever: his port was still erect, his hair was still raven black . . . not in one year's space, by any sorrow, could his athletic strength be quelled, or his vigorous prime blighted. But in his countenance, I saw a change . . . that reminded me of some wronged and fettered wild beast or bird, dangerous to approach. . . . The caged eagle . . . might look as looked that sightless Samson" (434). This is not a Philip Wakem, whose crippled helplessness evokes in Maggie Tulliver pitiful images of "wry-necked lambs."[27] An eagle, later "a royal eagle," or a lion (439, 441), Rochester is still commanding, still a king beneath the metamorphoses that but enhance his animal vitality. Human analogues, too, contribute to the impression of virile strength: Rochester is a Samson, "a Vulcan . . . brown, broad-shouldered" (389). In perhaps their most telling metaphorical exchange Rochester, comparing himself to the lightning-struck chestnut tree in his garden, hesitates to ask Jane, "a budding woodbine," to twine around him. He is not a ruin, Jane assures him, but a strong tree, "green and vigorous. Plants will grow about your roots . . . they will lean towards you, and wind round you, because your strength offers them so safe a prop" (391). A girl need not learn to stand on her own two feet if she can drape her sweetness round a man's oak-like strength. Brontë's images, appealing directly to the level of unconscious fantasy, repeat a familiar combination of paternal strength and graceful girlhood, belying the reassuring surface fantasy of a new balance of power.

Brontë has managed to shape her ending to satisfy both extremes of female ambivalence toward fathers: while Jane gets a Rochester with patriarchal sex appeal undiminished, Bertha's revenge nevertheless reduces him, with satisfying symmetry, to a position of female weakness, "humbled," "dependent," "powerless," and, cruellest parallel of all, confined (by blindness) to the house (435, 442, 450).[28] Rather than equality developing through a woman's entry into the world of work and adventure, it comes about through Rochester's loss of mobility and ambition. Rather than Jane expanding into the wide field of endeavor that she earlier claimed as the prerogative of a talented and ambitious woman, Rochester has been shrunk till he is available for enclosure in the romantic fulfillment that "makes one little room an everywhere," to borrow Donne's phrase.[29]

What has become of the fantasy of autonomy and adventure in the wide world that Jane used to hold dear? Brontë projects it onto a male figure. While Jane melts into passionate union, St. John explores the world alone: "resolute, indefatigable pioneer . . . amidst rocks and dangers . . . he labors for the race" (455). *Jane Eyre* ends, it seems, with a confirmation of Freud's assertion that men and women dream differently: "In young women erotic wishes dominate the phantasies almost exclusively, for their ambition is generally comprised in their erotic longings; in young men egoistic and ambitious wishes assert themselves plainly enough alongside their erotic desires."[30] Freud probably accepted only erotic fantasies in women as normal because he defined normal women as passive, and romantic love, as we have seen, gives women a passive role; ambitious fantasies Freud dismissed as "penis envy," consigning their possessors to the pathological condition of "masculinity complex."[31] Freud's establishment of a passive norm for female fantasy, like his description/prescription of passivity as the norm for female personality structure, has the effect of limiting possibilities for women. Since we can become only what we first wish to become, the allocation of love fantasies to girls, adventure stories to boys, reinforces gender distinctions by making girls long for love and marriage, boys for autonomy and adventure. The ending of *Jane Eyre* splits the human possibilities of life between the two sexes, reinstating the old gender definitions that the whole novel has demonstrated to be painfully restrictive.

To return to my original question: what accounts for readers' lifelong attachment to *Jane Eyre*? Perhaps it is Brontë's combination of fantasies that often seem, in life as in novels, incompatible: she presents a passionate assertion of autonomy and at the same time a passionate commitment to romantic love, mirroring her readers' conflicting wishes and endeavoring, like them, to have it all. Jane's defiant autonomy, together with Bertha's cruder but violently effective protests against patriarchal domination, must energize a reader's revolutionary passion by appealing to a deep level of anger against existing family structures: Jane Lazarre attests to the courage *Jane Eyre* gave her to assert her own rebel identity in the face of patriarchal definitions of the good girl; and Adrienne Rich claims to have been inspired, in a way that lasted all her life, by *Jane Eyre*'s model of female integrity supported by nurturant models of female strength.

But I suspect that many modern readers, including feminists like myself, are attached to *Jane Eyre* because it reflects so well our ambivalence. On the level of lucid and compelling rhetoric, Brontë advocates feminist ideals — arguing against patriarchal structures that confine and subordinate women and for a wider field for women's endeavors — while underneath flows, unchecked, a passionate desire for the fusions of romantic love. Those of us who, like Brontë, grew up in patriarchal family structures with an attachment like hers to a strong father[32] probably share with her a susceptibility to the ideology of love at odds with ideological conviction. I suspect that the way conscious autonomous and egalitarian structures operate as covers for unconscious desire throughout the last two chapters mirrors our genuine efforts to structure our lives differently, only to be sabotaged by our own unregenerate desires for fusion with a patriarchal figure. Jane founds a broad base for autonomy at Moor House, but abandons it for Rochester's narrow embrace: evidently a community that offers only respect and self-respect based on productive work and financial independence, along with family warmth and female solidarity grounded in shared intellectual pursuits and emotional kinship, isn't enough; passionate love is. The careful restructuring of power that seems to promise something new — an egalitarian basis for marriage with a bit of leeway for wifely autonomy — gives way to the rhapsody on marital fusion. The superficial political fantasy of redistributed power covers underlying images of symbiosis with a strong oak of a man. I suspect that just as erecting a new structure for marriage enables Brontë to dream an old dream, so the apparently revolutionary nature of Jane's egalitarian marriage allows an old fantasy to get by the ideological censors of her readers, so that we all, feminists and Harlequin romance readers alike, can enjoy the unending story of having one's patriarch all to oneself forever.

Notes

1. *The Madwoman in the Attic* (New Haven: Yale University Press, 1979). I am indebted to Gilbert and Gubar's analysis of Brontë's structures of confinement and rage, and more generally to the inspiration of their example in unearthing the female psychic patterns reflected in women's literature.

2. Quoted from Martineau's *Autobiography* (1877) in Ellen Moers, *Literary Women* (Garden City, New York: Doubleday, 1977), 99.

3. "*Jane Eyre:* The Temptations of a Motherless Woman," *Ms.* 2 (October, 1973), 68.

4. " 'Charlotte's Web': Reading *Jane Eyre* over Time," in *Between Women* (Boston: Beacon Press, 1984), 223.

5. Dianne Sadoff points out the father-daughter configurations in *Villette* and *Shirley* as well as *Jane Eyre,* arguing persuasively that Brontë's dependence on her own father as well as her angry need to free herself from that dependency inspire certain recurrent patterns of interaction with father figures (or real fathers, in the case of Polly Home in *Villette*). Sadoff focuses on a different set of parallels with father-daughter arrangements than I do, highlighting patterns of fathers abandoning and punishing their daughters and daughters in turn punishing their fathers in "narrative castrations [that] appear to be an exaggerated attempt to free [Brontë's] heroines from dependence on fathers." *Monsters of Affection* (Baltimore: Johns Hopkins University Press, 1982), 151.

6. *The Dynamics of Literary Response* (New York: Oxford University Press, 1968), 52, 334, 340.

7. The popular appeal of romantic fantasy to modern women has been widely documented. See *The New Yorker* (9 May 1983), 39.

8. Tania Modleski makes the same point in her introduction to *Loving with a Vengeance* (Hamden, Connecticut: Shoe String Press, 1968), 14. Modleski's analysis of the basis in male-dominant family patterns of many of the fantasy patterns in Harlequin Romances and modern Gothics was inspiring and helpful to me in writing this essay.

9. *Love in the Western World* (New York: Doubelday, 1957).

10. "The Most Prevalent Form of Degradation in Erotic Life," in *Sexuality and the Psychology of Love* (New York: Macmillan, 1978), 67.

11. *The Second Sex* (New York: Random House, 1974), 328.

12. See Nancy Chodorow, *The Reproduction of Mothering* (Berkeley: University of California Press, 1978), 80, 195. Further references to this text are cited parenthetically in the text.

13. Charlotte Brontë, *Jane Eyre* (New York: New American Library, 1960), 137, 142, 439. Further quotations from this edition are cited parenthetically in the text.

14. David Smith, in "Incest Patterns in Two Victorian Novels," maintains that a battle between incestual desire and the incest taboo occupies Jane's unconscious and structures the whole novel. His analysis of the Red Room incident in terms of the incest theme is especially interesting. See *Literature and Psychology*, 15 (Summer, 1965), 135–44.

15. I do not mean to suggest that Brontë's picture of an inaccessible, mysterious man came from her father's absence from the home: as a minister, his place of work was the parsonage where the family lived. Nevertheless, his authoritarian manner and his "paradoxical absence and hovering presence somewhere in the godlike upper reaches of the parsonage," in Sadoff's words (139), endowed him with power and mystery. Probably more central to Rochester's makeup, though, is his literary ancestry, the line of Byronic heros the Brontë children knew and loved. See Helene Moglen's description of the Byronic hero in *Charlotte Brontë: The Self Conceived* (New York: Norton, 1976). Further references to this text are cited parenthetically in the text.

16. Holland elaborates this model throughout *The Dynamics of Literary Response*. See especially 189 and 311–14. Jameson restates Holland's theory in "Reification and Utopia in Mass Culture," *Social Text* 1 (1979), 136.

17. Gilbert and Gubar have brilliantly illuminated the psychological and sexual relevance of *Jane Eyre*'s houses and rooms, an imagery they find central to women's nineteenth century novels (83–92, 340–41, 347–49). Elaine Showalter notes the sexual connotations of the Red Room and its symbolic identity with Bertha's den, in *A Literature of Their Own* (Princeton: Princeton University Press, 1977), 114–15. Gilbert and Gubar also demonstrate how Bertha, "Jane's truest and darkest double," acts out Jane's anger against Rochester on several fiery occasions, including her final incendiary feat, which realizes "Jane's profound desire to destroy Thornfield, the symbol of Rochester's mastery and her servitude" (360).

18. Modleski describes a similar combination of unconscious fantasy with rational social analysis in Mary Wollstonecraft's *Maria* (83).

19. Maurianne Adams makes this point in "*Jane Eyre:* Woman's Estate," in *The Authority of Experience: Essays in Feminist Criticism*, eds. Arlyn Diamond and Lee Edwards (Amherst: University of Massachusetts Press, 1977), 145.

20. *Parallel Lives: Five Victorian Marriages* (New York: Knopf, 1983).

21. Rachel Brownstein, in *Becoming a Heroine*, finds in Jane's masterful use of the active voice an indication that her marriage "defiantly affirms not the heroine's transformation but her remaining herself." (New York: Random House, 1982), 156–57.

22. " 'Fairy-born and Human-Bred': Jane Eyre's Education in Romance," in *The Voyage In: Fictions of Female Development*, eds. Elizabeth Abel, Marianne Hirsch, and Elizabeth Langland (Hanover, N.H.: University Press of New England, 1983), 89.

23. *Reading the Romance* (Chapel Hill: University of North Carolina Press, 1984). Radway bases her explanation of readers' satisfaction with fictional lovers who offer a combination of traditional manly qualities and nurturing tenderness on the triangular pattern of the female oedipal stage described by Chodorow. Chodorow makes clear that when a girl turns from primary love for her mother to oedipal love for her father, she by no means leaves her mother behind. "Every step of the way . . . a girl develops her relationship to her father while looking back at her mother. . . . A girl is likely to maintain both her parents as love objects and rivals throughout the oedipal period" (127). Radway then argues that "the ideal male partner . . . is capable of fulfilling both object roles in a woman's triangular inner-object configuration. His spectacular masculinity underscores his status as her heterosexual lover . . . [but] his extraordinary tenderness and capacity for gentle nurturance means she does not have to give up the physical part of her mother's attentions because his 'soft' sexual attention allows her to return to the passive state of infancy where all of her needs were satisfied and her fears erased at her mother's breast" (147). Although Radway's argument is certainly winning—and certainly accurate, too, in assessing what women want—the women readers she surveyed all insist on the *dyad* of heroine and lover: they dislike romances that divert attention from the developing relation between male and female leads by introducing secondary characters (122–23). (The one fascinating exception, *Green Lady*, is a romance written by a mother-daughter team that ends with a mother-daughter merger that displaces

the women's male lovers altogether.) Women readers' preference for the pure intensity of a single developing relationship rather than a love triangle shows, I think, that the fantasy of romantic love, and oedipal love beneath it, has taken over the form of intense and complete union with one person from the mother-infant dyad, but has substituted the father or male object for the original mother object.

24. *Sexuality and the Psychology of Love* (New York: Macmillan, 1978), 199.

25. Patricia Beer, in *Reader, I Married Him,* also says this is "a marriage of equality as well as ecstasy" (New York: Harper and Row, 1974), 107. Maurianne Adams presents the most comprehensive analysis of the complex class, status and economic issues interlocking with the romantic dream, to conclude like me that finally questions of economic status and autonomy are secondary to "the fantasy that love is a fusion of souls" (157).

26. Terry Eagleton analyzes the complex blend of submissiveness and control in Jane's final power relations with Rochester in *Myths of Power: A Marxist Study of the Brontës* (London: Macmillan, 1975), 29–30.

27. George Eliot, *The Mill on the Floss* (New York: New American Library, 1965), 191.

28. Sadoff says that Rochester's "symbolic castration represents the daughter's surreptitious punishment of the domineering master-father . . . and gains the daughter a qualified mastery over him" (145).

29. Adams thinks the closeness at Ferndean has a sinister "hemmed-in, stagnant" undercurrent that indicates the price of Jane's surrender of ambition and curiosity to domestic romance (139).

30. "The Relation of the Poet to Day-dreaming," in *On Creativity and the Unconscious* (New York: Harper and Row, 1958), 47–48.

31. See Freud's "Femininity," reproduced in *Women and Analysis,* ed. Jean Strouse (New York: Grossman, 1974), and "A Case of Homosexuality in a Woman" in *Sexuality and the Psychology of Love* (New York: Macmillan, 1978).

32. Sadoff argues convincingly that Brontë's relationship with her father was the cornerstone of her emotional life: "She remained emotionally tied to him — dependent upon him even when he was dependent upon her — for life" (152).

Shirley

Currer Bell's *Shirley*

G. H. Lewes*

. . . *Shirley* is inferior to *Jane Eyre* in several important points. It is not quite so true; and it is not so fascinating. It does not so rivet the reader's attention, nor hurry him through all obstacles of improbability, with so keen a sympathy in its reality. It is even coarser in texture, too, and not unfrequently flippant; while the characters are almost all disagreeable, and exhibit intolerable rudeness of manner. In *Jane Eyre* life was viewed from the standing point of individual experience; in *Shirley* that standing point is frequently abandoned, and the artist paints only a panorama of which she, as well as you, are but spectators. Hence the unity of *Jane Eyre* in spite of its clumsy and improbable contrivances, was great and effective: the fire of one passion fused the discordant materials into one mould. But in *Shirley* all unity, in consequence of defective art, is wanting. There is no passionate link; nor is there any artistic fusion or intergrowth, by which one part evolves itself from another. Hence its falling-off in interest, coherent movement, and life. The book may be laid down at any chapter, and almost any chapter might be omitted. The various scenes are gathered up into three volumes, — they have not grown into a work. The characters often need a justification for their introduction; as in the case of the three Curates, who are offensive, uninstructive, and unamusing. That they are not *inventions*, however, we feel persuaded. For nothing but a strong sense of their reality could have seduced the authoress into such a mistake as admitting them at all. We are confident she has seen them, known them, despised them; and *therefore* she paints them! although they have no relation with the story, have no interest in themselves, and cannot be accepted as types of a class, — for they are not *Curates* but *boors:* and although not inventions, we must be permitted to say that they are *not true.* Some such objection the authoress seems indeed to have anticipated; and thus towards the close of her work defends herself against it. "Note well! wherever you present *the actual simple truth, it is somehow always denounced as a lie:* they disown it, cast it off, throw it on

*Reprinted from the *Edinburgh Review* 91 (January 1850): 84–88, 92.

the parish; whereas the product of your imagination, the mere figment, the sheer fiction, is adopted, petted, termed pretty, proper, sweetly natural." Now Currer Bell, we fear, has here fallen into a vulgar error. It is one, indeed, into which even Miss Edgeworth has also fallen: who conceived that she justified the introduction of an improbable anecdote in her text, by averring in a note that it was a "fact." But the intrusion is not less an error for all that. Truth is never rejected, unless it be truth so exceptional as to stagger our belief; and in that case the artist is wrong to employ it, without so *preparing* our minds that we might receive it unquestioned. The coinage of imagination, on the other hand, is not accepted *because* it departs from the actual truth, but only because it presents the recognised attributes of our nature in new and striking combinations. If it falsify these attributes, or the known laws of their associations, the fiction is at once pronounced to be *monstrous*, and is rejected. Art, in short, deals with the broad principles of human nature, not with idiosyncracies: and, although it requires an experience of life both comprehensive and profound, to enable us to say with confidence, that "*this* motive is unnatural," and "*that* passion is untrue," it requires no great experience to say "this character has not the air of reality; it may be copied from nature, but it does not *look* so." Were Currer Bell's defence allowable, all criticism must be silenced at once. An author has only to say that his characters *are copied from nature*, and the discussion is closed. But though the portraits may be like the oddities from whom they are copied, they are faulty as works of art, if they strike all who never met with these oddities as unnatural. The curious anomalies of life, which find their proper niches in Southey's *Omniana, or Commonplace Book*, are not suitable to a novel. It is the same with incidents.

Again we say that *Shirley* cannot be received as a work of art. It is not a picture; but a portfolio of random sketches for one or more pictures. The authoress never seems distinctly to have made up her mind as to what she was to do; whether to describe the habits and manners of Yorkshire and its social aspects in the days of King Lud, or to paint character, or to tell a love story. All are by turns attempted and abandoned; and the book consequently moves slowly, and by starts—leaving behind it no distinct or satisfactory impression. Power is stamped on various parts of it; power unmistakable, but often misapplied. Currer Bell has much yet to learn,— and, especially, the discipline of her own tumultous energies. She must learn also to sacrifice a little of her Yorkshire roughness to the demands of good taste: neither saturating her writings with such rudeness and offensive harshness, nor suffering her style to wander into such vulgarities as would be inexcusable—even in a man. No good critic will object to the homeliness of natural diction, or to the racy flavour of conversational idiom; but every one must object to such phrases as "Miss Mary, *getting up the steam* in her turn, now asked," &c., or as "making hard-handed worsted spinners *cash up to the tune of* four or five hundred per cent.," or as "Malone much chagrined at hearing him *pipe up in most superior style*;" all which phrases occur within the space of about a dozen pages, and that not in dialogue, but in the authoress's own narrative. And while touching on this minor, yet not trivial point, we may also venture a word of quiet remonstrance against a most inappropriate obtrusion of French phrases. When General Moore and his sister talk in French, *which the authoress translates*, it surely is not allowable to leave scraps of French in the translation. A French word or two may be introduced now and then on account of some peculiar fitness, but Currer Bell's use of the language is little better than that of the "fashionable" novelists. To speak of a grandmother as *une grand'-mère*, and of treacle of *mélasse*, or of a young lady being angry as *courroucée*, gives an air of affectation to the style strangely at variance with the frankness of its general tone.

We scarcely know what to say to the impertinence which has been allowed to mingle so largely with the manners, even of the favourite actors in this drama. Their frequent harshness and rudeness is something which startles on a first reading, and, on a second, is quite inexplicable. Is this correct as regards Yorkshire, or is the fault with the artist? In one place she speaks with indignant scorn of those who find fault with Yorkshire manners; and defies the "most refined of cockneys to presume" to do such a thing. "Taken as they ought to be," she assures us "the majority of the lads and lasses of the West Riding are gentlemen and ladies, every inch of them: and it is only against the weak affectation and futile pomposity of a would-be aristocrat that they even turn mutinous." This is very possible; but we must in that case strongly protest against Currer Bell's portraits being understood to be resemblances; for they are, one and all, given to break out and misbehave themselves upon very small provocation. The manner and language of Shirley towards her guardian passes all permission. Even the gentle, timid, shrinking Caroline enters the lists with the odious Mrs. Yorke, and the two *ladies* talk at each other, in a style which, to southern ears, sounds both marvellous and alarming. But, to quit this tone of remonstrance, — which after all is a compliment, for it shows how seriously we treat the great talents of the writer, — let us cordially praise the real freshness, vividness, and fidelity, with which most of the characters and scenes are depicted. There is, perhaps, no single picture representing one broad aspect of nature which can be hung beside two or three in *Jane Eyre*; but the same piercing and loving eye, and the same bold and poetic imagery, are here exhibited. . . .

Similar power is manifested in the delineation of character: her eye is quick, her hand certain. With a few brief vigorous touches the picture starts into distinctness. Old Helstone, the copper-faced little Cossack parson, straight as a ramrod, keen as a kite; Yorke, the hard, queer, clever, parson-hating, radical-Gentleman; the benevolent Hall; the fluttering, good, irresolute Mrs. Pryor; the patient, frugal, beneficent old maid, Miss Ainley; Hortense and Moore, and the Sympson family, — are all set with so much life before us, that we seem to *see* them moving through the rooms and across the moor. As a specimen of the nervous, compact writing which not unfrequently occurs to relieve the questionable taste of the rest, take the sentence describing the Sympsons: — "Mr. Sympson proved to be a man of spotless respectability, worrying temper, pious principles, and worldly views. His lady was a very good woman, patient, kind, well-bred. She had been brought up on a narrow system of views—starved on a few prejudices; a mere handful of bitter herbs."

The two heroes of the book, however, — for there are two—are not agreeable characters; nor are they felicitously drawn. They have both something sordid in their minds, and repulsive in their demeanour. Louis Moore is talked about as if he were something greater than our ordinary humanity; but, when he shows himself, turns out to be a very small person indeed. Robert, more energetic, and more decisively standing out from the canvas, is disgraced by a sordid love of money, and a shameless setting aside of an affection for Caroline in favour of the rich heiress. *He* will be universally condemned: for all our better instincts rebel against him. The authoress will appeal in vain here to *the truth* of such sordidness—the truth of thus discarding a real passion in favour of an ambitious project. True it is: *true of many men;* but *not true of noble natures*—not true of an ideal of manhood. In a subordinate character such a lapse from the elevation of moral rectitude, might have been pardoned; but in a hero—in the man for whom our sympathies and admiration are almost exclusively claimed—to imagine it possible, is a decided blunder in art—as well as an inconsistency in nature. A hero may be faulty, erring, imperfect; but he must not be sordid, mean, wanting in the statelier virtues of our kind. Rochester was far more to be respected than this Robert Moore! Nor is Louis Moore much better. On any generous view of life there is almost as much sordidness in his exaggerated notions of Shirley's wealth, and of the *distance* it creates between his soul and hers, as there is in Robert's direct and positive greed of the money. That Louis, as a tutor, should be sensitive to any personal slight, should deeply feel that he was no "match" for the heiress, we can readily understand; but if he thought so meanly of *her* as to suppose that her wealth was any barrier to her affection, then he was unworthy of her.

The heroines are more loveable. Shirley, if she did not occasionally use language one would rather not hear from the lips of a lady, and did not occasionally display something in her behaviour, which, with every allowance for Yorkshire plainness, does imply want of breeding, — Shirley, we say, would be irresistible. So buoyant, free, airy, and healthy in her nature, so fascinating in her manner, she is prettily enough described by her lover as a "Peri too mutinous for heaven, too innocent for hell." But if Shirley is, on the whole, a happy creation, Caroline Helstone, though sometimes remarkably sweet and engaging, is—if we may venture to say so—a failure. Currer Bell is exceedingly scornful on the chapter of heroines drawn by men. The cleverest and acutest of our sex, she says, are often under the strongest illusions about women—we do not read them in their true light; we constantly misapprehend them, both for good and evil. Very possibly. But we suspect that female artists are by no means exempt from mistakes quite as egregious when *they* delineate their sex; nay, we venture to say, that Mrs. Pryor and Caroline Helstone are as untrue to the universal laws of our common nature as if they had been drawn by the clumsy hand of a male: though we willingly admit that in both there are little touches which at once betray the more exquisite workmanship of a woman's lighter pencil.

Mrs. Pryor, in the capital event of her life—at least as far as regards this story—belies the most indisputable laws of our nature, in becoming an unnatural mother,—from some absurd prepossession that her child *must* be bad, wicked, and the cause of anguish to her, because it is pretty! The case is this. She marries a very handsome man, who illtreats her; the fine gentleman turns out a brute. A child is born. This child, which universal experience forces us to exclaim must have been the darling consolation of its miserable mother; this child, over whom the mother would have wept scalding tears in secret, hugging it closer to her bosom to assure her fluttering heart, that in the midst of all her wretchedness, *this* joy remained, that in the midst of all the desolation of home, *this* exquisite comfort was not denied her:—yet this child, we are informed, she parts with, *because* it is pretty! "I feared your loveliness, deeming it the sign of perversity. They sent me your portrait, taken at eight years old; that portrait confirmed my fears. Had it shown me a sunburnt little rustic—a heavy, blunt-featured, commonplace child—I should have hastened to claim you; but there, under the silver paper, I saw blooming the delicacy of an aristocratic flower: "little lady" was written on every trait. . . . In my experience I had not met with truth, modesty, good principle, as the concomitants of beauty. A form so straight and fine, I argued, *must* conceal a mind warped and cruel!" Really this is midsummer madness! Before the child had shown whether its beauty *did* conceal perversity, the mother shuts her heart against it! Currer Bell! if under your heart had ever stirred a child, if to your bosom a babe had ever been pressed,—that mysterious part of your being, towards which all the rest of it was drawn, in which your whole soul was transported and absorbed,—never could you have *imagined* such a falsehood as that! It is indeed conceivable—under some peculiar circumstances, and with peculiar dispositions—that the loathing of the wife for the husband, might extend to the child, because it was the husband's child; the horror and hate being so intense as to turn back the natural current of maternal instincts; but to suppose that the mere beauty and "aristocratic" air of an infant could so wrest out of its place a woman's heart,—supposing her not irretrievably insane,—and for eighteen years keep a mother from her child, is to outrage all that we know of human nature.

Not quite so glaring, and yet very glaring, is the want of truth in Caroline. There are traits about this character quite charming; and we doubt not she will be a favourite with the majority of readers. But any one examining *Shirley* as a work of art, must be struck with the want of keeping in making the gentle, shy, not highly cultivated Caroline *talk* from time to time in the strain of Currer Bell herself rather than in the strain of Helstone's little niece. We could cite several examples: the most striking perhaps is that long soliloquy at pages 269–274, of the second volume, upon the condition of women, — in which Caroline takes a leaf out of Miss Martineau's book. The whole passage, though full both of thought and of eloquence, is almost ludicrously out of place. The apostrophes to the King of Israel, to the fathers of Yorkshire, and to the men of England, might have rounded a period in one of the authoress's own perorations; but to introduce them into a soliloquy by Caroline Helstone is an offence at once against art and against nature.

This, however, is but one point in the faulty treatment of the character. A graver error, — one implying greater forgetfulness of dramatic reality and probability, — is the conduct of Caroline in her love for Moore. The mystery kept up between the two girls is the trick of a vulgar novelist. Shirley must have set Caroline's mind at rest; *must* have said, "Don't be unhappy about Moore and me; I have no love for him — nor he for me." Instead of this, she is allowed to encourage the delusion which she cannot but perceive in Caroline's mind; but what is more incredible still, Caroline — who believes that Moore loves Shirley and will marry her — never once feels the sharp and terrible pang of jealousy! Now, unless we are to be put out of court as men, and consequently incompetent to apprehend the true nature of woman, we should say that this entire absence of jealous feelings on Caroline's part, is an omission, which, conscious or unconscious, we cannot reconcile with any thing we have ever seen, heard, or read of about the sex. That a girl like Caroline might be willing to resign her claims, might be willing even to submit in silence to the torture of her disappointment, is conceivable enough; and a fine theme might this have afforded for some profound psychological probings, laying open the terrible conflict of irrepressible instincts with more generous feelings, — the conflict of jealousy with reason. But Caroline Helstone merely bows her head in meekness, and loves and clings to Shirley all the more; never has even a moment's rebellion against her, and behaves like pattern young ladies in "good" books!

We have been more than once disturbed by what looked like wilful departures from probability in this novel. We are by no means rigorous in expecting that the story is to move along the highway of every-day life. On the contrary, we are willing to allow the imagination full sweep; but we demand, that into whatever region it carry us, it must be at least consistent: if we are to travel into fairy land, it must be in a fairy equipage, *not* in a Hansom's cab. Now there are many regions in *Shirley* where we were glad enough to find ourselves; it is against the method by which we are transported to them that we protest. Thus in the second volume there is a really remarkable tirade about Milton's Eve: as an eloquent rhapsody we can scarcely admire it too much; but to be asked to believe that it was uttered in a quiet conversation between two young ladies, destroys half our pleasure. . . .

Our closing word shall be one of exhortation. Schiller, writing to Goethe about Madame de Stael's *Corinne*, says "This person wants every thing that is graceful in woman; and, nevertheless, the faults of her book are altogether womanly faults. She steps out of her sex — without elevating herself above it." This brief and pregnant criticism is quite as applicable to Currer Bell: For she, too, has genius enough to create a great name for herself; and if we seem to have insisted too gravely on her faults, it is only because we are ourselves sufficiently her admirers to be most desirous to see her remove these blemishes from her writings, and take the rank within her reach. She has extraordinary power — but let her remember that *"on tombe du côté où l'on penche!"*

Public Themes and Private Lives:
Social Criticism in *Shirley*   Arnold Shapiro*

From the outset, critics of Charlotte Brontë's third novel, *Shirley* (published in 1849), have said that the book lacks unity. It has been charged repeatedly that there is no correlation in it between the social themes — for example the Luddite rioting of the turn of the nineteenth century — and the private ones — the two love stories at the center of the book. Thus, G. H. Lewes asserts: *"Shirley* . . . is not a picture; but a portfolio of random sketches for one or more pictures. The authoress never seems distinctly to have made up her mind as to what she was to do; whether to describe the habits and manners of Yorkshire and its social aspects in the days of King Lud, or to paint character, or to tell a love story."[1] More recently, Miss Ratchford calls *Shirley* "the poorest of Charlotte Brontë's novels": ". . . it is cumbered and weighted down by too much that is taken directly from observation and the *Leeds Mercury* . . . ."[2] Asa Briggs, who sympathizes with Charlotte Brontë's intention in the book, states: ". . . it is not concerned with one theme but with a bundle of loosely connected — sometimes unconnected — themes. It lacks compactness and integration."[3] Finally, R. B. Heilman implies that there is a tug-of-war in the novel between Charlotte Brontë's social concerns and

*Reprinted from *Papers on Language and Literature* 4, no. 1 (Winter 1968), 74–84, © 1968 by the Board of Trustees, Southern Illinois University. Printed by permission.

her private ones: ". . . Charlotte cannot keep it a social novel. Unlike [Robert Penn] Warren, who in the somewhat similar *Night Rider* chose to reflect the historical economic crisis in the private crisis of the hero, Miss Brontë loses interest in the public and slides over into the private."[4]

One cannot separate the public and private themes of *Shirley,* just as one cannot separate the public and private lives of its central characters. Rather, the "historical economic" crises of the outer world of the novel are exactly reflected in the private crises of these characters. On the one hand, against the historical background of the Luddite rioting and Wellington's campaign against Napoleon in the Peninsula, Charlotte Brontë depicts a completely selfish society. On the other hand, in the love stories, she presents individuals who either embody the false values of that society, or who are victimized by them. She shows a society torn apart by conflicting motives—business vs. labor, Tory vs. Whig, manufacturer vs. patriot. She shows us characters who are similarly torn apart. Robert Moore cannot be a complete human being, because he is a businessman first. Caroline Helstone cannot fulfill herself as a woman because she is not rich enough to marry. Robert does not share her view that human feeling is at least as important as profits. Shirley Keeldar and Louis Moore are each so proud, in their different ways, that the class barriers which separate them seem unbridgeable. A central statement describing the world of *Shirley* is made about halfway through the book by William Farren, almost a touchstone character. Farren, a workingman, notes that most people are too bound by self-interest and social conventions to try to know each other: " 'Human natur' [he tells Caroline and Shirley] . . . is nought but selfishness. It is but excessive few, it is but just an exception here and there . . . that being in a different sphere, can understand t' one t' other, and be friends wi'out slavishness o' one hand, or pride o' t' other' " (II, 9).[5] This theme, selfishness, the lack of sympathy between people, connects everything— public or private—in the novel.[6]

Charlotte Brontë begins by indicting national selfishness. She casti-gates the people of England because, during the troubled period of the novel, they had sacrificed patriotism and honor to their bellies and pocket-books: "National honour was become a mere empty name, of no value in the eyes of many, because their sight was dim with famine; and for a morsel of meat they would have sold their birthright." The author especially criticizes those who ignore human concerns—the businessmen, for instance, who think that their machines are more important than people: ". . . it would not do to stop the progress of invention, to damage science, by discouraging its improvements. The war could not be termi-nated, efficient relief could not be raised—there was no help then—so the unemployed underwent their destiny: ate the bread and drank the waters of affliction" (I, 30). The nation was split because everyone was looking to his self-interest. The businessman "loved" his machines; the workingman was almost ready for revolution: "Misery generates hate. These sufferers hated the machines which they believed took the bread from them; they hated the buildings which contained those machines; they hated the manufacturers who owned those buildings" (I, 30–31).[7]

The businessman's attitude toward his workers has its counterpart in the attitude of gentlefolk toward their "inferiors." Just as the manufacturer uses his laborer as a tool, so the fine lady uses her governess as though she were not human. As one of these fine ladies reportedly says: " 'There were hardships . . . in the position of governess: doubtless they had their trials; but . . . it must be so. . . . Governesses . . . must ever be kept in a sort of isolation; it is the only means of maintaining that distance which the reserve of English manners and the decorum of English families exact' " (II, 65).[8]

Ironically, when it comes to human relationships, Tories turn out to be the same as liberals. Old Helstone, Caroline's uncle, is a professed Tory, a believer in King and country, right and might, law and order. Though he is a minister of the Gospels, he is "a man almost without sympathy, ungentle, prejudiced, and rigid" (I, 37). He is no Christian, therefore. Complacent and self-righteous, he has no idea of the sorrows of others, especially of women, whom he regards as an inferior species. On the other hand, Hiram Yorke, a wealthy landowner and a more or less typical Yorkshireman, is a "liberal." He claims to believe in the doctrines of the French and American revolutions. But in practice he upholds only the "equality" of those who are no threat to him: ". . . at heart he was a proud man: very friendly to his workpeople, very good to all who were beneath him, and submitted quietly to be beneath him, but haughty as Beelzebub to whomsoever the world deemed . . . his superior." Exactly like his political enemy, Helstone, he lacks sympathy for others: "The want of general benevolence made him very impatient of . . . all faults which grated on his strong, shrewd nature. . . . As he was not merciful, he sometimes could wound and wound again, without noticing how much he hurt, or caring how deep he thrust" (I, 48–49).

This is a world where utilitarianism is the official creed. All the men in the novel, no matter what their political views, agree with the view of marriage expressed by Peter Malone, a hardheaded curate: " 'If there is one notion I hate more than another, it is that of marriage . . . in the vulgar weak sense, as a mere matter of sentiment; two beggarly fools agreeing to unite their indigence by some fantastic tie of feeling. . . . But an advantageous connexion, such as can be formed in consonance with dignity of views, and permanency of solid interests, is not so bad . . .' " (I, 22). In the novel, men and women seem to have nothing in common. Old Helstone is most attentive to the least intelligent of the Sykes girls, because "at heart, he could not abide sense in women: he liked to see them as silly, as light-headed, as vain, as open to ridicule as possible; because they were then in reality what he held them to be, and wished them to be — inferior . . ." (I, 127). Caroline Helstone is completely separated from

Robert Moore, the man she loves, because she has no access to his thoughts or feelings: ". . . he was rapt from her by interests and responsibilities in which it was deemed such as she could have no part" (I, 190).

Certainly at this point one observes the relationship between public and private themes in *Shirley*. The "responsibilities" which keep Moore from Caroline are his all-consuming desire to succeed in business and to restore his family's fortune and honor. In describing Moore, Charlotte Brontë lashes out at the selfish individual, the man who substitutes materialistic for human values. Robert Moore, who reflects society's values, is the very embodiment of the social criticism of *Shirley*.

Moore is the complete businessman. His trade, mill, and machinery are his "gods"; the Orders in Council are "the seven deadly sins"; Castlereagh is his "Antichrist"; and "the war-party his legions" (I, 23). He sees existence in terms of the business relationship of profits: "Not being a native, nor for any length of time a resident of the neighbourhood, he did not sufficiently care when the new inventions threw the old work-people out of employ: he never asked himself where those to whom he no longer paid weekly wages found daily bread . . ." (I, 29).[9] Like other business-men of his day, he opposes the war against Napoleon, and criticizes Wellington's efforts in the Peninsular campaign: ". . . Moore was a bitter Whig—a Whig, at least, as far as opposition to the war-party was concerned: that being the question which affected his own interests; and only on that question did he profess any British policies at all" (I, 37–38). Finally, he has no time for personal relationships. Marriage too is a business proposition. He will not consider marrying Caroline, who he knows is penniless, because he realizes that such a match would mean "downright ruin" for him.

Moore is that phenomenon so common to Victorian literature—the divided man. As Caroline tells him, he is one person to the people in his house, and a completely different person to his workers. He is one thing in his parlor, reading aloud: "almost-animated, quite gentle and friendly" and something else the next morning in his mill—"frozen up again" (I, 84). He can talk to Caroline one evening, because as he says, " 'I have left the tradesman behind me in the Hollow. Your kinsman alone stands before you.' " There is, as he realizes, a sharp cleavage between "cousin Robert" and "Mr. Moore" (I, 136).

His view of life will not allow him to be whole. In his eyes, " 'Men in general are a sort of scum' " (I, 91). He is closed: "The secrets of business— complicated and often dismal mysteries—were buried in his breast, and never came out of their sepulchre . . ." (I, 137). He feels as though he "were sealed in a rock" (I, 180). He is blind and deaf. When he sees Miss Mann, an old spinster, all he notes is that she is "shrivelled . . . livid, and loveless." All he hears is her "vinegar discourse." He makes no attempt to understand her life; worst, he does not see the kindness beneath her unpleasant exterior (I, 197).

Though not affected in the same way as is Robert Moore, the other major characters in *Shirley* are nevertheless as deeply affected by the selfish society they live in and have to respond to. Thus, Louis Moore, Robert's brother, is simply a "satellite" to the snobbish Sympson family, his employers. Since he is a lowly tutor, no one in the family has to notice him or treat him like a human being (here is another version of the "governess theme" or the relationship of the businessman to his workers). Though his pupil, Harry, admires him, for the rest of the family Louis does not even exist. The Sympson "daughters saw in him an abstraction, not a man. It seemed, by their manner, that their brother's tutor did not live for them. . . . The most spirited sketch from his fingers was a blank to their eyes, the most original observation from his lips fell unheard on their ears" (II, 147).

Like his brother, however, Louis is partially to blame for his isolation. He accepts a view of the world that is almost exactly like Robert's: " 'I approve nothing Utopian,' " he tells his pupil. " 'Look life in its iron face: stare Reality out of its brassy countenance' " (II, 193). He has the strong pride of the poor man, who refuses to reveal his feelings for fear that he will look as though he is begging for favors. He cannot express his love for Shirley, since he fears a rebuff: ". . . it is well for a Sir Philip Nunnely to redden when he meets [Shirley's] eye: he may permit himself the indulgence of submission . . . but if one of her farmers were to show himself susceptible and sentimental, he would merely prove his need for a strait waistcoat. . . . no serf nor servant of hers have I ever been; but I am poor, and it behoves me to look to my self-respect — not to compromise an inch of it" (II, 203). Louis' pride here leads him astray. He misinterprets remarks, suffers imaginary slights. In effect, he is guilty of the false pride he thinks he is struggling against; he himself makes wealth and caste a barrier to love.

The woman Louis loves, Shirley Keeldar, seems at first to be the character most free of the ties of the world. She has glorious visions of the role of woman, seeing woman as coequal with life, with strength, with power. Yet even Shirley has limitations which make her guilty of inhumanity. For example, though she castigates Mr. Yorke for his pride that only serves to separate people, she has great pride herself. She berates her companion, Mrs. Pryor, for not flinging open her manor, Fieldhead, at a time of crisis: "That at such a time Fieldhead should have evinced the inhospitality of a miser's hovel, stung her haughty spirit to the quick . . ." (II, 44). She hurts Mrs. Pryor terribly. As the latter says, Shirley "should have known my character well enough by this time," should have known her shyness and painful lack of self-confidence (II, 51).

Worst of all, Shirley is not always true to herself, true to her own visions. In her long story, "The First Blue-Stocking," composed when she was a young girl, Shirley pictured the "marriage" of Genius with humanity, whom she represented as an orphan girl. But she seems content to preserve Genius for herself, and to forget about humanity. Even though she is a person, who, if she wants, can get along with everyone, in her pride she sometimes cuts herself off from people. For example, when she thinks that she has been bitten by a mad dog, she refuses to seek help from anyone. There is some truth in Louis Moore's attack: " 'You disdain sympathy . . . all must be locked up in yourself. . . . nobody can give the high price you require for your confidence. . . . Nobody has the honour, the intellect, the power you demand in your adviser. There is not a shoulder in England on which you would rest your hand for support. . . . Of course you must live alone' " (II, 210–11). Pride dictates Shirley's behavior toward Louis. Because she is not sure how Louis feels about her, she alternates between hauteur and humility— ". . . now sweeping past him in all the dignity of the monied heiress and prospective Lady Nunnely, and anon accosting him as abashed school-girls are wont to accost their stern professors . . ." (II, 174).

Shirley's friend, Caroline Helstone, on the other hand, has little pride. Closer to the typical Brontë heroine, she is the victim of society. Though she is not literally an orphan like Jane Eyre, she is virtually one. She does not know her mother; she has only the bitterest memories of her father. She lives with her uncle, who, though he treats her kindly—in the sense of feeding and clothing and sheltering her—never really talks to her. Since she is "just" a woman, he makes no attempt to understand what she thinks or feels.

Caroline is the victim of a society which gives her nothing to do— since she is "respectable"—and has no understanding of her needs. She is the victim of this world where selfish men dominate and "feeling" is ignored. She is the victim—again because she is respectable—of a world where she cannot speak out and express her love freely. In Caroline's story, therefore, the social and private themes of *Shirley* again coalesce. In Chapter 10, called "Old Maids," Charlotte Brontë places Caroline's dilemma—her unrequited love—in its social context. The chapter opens with an account of the progress of the war in Spain. Napoleon at this point is still victorious. English businessmen are crying for the war to end: ". . . they demanded peace on any terms; men like Yorke and Moore—and there were thousands whom the war placed where it placed them, shuddering on the verge of bankruptcy—insisted on peace with the energy of desperation." This, the author feels, indicates a national selfishness— "All men, taken singly, are more or less selfish, and taken in bodies they are intensely so" (I, 84). Against such a social background, Caroline's protest in the chapter takes on a larger significance. When she describes the "hollowness, mockery, want, craving" that mark the life of an old maid, one feels that Caroline is not simply a lonely women, who thinks she is fettered by her life and circumstances. She has become Charlotte Brontë's symbol of all those victimized, of all people who are at the mercy of the selfish men, who, having no honor themselves, will sacrifice everything to their own interests.

Typically, Charlotte Brontë offers her cure for this society in individual, human terms. Society can change only when the people in it change. The novelist thus calls for the breakdown of reserve and pride, for the opening of the heart to the needs of others, and for a new way of seeing.

Robert Moore, for example, quite literally is made to see what life is like for the poor:

"While I was in Birmingham [he tells Yorke] I looked a little into reality, considered closely . . . the causes of the present troubles of this country. . . . I went where there was no occupation and no hope. I saw some, with naturally elevated tendencies and good feelings, kept down amongst sordid privations and harassing griefs. I saw many, originally low, and to whom lack of education left scarcely anything but animal wants, disappointed in those wants . . . and desperate as famished animals; I saw what taught my brain a new lesson, and filled my breast with fresh feelings. I have no intention to profess more softness or sentiment that I have hitherto professed. . . . I should resist a riotous mob just as heretofore . . . but I should do it now chiefly for the sake and security of those . . . misled. Something there is to look to . . . beyond a man's personal interest, beyond the advancement of well-laid schemes, beyond even the discharge of dishonouring debts. To respect himself, a man must believe he renders justice to his fellow-men." (II, 245–46).

In much the same way, Moore is made to perceive that his view of love as another sort of business relationship is wrong. He had thought of Shirley as a possible wife because she was rich and could help him in his business, whereas Caroline, dowryless, could not. Like a lesser Oedipus, Robert had let his pride blind him to the truth. He had thought that when Shirley was friendly to him she was in love and would be an easy conquest. As soon as Shirley discovered his feelings, however, she removed his blinkers: " 'Your sight is jaundiced: you have seen wrong; your mind is warped: you have judged wrong; your tongue betrays you: you now speak wrong. I never loved you. . . . My heart is as pure of passion for you as yours is barren of affection for me' " (II, 237–38). Moore is overcome. What he had thought was the only reality—hard cash, profits, his interests—has proved to be unimportant, at least as measured against the terrible conditions he saw when he broke out of his narrow limits. Similarly, his pride has been crushed by Shirley. As he tells Yorke, in an apt metaphor: " 'The machinery of all my nature; the whole enginery of this human mill: the boiler, which I take to be my heart, is fit to burst' " (II, 233).

Robert's punishment fits his crime. He is shot by a leader of the faction opposed to him, and now he learns, through experience, what it is like to be helpless in someone's hands, to be totally dependent. The only reason Yorke takes him in after the attack is that he *is* helpless: "Well did Mr. Yorke like to have power, and to use it: he had now between his hands power over a fellow-creature's life; it suited him" (II, 267). Once inside the Yorke house, Robert is treated like a baby by the "dragon" nurse, Mrs. Horsfall. In a complete reversal of roles, his doctor treats him as he, Robert, had formerly treated his workers. Dr. MacTurk regards him "as a damaged piece of clock-work, which it would be creditable . . . to set a-going again" (II, 271).

At the end, then, there is a transformation of Robert's values. Whereas earlier, his home had not meant much to him — "its air of modest comfort seemed to possess no particular attraction for its owner" (I, 66) — after his long stay with the Yorkes he tells his sister, " 'I am pleased to come home' " (II, 306). Whereas earlier, "progress" had meant only the improvement of his own business; after he has seen Birmingham, he has enlarged his view to include everyone. He envisions the transformation of the valley, with the idea that there will be work for all men who want it: " 'Caroline, the houseless, the starving, the unemployed, shall come to Hollow's Mill from far and near, and Joe Scott [his foreman] shall give them work, and Louis Moore, Esq., shall let them a tenement, and Mrs. Gill [Shirley's housekeeper] shall mete them a portion till the first pay-day' " (II, 360).

It is significant that Robert sees Louis Moore as his coruler, for Charlotte Brontë uses the language of government to depict the break-down of pride between Louis and Shirley. Obviously, she here means to underline the connection between political and personal themes. In the scene where they finally reveal their feelings, Louis and Shirley try to form the basis for a relationship between equals. She asks him to "be good" to her, to "never tyrannize." In turn, he asks her to let him breathe, to "not bewilder" him (II, 336). She denies that her wealth and his poverty will make any difference between them. She asks for his aid: " '. . . teach me and help me to be good. I do not ask you to take off my shoulders all the cares and duties of property; but . . . to share the burden, and to show me how to sustain my part well. . . . Be my companion through life; be my guide where I am ignorant; be my master where I am faulty; be my friend always.' " (II, 338). Up to this point, Shirley, as the mistress of Fieldhead, has been the ruler of a considerable property, but now "she abdicated without a word of struggle" (II, 352). She sees her marriage not only as the consummation of her love, but as a change almost political in its implications: " 'Louis [she commented later] . . . would never have learned to rule, if she had not ceased to govern: the incapacity of the sovereign had developed the powers of the premier' " (II, 353). Louis, at the end, is a wise judge who helps solve the problems of all the people in the area. He is a wise governor who never would have come to power and fulfillment if he had not learned to look at reality differently and to break the shell of his isolating pride.

In this way, the reader is prepared for the conclusion of *Shirley*, where history and private life come together. Writing an historical novel, Charlotte Brontë shows her awareness that time does not stop with the close of her book. She indicates that Wellington, a hero at the end of the Peninsular campaign, was later reviled. She indicates that Robert Moore's idea of progress—his cottages and mills and highways—was not totally beneficent, since it despoiled much of the beauty of the countryside. She even notes that men like Moore had to continue to struggle to make a living, since times were not always as good as they were after the Napoleonic wars. But she at least points the way to a better society. Having shown that people can change, she implies that society's values can also change. Thus, unlike *Jane Eyre*, *Shirley* has a double happy ending, involving both the central characters and society, the private and the public themes.

With the end of the war in the Peninsula, and the revocation of the Orders in Council, the lovers can be united. The dreary past is over; the concluding words are couched, symbolically, in the present tense: "It is August: the bells clash out again, not only through Yorkshire but through England: from Spain, the voice of the trumpet has sounded long: it now waxes louder and louder; it proclaims Salamanca won. This night is Briarfield to be illuminated. On this day the Fieldhead tenantry dine together; the Hollow's-mill work-people will be assembled for a like festal purpose; the schools have a grand treat. This morning there were two marriages solemnized in Briarfield church . . ." (II, 360–61). With the end of the war has come the end of Robert's struggles, the end of selfishness—in the individual and in society—and love can prevail.

Notes

1. "Currer Bell's *Shirley*," *Edinburgh Review*, XCI (1850), 85.

2. Fannie E. Ratchford, *The Brontë's Web of Childhood* (New York, 1941), p. 214. Miss Ratchford goes on to say that *Shirley's* "leading characters save it from actual failure," but this only implies that there is a split between the characters in the novel and its social and historical background.

3. "Private and Social Themes in *Shirley*," *Brontë Society Transactions*, XIII (1958), 206.

4. "Charlotte Brontë's 'New' Gothic," in *From Jane Austen to Joseph Conrad: Essays Collected in Memory of James T. Hillhouse*, eds. Robert C. Rathburn and Martin Steinmann, Jr. (Minneapolis: University of Minnesota Press, 1958), p. 123.

5. T. J. Wise and J. A. Symington, eds. *Shirley: A Tale*, The Shakespeare Head Brontë, 2 vols. (Oxford, 1931). All references in the text are to this edition.

6. Jacob Korg thinks the theme is "romantic egoism." Korg divides the characters into groups, with those who "choose to be guided by feeling" opposed to those who "conform to custom or common sense" ("The Problem of Unity in *Shirley*," *NCF*, XII [1957], 126–27). Korg's approach to the novel is completely different from mine, since for the most part he is not really concerned with Charlotte Brontë as a social critic.

7. Asa Briggs notes that Charlotte Brontë's primary concern here was human: "She was completely uninfluenced by political economy. . . . She concentrated on the human plight of the poor. . . ." He points out the power of her statement, "Misery generates hate," noting that it was used as a motto by Sir William Beveridge, one of the architects of Britain's welfare state ("Private and Social Themes in *Shirley*," p. 215).

8. Briggs, then, is wrong when he says that the governess theme "is not related at all . . . to the Luddite background" ("Private and Social Themes in *Shirley*," p. 217). They are both manifestations of the selfishness that pervades society.

9. Passages such as this convince me that Korg is incorrect when he says that despite his stand, Robert is a heroic figure: "Moore's stand against his workmen is noble because it is an individual action . . ." ("The Problem of Unity in *Shirley*," p. 133). G. H. Lewes is closer to the truth, I think, when he says that Robert is "sordid." "*He* will be universally condemned for all our better instincts rebel against him." It is interesting that Lewes goes on to condemn Charlotte Brontë for making such a man her hero: "The authoress will appeal in vain here to *the truth* of such sordidness—the truth of thus discarding a real passion in favour of an ambitious project" ("Currer Bell's *Shirley*," p. 87).

The Genesis of Hunger, According to *Shirley*

Susan Gubar*

Charlotte Brontë's second published novel, *Shirley*, begins with three clergymen at table: complaining that the roast beef is tough and the beer flat, they nevertheless swallow enormous quantities of both, calling for "More bread!" and ordering their landlady to "Cut it, woman."[1] They also consume all her vegetables, cheese and spice cake. Is it merely a scene of local color, part of the wrong-headed impulse that led Brontë to write an historical novel set during England's war-time depression of 1811–1812? Is it just one example of the multiple ways in which the wide-ranging omniscient point of view allowed her to digress with irrelevant characters and vulgar dialogue included only because she wanted to be faithful to her real-life models? This is what many of her critics have claimed.[2] Yet, the voracious curates begin a novel very much about the expensive delicacies of the wealthy, the eccentric cookery of foreigners, the abundant provisions due soldiers, the scanty dinner baskets of child laborers, the starvation of the unemployed. Indeed, the hunger of the exploited links them to all those excluded from an independent and successful life in English

*This article is reprinted from *Feminist Studies*, 3, no. 3/4 (Spring–Summer 1976): 5–21, by permission of the publisher, *Feminist Studies* Inc., c/o Women's Studies Program, University of Maryland, College Park, MD. 20742.

society: one of the workers lucidly explains that "starving folks cannot be satisfied or settled folk" (p. 257). Although Matthew Arnold (like many of Brontë's male readers) was repulsed, he recognized that the rebellion and rage of her fiction is inextricably linked to her hunger.[3]

Shirley has been attacked as muddled in subject and point of view, marked by hysterical fustian and marred by a sexist, reactionary ending.[4] Yet, the novel is much more coherent, ambitious, and revolutionary than its critics have yet realized. Contemporary reviewers disliked the novel precisely because they could discern so clearly in "unladylike" *Shirley* the female identity of Currer Bell. Discouraged, no doubt, by a female writer who refused to be "feminine," Brontë's first readers reacted against the militancy of the novel. They possibly even sensed how this book about the "woman question" uses the workers' wrath to enact the women's revenge against the lives of enforced emptiness, of starvation. Far from being merely feverish or hectic, *Shirley* justifies and embodies Brontë's feminist consciousness. Many of the so-called purple passages are passionate protests, authenticated by her radical attack on the sexism of mercantile capitalism. Using imagery of imprisonment and starvation, Brontë traces the suicidal effect of female confinement and submission in order to explore how traditional sex roles destroy women. Finally, she examines the connections between sexist socio-economic institutions and the patriarchal myths of the voracious curates, of Christianity itself.

Still, in spite of her successful use of both spatial and food imagery, in spite of her brilliant analysis of the sexism of both capitalism and Protestantism, Brontë does fail to create an integrated, coherent novel. Yet this very failure illuminates crucial issues. Perhaps Brontë was reacting against the Gothic intensity of *Jane Eyre* because of the notoriety and censure it brought her both as a woman and as a female writer. Undoubtedly, in the writing of *Shirley,* she was affected by the decline and death of Branwell, Emily, and Anne. But, for whatever reason, in *Shirley* she seems to have tried for the objectivity and breadth and neutrality she admired in the fiction of Scott and Thackeray. And the result was a loss of coherence and fusion. Just as she explores in the character of Shirley a woman who fails to fulfill her potential as a romantic poet, Brontë explains her own failures and, implicitly, her own ultimate rejection of the omniscient and omnipotent narrative strategy she had been tempted to employ: she herself, she shows, has become enmeshed in essentially the same male-dominated structures that imprison the characters in all her books.

Shirley is worth studying, then, not only because, like Brontë's other works, it voices her sometimes overt and sometimes secret rejection of patriarchy, but because its very failure defines the contradictions experienced by women writing within male literary culture. This study will try to come to terms with the process of Brontë's plot, with the sequential development of her themes and images, because it is in this way that we can see most clearly her struggles as a writer. What Harold Bloom has defined as "the anxiety of influence" experienced by all great writers who must come to terms with their predecessors' achievement is particularly painful and difficult for women who have been discouraged from writing or have been categorized as inferior "women writers."[5] As is the case with so many other female writers, Brontë's "anxiety of influence" involves her recognition that to be true to her own female perspective she must use and subvert the traditions at her disposal. While committed in *Shirley* to the generic conventions of the historical novel, Brontë remains primarily interested in women who exist privately, confined precisely by those morals and manners that prevent them from participating in public life. In trying to deal historically with a caste denied any historical existence, Brontë must set up the traditional historical heroes in such a way as to dispense with them as insignificant subjects. Similarly, she is committed to exploring the great distance between historical change and the seemingly unrelated, lonely struggles of her heroines. When this kind of juggling results in a loss of artistic fusion — even though Brontë uses it to trace the tragic consequences that occur when women are unable to shape the public history that necessarily and inalterably affects their lives — from our vantage in time we can see that the pain of female confinement is not merely her subject in *Shirley*; it is an integral aspect of her artistry.

How to plot a story about characters defined by their very inability to initiate action — this is the problem Brontë faced. *Shirley* focuses on impotence, the stasis that derives from hopelessness. Every class has been affected: unable to win the war against France, the English are merely trying to maintain their positions. Neither the violence of the workers nor the prayers of the clergy can alleviate the situation. In Yorkshire, the manufacturers suffer because the Orders of Council have cut off the principal markets of trade. To underline this point, the novel begins with mill-operator Robert Moore waiting for the arrival of machinery that finally shows up smashed by the angry workers. Throughout the novel, Robert Moore waits — hoping to alter his waning fortunes but unable to take any real initiative. He can revenge himself on the workers by bringing them to trial, but this does not help business. He is reduced to the morally reprehensible and pitifully ineffective decision not to marry Caroline Helstone because she is poor, to propose to Shirley Keeldar because she is rich. The egotism which leads him unscrupulously to use women links him to all the other men in the novel.

The best of the Yorkshire leaders, those most dedicated to shaping their lives through their own exertions, are two men who are bitter political enemies. Hiram Yorke, a rebellious blasphemer, rants against a land "king-ridden, priest-ridden, peer-ridden" while Mr. Helstone, an ecclesiastic, defends God, King and "the judgment to come" (p. 42). Radical and conservative, each thinks the other damned. They are barely on speaking terms, yet they share uncommon personal courage and honesty. Yorke's democratic and blunt generosity is as admirable as Helstone's loyal fearlessness. Whig and Tory, manufacturer and clergyman, family man and childless widower, one a wealthy landowner and the other comfortably well-off from a living—these two pillars of the community remain unaffected by the poverty and bankruptcy of their neighbors. Secure about their future, representative of the best in their society, they share a common past. Early in the novel we discover that they were rivals in their youth for a young woman, a girl of "living marble," really "a monumental angel" (p. 39).

This ominously named Mary Cave was completely ignored by her clergyman-husband: she was no companion for Mr. Helstone, belonging as she did to "an inferior order of existence" (p. 40). After a year or two of marriage, she dies of neglect leaving behind a "still beautiful-featured mould of clay . . . old and white" (p. 40). We must wait almost four hundred pages to learn more about her. Yorke finally admits that he too would have rejected her if he had won her. Neither of these men respect or like the female sex: Helstone prefers them as silly as possible, to serve as playthings, while Yorke eventually chooses a morose, self-righteous, and tyrannical woman to breed and rear his brood. The best and the brightest among the powerful are obsessed with delusive and contradictory images of women that are powerful enough to cause Mary Cave's death. She is an emblem, a warning that the fate of women inhabiting a male-controlled society involves suicidal self-renunciation.

Inheriting her aunt's place in Helstone's esteem, Caroline Helstone lives invisibly in her uncle's house, received with the same chilly indifference because of her inferiority. But, Caroline is thankful that her life with Helstone is at least calmer than her past existence with her father: voluntarily enclosed in an upstairs bedroom of Helstone's house, Caroline remembers how her father locked her up day and night in a high garret room without companion, carpet, curtains or furniture, a room where "she waited for his return knowing he would be a madman or a senseless idiot" (p. 80). Although Helstone merely ignores her, he always supplies adequate physical surroundings. And she can visit her cousins, the Moores. This too is a mixed blessing, however, since Hortense Moore tries to train her insufficiently submissive friend in the duties of women, by providing her with tedious grammatical problems in French matched in complexity by arduous stocking-mending. While Caroline discretely considers her own convictions (her feeling that Robert is unjustly cruel to the workers, her wish to earn her own living), Hortense dedicates herself wholeheartedly to rummaging, arranging, and disarranging her drawers. Yet even this rather confining escape from Helstone's house is denied Caroline when her uncle's political feuding coupled with Robert's rejection of her make these visits impossible.

When Robert rejects Caroline on financial grounds, his withdrawal—a mere glance, distant and cousinly—is immediately apparent to her. As a female who has loved without being asked to love, she is chastised by the narrator. She can say nothing. Spurned, she is admonished to "ask no questions; utter no remonstrances" (pp. 81–82). She must suffer and be still. The narrator is pitiless. Since this tirade brings together all of the imagery that has developed around the opposition of food and stone, as well as the necessity of self-enclosure and self-containment for women, it is worth quoting at length:

> Take the matter as you find it; ask no questions; utter no remonstrances: it is your best wisdom. You expected bread, and you have got a stone; break your teeth on it, and don't shriek because the nerves are mar-tyrised: do not doubt that your mental stomach — if you have such a thing — is strong as an ostrich's: the stone will digest. You held out your hand for an egg, and fate put into it a scorpion. Show no consternation: close your fingers firmly upon the gift; let it sting through your palm. Never mind: in time, after your hand and arm have swelled and quivered long with torture, the squeezed scorpion will die, and you will have learned the great lesson how to endure without a sob. For the whole remnant of your life, if you survive the test — some, it is said, die under it — you will be stronger, wiser, less sensitive. (pp. 81–82)

With what fury the lesson of repression is given. Endurance and submission, silence and suffering involve pain and self-destruction. When Brontë describes the transubstantiation of bread into stone, of egg into scorpion, she explains the cause and result of female suffering: with no sustaining nourishment, growth is impossible and so is escape; the woman can only witness her imprisonment and withdraw into it with the ambiguous solace that comes from being hidden. Like the ballad heroine, *Puir Mary Lee*, she can only ask to be buried, graved up by a wreath of snow. The woman who cannot hide away her pain within a clenched hand must contain her grief through death, by taking nothing in. Like Mary Cave, Caroline withdraws first into her room and then more dangerously into herself until she literally begins to disappear from lack of food and love. Despised and rejected by all the men who control her life, Caroline *Hel/stone* is destined to stand in shadows, shrinking into the concealment of her own mind until (like her aunt before her) she too becomes "a mere white mould, or rigid piece of statuary" (p. 318).

Caroline has nothing left but to attempt the rites and duties of the lady at her uncle's tea table and Sunday school. As if to emphasize this fact, the first and extremely detailed scene after Robert's look of rejection pictures Caroline tending the jews-basket ("that awful incubus" [p. 87]) while entertaining those paragons of propriety — the Mrs. and Misses Sykes. Wearied by the vacancy of such ladylike activity, tired of the lethargy caused by the tasteless rattle of the piano and the interminable gossip, Caroline retreats to a quieter room only to be unexpectedly caught in a meeting with Robert. There is something foreboding in her warning that his harshness to the mill laborers will lead to his own destruction. She wants him to know "how the people of this country bear malice: it is the boast of some of them that they can *keep a stone in their pocket* seven years, turn it at the end of that time, keep it seven years longer, and hurl it and hit their mark 'at last' " (p. 96) [italics mine]. The man who offers stones instead of sustenance in return for the woman's love will receive as his punishment the rocks and stones cast by the other victims of his competitive egotism, the workers.

What connects the workers to the women is their vulnerability, their common victimization and invisibility. Brontë contrasts Robert's business zeal with the workers' Wesleyan faith as it is voiced in their hymns:

> Sleeping on the brink of sin,
> Tophet gaped to take us in;
> Mercy to our rescue flew, —
> Broke the snaire, and brought us through.
>
> Here, as in a lion's den,
> Undevour'd we still remain;
> Pass secure the watery flood,
> Hanging on the arm of God.
>
> [p. 115]

The workers feel just as enclosed by the lion's den as they do by Tophet's snare and it is this feeling of imprisonment and impotence that links them to the women in the book. This recognition of their own helplessness is diametrically opposed to the attitude of industrialists like Robert who think they are the free masters of their own future and the future of society. Priding himself on his exertions, on work and self-reliance, Robert embodies the faith of the English shopkeepers who view all activity except trade in the light of "eating the bread of idleness, of passing a useless existence" (p. 132). With these standards Robert necessarily despises women: self-help means sexism. It means, also, that he will oppose the continuation of a war that he knows must be fought to insure British liberty: self-actualization through work means selfishness. Finally, it means damnation and unhappiness because no self-respecting self-made man (be he millowner or clergyman) can pass secure by "hanging on the arm of God." As Brontë says in one of her many addresses to the reader, "Long may it be ere England really becomes a nation of shopkeepers!"

Living in a world with no place for her, Caroline must curb her remembrances of a romantic past, returning to her present lonely condition: she must replace visions of feeding Moore berries and nuts in Nunnely Wood with a clear-sighted recognition of her own narrow chamber; for the songs of birds, she must listen to the rain on her casement and she must exchange Moore's companionship for the illusion of her own dim shadow on the wall (pp. 137–38). She knows that virtue does not lie in self-abnegation, but what is left to her except imprisonment and martyrdom? There seem to be no answers in the world she inhabits other than those detailed by the narrator. The bitten who survive will be stronger because less sensitive. They will become a Miss *Mann*. Caroline visits her in order to learn the secrets of old maids. What she discovers is a Medusa whose gaze turns men to *stone*, to whom "a crumb is not thrown once a year"; a woman who exists "ahungered and athirst to famine" (p. 143). Miss Ainely manages to live more optimistically through religious devotion and self-denial. These lives are not attractive to Caroline. They are the very lives scorned by Robert. Yet Caroline sees no other option: life for women means nerves martyrized because "all men, taken singly are more or less selfish; and taken in bodies they are intensely so" (p. 132). With clenched hands Caroline decides to follow Miss Ainely's example, to work hard at keeping down her anguish, although haunted by a "funereal inward cry" (p. 146).

Caroline Helstone's case history provides positive proof, in Brontë's eyes, that the source of female tribulation is the dependent status of women. Unlike Jane Eyre, Caroline is quite beautiful. She is protected from penury by her uncle's generosity and he promises an annuity to provide for her after his death. She *need* not go out into the frozen world but, ironically, such a need would provide relief. In some ways, Caroline is worse off than Jane: Jane, after all, does travel from the Reeds to Lowood, from Thornfield to Marsh End and finally to Ferndean while Caroline never leaves Yorkshire. She would welcome what she knows to be an uncomfortable position as governess because it would at least alleviate an inertia that can only increase her mental suffering. Of course such an option is rejected by her friends as improper. And Caroline's complete immobility makes it seem quite probable that she will not survive the test, that her mental stomach cannot digest the stone nor her hand endure the grasped torture. It is only at this point of total paralysis that Brontë introduces Shirley Keeldar—a heroine who in all ways serves as a contrast to Caroline.

Brilliant while Caroline is colorless, as out-going as Caroline is retiring. Shirley is not a dependent inmate or a surrogate male: she is not a mere housekeeper or housewife. On the contrary, she is a wealthy heiress who owns her own house, the ancestral mansion usually allotted to the hero, complete with old latticed windows, stone porch, and a shadowy gallery with carved stags' heads hung on its walls. A true Lady Bountiful, strong yet loving, Shirley seems to have all the provisions necessary to cure the entire parish. She is a provider who enjoys laying out impromptu regales in the garden, or gastronomic feasts in the dining room. Her dairy feeds the cottages, supplying all with milk and butter. She knows her cook, Mrs. Gill, cheats her of meat, bread, candles, and soap, but she only wonders aloud about the bills. Caroline is given sustenance—new life, new vibrancy, and comfort—from her companionship with Shirley who poses as a flirtatious suitor, as lord of the manor. Shirley scorns lap dogs, romping instead with a huge mastiff reminiscent of Emily's hound, Keeper. She enjoys the ambiguous effect of her status on her sexual role: "Business! Really the word makes me conscious I am indeed no longer a girl, but quite a woman and something more. I am an esquire! Shirley Keeldar, Esquire, ought to be my style and title. They gave me a man's name; I hold a man's position: it is enough to inspire me with a touch of manhood, and when I see such people as that stately Anglo-Belgian — that Gerard Moore before me, gravely talking to me of business, really I feel quite gentleman-like" (p. 160). Part of this is teasing, because Shirley is speaking to someone unsympathetic to her independence — Mr. Helstone. Yet, it is more than unfortunate that independence is so closely associated with masculinity that it confines Shirley to a kind of male-mimicry.

The fact that Shirley emerges only when Caroline has been completely immobilized through her own self-restraint and self-submission is reminiscent of the ways in which Bertha Mason Rochester offers a means of escape to the otherwise boxed-in Jane Eyre. Here in *Shirley*, repression signals the emergence of a free and uninhibited self that is not criminal. That Shirley *is* Caroline's double, a projection of all her repressed desire, becomes apparent in the acts she performs "for" Caroline. What Shirley *does* is what Caroline would like to do: Caroline's secret hatred for the curates is gratified when Shirley angrily throws them out of her house after they are attacked by her dog; Caroline needs to move Helstone, and Shirley bends him to her will; Caroline wishes early in the novel that she could penetrate the business secrets of men while Shirley reads the newspapers and letters of the civic leaders; Caroline wants to lighten Robert's financial burden and Shirley secures him a loan; Caroline tries to repress her desire for Robert while Shirley gains his attention and proposal of marriage; Caroline has always known that he needs to be taught a lesson (consider her explication of *Coriolanus*) and Shirley gives it to him in the form of a humiliating rejection of his marriage proposal. This last we do not find out until quite late in the novel. It is withheld by the narrator. But it is far from the most dramatic way in which Shirley acts as an implement of Caroline's will: Caroline wishes above all else for her long-lost mother and Shirley supplies her with just this person in the figure of Mrs. Pryor.

For all the seeming optimism implied in this double, for all the release that Shirley seems to provide Caroline, Brontë undercuts the reader's expectations. In spite of her independent activity and exuberant liveliness, Shirley seems slightly unreal to most readers and this very unreality serves to remind us that she is part of a fantastic wish-fulfillment, an affirmation of what ought to be possible for women. We need not look only to Brontë's admission that Shirley is a portrait of what Emily Brontë might have been if born under luckier circumstances[6] — we need not because Shirley is also a projection of Caroline's mind, a double who seems to contradict her own hopeless situation, making her fate "merely" psychological and therefore idiosyncratic. Caroline's isolation, her discontent must be her own fault. If not, the very structure of English society must be found guilty, and a triumph like that of Jane Eyre's would be very exceptional indeed. If not, the source of tribulation is not merely the dependent status of women but the very ways in which male society defines even those few women upon whom it confers independence. When even Shirley is shown to be incapable of escaping the confines of being born female, just such a lesson seems implied.

While none of the male characters can initiate effective action because of the contingencies of a costly war abroad, Brontë's heroines really cannot act in their own behalf at all. *Shirley* falls into two parts. In the first half, we are centrally concerned with Robert's rejection of Caroline and, in the second, we shift our attention to Louis' hesitancy in courting Shirley. This division illustrates how the men are impeded while the women are completely immobilized by the constraints imposed by their society. Circumscribed principally by their gender, the women are necessarily passive and this is reflected in the plot which consistently calls attention to its own inorganic development, its dependence on the manipulations of the narrator who keeps secrets, pushes characters in and out of the neighborhood, and engineers fortuituous misunderstandings, riots, and reunions. Our initial insight into Shirley's confinement is produced through the juxtaposition of two central episodes: the Sunday school feast and the attack on the Mill.

Caroline and Shirley play a central role in the Whitsuntide celebration in which the three parishes of Briarfield, Whinbury, and Nunnely march in procession to a feast for all the school children and their parents in the parish. Caroline has changed a great deal. Instead of behaving like "an imprisoned bird" (p. 196), she dresses carefully and then helps Shirley do the same. Together they look "very much like a snow-white dove and gem-tinted bird-of-paradise joined in social flight" (p. 134). They head the Briarfield contingent of women and children. In spite of the religious nature of the parade, Shirley dreams of battles and stirring victories. They do meet up with a threat. In a narrow lane in which only two can walk abreast, they confront an opposition procession of Dissenters. Shirley very accurately terms them "our double" (p. 239). In a scene reminiscent of *Casablanca* (where French patriots and German troops try to outsing each other), Helstone's group bellows "Rule, Britannia" while the Dissenters hymn one of their most dolorous canticles. Helstone and Shirley keep all from faltering on their side and are rewarded with victory; the Dissenters are forced to flee. The final feast, far from being a celebration of Christian piety, is a victory celebration.

Even if Brontë had not linked this scene to the defense of the Mill, its military and national overtones would have been apparent: the Church is the State's arm. That both Church and State depend on exclusion and coercion which are not merely economic and social but also sexual — this is detailed through the taking of toast and tea. In the midst of merriment and cheer, Shirley has to resort to the most inane feminine wiles in order to preserve a seat for Moore: "accidently" staining her dress, she even threatens to swoon. Meanwhile, Caroline is silently tortured by her friend's intimacy with the man she still loves and Shirley either is or pretends to be insensitive to Caroline's humiliation. Above all the imbibing, suspended in at least some twenty cages, sit as many canaries, placed there by a clerk who "knew that amidst confusion of tongues they always carolled loudest" (p. 230). As Caroline is forced to serve and Shirley to consume tea, the canary birds sing shrilly in their high-hung cages. They are a mocking symbol of the girls' chatter and finery, their social roles.

Both Caroline and Shirley are excluded at the end of the feast day when the men will not trust her and "that is always the way when it comes to the point" (p. 248). Caroline and Shirley, obedient to orders, lock themselves into Helstone's house provided with a knife and some pistols in case of trouble. That night, when the marching workers decide to pass by without molesting the inhabitants, the girls jump hedges, ford streams, and leap over walls in an effort to warn Moore of the advancing rioters. Of course they are neither necessary nor welcome, as they themselves realize. Instead of delivering the message, they watch the battle at a distance as the workers break down gates and doors, hurling volleys of *stones* at the mill, breaking every pane of every lattice into shattered fragments. This is the real confrontation, perpetrated by their "doubles" — that same excluded group whose counter-parade was a kind of ceremonial proem. Moore, Helstone, and their male cohorts will only accept limited succor from the women, and then only after the fact. Shirley understands this even better than Caroline. Indeed, by this point, Shirley exchanges roles with Caroline and restrains her friend from going to help Moore, knowing that their presence would only infuriate him.

To understand the eruption of violence at the Mill, the anger that results in wounded men writhing in the bloodied dust, to understand the workers' wrath in terms of the women's revenge, it is necessary to recall the meditations of Shirley and Caroline after they refuse to follow the rest of the Sunday school into the Church at the close of the day and before the nighttime battle. Moved by the beauty of nature, Shirley offers Caroline an alternative to Milton's story of creation. Milton, it seems, saw Satan and Sin, angels and devils, but he never saw Eve: "It was his cook that he saw; or it was Mrs. Gill" (p. 252). Instead of the domesticated housewife pictured by Milton, Shirley describes the vitality and life of "a woman-Titan" who could conceive and bring forth a Messiah (p. 253). Her Eve, Nature, was heaven-born: "vast was the heart whence gushed the well-spring of the blood of nations, and grand the undegenerate head where rested the consort-crown of creation" (p. 253). It is this sexually charged earth mother who can only be worshipped outside that Shirley considers an Amazon-Eve and, just in case we have forgotten how radical a departure this is from the Bible, Brontë almost immediately introduces Moore's foreman to remind us. He quotes the second chapter of St. Paul's first Epistle to Timothy: " 'Let the woman learn in silence, with all subjection. I suffer not a woman to teach, nor to usurp authority over the man; but to be in silence. For Adam was first formed, then Eve.' " When Shirley does not receive the lesson immediately, Joe continues: " 'Adam was not deceived; but the woman, being deceived, was in the transgression' " (p. 260). There is a confusion of tongues here. Shirley can no more accept Joe's Eve than he could have understood her Titan-woman. Shirley knows that men keep secrets from women precisely because of the Christian myths they, like Joe, have inherited and the images that derive from them.

All of the characters are affected by the myths of their culture, specifically by the myth of the garden: Caroline wants to return to Hollow's Cottage "as much almost as the first woman, in her exile, must have longed to revisit Eden" (p. 196); Moore feels the future opening up "like Eden" (p. 228); for Shirley, the beauty of the twilight sky seems to make of earth an Eden (p. 307).[7] Shirley and Caroline know the power of myth; they are aware of inhabiting a male culture that cannot really accept or understand them. They know that men think in terms of a silent, deceived Eve—the cause of sin and suffering—or a domesticated little helper cooking up messes in the cottage kitchen. Shirley explains to Caroline that men conceal danger from women, keeping the most important facts of their existence a secret, because they fancy women have minds like children: "The cleverest, the acutest men are often under an illusion about women: they do not read them in a true light: they misapprehend them, both for good and evil: their good woman is a queer thing, half doll, half angel; their bad woman almost always a fiend" (p. 278). This is no less true of recent literature, according to Shirley, than of the ancient origin of most stories—the Bible.

Forced to present themselves as children/dolls/servants/angels, women experience their anger as daemonic. Thus Shirley pictures to Caroline the destructive rage of a North Atlantic mermaid:

> I show you an image, fair as alabaster, emerging from the dim wave. We both see the long hair, the lifted and foam-white arm, the oval mirror, brilliant as a star. It glides nearer: a human face is plainly visible—a face in the style of yours, whose straight, pure (excuse the word, it is appropriate), —whose straight, pure lineaments, paleness does not disfigure. It looks at us, but not with your eyes. I see a preternatural lure in its wily glance: it beckons. Were we men, we should spring at the sign, the cold billow would be dared for the sake of the colder enchantress; being women, we stand safe, though not dreadless. (p. 192)

In part, Shirley is merely parodying the rather absurd images of women held by men who see women as unnatural monsters, the cause of original sin and exile from Eden. But, she is also describing the effect of those images on women themselves. Locked into bodies termed unnatural or inferior, desexed as only a mermaid can be, women work their cold enchantment in order to destroy the men who have enslaved them. This is a portrait of the fury of Miss Mann, Miss Moore, Mrs. Pryor—all those Gorgon-Medusas whose ugliness turn men to stone. This "Temptress-terror!" is also, Shirley tells Caroline, a "monstrous likeness of ourselves!" It is a being with pure lineaments and a lure in its glance, straight and wiley, fair and preternatural. It is an angel-fiend whose star is a mirror: the other side of the Titan-woman who gives birth to all creation is the terrible, avenging devourer of men.

Because Shirley is not trapped in the coercive myths that imply and even condone inequality and exploitation, because she sees through the patriarchal culture she inhabits so comfortably, Shirley is the only wealthy person in the novel who "cannot forget, either day or night, that these embittered feelings of the poor against the rich have been generated in suffering" (p. 210). This does not mean she has a solution to the class conflict she watches with such ambivalence; sympathizing with Moore as he defends her property, she knows that his cruelty and the workers' misery have erupted in violence she can only decry. Her own rather maternal relationship with the laborers allows for more communication and kindness between the classes, but it is fraught with potential violence too, since she retains economic control over their lives and they, in their masculine pride, are revolted by what they see as her unnatural position of authority. Still, she alone rejects "all arraying of ranks against ranks, all party hatreds, all tyrannies disguised as liberties" (p. 291). Her revolt against injustice only causes her listener, here Hiram Yorke, to undermine her position by ridiculing her gender. He seeks to embarrass her, by asking when she will marry Robert Moore and thereby intimating that her entire position is merely a result of infatuation. Shirley's response entirely baffles him. He cannot read the language of her look; it is untranslatable; a fervid lyric in an unknown tongue. This does not surprise Shirley, who knows that her real opinions, if fully expressed, would probably lead to her being *stoned* (p. 278). Hers is the language of a new woman; it is either repugnant or incomprehensible to those it seeks to expose and transform. It is during this most interesting impasse that we learn a fact never developed in the novel but highly suggestive: Shirley's father's name was Charles *Cave* Keeldar. Mary Cave, symbol of female protest through suicide, is an ancestor of Shirley's and yet another link with Caroline.

Although Shirley lives a life of freedom reminiscent of her own Titan-woman, a pastoral and idyllic existence spent out-of-doors reviewing the cows and feeding the chickens, there *is* something untranslatable not only about her fervid lyrics but about all of her gestures and talk. There is an extravagance about her behavior, an edge that makes it seem as if Shirley is playing the roles provided with some degree of distance. Whether she is the courtly gentleman, the coy coquette, the lady bountiful, the tomboy, the little lady or the touched bard, Shirley seems to be conscious of each role and its ludicrous limits. Although she can parody these roles, she is still condemned to play them. That she is continuously hampered in this way makes her mysterious decision to invite the Sympson family into her home less surprising. They are a pattern family well-supplied with "pattern young ladies, in pattern attire, with pattern deportment" (p. 308). They are the cause of her separation from Caroline since they confine her to their company and yet another sign that in some still undisclosed way Shirley is not as free or as independent as she first seemed. And, of course, *her* lack of freedom effects Caroline's further decline.

Far from being merely love sick, Caroline is discontent. Her illness is a result of her misery at her own impotence. She seems to have no alternative except resignation as she sits "still as a garden statue" (p. 308). Again she visits the old maids to learn submission, but now she sees Miss Ainly's religious faith in terms of nuns who are enclosed in close cells and robes straight as shrouds and beds narrow as coffins. The problem is that society demands that "Old maids, *like the houseless and unemployed poor, should not ask for a place and an occupation* in the world" (p. 310) [italics mine]. It is the narrowness of woman's lot that makes her scheme in the marriage market where she is as much a commodity as the workers in the mercantile market. Caroline's thoughts on the subject of the woman question pitifully conclude with an impassioned plea directed, of course, to the "Men of England!" It is they who keep female minds fettered. Presumably it is only they who have the power to alter the situation.

Directly after this outburst, almost as if her own anger is taken up and expressed through their mouths, Caroline is verbally attacked by Rose Yorke and her mother. Rose rises up against Caroline's submission, using language that exploits all of the imagery of imprisonment in a context that illustrates how woman's domestic lot enlists her as a jailor of herself. Rose will not live "a black trance like the toad's, buried in marble" and she will not be "for ever shut up" in a house that reminds her of a "windowed grave" (p. 316). She would rather "try all things and find them empty" than leave life a blank. She takes as her text the parable of the talents:

> And if my Master has given me ten talents, my duty is to trade with them, and make them ten talents more. Not in the dust of household drawers shall the coin be interred. I will *not* deposit it in a broken-spouted tea-pot, and shut it up in a china-closet among tea-things. I will *not* commit it to your work-table to be smothered in piles of woolen hose. I will *not* prison it in the linen press to find shrouds among the sheets: and least of all, mother" — (she got up from the floor) — "least of all will I hide it in a tureen of cold potatoes, to be ranged with bread, butter, pastry, and ham on the shelves of the larder. (p. 317)

The pun on the word "talent" is a functional one since Rose's point is precisely the connection between the financial dependence of women and the destruction of their creative potential. Rose will not bury her talent because she knows that "The tea-pot, the old stocking-foot, the linen rag, the willow-pattern tureen, will yield up their barren deposit in many a house." Each and every one of these drawers, chests, boxes, closets, pots and bags represents the pitiful pride of the housekeeper whose very control and skill at managing and maintaining the house is a form of self-enclosure, self-denial, even self-burial.

Ironically, Rose's counsel is as repressive as that of her mother. One advises women to enter the mercantile market; the other advocates stoicism when the marriage market fails. Both counsel the competitive exertion which (we have seen in the novel) dehumanizes and degrades both sexes. That the fury of these two women supplies no answer or solution to Caroline becomes clear when Louis Moore enters, since his appearance is one more step in Shirley's increasing subjugation. When Caroline hears only of escapes purchased by exile and restraint, when her "free" double keeps secret her wiles to gain the presence of a suitor, then Caroline's decline must hasten into a dying. That the "well-lit fire" of the fever consumes her "like any snow-wreath in thaw" (pp. 330–31) shows it to be a release from her earlier endurance.

During her illness Caroline cannot eat. She received stones, instead of food. She has been deprived of maternal care and familial love so she denies herself the traditional symbol of that care and love. Of course her starvation is also a sign that she is being eaten away, consumed by sorrow. Brontë has carefully associated Caroline's eating of food with the voracious curates, with the Sunday school feast and Mr. Helstone's table, so in some ways Caroline in rejecting food is rejecting these characters and, with them, communion and redemption as they define it. A Father whose love and approbation must be earned by well-invested talents is not worth having.

Besides, a girl surrounded by selfish men has no reason to believe that paternal benevolence exists. Christ, the cornerstone of the Church, has not sustained Caroline. And so it is at this point in the novel that Caroline questions the existence of the other world and the purpose of this one. The Christian version of Genesis has already been attacked by Shirley. Now it becomes clear how that myth in which a woman is condemned for eating reflects male hatred of the female and fear of her sustaining and strengthening herself. From the male point of view, all fruit — indeed, all food — should be forbidden to woman: he has fallen because he harkened to her; when she spoke, it was to justify her own and encourage his eating. From the male point of view, then, the woman is guilty of being born female. Instead of asserting herself, she should be ashamed of her own physicality.

Yet, fasting is also an act of revolt. Since eating maintains the self, in a discredited world it is a compromise that implies acquiescence. It is truly a guilty act. In a male-defined world, the mouth of the woman should be reserved to forge a new language. Women *will* starve until new stories are created that confer upon them the power of naming and controlling their world. Brontë's style, like Shirley's, becomes more rhapsodic and fervid, more exotic, as her writing progresses and she seeks to create a new word, a new genre for her sex. In *Shirley* as in *Jane Eyre* before it, one heroine silently starves while the other raves. Both are involved in a militant rejection of the old myths and the degrading roles they provide. *Shirley* is very much an attack on the religion of the patriarchs. Caroline, in her illness, searches for faith in God, the Father. She finds instead the encircling arms of her mother.

Mrs. Pryor is a suitable mother. Aloof and withdrawn in public, she has survived the test of "a man-tiger" (p. 351) whose gentlemanly soft speech hid private "discords that split the nerves and curdled the blood — sounds to inspire insanity" (p. 342). Although formal and reticent, she has survived to endure with greater strength. She is the prior woman — prior to Shirley, as well as Caroline. She has been the closest friend and companion to Shirley. And Shirley increasingly shows herself to be as reticent and discreet as Mrs. Pryor, when she keeps secrets from Robert, Caroline, Louis, and all of her visiting relatives. Shirley's reserve reaches its heights when she is bitten by a dog she believes to be mad. Caroline was admonished to show no consternations over the figurative bite of the scorpion, but it is Shirley who epitomizes the horror of self-containment and repression when she actually remains silent about her terrifying fears of hydrophobia and begins to waste away from anxiety. Even as she becomes more reserved, Shirley also grows docile in the schoolroom with her old tutor. When she cannot master the French, she takes it from his mouth finding "lively excitement in the pleasure of making his language her own" (p. 388).

Why does Caroline's reunion with her mother, her virtual rebirth, lead to this decline in Shirley's honest independence and assertiveness? Mrs. Pryor, not the Titan-woman, is the mother of both heroines because her experience is archetypically female. Both Caroline and Shirley, like most girls, will grow into womanhood through marriage which, Mrs. Pryor warns, is a horrible, a shattering experience. She never details the terror of male potency but it is all the more dreadful for remaining so mysterious. Her experience, her pain in marriage and eventual flight from it, is central to the initial split between Caroline and Shirley — the split between suicidal, "feminine" passivity and "masculine" self-assertion. This definition of sexual roles is precisely what imprisons both women and men. This is the true Fall. Mrs. Pryor has in some ways perpetuated this dichotomy (and exemplifies it even within herself) because her dread of the male has caused her to reject his daughter, but since his daughter is also *her* daughter and part of herself, she has contributed to her own mutilation. Psychologically, she is the cause of Caroline's passivity because she has withheld from her child the love that allows for a strong sense of self. But, perhaps more importantly, by experiencing men as evil, by seeing herself as a victim who can only submit to male degradation or flee from it, Mrs. Pryor defines the woman's role as a tragic one. With her emergence, both heroines — now sisters — are wooed by the brothers Moore. Their initiation into their own sexuality is bound to be humiliating.

That Shirley does submit over and over again is unmistakable. The Titan-woman has been subdued. And by no one less than the first man. "With animals," Louis declares proudly, "I feel I am Adam's son: the heir of him to whom dominion was given over 'every living thing that moveth upon the earth' " (p. 359). It is no surprise, then, to come across an old *devoir* on *"La Premiere Femme Savante"* which differs from Shirley's earlier portraits of Titan-Eve. She is now described as passive and powerless. *This* first woman is forsaken and lost. She calls out for comfort and a spirit loosens the fetters from her faculties, the darkness from her vision. The liberating force is the Godly male spirit called Genius. The subsequent sexual fantasy depends on the woman receiving the God who infuses her with his power. It is Genius who fights for Humanity's place in heaven and wins it for her. She is left to pant in ecstatic thankfulness at being thus saved.

Brontë has already presented us with a fair, pale heroine full of rage at the men of England. Now she shows us a dark and romantic woman who is self-contained and silent about her true feelings. Not only have Shirley and Caroline exchanged roles in the course of the novel, Shirley and Louis Moore undercut traditional novelistic expectations. Indeed, as many readers have noted, they reverse the types exploited in *Jane Eyre*. Just as Shirley possesses all the accoutrements of the aristocratic hero, Louis Moore is the male counterpart of a governess — a private tutor. Invisible and hungry (p. 493), his faculties and emotions are pent in, walled up (pp. 356, 397). In his locked desk, he keeps a journal to record a hopeless passion which even causes him to temporarily fall ill of a fever. He refers to this exchange of traditional roles himself when he remembers "the fable of Semele reversed" (p. 413). Yet, for all this seeming reversal of roles, Louis loves Shirley because she requires his mastery, his advice and checking. He is older and wiser. As her teacher, he values the perfect lady in her, her maidenly modesty, as well as her need to be bent and curbed. By the end of the novel, Shirley is a bondswoman in the hands of the hero of a patriarch (p. 477).

It looks as if Brontë began *Shirley* with the intention of parodying not only the sexual images of literature but the courtship roles and myths from which they derive. However, no models existed for this kind of fiction. On the contrary, as she herself explains in her use of the Genesis myth, the stories of her culture actively endorse traditional sexual roles, even as they discourage female dissent, female talk and assertion. When Brontë rejects silence, when she refuses to practice her art as a recluse (by forging a private language, for instance, like Emily Dickinson), she finds herself trapped in the conventions of a genre shaped by men. At the instigation of G. H. Lewes, Brontë in *Shirley* tries the disinterested omniscient stance of the historical novelist.[8] Her discomfort is evident each time she slips back into the partisan passion of her heroines. Similarly, she finds herself confined by the traditions of the historical novel; she is influenced, for example, by the romantic conservatism of a writer like Scott, although it contradicts both her general attack on sexism and her more specific satiric criticism of characters like Hiram Yorke. The tension between Brontë's personal allegiance and the dictates of literary conventions is especially evident when she seeks to write something altogether new — a story of female strength and survival. Nowhere does her writing reflect how greatly she was encumbered by the male conventions she inherits than in the endings of her novels. What kind of ending could conclude *Shirley* except submission or flight? Don't both of these contradict her own optimism about finding an adequate solution to the woman's dilemma — an optimism implied by her own literary efforts? Jessy and Rose Yorke do flee to death on foreign soil, but understandably Brontë wants to save her heroines from that fate. She has herself explained to the reader in the course of the novel why the only "happy ending" for women in her society is marriage. She gives us that ending, but she never allows us to forget that marriage is a suspect institution based on degradation. She never allows us to forget that Caroline and Shirley are saved only by the good offices of the narrator and that women who are not novel heroines probably do not fare even this well.

Brontë cannot avoid the conventional "happy ending," as bankrupt as she knows it to be. Having recognized that the inherited novelistic conventions assign to characters a degree of freedom that contradicts her own sense of the female condition, she can only call attention to this by describing remarkably improbable escape routes. At least part of what makes the ending seem so unreal is the way in which the plot metes out proper rewards and punishments to all the characters. Not only do the reader's wishes get totally fulfilled, there is extraordinary symmetry in the way this is done. Robert Moore, for instance, has erred both in his cruelty to the workers and in his mercenary proposal of marriage to Shirley so he is shot down "like some wild beast from behind a wall" (p. 441) by a half-crazed weaver who is a leveller and an Antinomian. Robert has made himself into a business machine so he must be taught the limits of self-reliance, the need for charity. He is imprisoned by a female monster, a dragon. Locked up in an upstairs bedroom, he is taught docility by the terrible Mrs. *Hors/falls*. She is an embodiment of female rage, a revengeful giantess who recalls the wily mermaid. Since Robert has made Caroline ill by withholding his love, he is made to waste away at the hands of a woman who is said to starve him. He cannot eat and he grows as hollow and pale as Caroline.

The entire episode recalls childhood fantasies and fears that are further emphasized by the introduction of Martin Yorke, a young boy who is enthralled by a contraband volume of fairy tales. In the moonlight, he meets Caroline wandering lost about his father's wood and she reminds him of an apparition, a wood nymph. She also recalls a blackbird lamenting her nestlings which were *stoned* to death by his brother. Initially a misogynist, Martin's experience of Caroline causes him to question his previous notion that all females are selfish and shallow. He teases and tests, even while helping her. But he does seem endowed with some puckish powers since he is able to trick his mother, Hortense Moore, and even Zillah Horsfalls. Casting the entire household under a spell, Martin makes it possible for Caroline to slip upstairs unobserved for an interview with Robert. Because he is still only a boy, Martin has the sympathy and the imagination to help Caroline. A parody of the author, he is corrupt enough to enjoy controlling the lovers with his fictions when he views them as characters in a romance of his own making. By returning to the fairy tale motifs that worked so well in *Jane Eyre*, Brontë marks the redemptive education of the capitalist as mere wish-fulfillment.

Shirley's path to happiness is no less amazing than Caroline's. Just as Caroline employs Martin, Shirley uses poetic Henry's admiration to enchant Louis. She receives and rejects three marriage proposals of increasing material advantage. Her rejection of the last and most financially attractive offer manages to transform Louis from an ugly old duck into a youngish swain. In a set-piece of passion, Shirley rebukes the wicked stepfather and Louis exorcises him from the house; however, the imagery undercuts this explicitly joyous scene when Louis is described as desisting from violence, feeling all the time "as cool as stone" (p. 489). Even more malevolently, Shirley claims that he looks like an Egyptian God, "a great sand-buried stone head" (p. 489). He is Shirley's keeper, by her own admission. She has become a "Pantheress!" He, the first man, must prove his dominion over her as "she gnaws at the chain" (p. 496). With the total collapse of Shirley as an independent, self-defined woman the reader sees substantiated Mrs. Pryor's prediction that "Two people can never literally be as one" (p. 300). Whether tactical or obsessive, Shirley's submission is the complete and necessary prelude to her marriage.

Brontë calls attention to the ridiculous fantasy that is the novel's end by entitling her final chapter "The Winding-Up." As if that were not enough to qualify the happy ending, she ties up loose ends, proclaiming that she thinks "the varnish has been put on very nicely" (p. 500). With Shirley on the brink of marriage, it is no surprise that Robert Moore starts perceiving Caroline's resemblance to the Virgin Mary — although for those readers who remember Mary Cave the echoes are less than cheering. Brontë is careful to develop the imagery she has established from the beginning of the novel, most especially the connection between stones, patriarchal Christianity and male lovelessness. The marriage proposal is set near a wall, next to the fragment of a sculptured stone, perhaps the base of a cross. Robert wonders if Caroline can care for him "as if that rose should promise to shelter from tempest this hard, grey stone" (p. 507). He is, in other words, still unable to love anyone except himself. He pictures Caroline as the perfect Sunday school mistress for the cottagers he will employ at his expanded Mill. His is the spirit of the nineteenth century, that "Titan-boy" who "hurls rocks in his wild sport" (p. 502). The salvation of England has been effected by a similar "demigod," named Wellington. The final victory and vision is Robert's. He describes how the "green natural terrace shall be a paved street: there will be cottages in the dark ravine, and cottages on the lonely slopes: the rough pebbled track shall be an even, firm, broad, black, sooty road" (p. 509). The future has been won by and for the men. The narrator confirms the truth of the prophesy. She returns to the Hollow to witness the stones and bricks, the mill as ambitious as a tower of Babel. In mercantile, postlapsarian England, the natural world has been subdued and there are no more fairies. Happy endings will not be quite so easily arranged in this fallen world: history replaces mere romance in the world of stony facts.

Notes

1. Charlotte Brontë, *Shirley* (London: Everyman's Library, 1970), pp. 3–4. All subsequent page references will appear parenthetically in the text.

2. For the best and perhaps the earliest illustration of this view, see G. H. Lewes' review of *Shirley* in the *Edinburgh Review* of 1850, reprinted in *The Brontës: The Critical Heritage*, ed. Miriam Allott (London and Boston: Routledge & Kegan Paul, 1974), p. 164. In this same review, Lewes terms the novel "over-masculine" in its vigor. The review of *Shirley* that appeared in *Church of England Quarterly Review*, January 1850, uses the three clergymen to illustrate Currer Bell's ignorance of religious subjects. This is also reprinted in *The Brontës*, p. 156.

3. Matthew Arnold's letter to Mrs. Foster, dated April 14, 1853, is reprinted in *The Brontës*, p. 201. More recently, Margot Peters comments on imagery of hunger and nourishment in *Charlotte Brontë: Style in the Novel* (Madison: The University of Wisconsin Press, 1973), p. 76.

4. Patricia Beer, *Reader, I Married Him* (London: The MacMillan Press, 1974), pp. 106–109; Charles Burkhart, *Charlotte Brontë: A Psychosexual Study of Her Novels* (London: Victor Gollancz Ltd., 1973), pp. 78–95; Terry Eagleton, *Myths of Power: A Marxist Study of the Brontës* (London: The MacMillan Press, 1975), pp. 45–60; Patricia Meyer Spacks, *The Female Imagination* (New York: Alfred A. Knopf, 1975), pp. 58–63.

5. Elaine Showalter describes the ways in which Victorian women were labelled and, thereby, inhibited by reviewers in "Women Writers and the Double Standard," *Woman in Sexist Society*, eds., Vivian Gornick and Barbara K. Moran (New York: Basic Books, 1971), pp. 323–43. For a discussion of the male artist's ambiguity over the traditions he inherits, see Harold Bloom, *The Anxiety of Influence* (New York: Oxford University Press, 1973).

6. Laura J. Hinkley explores the relationship between Shirley and Emily Brontë in *The Brontës, Charlotte and Emily* (New York: Hastings House, 1945), pp. 290–92.

7. Burkhart, *Charlotte Brontë*, pp. 82–83. Also, M. A. Blom, "Charlotte Brontë, Feminist *Manquée*," *Bucknell Review* 21, no. 1 (1973): 87–102.

8. Lewes' attack on the melodrama and improbability of *Jane Eyre*, which appeared originally in his unsigned review for *Fraser's Magazine*, December 1847, is reprinted in *The Brontës*, pp. 83–87. Burkhart, in *Charlotte Brontë*, discusses the influence of Lewes' letters on Brontë.

Villette

Review of *Villette* by Currer Bell   Harriet Martineau*

Everything written by Currer Bell is remarkable. She can touch nothing without leaving on it the stamp of originality. Of her three novels, this is perhaps the strangest, the most astonishing, though not the best. The sustained ability is perhaps greater in *Villette* than in its two predecessors, there being no intervals of weakness, except in the form of a few passages, chiefly episodical, of over-wrought writing, which, though evidently a sincere endeavour to express real feeling, are not felt to be congenial, or very intelligible, in the midst of so much that is strong and clear. In regard to interest, we think this book will be pronounced inferior to *Jane Eyre*, and superior to *Shirley*. In point of construction it is superior to both; and this is a vast gain and a great encouragement to hope for future benefits from the same hand which shall surpass any yet given. The whole three volumes are crowded with beauties — with those good things for which we look to the clear sight, deep feeling, and singular, though not extensive, experience of life which we associate with the name of Currer Bell. But under all, through all, over all, is felt a drawback, of which we were anxious before, but which is terribly aggravated here — the book is almost intolerably painful. We are wont to say, when we read narratives which are made up of the external woes of life, such as may and do happen every day, but are never congregated in one experience — that the author has no right to make readers so miserable. We do not know whether the right will be admitted in the present case, on the ground of the woes not being external; but certainly we ourselves have felt inclined to rebel against the pain, and, perhaps, on account of its protraction, are disposed to deny its necessity and its truth. With all her objectivity, Currer Bell here afflicts us with an amount of subjective misery which we may fairly remonstrate against; and she allows us no respite, even while treating us with humour, with charming description, and the presence of those whom she herself regards as the good and gay. In truth, there is scarcely anybody that is good — serenely and cheerfully good, and the

*Reprinted from the London *Daily News* (3 February 1853): 2, col. 1.

gaiety has pain in it. An atmosphere of pain hangs about the whole, forbidding that repose which we hold to be essential to the true present- ment of any large portion of life and experience. In this pervading pain, the book reminds us of Balzac; and so it does in the prevalence of one tendency, or one idea, throughout the whole conception and action. All the female characters, in all their thoughts and lives, are full of one thing, or are regarded by the reader in the light of that one thought—love. It begins with the child of six years old, at the opening—a charming picture—and it closes with it at the last page: and, so dominant is this idea—so incessant is the writer's tendency to describe the need of being loved, that the heroine, who tells her own story, leaves the reader at last under the uncomfortable impression of her having either entertained a double love, or allowed one to supersede another without notification of the transition. It is not thus in real life. There are substantial, heartfelt interests for women of all ages, and under ordinary circumstances, quite apart from love: there is an absence of introspection, an unconsciousness, a repose in women's lives—unless under peculiarly unfortunate circum- stances—of which we find no admission in this book: and to the absence of it may be attributed some of the criticism which the book will meet with from readers who are no prudes, but whose reason and taste will reject the assumption that events and characters are to be regarded through the medium of one passion only.

And here ends all demur. We have thought it right to indicate clearly the two faults in the book, which it is scarcely probable that any one will deny. Abstraction made of these, all else is power, skill, and interest. The freshness will be complete to readers who know none but English novels. Those who are familiar with Balzac may be reminded, by the sharp distinctness of the pictured life, place, and circumstances of some of the best of his tales: but there is nothing borrowed; nothing that we might not as well have had if Currer Bell had never read a line of Balzac—which may very likely be the case. As far as we know, the life of a foreign *pension* (Belgian, evidently), and of a third-rate capital, with its half-provincial population and proceedings, is new in purely English literature; and most lifelike and spirited it is. The humour which peeps out in the names—the court of Labassecour, with its heir-apparent the Duc de Dindonneau—the Professors Boissec and Rochemorte—and so forth—is felt throughout, though there is not a touch of light-heartedness from end to end. The presence of the heroine in that capital and *pension* is strangely managed; and so is the gathering of her British friends about her there; but, that strangeness surmounted, the picture of their lives is admirable. The reader must go to the book for it; for it fills two volumes and a half out of the three. The heroine, Lucy Snowe, tells her own story. Every reader of *Jane Eyre* will be glad to see the autobiographical form returned to. Lucy may be thought a younger, feebler sister of Jane. There is just enough resemblance for that: but she has not Jane's charm of mental and moral health, and consequent repose. She is in a state of chronic nervous fever, for the most part; is usually silent and suffering; when she speaks, speaks in enigmas or in raillery, and now and then breaks out under the torture of passion; but she acts admirably—with readiness, sense, conscience, and kindliness. Still we do not wonder that she loved more than she was beloved; and the love at last would be surprising enough, if love could ever be so. Perhaps Paulina and her father are the best-drawn characters in the book, where all are more or less admirably delineated. We are not aware that there is one failure.

A striking peculiarity comes out in the third volume, striking, from one so large and liberal, so removed from ordinary social prejudices as we have been accustomed to think Currer Bell. She goes out of her way to express a passionate hatred of Romanism. It is not the calm disapproval of a ritual religion, such as we should have expected from her, ensuing upon a presentment of her own better faith. The religion she invokes is itself but a dark and doubtful refuge from the pain which compels the invocation; while the catholicism on which she enlarges is even virulently reprobated. We do not exactly see the moral necessity for this (there is no artistical necessity); and we are rather sorry for it, occurring as it does, at a time when catholics and protestants hate each other quite sufficiently; and in a mode which will not affect conversion. A better advocacy of protestantism would have been to show that it can give rest to the weary and heavy laden; whereas it seems to yield no comfort in return for every variety of sorrowful invocation. To the deep undertone of suffering frequent expression is given in such passages as this—beautiful in the wording, but otherwise most painful: —

> Now a letter like that sets one to rights. I might still be sad after reading that letter, but I was more composed; not exactly cheered, perhaps, but relieved. My friends, at least, were well and happy: no accident had occurred to Graham; no illness had seized his mother—calamities that had so long been my dream and thought. Their feelings for me too were—as they had been. Yet, how strange it was to look on Mrs. Bretton's seven weeks and contrast them with my seven weeks! Also, how very wise it is in people placed in an exceptional position to hold their tongues, and not rashly declare how such position galls them. The world can understand well enough the process of perishing for want of food; perhaps few persons can enter into or follow out that of going mad from solitary confinement. They see the long buried prisoner disinterred, a maniac or an idiot!—how his senses left him—how his nerves, first inflamed, underwent nameless agony, and then sunk to palsy—is a subject too intricate for examination, too abstract for popular comprehension. Speak of it! you might almost as well stand up in an European market place and propound dark sayings in that language and mood wherein Nebuchadnezzar, the imperial hypochondriac, communed with his baffled Chaldeans. And long, long may the minds to whom such themes are no mystery—by whom their bearings

are sympathetically seized—be few in number, and rare to encounter. Long may it be generally thought that physical privations alone merit compassion, and that the rest is a figment. When the world was younger and haler than now, moral trials were a deeper mystery still; perhaps in all the lands of Israel there was but one Saul—certainly but one David to soothe or comprehend him—Vol. II, pp. 220-222.

We cannot help looking forward still to other and higher gifts from this singular mind and powerful pen. When we feel that there is no decay of power here, and think what an accession there will be when the cheerfulness of health comes in with its bracing influence, we trust that we have only to wait to have such a boon as *Jane Eyre* gives us warrant to expect, and which Currer Bell alone can give.

[From *Sexual Politics*]   Kate Millett*

. . . Lucy Snowe, the heroine of Charlotte Brontë's *Villette*,[1] a book too subversive to be popular, is another matter. In Lucy one may perceive what effects her life in a male-supremacist society has upon the psyche of a woman. She is bitter and she is honest; a neurotic revolutionary full of conflict, backsliding, anger, terrible self-doubt, and an unconquerable determination to win through. She is a pair of eyes watching society; weighing, ridiculing, judging. A piece of furniture whom no one notices, Lucy sees everything and reports, cynically, compassionately, truthfully, analytically. She is no one, because she lacks any trait that might render her visible: beauty, money, conformity. Only a superb mind imperfectly developed and a soul so omnivorously large it casts every other character into the shadows, she is the great exception, the rest only the great mediocre rule.

Lucy is a woman who has watched men and can tell you what they are as seen by the woman they fail to notice. Some are like John Graham Bretton, charming egoists. Their beauty, for Brontë is perhaps the first woman who ever admitted in print that women find men beautiful, amazes and hurts her. Bretton is two people: one is Graham the treasured and privileged man-child seen through the eyes of a slighted sister, whether the distant idolator be Lucy or Missy Home. Brontë keeps breaking people into two parts so we can see their divided and conflicting emotions; Missy is the worshipful sister, Lucy the envious one. Together they represent the situation of the girl in the family. Bretton is both the spoiled son Graham, and the successful doctor John, and in both roles

*[Excerpts from *Sexual Politics*] by Kate Millett, 140-47. © 1969, 1970 by Kate Millett. Reprinted by permission of Doubleday, a division of Bantam, Doubleday, Dell Publishing Group, Inc.

Lucy envies, loves and hates him. Never does the situation permit her to love him in peace, nor him to take notice of her in any but the most tepid and patronizing good humor: sterile, indifferent. His beauty and goodness make him lovable; his privilege and egotism make him hateful. The enormous deprivation of her existence causes Lucy to resemble a ghetto child peering up at a Harvard man—envy, admiration, resentment and dislike; yet with a tremendous urge to love—if it were possible to love one so removed, so diffident, so oppressive, so rich, disdainful and unjustly superior in place.

If the male is not the delightful and infuriating egoist whom maturity means learning to relinquish one's "crush" on, he is the male one encounters a bit later in life when one tries to make one's way. He is Paul Emanuel, the voice of piety, conventionality, male supremacy, callow chauvinism terrified of female "competition." John is unconquerable; he will never acknowledge any woman who is not beautiful or rich, his only qualifications; he loved Fanshawe's stupidity just as readily as Paulina Mary's virtue. Women are decorative objects to him. Paul is easier to cope with; in his sexual antagonism there is something more tractable. John Graham never saw Lucy; Paul sees her and hates her. Here it is possible to establish contact and, as the story is all a fantasy of success (a type of success utterly impossible to achieve in Brontë's period, and so necessarily fantastic) Paul is met and persuaded. To his sneer that she is ignorant and women are dolts, Lucy replies with phenomenal intellectual effort. Despite the impossible atmosphere he gives off as a pedagogue, the bullying, the captivity in overheated rooms, the endless spying, the bowdlerizing of her texts—she learns. It is his ridicule that forces her to achieve, pokes her into development, deprives her of the somnolence of ladyhood, its small ambitions, timidity, and self-doubt.

Lucy watches women—again from a double and even more complicated point of vantage. She studies Ginevra Fanshawe the flirt, an idiot beauty callously using men to acquire what she has been carefully taught to want: admiration, money, the petty power of dominating a puppy. Fanshawe is beautiful too, and Lucy, in every respect the product of her society as well as its enemy and rebel, has been schooled to love this beauty. It stirs her. The book is full of references to the desire such beauty arouses in her. To express it, Brontë invents the device of an afternoon of amateur theatrics. Lucy is dragged into them at the last moment to play Fanshawe's lover. It is another of Paul's bullying schemes (he locks her in an attic in the July heat to be sure she learns her lines) to coerce her into courage and achievement. Lucy succeeds miraculously, and she makes love to Fanshawe on stage in one of the most indecorous scenes one may come upon in the entire Victorian novel. (Brontë is too much an insurrectionary to acknowledge any convention beyond the literary and the most astonishing things occur continuously in her fiction.) Just as maturity and success lie in outgrowing an infatuation with Graham's masculine egotism, or

Paul's bullying but productive chauvinism, they are also a matter of renouncing a masculine lust for Fanshawe. She is too dumb to love, too silly to want or to permit oneself to be wounded by. The dialogue between the two young women is brutal; Fanshawe parades her beauty with the double purpose of making Lucy capitulate before it, acknowledge herself an ugly woman and therefore inferior; or propose herself a suitor to it and therefore a captive through desire. For Ginevra knows critical Lucy would be the best catch of all, the biggest conquest. Lucy holds her own in these cruel sessions and won't be had either way. Ultimately, she transcends them and Fanshawe altogether, who fades into the mere butterfly she is and disappears from the book.

The other women Lucy watches are Madame Beck and Mrs. Bretton. Both are older women, one a mother, one a businesswoman and head of a school. They are two of the most efficient women one can meet anywhere in fiction. Lucy, who, like Charlotte Brontë, lacked a mother, regards older women as the embodiment of competence, and what she loves in them is their brilliant ability to manage. While Victorian masculine fantasy saw only tender, quivering incapacity in such women, Lucy perceives them as big, capable ships and herself only a little boat. But the big ships are afloat because they knew how to compromise; Lucy does not plan to. The big ships are convention. For all the playful banter of her relationship with her son, Mrs. Bretton stands for a stale and selfless maternity, bent on living vicariously through her adored boy's success. Pleasant matron that she is, she would sacrifice any daughter in the world for the comfort of his lordly breakfast, and Lucy knows it. Mrs. Bretton's conventional motherhood is only the warm perfection of chauvinist sentiment. Then there is Madame Beck, a tower of convention, the tireless functionary of European sexual inhibition, watching every move of the young women under her Jehovah-like and unsleeping surveillance; getting up at night to examine Lucy's underwear, reading her letters to sniff out traces of sex in them, watching for missives thrown from windows to her pupils. Both these women are still young and ripe for sexuality. Mrs. Bretton fulfills her own in flirtation with her son:

"Mamma, I'm in a dangerous way."

"As if that interested me," said Mrs. Bretton.

"Alas! the cruelty of my lot!" responded her son. "Never man had a more unsentimental mother than mine; she never seems to think that such a calamity can befall her as a daughter-in-law."

"If I don't, it is not for want of having that same calamity held over my head; you have threatened me with it for the last ten years. 'Mamma, I am going to be married soon!' was the cry before you were well out of jackets."

"But mother, one of these days it will be realized. All of a sudden, when you think you are most secure, I shall go forth like Jacob or Esau, or any other patriarch, and take me a wife, perhaps of these which are of the daughters of the land."

"At your peril, John Graham! that is all."[2]

Beck is more sensually alive and would be delighted to take on John Graham, but of course she is not sufficiently young, beautiful, or socially prominent for his tastes. Real as her own sexuality is, she will gracefully acknowledge his rejection, and serenely carry on the business, while cheerfully stamping out the intrusion of the least hint of sex in any corner of her establishment. As the educator of young females, Madame Beck is a perpetual policewoman, a virtual forewoman of partriarchal society. No system of subjection could operate for two seconds without its collaborators, and Beck is a splendid example of the breed.

Finally, there is Paulina Mary, the golden one, the perfect woman, John Graham's pretty Polly, the apple of her daddy's eye. Lucy had no father to dote upon her, nor any John to court her, and she is painfully aware that Paulina is lucky. Yet there is one flaw in this female paragon — she is a child of eight — delightful when she appears as Missy Home at the beginning of the book; clever, affectionate, precocious — but nauseating when she reappears as a woman of nineteen and still a mental infant. Paulina is well-meaning and well loved. Even Lucy is fond of her from time to time, but she is also appalled that society's perfect woman must be a cute preadolescent. Having surveyed the lot, Lucy prefers to be like none of them. Looking over all the "role models" her world presents, the adoring mother, the efficient prison matron, the merciless flirt, the baby-goddess, Lucy, whose most genuine trial is that she has been born into a world where there are no adequate figures to imitate so that she is forced to grope her way alone, a pioneer without precedents, turns her back on the bunch of them. Better to go back to something solidly her own — deal with mathematics, Paul Emanuel, and the job.

Lucy has watched men look at women, has studied the image of woman in her culture. There is probably nothing so subversive in the book as that afternoon in the Brussels museum when she scrutinizes the two faces of woman whom the male has fashioned, one for his entertainment, one for her instruction: Rubens' Cleopatra and the Academician's four pictures of the virtuous female. Lucy's deliberately philistine account of Cleopatra is very entertaining:

> It represented a woman, considerably larger, I thought, than the life. I calculated that this lady, put into a scale of magnitude suitable for the reception of a commodity of bulk, would infallibly turn from fourteen to sixteen stones. She was indeed extremely well fed. Very much butchers' meat, to say nothing of bread, vegetables, and liquids, must she have consumed to attain that breadth and height, that wealth of muscle, that affluence of flesh. She lay half-reclined on a couch, why, it would be difficult to say; broad daylight blazed round her; she appeared

in hearty health, strong enough to do the work of two plain cooks; she could not plead a weak spine; she ought to have been standing, or at least sitting bolt upright. She had no business to lounge away the noon on a sofa. . . . Then, for the wretched untidiness surrounding her, there could be no excuse. Pots and pans, perhaps I ought to say vases and goblets, were rolled here and there on the foreground; a perfect rubbish of flowers was mixed amongst them, and an absurd and disorderly mass of certain upholstery smothered the couch, and cumbered the floor.[3]

This "coarse and preposterous canvas," the "enormous piece of claptrap," as Lucy nominates the masturbatory fantasy she perceives in it, is the male dream of an open and panting odalisque, the sheer carnality floating always in the back of his mind, and can be matched only by its obverse — the image of woman he would foist on the woman herself. Cleopatra is for masculine delectation only, and when Paul catches Lucy contemplating the painting he is deeply shocked: "How dare you, a young person, sit coolly down, with the self-possession of a garçon and look at *that* picture?"[4] A despot, as Lucy describes him so often, he is deeply offended, even affronted, that a young woman should see what he immediately settles down to gaze at. Paul forbids Lucy to look upon Cleopatra, and forces her to sit in a dull corner and study several mawkish daubs the conventional mind has designed for her.

. . . a set of four, denominated in the catalogue, "La vie d'une femme." They were painted in a remarkable style, flat, dead, pale and formal. The first represented a "Jeune Fille," coming out of a church door, a missal in her hand, her dress very prim, her eyes cast down, her mouth pursed up — the image of a most villainous, little, precocious she-hypocrite. The second, "a Mariée" with a long white veil, kneeling at a prie-dieu in her chamber, holding her hands plastered together, finger to finger, and showing the whites of her eyes in the most exasperating manner. The third a "Jeune Mère" hanging disconsolate over a clayey and puffy baby with a face like an unwholesome full moon. The fourth, a "Veuve," being a black woman, holding by the hand a black little girl [black because in mourning] and the twain studiously surveying an elegant French monument. . . . All these four "Anges" were grim and grey as burglars, and cold and vapid as ghosts. What women to live with! insecure, ill-humored, bloodless, brainless nonentities! As bad in their way as the indolent gipsy giantess, the Cleopatra, in hers.[5]

In this comic instance of sight taboo, the social schizophrenia within masculine culture, not only the hypocrisy of the double standard, but its purpose and intentions are exposed. It has converted one woman into sex symbol, flesh devoid of mentality or personality, "cunt" — this for itself to gaze upon. And unto woman herself is reserved the wearisome piety of academic icons with their frank propaganda of serviceable humility.

The disparity in the contradiction of images represented by the two pictures explains the techniques of *Villette* better than any other moment in the novel. It is a division in the culture which Brontë is retorting to by splitting her people in half and dividing Lucy's own responses into a fluctuating negative and positive. The other dichotomy is between her newness, her revolutionary spirit, and the residue of the old ways which infects her soul. This inner conflict is complemented by an exterior one between her ambitions and desires and the near impossibility of their fulfillment. There are obstacles everywhere, social and financial. The hard realities of the sexual caste system frustrate her as well as its mentality. Curiously enough, the obstacles drive her on. Lucy represents not only Brontë's, but what must have been, and probably still remains, the ambition of every conscious young woman the world. She wants to be free; she is mad to escape, to learn, to work, to go places. She envies every man his occupation, John his medicine, Paul his scholarship, just as she envied them their education. Both had the finest obtainable and it was given to them as a preparation for life. Lucy was given nothing so substantial: ". . . picture me for the next eight years, as a bark slumbering through halcyon weather, in a harbour as still as glass—the steersman stretched on the little deck, his face up to heaven, his eyes closed. . . . A great many women and girls are supposed to pass their lives something in that fashion; why not I with the rest? . . . However, it cannot be concealed that in that case, I must somehow have fallen overboard, or there must have been a wreck at last."[6] She is traumatically cast out of the middle class quite unprepared to live, for all the world had expected her to exist parasitically. She now lacks the prerequisites: a face, respectable social connections, and parents to place her. She is a serf without a proprietor who must become a wage slave, namely a governess or teacher. The only way out, and it's a desperate track, is to learn in the world and books. *Villette* chronicles her formal and informal education in the acquisition of her own competence through both.

But what work can Lucy do; what occupations are open to her? Paid companion, infant nurse, governess, schoolteacher. As they are arranged, each is but another name for servant. Each involves starvation wages which only a lifetime of saving could ever convert to ransom. There is another humiliation in the fact of servant status which rested with particular severity on middle-class women who in taking employment are falling a step below the class of their birth. (While a paid companion, Lucy encounters a schoolmate now the mistress of a household—Lucy had been visiting another servant in the kitchen.) Furthermore, these occupations involve "living-in" and a twenty-four-hour surveillance tantamount to imprisonment. The only circumstances under which Lucy is permitted an occupation are such that they make financial independence and personal fulfillment impossible. It is not very hard to understand her envy at the gratification and status which Paul and John are given automatically in their professions. One might well ask, as Lucy does unceasingly, is it worth it then, under these conditions, to work? Is it not easier to keep falling into daydreams about prince charmings who will elevate one to royalty, or so they claim? At any rate, they could provide easy security and a social position cheaply attained. They will provide, if nothing else, the sexual gratification which women occupied like Lucy are utterly forbidden to enjoy.

Villette reads, at times, like another debate between the opposed mentalities of Ruskin and Mill. Lucy is forever alternating between hankering after the sugared hopes of chivalric rescue, and the strenuous realism of Mill's analysis. Brontë demonstrates thereby that she knows what she is about. In her circumstances, Lucy would not be creditable if she were not continuously about to surrender to convention; if she were not by turns silly as well as sensible. So there are many moments when she wishes she were as pretty as Fanshawe, as rich as Polly, occasions when she would happily forgo life itself at a sign that Graham recognizes she was alive. Born to a situation where she is subject to life-and-death judgments based on artificial standards of beauty, Lucy is subject to a compulsive mirror obsession, whereby each time she looks in the glass she denies her existence—she does not appear in the mirror. One of the most interesting cases of inferiority feelings in literature, Lucy despises her exterior self, and can build an inner being only through self-hatred. Yet living in a culture which takes masochism to be a normal phenomenon in females, and even conditions them to enjoy it, Lucy faces and conquers the attractions Paul's sadism might have held.

Charlotte Brontë has her public censor as well as her private one to deal with. This accounts for the deviousness of her fictional devices, her continual flirtation with the bogs of sentimentality which period feeling mandates she sink in though she be damned if she will. Every Victorian novel is expected to end in a happy marriage; those written by women are required to. Brontë pretends to compromise; convention is appeased by the pasteboard wedding of Paulina Mary and Prince John; cheated in Lucy's escape.

Escape is all over the book; *Villette* reads like one long meditation on a prison break. Lucy will not marry Paul even after the tyrant has softened. He has been her jailer all through the novel, but the sly and crafty captive in Lucy is bent on evading him anyway. She plays tame, learns all he has to teach her of the secrets of the establishment—its mathematics and Latin and self-confidence. She plays pupil to a man who hates and fears intelligent women and boasts of having caused the only woman teacher whose learning ever challenged his own to lose her job. Lucy endures the baiting about the "natural inferiority of females" with which Paul tortures her all through the lesson, and understands that only the outer surface of his bigotry melts when she proves a good student and thereby flatters his pedagogic vanity. Yet in his simplicity he has been hoodwinked into giving her the keys. The moment they are in her hand, and she has beguiled him into lending her money, renting her a school of her own, and facilitated her daring in slipping from the claws of Madame Beck—she's gone. The keeper turned kind must be eluded anyway; Paul turned lover is drowned.

Lucy is free. Free is alone; given a choice between "love" in its most agreeable contemporary manifestation, and freedom, Lucy chose to retain the individualist humanity she had shored up, even at the expense of sexuality. The sentimental reader is also free to call Lucy "warped," but Charlotte Brontë is hard-minded enough to know that there was no man in Lucy's society with whom she could have lived and still been free. On those occasions when Brontë did marry off her heroines, the happy end is so fraudulent, the marriages so hollow, they read like satire, or cynical tracts against love itself. There was, in Lucy's position, just as in the Brontë's own, no other solution available.

As there is no remedy to sexual politics in marriage, Lucy very logically doesn't marry. But it is also impossible for a Victorian novel to recommend a woman not marry. So Paul suffers a quiet sea burial. Had Brontë's heroine "adjusted" herself to society, compromised, and gone under, we should never have heard from her. Had Brontë herself not grown up in a house of half-mad sisters with a domestic tyrant for father, no "prospects," as marital security was referred to, and with only the confines of governessing and celibacy staring at her from the future, her chief release the group fantasy of "Angria," that collective dream these strange siblings played all their lives, composing stories about a never-never land where women could rule, exercise power, govern the state, declare night and day, death and life—then we would never have heard from Charlotte either.[7] Had that been the case, we might never have known what a resurrected soul wished to tell upon emerging from several millennia of subordination. Literary criticism of the Brontës has been a long game of masculine prejudice wherein the player either proves they can't write and are hopeless primitives, whereupon the critic sets himself up like a schoolmaster to edit their stuff and point out where they went wrong, or converts them into case histories from the wilds, occasionally prefacing his moves with a few pseudo-sympathetic remarks about the windy house on the moors, or old maidhood, following with an attack on every truth the novels contain, waged by anxious pedants who fear Charlotte might "castrate" them or Emily "unman" them with her passion. There is bitterness and anger in Villette—and rightly so. One finds a good deal of it in Richard Wright's Black Boy, too. To label it neurotic is to mistake symptom for cause in the hope of protecting oneself from what could be upsetting.

What should surprise us is not Lucy's wry annoyance, but her affection and compassion—even her wit. Villette is one of the wittier novels in English and one of the rare witty books in an age which specialized in sentimental comedy. What is most satisfying of all is the astonishing degree of consciousness one finds in the work, the justice of its analysis, the fairness of its observations, the generous degree of self-criticism. Although occasionally flawed with mawkish nonsense (there is a creditable amount of Victorian syrup in *Villette*), it is nevertheless one of the most interesting books of the period and, as an expression of revolutionary sensibility, a work of some importance. . . .

Notes

1. Charlotte Brontë, *Villette*, first published in 1853 under the pseudonym Currer Bell. Reprinted by the Gresham Publishing Company, London, undated. Page numbers refer to this edition. Throughout my remarks I am indebted to an unpublished essay on Charlotte Brontë's *Shirley* written by Laurie Stone.

2. *Ibid.*, p. 193.

3. *Ibid.*, p. 183.

4. *Ibid.*, p. 184.

5. *Ibid.*, p. 185.

6. *Ibid.*, p. 32.

7. See Fannie Ratchford, *The Brontës' Web of Childhood* (New York: Columbia University Press, 1941).

The Face in the Mirror: *Villette* and the Conventions of Autobiography

Janice Carlisle*

Recounting one of the more famous anecdotes of the fabled life at Haworth parsonage, Patrick Brontë once described the result of his desire to know what his very young children were thinking: "happening to have a mask in the house, I told them all to stand and speak boldly from under the cover of that mask." The father suspected that the everyday behavior of his children was itself a mask, an assumed pose of innocence that veiled "more than [he] had yet discovered."[1] By means of his ruse he hoped to counter that deception; the mask would conceal the face and identity of the speaker in order to reveal the child's heart. The episode is one of those telling revelations of both character and the forces that mold character. Even at the age of eight, Charlotte Brontë was being encouraged to adopt subversive modes of self-expression. The form of this little drama would become the form of her art. Like Thackeray, who fled the responsibilities of speaking in propria persona by creating narrators such as Barry Lyndon or Arthur Pendennis, Brontë was most comfortable when presenting narrative mediated through a consciousness other than her own; from the

*Reprinted from *ELH* 46 (Summer 1979): 262–89, by permission of the Johns Hopkins University Press.

earliest extant juvenilia to the fragment of the novel begun just before her death, she spoke with most freedom when she spoke through the voices of characters like Captain Tree or Charles Wellesley Townshend, Jane Eyre or Mrs. Chalfont. This mode was never more central to Brontë's art than in the case of *Villette*. Lucy Snowe is the mask under cover of which Brontë conceals her identity in order to reveal the unappealing reality of her emotional life and its central figures, M. Heger and George Smith. The mask, however, performs this function in the service of art. The novel is a mirror in which reality is transformed to grant the emotional and aesthetic satisfactions that life invariably withholds.

Villette, the result of this process, is indeed a private document, but its privacy is a function of Lucy Snowe's life and character, not its author's. Brontë was able to distance herself from her own experience and even from facets of her own personality so that we do not need the facts of her life to explain or justify the novel. Yet *Villette* is genuinely puzzling, and it presents mysteries that we might be tempted to unlock with the key of biography. Its first reader, George Smith, responded to the manuscript with a pained silence so prolonged that it almost induced Brontë to journey to London to discover what had gone amiss. Even she seemed at least partially unaware of the implications of her novel. Like Lucy naïvely suggesting that her cold exterior represents her true identity, Brontë commented soon after finishing *Villette*, "Unless I am mistaken the emotion of the book will be found to be kept throughout in tolerable subjection."[2] She was, of course, mistaken, and one might say of Charlotte and *Villette* what Charlotte said of Emily and *Wuthering Heights*, "Having formed these beings, she did not know what she had done." Charlotte Brontë firmly believed that writers are mastered by a force that they themselves do not comprehend—"something that at times strangely wills and works for itself"[3]—but even the powers of unconscious creative agency do not explain the questions the novel raises. What are we to make of its disjointed chronology, its shifts of tone and subject, its patent evasions, and the inconclusiveness of its ending? Does the novel reveal the view of a woman who accepts suffering as the dispensation of a just Providence? Or does it, in Matthew Arnold's words, display the author's "hunger, rebellion, and rage"? On a first reading, the novel almost always seems as "preternatural in its power" as George Eliot found it,[4] but most readers—and here I speak for myself and my students—wonder if its power is not the result of emotions profoundly confused and confusing. Yet if we begin to look more closely at Lucy Snowe, at the shape and form of Brontë's mask, what has seemed perplexing or contradictory about her story reveals a clarity and persuasive emotional logic that shine through even the most apparently trivial or irrelevant detail.

The qualities that Lucy displays as the narrator of her own life and the qualities of *Villette* as the mirror of her experience are most easily defined if we set the novel in the context of its contemporary tradition, the art of autobiography at the Victorian midcentury. As Leigh Hunt noted in 1850, autobiography had "abounded of late years in literary quarters,"[5] and the trend only continued to increase in the early years of the 1850's. The popularity of *Jane Eyre* (1847) had been an important impetus to the widespread adoption of the form. Because of the generous gifts of books from her publishers and a growing circle of literary friends, Charlotte Brontë was well aware of this development. During the fall of 1849, when *Shirley* was being published, she began reading Dickens' *David Copperfield*, the first in a number of autobiographical works that she read before starting *Villette*. If "autobiographical" is defined formally in terms of first-person narration, then this group of works includes memoirs and poetry as well as fiction: the "Recollections" that preface Southey's *Life and Correspondence*, Hunt's *Autobiography*, and Tennyson's *In Memoriam*. The most significant work, however, was the posthumous 1850 edition of Wordsworth's *Prelude*.[6] In all the autobiographical works that Charlotte Brontë read in 1849 and 1850, the central issues of memory and the past are treated in a highly self-conscious manner. To each of these writers, memory is the source and proof of personal identity: as Southey comments, "at two years old . . . my recollection begins; prior identity I have none" ("Recollections," p. 23). The effect of this widespread emphasis on memory seems clear. Though Jane Eyre had been called upon to recount her past experience, only in *Villette* and one of the sketches that preceded it does Brontë treat memory as a problematic function. *Henry Esmond*, a novel that Brontë read in manuscript as she was writing *Villette*, testifies to the predominance of the same concerns: for the first time in Thackeray's career, memory itself becomes the subject of analysis and description.

Autobiography is, almost by definition, a form that strives to accommodate fact and desire, circumstances as they actually occurred and the longing that they—or oneself—had been somehow different. The complexity of memory is beautifully imaged in Wordsworth's well-known comparison of the man who looks through the "surface of the past" to a man looking over the side of a boat on a still lake: he

> . . . often is perplexed and cannot part
> The shadow from the substance, rocks and sky,
> Mountains and clouds, reflected in the depth
> Of that clear flood, from things which there abide
> In their true dwelling; now is crossed by gleam
> Of his own image, by a sun-beam now,
> And wavering motions sent he knows not
> whence. . . .
>
> (IV, 263–69)

The past self is the product of a number of refracted images: the uneven mirror of the lake reflects the sky, the sun, and the face of the watcher as it communicates the ever-moving objects on its bottom: shadow and substance merge indistinguishably. Most potent are the shadows cast by the longing to perceive an image of self that is acceptable if not flattering. Biographical research has shown us the extent to which such feelings can shape the "facts" recorded in autobiographical documents. Wordsworth omits the story of Annette Vallon from *The Prelude,* perhaps because she had little relevance to the account of his poetic discipline, more probably because his own part in the affair involved unattractive qualities that he did not care to reveal. In his *Confessions* Rousseau similarly distorts the chronology of his sojourn at Les Charmettes so that he does not have to acknowledge the quality of Mme. de Warens' less than exclusive affection for him. Not constrained even as much as Wordsworth or Rousseau by the need to be faithful to actual events, Brontë uses the freedom of her fictional autobiography to increase the complexity of interpenetrating and refracted images of self. Why she would need to do so seems clear. For neither Brontë nor Lucy Snowe can the facts or circumstances of experience offer any satisfaction. Family is gone; suitors have disappeared. M. Paul is dead; Graham Bretton, married to another woman, is dead to Lucy. Memory can only reveal a past of promise and hope turned to present deprivation; it is primarily a record of losses and humiliations. David Copperfield or Jane Eyre can see every untoward event in their lives as a step in the direction of the happy resolution of past difficulties — Agnes and Rochester wait at the end of their narrative journeys. No such consolation is available to Lucy. Her dilemma is like that of *In Memoriam:* events can yield fulfillment only through a change in the perspective of the individual who has suffered through them. Lucy must find the little satisfaction that her life affords through the pattern which she imposes on it, through the way in which she chooses to relate events: memory must mold experience into a form that is acceptable, a form that will "suffice," if not actually console. Lucy must depend on essentially subversive ways of appeasing memory.

Commenting on other people and their petty vanities, Lucy notes "wherever an accumulation of small defences is found . . . there, be sure, it is needed."[7] *Villette* is a carapace of defenses against the almost intolerable pain of memory, and the first of the ways in which Lucy tries to assuage that pain is the simplest: she ignores one of the most prominent themes of midcentury autobiography by flatly refusing to acknowledge the cost of retrospection. Even in a treatment of the past as unremittingly cheerful as Leigh Hunt's, the writer still looks back on his narrative and notes, "I can never forget the pain of mind which some of the passages cost me" (I, iv). Likewise, Southey claims with calm satisfaction, "I have lived in the sunshine, and am still looking forward with hope," while he speaks of the "courage" he has had to find "to live again in remembrance with the dead, so much as I must needs do in retracing the course of my life" (17). The pain of loss is the predominant tone in much of David Copperfield's narrative, and the valiant, but futile efforts of Mr. Dick illustrate the frustrations faced by any man who tries to write "a Memorial about his own history" (205). But Lucy does not deal with the problem so directly. Indeed she never lets us know that for her recollection is something less than an occasion for tranquillity. In the context of her character, such evasions make sense. She has been trained by untoward circumstances to hide her feelings, to pretend that she is the "unobtrusive article of furniture" (I, 120) that the other characters take her to be. Throughout her earlier experience in Bretton and at Mme. Beck's, she has learned the benefit of "telling tales," of presenting elliptical accounts of events that do not involve any embarrassing revelations of her feelings. In one rather comically self-conscious instance, she tells Ginevra that her callous mockery of Graham and his mother has caused him acute suffering—she has told a tale, a lie, to satisfy Ginevra's expectations. Lucy often treats the reader and his conventional demands for a gratifying story as cavalierly as she has treated Ginevra. She buries her feelings in her "heretic narrative" (I, 205) as surely as she has buried her affections in the jar she entombs beneath the pear-tree in Mme. Beck's garden. She tells us that one must struggle "with the natural character, the strong native bent of the heart," that one must follow the dictates of Reason rather than Feeling and present to the world a surface that is "regulated," quiet, and "equable" (I, 225). To see beyond the supposedly imperturbable, opaque surface of Lucy's story is the reader's most challenging responsibility. Only by examining a crucial event from the narrator's earlier experience can we begin to understand the pain she inevitably feels whenever she thinks of her past.

At the opening of Volume II, Brontë presents one of the most complete of Victorian speculations on the dangers and terrors of memory, but her analysis is as remarkable for its indirection as for its power. Instead of letting the older Lucy tell us what it means to revive thoughts of the past, Brontë subjects the younger Lucy to a literal return of the "scenes and days" of her "girlhood" (I, 210). The effect is something like watching Alice fall down the rabbit-hole of imagination: mental phenomena are rendered as physical objects and sequences of narrative. Brontë sets this scene in "Auld Lang Syne" at a moment of crisis. Lucy has been left to spend the long vacation alone at Mme. Beck's *pensionnat*. After fainting in a street beyond the church where she has attended confession, she wakes to experience an involuntary and unexpected rebirth into a strangely familiar world. "With pain, with reluctance, with a moan and a long shiver," Lucy finds herself in an environment that seems ghostlike. At one of those oddly resonant moments so frequent in *Villette*, Lucy faces a mirror and sees the skull-like image of a dead self: "In this mirror . . . I looked spectral; my eyes larger and more hollow, my hair darker than was natural, by contrast with my thin and ashen face" (I, 208). As she begins to recognize the objects in the drawing room as the furniture from her godmother's house in Bretton, Lucy becomes increasingly skeptical about her own identity or sanity. She then falls asleep — only to wake in another room that intensifies her earlier sense of uncanny recognition. Again, Lucy looks into a mirror; instead of seeing a ghostly image of herself, she sees the past: "Bretton! Bretton! and ten years ago shone reflected in that mirror. And why did Bretton and my fourteenth year haunt me thus? Why, if they came at all, did they not return complete?" To return to the past, as Lucy literally does here, is to journey into a world that is spectral because it is dead, a world that calls into question the stability and substantiality of one's identity.

There is, of course, a logical explanation for Lucy's hallucinatory vision of "auld lang syne." After recognizing a portrait of Graham Bretton, Lucy soon discovers his mother sitting by her bedside. Although Lucy chooses not to reveal her identity, she learns that the past has been revived in the present simply because the Brettons have moved themselves and their belongings from England to Labassecour. As she becomes accustomed to her reinstatement in the world of her childhood, she describes even its comforts in a way that again suggests the emotional cost of memory. She rests in her bedroom and thinks of her "calm little room" as a "cave in the sea":

> There was no colour about it, except that white and pale green, suggestive of foam and deep water; the blanched cornice was adorned with shell-shaped ornaments, and there were white mouldings like dolphins in the ceiling-angles. Even that one touch of colour visible in the red satin pincushion bore affinity to coral; even that dark, shining glass might have mirrored a mermaid. When I closed my eyes, I heard a gale, subsiding at last, bearing upon the house-front like a setting swell upon a rock-base. I heard it drawn and withdrawn far, far off, like a tide retiring from a shore of the upper world — a world so high above that the rush of its largest waves, the dash of its fiercest breakers could sound down in this submarine home, only like murmurs and a lullaby.   (I, 228)

La Terrasse literally offers Lucy a refuge in the past. The scene evokes some of the most eloquent language in *Villette*, yet its lyrical qualities are themselves warnings against the seductive and potentially dangerous powers of memory. Like other Victorian descriptions of the past, this passage is an image of a withdrawal that is also a regression. In the womblike "submarine home" of memory, one is protected from the storms of adult experience; there the sound of conflict is magically transformed into a lullaby. The context of the passage offers further warning that the peace of this withdrawal is deceptive and its comfort merely temporary. Like every other retreat Lucy finds, it must be abandoned; like every moment of calm, it will be disturbed. Only four chapters later, Lucy suffers a "Reaction" when she returns to Mme. Beck's school: the responsibilities of maturity must inevitably replace the joys and security of childhood. Lucy now must live by "imperious rules, prohibiting under deadly penalties all weak retrospect of happiness past; commanding a patient journeying through the wilderness of the present" (I, 292).

From these events the twenty-three-year-old character learns an impressive lesson that the older narrator is not likely to overlook. To relive the sorrows of the past is to revive their pain; to relive its joys is to relinquish them once more. Though Lucy's retreat to La Terrasse, to the cave in the sea, is a time of peace and fulfillment, it renders more unbearable the present solitude and struggle which she must endure. Like Vashti, Lucy remembers the heaven she has left, and "Heaven's light" can only serve to disclose the "forlorn remoteness" of her "exile" (II, 8). By making a narrative return to the scenes of her past, the older Lucy is forcing herself to do what Graham unwittingly does to her when he brings to La Terrasse the sick English schoolteacher he does not recognize. In the face of such difficulties, simple reticence is no adequate defense. Without giving the reader any direct indication of the principles that underlie her treatment of the past, the narrator responds to the events or characters she recalls in ways that vary according to the emotional challenges they entail. Like the young woman responding to the unfolding revelations of her stay at La Terrasse, the older woman allows her attitudes toward the past to develop according to a coherent "plot" roughly equivalent to the volume divisions of the novel: her visit to Bretton when she was fourteen and her first term at Mme. Beck's *pensionnat* in Volume I; her renewed acquaintance with the Brettons and the Homes in the second volume; and the relationship with M. Paul that dominates the action of the third volume. But the narrator never acknowledges that such a development is taking place. The reader must discover for himself how and why these psychological processes are at work. Again the practice of Brontë's contemporaries helps define Lucy's more unconventional modes of dealing with the past.

Dickens, Hunt, Southey, Wordsworth and Tennyson all agree on the central problem that memory presents: the difficulty of defining one's temporal perspective on the past. Wordsworth is, of course, the subtlest commentator on this question. As he explains, the man who tells his own story may feel that the difference between his past and present selves creates in him "two consciousnesses" (II, 32), separate identities with no relation to each other. Conversely, these two selves may interpenetrate. Speaking of his undergraduate days, Wordsworth admits: "Of these and other kindred notices / I cannot say what portion is in truth / The naked recollection of that time, / And what may rather have been called to life / By after-meditation" (III, 612–16). The narrator may present his "naked recollection" — his initial impressions of an event — or the product of his "after-meditation": his first impressions may be altered or effaced by his knowledge of later events or his more mature understanding of himself. Although they may not be as dismayed by their autobiographical tasks as Mr. Dick, all these writers openly admit that they are often baffled by the relation between their past and present selves. Like Wordsworth, they conscientiously warn us when, in Hunt's words, they "bring [their] night-thoughts into the morning of life" (I, 59). Southey, for instance, speaks of an acquaintance: "I look back upon his inoffensive and monotonous course of life with a compassion which I was then not capable of feeling" (40). The Prologue to *In Memoriam* notifies the reader that the present-tense lyrics that follow are actually records of the first impressions of a past experience of grief. Dickens' careful handling of tenses is an even more remarkable indication of the care with which an author may balance the presentation of the narrator's first impressions against his later understanding of them. The use of the historical present is, of course, frequent in *David Copperfield*, especially in the first half of the novel as David tries to recapture the feelings of childhood. David's evolving identity is defined by present-tense chapters such as "I Observe" and his various "Retrospects." Yet the use of the tense can also express the strength of the older narrator's feelings about his past experience: the warehouse where David works as a child contains "things, not of many years ago, in my mind, but of the present instant" (154). Dickens is exceedingly careful to distinguish between the historical present of the revivified past and the present tense appropriate to his narrative activity. David adds qualifications such as "according to my present way of thinking" (273) whenever his "later understanding comes . . . to [his] aid" (18). At one point, he even employs the two uses of the tense in one sentence so that he can distinguish between them: "I am a sensible fellow [at seventeen years], I believe — I believe, on looking back, I mean — " (270). Here irony emphasizes the demarcation between past and present; the narrator's "I believe" becomes a telling comment on the sense with which the seventeen-year-old credits himself.

Such self-conscious treatments of memory and its perplexing effects are characteristic of the autobiographical works Charlotte Brontë read as she approached the writing of *Villette*. By comparison Lucy Snowe's attitude toward her retrospective activity seems almost naïve. Again she simply avoids the issue. Her reticence about her narrative role suggests that, for her, memory involves neither pain nor complicated temporal perspectives. Indeed her most straightforward comment on the question — the one too often accepted as definitive — implies that *Villette* is entirely the product of mature "after-meditation": "(for I speak of a time gone by: my hair which till a late period withstood the frosts of time, lies now, at last white, under a white cap, like snow beneath snow)" (I, 52). Lucy, now an old woman, tells the story of her younger self. The passage is reminiscent of Southey's comments on his old age or David's reference to the twenty years that separate his present self from the events he recounts. We are asked to believe that Lucy brings to the story of her youth all the serenity and calm resignation implicit in the image of her whitened hair. As we have learned from "Auld Lang Syne," however, memory has not always been a capacity that Lucy has been able to exercise with such painless ease. In another passage describing the attitudes of her younger self, Lucy has noted, "Oh, my childhood! I had feelings: passive as I lived, little as I spoke, cold as I looked, when I thought of past days, I *could* feel" (I, 134). The older narrator differs in no essential way from the young woman who makes this statement. A look at the first three chapters of *Villette* reveals the complex distortions of temporal perspective that her feelings create.

As conventional autobiography, these chapters are woefully inadequate. As an indication of the essential qualities of Lucy's relation to her past, they display an admirable degree of emotional logic. Reticence, of course, predominates. Neither the narrator's past nor present self is the ostensible subject here. Lucy refuses to tell us about her own childhood; rather she depicts her adolescent acquaintance with the child Paulina Home. We are asked to assume that Lucy offers us her first impressions of this relationship. Her apparently detached, yet ultimately hostile attitude toward this child creates the main difficulty. In Lucy's view of her, Paulina is scarcely human. She arrives in Bretton a "shawled bundle"; even when she emerges, Lucy repeatedly calls her "it" or the "creature" or a "mere doll" (I, 4–5). She continually views Paulina's love for her father or Graham as "absurd" or grotesquely dehumanizing. At one point Lucy even suggests that Paulina, the "little Odalisque" (I, 32), is faintly immoral. We might be tempted to attribute these shrewish comments to Lucy's adolescent jealousy. There is reason enough for that response. Before Paulina arrives, Lucy reigns supreme in Mrs. Bretton's affections. Paulina causes a "change" in this situation that is all the more disturbing because it is so "unexpected" (I, 2). This quaint child takes Lucy's place, and Lucy is forced to watch as Mrs. Bretton lavishes her attention on Paulina. Lucy finds the reunion between Paulina and her father "oppressing" simply because she is excluded from that or any other scene of parental fondness. Yet there are at work here forces — covert emotions, confused perceptions — that simply cannot be explained as the first impressions of even the most jealous of fourteen-year-old girls.

Though the narrator betrays no emotional involvement in the Bretton scenes she recalls, we need to know why she would begin her own story at that point in her experience. One answer is obvious: like the vignettes of the child and nature in *The Prelude*, like David Copperfield's precocious fascination with the subject of marriage, Paulina's stay in Bretton has a central thematic role in *Villette*. It illustrates what Lucy knows to be the basic structure of human relationships: emotional bonds are forged by the pressure of a woman's great need, and they are inevitably disrupted by "fate" or a man's fickle indifference. More importantly, Lucy's depiction of Paulina defines a central quality of her own memory: the emotional resonance of a particular scene often has little relation to Lucy's "naked recollection," and the narrator's temporal perspective on an event usually becomes apparent only after she has moved on to recount later incidents in her life. Without giving the reader any warning, Lucy allows her "later understanding" to efface her first impressions of Paulina. Only after we have read well into the second volume of *Villette* do we realize that Lucy's memory of the Bretton scenes elicits an extremely defensive response because they prophesy the most disturbing crisis in her later experience.

The events of Volume II recapitulate those in the first three chapters and explain why Lucy should find those earlier events significant. The incidents that occur when Lucy is fourteen are exactly reenacted when she is twenty-three. After the distressing isolation of the long vacation — comparable to the "unsettled sadness" (I, 2) of her kinfolk's home when she is fourteen — Lucy again finds herself with her godmother, "happier, easier, more at home" (I, 236) than she has been for years. Bretton and the past have been revived for her. She is again pampered by Mrs. Bretton and treated to sight-seeing and entertainments by John. Again Paulina usurps Lucy's place. When Graham first meets the Homes at the theatre, he tells them that the lady with him, Lucy, is "neither hindrance nor incumbrance" (II, 12). She is certainly no incumbrance on his affections. She is completely forgotten for seven weeks after the renewal of the relationship between the Brettons and the Homes. Even the seemingly insignificant details of the second volume have their precursors in the first three chapters. When Lucy finally returns to her "own little sea-green room" at La Terrasse, she finds that Paulina has installed herself there and that she is herself the "intruder" (II, 30), just as she has earlier gone up to her bedroom at Bretton and found, without warning, that a crib and a chest have been added for another child's use. Paulina's sewing, her lisping speech, her servile and tender doting on the men, all repeat her earlier behavior. Lucy even uses the same allusion to describe the two episodes in her life. Her visits in Bretton "resembled the sojourn of Christian and Hopeful beside a certain pleasant stream" (I, 2). Later, Graham's attention is "a goodly river on whose banks I had sojourned, of whose waves a few reviving drops had trickled to my lips." In both cases the comfort is taken away: the river "bend[s] to another course," Paulina (II, 54). Lucy's treatment of the earlier Bretton scenes must bear all the weight of a mature woman's jealousy, yet she cannot admit to herself — much less to her reader — that she has ever experienced such feelings.

To reticence, then, Lucy adds a second defense against her memories of the past: even the indirect revelation of both the narrator and the character's emotional involvement may be transferred from the scene which elicited it to another, less painful scene. Because the events recorded in the second volume of *Villette* are ultimately more significant than the events of Lucy's adolescence, she displaces her feelings about Paulina's second entry into her life onto the story of her first intrusion into the Bretton world of security and affection. The scene at Bretton, for all its pretence of calm objectivity, is a scene recollected so much in the light of later events that the initial emotions are ignored while the narrator tries to avoid depicting her own present response to her memory of the scene. The result of this process is a curious sort of freedom. By attributing to her adolescent experience all her harsh attitudes toward Paulina, Lucy can recount her rival's later role in the second volume as if it had no relation to her own hopes and desires. She can ignore the cruelty of Graham's indifference. The emotional energy appropriate to the later event has already been expended. The reader's response to this complex interweaving of temporal perspectives must be less immediately productive. The reader can begin to understand the considerations that have shaped Lucy's account of an event only long after she has finished relating that part of her story. *Villette* would seem to be a novel that must be read backwards or, at very least, reread if one is to judge the narrator's perspective accurately.

Lucy's unacknowledged love for Graham Bretton is, of course, the reason for her evasive treatment of the past in Volume II. Like Paulina, Lucy is naturally reticent about affection that is not reciprocated. In a characteristically deceptive parenthetical statement, she denies entertaining any "warmer feelings" for Graham (II, 2). Even years later when her hair has turned to gray, Lucy abides by the convention that a woman should not speak of love until she has been spoken to. Beyond such social prohibitions there is a more important reason for Lucy's silence. The memory of this unrequited love, the mere thought of which carries with it the certain knowledge of unfulfilled desires and wasted emotions, is so painful that it cannot be confronted openly. Like Paulina's letters to Graham, however, Lucy's narrative does "glow" with the "unconfessed confession" of her love (II, 225). Indeed, Thackeray, confusing Lucy with Charlotte Brontë, felt moved to make a condescendingly amused comment on the author's "naïve confession of being in love with 2 men at the same time."[8] Only as the novel reaches its conclusion, do we discover the full extent of the narrator's involvement with these concealed past emotions and, therefore, the justice of Thackeray's comment.

Four chapters before the end of *Villette*, when Lucy is describing her hallucinatory responses to the characters gathered at the fête in the park, she refers in an uncharacteristic fashion to events that occur after the close of her story. Here, for the first and only time in the novel, she confesses to the reader her past love for Graham Bretton and, more importantly, her present undiminished capacity to love him:

> I believe in that goodly mansion, his heart, he kept one little place under the skylights where Lucy might have entertainment, if she chose to call. It was not so handsome as the chambers where he lodged his male friends . . . still less did it resemble the pavilion where his marriage feast was splendidly spread; yet, gradually, by long and equal kindness, he proved to me that he kept one little closet, over the door of which was written "Lucy's Room." I kept a room for him, too — a place of which I never took the measure, either by rule or compass: I think it was like the

tent of Peri-Banou. All my life I carried it folded in the hollow of my hand — yet, released from that hold and constriction, I know not but its innate capacity for expanse might have magnified it into a tabernacle for a host.   (II, 265)

As Lucy has said of her younger self, "I *could* feel." This confession completely invalidates her earlier claim to the resigned objectivity of old age. At any time, presumably even as she tells her story, Graham could find in her heart a place splendid enough for a god. Coming as late as it does, offset by its placement among opium-induced visions, this avowal merely highlights the disconcerting complexity of the temporal perspectives in *Villette*.

This confession gives us the clue we need if we are to understand the narrator's earlier attitudes toward Graham and his place in her past. Because her feelings are so often at stake, she can never present her "naked recollections" of these events. The excessive emotions that typify her responses to Graham can be explained only by the later feelings she never mentions. Although her first meeting with Dr. John is too brief to allow her to realize that he is Graham Bretton, she reacts to this stranger who leads her through Villette with all the exaggerated trust that a Victorian wife might place in the husband who will lead her through life: "as to distrusting him, or his advice, or his address, I should almost as soon have thought of distrusting the Bible. There was goodness in his countenance, and honour in his bright eyes. . . . I believe I would have followed [his] frank tread, through continual night, to the world's end" (I, 74–75). The tone here is clearly inappropriate. Lucy's response seems proof of almost hysterical desperation of a naïve adoration of "bright eyes." Many chapters later we learn that her extravagant claims of faith in this stranger can be attributed to her later recognition of him as the man she would marry if she could. Memory has clearly responded to the pressures exerted on it by the knowledge of later events. The reader, however, is asked to accept this passage as the rendering of a first impression; there are no clues to the perspective from which the event is actually viewed. Such evasions continue. The most obvious was noticed by E. M. Forster.[9] Lucy violates the one essential convention of autobiographical form — if the reader does not demand to share the narrator's sense of late events, he does have the right to know what the character realizes at the time of any given event. For six chapters before she finds herself at La Terrasse, Lucy refuses to tell us that she knows that Dr. John and Graham Bretton are one and the same character.

In Volume II the pressures of memory result in the confusing gyrations in attitude that typify Lucy's comments on Dr. John. She often takes pleasure in rehearsing the shortcomings of this bright-eyed John Bull — his "cruel vanity," his "levity," and his "masculine self-love" (I, 249). The man we see beyond her biased presentation of him deserves perhaps better treatment. He may indeed be unimaginative, even sometimes unfeeling, but he can also be kindly, generous, and charming. His greatest shortcoming seems to be his failure to recognize just how attractive he is. Lucy surely is making him pay for his "frozen indifference" to her. Only once in the second volume does she come close to describing her original estimate of John. When he becomes disenchanted with Ginevra, when there is no other woman to claim his attention, Lucy allows herself another excessive statement, "I remember him heroic. Heroic at this moment will I hold him to be" (I, 313). Such ardor fades as soon as another woman arrives to captivate Graham's interest.

What Lucy recognizes as the "seeming inconsistency" (I, 242) of her treatment of John in Volume II disappears when she comes to describe the hero of Volume III, Paul Emanuel. M. Paul is the only character in *Villette* who is treated in anything like a consistent fashion by Lucy's memory. His avowed love for her is the confirmation and fulfillment that she has sought, and one would expect her to present him entirely from the perspective of "after-meditation." Quite the opposite is true. Paul's characterization depends on the attitudes and judgments of the younger Lucy Snowe. We learn to value Paul just as Lucy has done. At first he is hostile, malicious—an intriguer, a despot, "not at all a good little man" (I, 303). Slowly, however, a "face" replaces this "mask" (II, 89), and we are allowed to see his good qualities as Lucy discovers them.[10] Because the narrator can take comfort in looking ahead to the declaration of their mutual love in Volume III, she can afford to describe, with honesty and immediacy, those times in their relationship when even friendship seemed an impossibility. Paul's effect on Lucy has been not only to make her behavior in the past "placid and harmonious" (II, 101), but also to offer her a memory that she can later view in a placid and harmonious manner.

Lucy herself seems to understand that Paul's love has freed her from the emotional restraints that Graham's indifference has imposed on her. M. Paul, she tells the reader, "deserved candour, and from me always had it" (II, 304). When they reach the Faubourg Clotilde, she gives him a complete and accurate account of her feelings: " 'I want to tell you something,' I said; 'I want to tell you all.' . . . I spoke. All leaped from my lips. I lacked not words now; fast I narrated; fluent I told my tale; it streamed on my tongue. . . . All I had encountered I detailed, all I had recognized, heard, and seen . . . the whole history, in brief, summoned to his confidence, rushed thither truthful, literal, ardent, bitter" (II, 306–07). This description of Lucy's communication with M. Paul—"truthful, literal, ardent, bitter"—is an accurate account of the way she tells the part of the story in which he is involved. Again the quality of Lucy's initial behavior toward a character determines the quality of her memories. At the end of *Villette*, Lucy is finally able to be candid with both herself and the reader. She can say openly, "I loved him . . . with a passion beyond what I had yet felt" (II, 295). W. S. Williams had complained that the break between the second and third volumes of

Villette marks a transfer of interest from one set of characters to another. Such, indeed, is the case. Yet there is a more significant change: from one mode of memory—painful, evasive, confused—to another mode that permits an honest return to first impressions. The third volume of *Villette* is one of the finest achievements in Charlotte Brontë's fiction. For once the characters, not the attitudes of the "morbid" narrator, dominate and determine the action. The passion and the comedy that characterize the love between Lucy and Paul are given room to expand and develop. For once a clarity of tone, based on a secure temporal perspective, puts the reader at his ease.

David Copperfield provides a suggestive counterpoint here. Throughout David's "written memory" (690), the narrator is simultaneously "looking back" to the past and looking forward to a time "thereafter, when all the irremediable past [is] rendered plain" (434). Although he never offers more information than he as a character would have had at the time of any particular event, the whole narrative is dominated by his awareness of a future in which that event becomes part of the "irremediable past." We can accept David's frequently excessive responses because we know that he is aware of implications to which we are necessarily blind. Before he describes Steerforth's seduction of Emily, he speaks of the "dread" with which his narrative "journey" fills him: "I cannot bear to think of what did come, upon that memorable night; of what must come again, if I go on" (447). We may disagree with the judgments and attitudes that result from David's basic conventionality, but we trust him to define his perspective on his past. Yet even David can be evasive. His love for Agnes, "the most secret current of [his] mind" (817), is a secret kept from the reader's view. Because he knows that his feelings for Agnes are not merely sibling affection even while Dora is alive, he cannot reveal them until long after he has recounted the event of Dora's death. The older narrator cannot acknowledge a love which even his younger self represses; as Thackeray said of Brontë, David has loved two women at the same time. Lucy's difficulties are even more complex—she seems to look back on an isolated moment in the past as if nothing precedes or follows it simply because each event leads to Graham's ultimate rejection of her—but the basic pattern of reminiscence is the same. Evidences of guilty love, be it love for Agnes or Graham, must be suppressed. The narrator can afford to revive his first impressions only when his love has been the function of his innocence—as is David's infatuation with Dora—or when it has found later confirmation—as Lucy's does when M. Paul proposes to her.

Yet even Paul's response to the intensity and purity of Lucy's love does not account for the emotional clarity that the narrator achieves in Volume III. Here we find the direct and unrestrained honesty that is one of Jane Eyre's most attractive qualities. Here Lucy is able to confess her love for Graham. We are forced to recognize that Lucy has managed to put considerable distance between her narrating self and her earlier emotions;

paradoxically, this distance allows a revival of first impressions. At first this paradox seems inexplicable. The facts of Lucy's experience have again become an insurmountable barrier to emotional satisfaction. Unlike David, who writes his story with Agnes seated next to him, Lucy is another Miss Marchmont, alone with her memories. Yet she recounts the marriage of Paulina Home and Graham Bretton with such calm disinterest one might think that it causes her no pain. How does this situation come about? In one sense the answer to this question is very simple. Lucy's writing of her story in the first and second volumes is itself the activity that allows her to triumph over her earlier inability to confront the implications of memory. Both *The Prelude* and *In Memoriam* attest to the way in which the expression of confusion or sorrow may become the means to certainty or consolation. Unlike Wordsworth, however, Lucy can take no comfort in an artistic self that is the source of imperishable art. Nor is her perspective like Tennyson's; her focus, more comparable to that of Wordsworth's political hopes, is fixed on this world, "the place where, in the end, / We find our happiness, or not at all" (XI, 143–44). As Lucy tells us, if she were a nun, she would have no reason to write her confessions. The act of recording her past must, therefore, provide Lucy with the specifically temporal satisfactions that this world has denied her. The process by which this unlikely end is attained is again illuminated by an event from her earlier experience.

During her first term at Mme. Beck's, Paul forces Lucy to perform a man's role in a vapid comedy, and she turns an incident which seems to promise only embarrassment into an emotional harvest. This scene has made numbers of readers uneasy. It is less important, however, as a demonstration of covert androgyny or sexual perversity than as a key to the way in which Lucy's imagination allows her to triumph over apparently intractable circumstances. At this point in the story, Dr. John is in love with Ginevra, a woman Lucy judges unworthy of his affections. The role that M. Paul asks Lucy to play before an audience which includes Dr. John allows her to reverse the roles of actual experience. If Lucy cannot be successful as Ginevra's rival for Dr. John's affections, then she will become the image of Colonel de Hamal, Dr. John's rival for Ginevra. Here Lucy is fully aware of what she is doing: "my longing was to eclipse the 'Ours:' *i.e.*, Dr. John." Lucy's "idea" has "half-changed the nature of the rôle" and "recklessly altered the spirit" of the play (I, 176). She proves that Ginevra can be attracted to a "butterfly, a talker, and a traitor" (I, 167) by accepting that characterization as her own. She finds immense personal satisfaction in her part: "warming, becoming interested, taking courage, I acted to please myself" (I, 176). She mocks the facile nature of both John's love and its object. The "facts" of the play's script have been retained, but they have been molded to offer Lucy precisely the gratifying self-justification they would seem to preclude.

This incident is a remarkably clear emblem of the way in which Lucy recalls the most potentially painful junctures of her experience. She finds consolation in an otherwise barren past by systematically and continuously reversing the roles which the facts of her story impose on herself and her fellow characters. Particularly in Volume II, each of the major characters becomes an objectified version of Lucy's personality or experience — until together they become a way of positing at least a symbolic or vicarious fulfillment of her desires. *Villette* is less a narrative in which other characters are granted an autonomous existence than a hall of mirrors in which they are allowed to appear because they serve as facets reflecting the affective truth of Lucy's life. This process allows Lucy to set her identity at a distance for the purposes of honest scrutiny while she transforms that image of self into an emotionally satisfying prospect. Memory, for Lucy, achieves all the status that the Romantics attribute to the imagination. Indeed, Lucy's narrative is proof of the mental capacities whose power De Quincey found so overwhelming: "I feared . . . that some . . . tendency of the brain might thus be making itself . . . *objective*; and the sentient organ *project* itself as its own object."[11] The recreative power of Lucy's memory has precisely this effect: by "projecting" her past and present needs onto the portions of the narrative ostensibly concerned with other lives, her "sentient organ," her memory of the past finally achieves expression.

The role of Paulina de Bassompierre is central to the transformations wrought by Lucy's memory. The childhood scenes of the novel contain hints of a mysterious emotional identification between the two characters. At one point, Lucy notes, "I wished she would utter some hysterical cry, so that I might get relief and be at ease" (I, 13). Paulina is the main defense created by the quality of Lucy's vision because she is a projection of Lucy's most gratifying self-image. In an idealized and literally beautified manner, Paulina's "hoar-frost" and "pure, fine flame" (II, 159) recapitulate the fire and ice of Lucy's nature. The narrator explains, "In speaking of her attractions, I would not exaggerate language; but, indeed, they seemed to me very real and engaging" (II, 31). Indeed they should — for they are the attractions of sensibility and character that Lucy knows to be her own. If we take the assumptions behind the illusion of autobiographical fiction seriously, we must accept the premise that Lucy has no control over the action. John and Paulina will marry, whatever Lucy may feel about that event. By defining Paulina as a second self, Lucy can find satisfaction in the attraction that John feels for the qualities she shares with Paulina — even as she offers implicit criticism of his inability to recognize them in herself.

This process, however, would not work if Lucy's memory did not have another counter with which to work: Ginevra Fanshawe. During the action of the first volume, Ginevra serves as a way of putting Graham in his place — or, more precisely, of putting Graham in Lucy's place. Like Graham in his responses to Lucy, Ginevra dismissed his affection because he has none of the glamour of Colonel de Hamal; she claims, "Les penseurs, les hommes profonds et passionnés ne sont pas à mon gout," but her characterization of Graham is more appropriate to Lucy than to the charming young doctor (I, 112). At the beginning of the second volume, just as Graham suffers his final disillusionment about Ginevra, Lucy describes him in a way that exactly defines her own situation: "His lady-love beamed upon him from a sphere above his own: he could not come near her; he was not certain that he could win from her a look" (I, 272). Like Lucy, Graham finds himself loving someone both unattainable and worthless. Including Ginevra in her story is Lucy's way of making Graham suffer the pain that his indifference causes her. Here, perhaps, is one reason behind the inconsistency of Lucy's behavior when she responds to Graham's suspicions about Ginevra by becoming her "advocate" (I, 284). Here, as well, is the emotional logic behind the unacknowledged bond of intimacy between the spoiled schoolgirl and the reserved teacher at Mme. Beck's.

When Paulina enters the action in the second volume, Lucy's memory of events must again "half-change" and "alter" the roles of the various characters if this process of emotional fulfillment is to continue. If Lucy is not to hate her new rival Paulina — and she cannot hate the woman who is a perfected version of herself — then Lucy must attribute to Ginevra all the jealousy she cannot allow herself to feel. Ginevra therefore learns to value Graham's attentions only when he no longer feels anything for her. Like the Lucy who narrates the first three chapters of *Villette,* Ginevra dismisses Paulina as a "conceited doll" and finds "sickening" the domestic scenes enacted by the Brettons and the de Bassompierres. Lucy's evaluation of Ginevra's petulance is shrewd. She tells Ginevra, "It would not have been so [sickening] if the object of attention had been changed: if *you* had taken Miss de Bassompierre's place" (II, 23). Lucy, of course, is right about Ginevra's jealousy. Here temporal perspectives become complex indeed; the narrator's younger self is indirectly commenting on her own later attitude toward Paulina, an attitude that has made itself apparent in the earlier childhood scenes. Because Ginevra is acting out Lucy's jealousy, the narrator can understand its implications. Later when Ginevra expresses her disdain for Graham, a "hatred . . . expressed in terms so unmeasured and proportions so monstrous," she gives the schoolgirl a "sound moral drubbing" (II, 90). Ginevra receives the "taming" that Lucy's Jael so often must administer to the Sisera of her affections. To complete this circle of identifications, Paulina must assume the burden of Lucy's earlier jealousy of Ginevra. Long after Graham's actions cease to justify the fear, Paulina worries that he loves Ginevra. At the end of Chapter XXVI, she confesses this fear to Lucy. Lucy now can answer with all the calm and generous candor of the celibate who has been freed from the pressures of earthly desires — only because Paulina is acting out those desires for her. As the story of Graham and Paulina's engagement develops along the periphery of the central action of Volume III, Lucy can tell that part of the story with dignified objectivity — not because she is now the "mere looker-on at life" (I, 176) that she has claimed to be, not because the older woman no longer feels any love for Graham, but simply because she sees herself so thoroughly involved in Paulina's unquestionable triumph over Graham's heart.

Finding such fugitive modes of self-expression is a central convention of nineteenth-century autobiography. The writer whose work is a mirror of his experience naturally emphasizes those events or characters within it which serve as miniature reflections of self. The pretence of distance between the writer and his reflection is, however, absolutely essential to the success of this kind of self-analysis. Wordsworth, for instance, inserted in *The Prelude* a description of himself that he had written earlier, but he found he had to conceal it as a meditation on the dead Winander boy if he were to acknowledge that a facet of himself had likewise perished. On another occasion he refers to the story of Vaudracour and Julia because Vaudracour is a repressed version of the self who fell in love with Annette Vallon. *In Memoriam* is the record of similar processes. Tennyson continuously seeks out analogues for his feelings — he is variously defined as the widow, the linnet, the expectant or disappointed lover — and he explains this proliferation of analogues by noting that the love he feels "sees himself in all he sees" (XCVII, 4). In one passage he recalls a dream in which he has seen Hallam's troubled face. He wakes and realizes, "It is the trouble of my youth / That foolish sleep transfers to thee [Hallam]" (LXVIII, 15–16). The art of autobiography, like Tennyson's dream, rests on such projections of self. Patrick Brontë's mask, seemingly the bright idea of a concerned parent, is a device that has a natural role in autobiography. By exploring self as if it were another identity, the autobiographer can confront its hidden facets with honesty and often profoundly acute scrutiny. Lucy's use of this device is unusual only because it invariably achieves for her an otherwise unattainable emotional gratification.

Brontë defines even more clearly the tradition behind *Villette* when Lucy says of Paulina, "I wondered to find my thoughts hers: there are certain things in which we so rarely meet with our double that it seems a miracle when that chance befals" (II, 33). Lucy uses precisely the right word here. Paulina is her double, but that fact is a function of her own perception, not the result of the workings of Providence or fortune. Unlike Lucy, Brontë would not be blind to the psychological implications of that term. In *The Spell*, one of the more coherent works of the juvenilia, she had followed the model of Hogg's *Confessions of a Justified Sinner* (1824) when she created for the Duke of Zamorna a twin brother, an "alter-ego" and "repetition" to explain his "unfathomable, incomprehensible nature."[12] Lucy, a character considerably more advanced in complexity than even Zamorna, deserves and indeed requires a doppelgänger. Paulina, Ginevra, and even Vashti are extensions of a technique that Brontë would have remembered from her early reading of Romantic fiction and from her own adolescent Angrian works. Yet the psychological process involved in the creation of doubles is as much akin to the conventions of autobiography as it is characteristic of the Gothic or Romantic imagination expressed in *The Devil's Elixir* or Hogg's *Confessions*. Otto Rank defined the link between doubles and narcissism as the desire to perceive a version of self that triumphs over mortality;[13] autobiography, by definition a narcissistic endeavor, would seem the genre particularly suited to such modes of perception. In fact, both *David Copperfield* and *Villette* attest to the vitality and significance of the double in midcentury autobiography.

Like Tennyson and Wordsworth, both David and Lucy share the propensity to project versions of themselves onto other characters such as Steerforth, Traddles, Ginevra, or Miss Marchmont, but they also refuse to recognize the doubles who figure forth their own sexual identities — Uriah Heep and the Nun. This situation is not at all surprising. Both David and Lucy suffer from a similar inability to recognize themselves when they literally look into a mirror. David's hatred for Uriah is the only expression he can give the "secret current" of his emotions, his love for Agnes. Uriah's role in his story is consistently tied to David's attitude toward his adopted "sister." Uriah takes over David's bedroom in the Wickfield household; he aspires to Agnes' hand in marriage — all when David himself is involved in his courtship of Dora and their subsequent marriage. David acts out his self-disgust and punishes his own hidden desires when he slaps Uriah. If there were any question about the nature of David's feelings, it would be swept away by his response when Uriah announces his plan to marry Agnes:

> I believe I had a delirious idea of seizing the red-hot poker out of the fire, and running him through with it. It went from me with a shock, like a ball fired from a rifle: but the image of Agnes, outraged by so much as a thought of this red-headed animal's, remained in my mind. . . . He seemed to swell and grow before my eyes . . . and the strange feeling . . . that all this had occurred before, at some indefinite time, and that I knew what he was going to say next, took possession of me.
>
> (381)

David, of course, knows what Uriah will say next because Uriah expresses what he feels; the concatenation of libidinal energies in this passage is attributed to both charaters, not just to Uriah. Interestingly, Brontë inverts this use of the double — and indeed the larger tradition of which it is an example — in her treatment of the nun. While Dickens uses Uriah to objectify the sexual impulses that David must deny, Lucy Snowe's nun projects the refusal to express such energies: the sin in *Villette* is not desire, but the repression of desire. The nun first appears when Lucy receives a letter from Graham, when she is trying to summon reason to restrain emotion. As Graham quite accurately comments, the nun is specifically his enemy. Only after she has buried Graham's letter and her hope that he might reciprocate her feelings does Lucy welcome and even reach out to touch the spectral figure she has earlier fled. David leaves the side of Dora's deathbed so that he can travel to Dover and aid in the defeat of Uriah's ambitions; when it seems most likely that Dora's death will render his feelings for Agnes acceptable, David literally puts them in prison. Lucy, however, destroys her double when she recognizes the strength of her love for M. Paul; after seeing Justine Marie in the park with Paul, she can express her jealous desire to possess him and, later that evening, tear to pieces the clothes worn by the nun.

Yet memory must further complicate these earlier psychological processes. Brontë gives the tradition of the double a final and unconventional twist by turning Lucy's lover into yet another of her second selves. Paul is, first and foremost, Graham's replacement. If Graham is the romantic hero of *Villette*, Paul is its "Christian hero" (II, 188). Patterned after the initial tie between Lucy and Graham, Paul's love first finds expression in the idea of a sibling affection. Just as the Frenchman represents a more satisfying version of the young English doctor, he is also another Lucy. At one point he even forces her to look in a mirror so that she can see the "affinity" between them. His irritable actions, like Lucy's reserve, conceal the "inner flame" he shares with both Lucy and Paulina. This identification, in turn, affects Lucy's position. Paul's love, his frequently demonstrated jealousy, his fiery nature allow Lucy to assume the role that Graham has played in Volumes I and II. Like the earlier Graham, she becomes the unresponsive object of love: she is "placid" in the face of Paul's tempestuous emotions; she experiences "a certain smugness of composure, indeed, scarcely in my habits, and pleasantly novel to my feelings" (II, 101). That Paul, playing Lucy's earlier role, wins her affection and respect is, by analogy, a final triumph over Graham's indifference. By describing Paul as if he were going through a course of emotions that she herself has previously experienced, Lucy manages to have it both ways. Because Paul is a man, he can reveal his feelings and therefore act out the responses that Lucy has previously denied. Even the quality of Paul's speech depends on Lucy's actions and characterization. When he explains that his capacity for love "died in the past — in the present it lies buried — its grave is deep-dug, well-heaped, and many winters old" (II, 119), he is recapitulating the scene in which Lucy buries the symbol of her love for Graham under the pear-tree in the garden. Paul's exaggerated jealousy also reveals Lucy's carefully concealed responses to Graham. As Lucy allows herself to play the roles of both Paulina and Graham, Paul's character becomes identified with those of Graham and Lucy.

Late in *Villette* Lucy makes what seems to be a wholly gratuitous and nearly absurd statement that again emphasizes the transformations that her imagination perpetually effects. After asking Lucy for her friendship, Paul fails to meet her at their usual hour for lessons. Instead he works in the garden outside the schoolroom and "fondles" the spaniel Sylvie, "calling her tender names in a tender voice" (II, 207). Lucy describes the dog and then comments, "I never saw her, but I thought of Paulina de Bassompierre: forgive the association, reader, it *would* occur." This strange "association" is explained in the next sentence: "M. Paul petted and patted her; the endearments she received were not to be wondered at; she invited affection by her beauty and her vivacious life" (II, 211–12). Paulina must appear one more time as a threat to Lucy's hold on a man's affections. Here, however, her rival for Paul's love is no more likely to succeed than she herself could have succeeded against Paulina's claims on Graham. Her apology for this "association" is either disingenous or naïve. Such associations, doublings, and identifications are the distinguishing characteristic of a narrative which constantly mirrors back the images of Lucy's suppressed emotional life. At one point she says of Graham, "He was a born victor, as some are born vanquished" (II, 234). Lucy consistently sees herself as one of the vanquished. But if some victors are born, Lucy's narrative proves that others can be made. During the course of the third volume, the fact of Paul's love allows Lucy to triumph. More importantly, the way in which she describes that love, the form that memory imposes on events through "associations," allows her to triumph one last time over that "born victor," Graham Bretton.

During their first meeting at La Terrasse, Paulina explains herself to Lucy by paraphrasing a line from Wordsworth: "The child of seven years lives yet in the girl of seventeen." The rest of the epigraph to the "Intimations of Immortality" ode is equally applicable to Paulina: "And I would wish my days to be / Bound each to each by natural piety." Paulina's quite Wordsworthian sense of the past—as opposed to Graham's propensity to live in and for the present moment—elicits Lucy's unqualified approval and admiration: "Her eyes were the eyes of one who can remember; one whose childhood does not fade like a dream, nor whose youth vanish like a sunbeam. She would not take life, loosely and incoherently, in parts, and let one season slip as she entered on another: she would retain and add; often review from the commencement, and so grow in harmony and consistency as she grew in years" (II, 32). This passage recalls Wordsworth's desire to use the narration of his past experience to "understand [him]self": "my hope has been, that I might fetch / Invigorating thoughts from former years; / Might fix the wavering balance of my mind" (I, 627, 620–22). Memory, for both Paulina and Wordsworth, is literally a source of integrity, that sense of a self that is "consistent," "harmonious," and unwavering. The connections between past and present selves that are wrought by memory are proof of the organic growth of a distinct identity. Addressing Venus, the morning and the evening star, Tennyson makes the same point: "Thou, like my present and my past, / Thy place is changed; thou art the same" (CXXI, 17-20). By the end of *David Copperfield,* the narrator can claim a similar faith in the coherent patterns that memory imposes on his life. Earlier he has seen an absolute division between the young boy he was and the man he has become: "That little fellow seems to be no part of me; I remember him as something left behind upon the road of life—as something I have passed, rather than have actually been—and almost think of him as of some one else" (268). By the time he proposes to Agnes, however, his narrative "journey" has linked the two selves: "Long miles of road then opened out before my mind; and, toiling on, I saw a ragged way-worn boy forsaken and neglected, who should come to call even [Agnes'] heart now beating against mine, his own" (863). Paulina's sense of the past, then, embodies a common nineteenth-century ideal, one that would appear again as the central piety of *The Mill on the Floss.*

Paulina's ability to give "a full greeting to the Past" (II, 49) is yet another way in which she is a refined version of Lucy's less than ideal self. Lucy has said of her younger self that she has lived "two lives" (I, 92); that sense of division is appropriate to her narrative activity as well. The moments of clarity she achieves in Volume III fade in the "Finis" with which *Villette* ends. Here again memory too painful for expression must be evasively cloaked in vague generalizations and patently ironic statements of resolution. Earlier Lucy's childhood, unlike Paulina's, has "fade[d] like a dream." At the end of the novel, Lucy lets another "season slip" because its revival would be unbearable. Though the evasions at the end of *Villette* were a response to Patrick Brontë's demand for a happy ending, Charlotte Brontë's attempt to "veil the fate in oracular words," as Elizabeth Gaskell called the process,[14] is an appropriate final demonstration of the nature of Lucy's memory. The workings of memory implicit in her narrative correspond to the stages depicted in "Auld Lang Syne." During the childhood sections of *Villette,* Lucy is a ghost-like presence on the periphery of the action. Later she finds herself "happier, easier, more at home" in the past as she has felt during her stay at La Terrasse. But the comfort offered by memory is a promise of inevitable dispossession. The fact of Paul's death makes the past as uninhabitable as Lucy's earlier need to earn a living has made La Terrasse. Yet in the interval before she must acknowledge the fact of her ultimate and continuing deprivation, Lucy makes at least partial peace with her past. In her hands, the already highly developed conventions of autobiography reach a new level of complexity and subtlety. Both character and creator construct a narrative mirror in which self appears vindicated against the slights experience has dealt them and consoled for the indifference with which others have treated them.

Notes

1. Quoted by Elizabeth Gaskell, *The Life of Charlotte Brontë*, ed. Alan Shelston, (1857; Harmondsworth: Penguin, 1975), p. 94.

2. *The Brontës: Their Lives, Friendships and Correspondence*, ed. T. J. Wise and J. Alexander Symington (Oxford: Shakespeare Head, 1932), IV, 17–18. Cited as *Letters*.

3. "Editor's Preface to the New Edition of *Wuthering Heights*" (1850), rpt. *Wuthering Heights*, ed. William M. Sale (New York: Norton, 1972), pp. 10, 12.

4. *The Letters of Matthew Arnold, 1848–1888*, ed. George W. E. Russell (1895; rpt. London: Macmillan, 1900), p. 34. *The George Eliot Letters*, ed. Gordon S. Haight (New Haven: Yale Univ. Press, 1954), letter of 11 February [1853], II, 87.

5. *The Autobiography of Leigh Hunt* (New York: Harper, 1850), I, iii. Cited hereafter in the text.

6. Although Charlotte Brontë's correspondence gives no satisfactory account of her attitudes toward the books she read, her notes of thanks to George Smith and W. S. Williams and her letters to Mrs. Gaskell prove that she read at least part of each of these works. See *Letters*, III, 20, 98, 174, 150, 132. The following editions of these works will be cited in the text: *David Copperfield*, Oxford Illustrated Dickens (London: Oxford, 1971), by page; *In Memoriam, The Poems of Tennyson*, ed. Christopher Ricks (London: Longmans, 1969), lyric and line; *The Prelude* (1850), ed. Ernest de Selincourt and Helen Darbishire (Oxford: Clarendon, 1959), book and line; *The Life and Correspondence of Robert Southey*, ed. Charles Cuthbert Southey (New York: Harper, 1851), page.

7. *Villette*, 2 vols., Shakespeare Head Brontë (1853; rpt. Oxford: Shakespeare Head Press, 1931), II, 75. Future references to this edition are included in the text. When I refer to the volumes of *Villette*, I mean, of course, not the two volumes of the Shakespeare Head edition, but the three volumes of its original publication form: Volume I, Chapters I–XV; Volume II, Chapters XVI–XXVII; Volume III, Chapters XXVIII–XLII. As Charlotte Brontë's letters to her publisher attest, the novel was conceived and written according to these major structural divisions.

8. *The Letters and Private Papers of William Makepeace Thackeray*, ed. Gordon N. Ray (Cambridge, Mass.: Harvard, 1946), III, 233. On one occasion CB said of George Smith, "I should not in the least fear to go with him to China" (*Letters*, III, 120–21). Later she told him, "You are to keep a fraction of yourself – if it be only the end of your little finger – for *him* [Currer Bell] and that fraction you will neither let gentlemen or lady . . . take possession of" (*Letters*, III, 279). That both passages are echoed in the quotations offered in my next few pages suggests that Thackeray had gotten to the heart of the matter.

9. *Aspects of the Novel* (New York: Harcourt, Brace, 1927), pp. 139–40. Forster finds this "slip" too "trivial" to harm our sense of Lucy's integrity. More recent readers have been frankly skeptical about Lucy's reliability: see, for instance, Robert Bernard Martin, *Charlotte Brontë's Novels: Accents of Persuasion* (New York: Norton, 1968), p. 149; and Helene Moglen, *Charlotte Brontë: The Self Conceived* (New York: Norton, 1976), p. 196.

10. There is one exception to this rule. During the early part of her stay at the *pensionnat*, Lucy is given a bouquet of violets by a "stranger." In Volume III we learn that the stranger is M. Paul. I assume that this instance of reticence is characteristic of the evasions of Volumes I and II rather than her presentation of him in Volume III.

11. *Confessions of an English Opium Eater*, ed. Alethea Hayter (1821; rpt. Harmondsworth: Penguin, 1973), p. 107. De Quincey's *Confessions* are, of course, another autobiographical model that Charlotte Brontë might have had in mind as she was writing *Villette*. His comments on memory have particular relevance to Lucy's highly selective treatment of her past: "there is no such thing as *forgetting* possible to the mind"; there is rather a "veil between our present consciousness and the secret inscription on the mind" (p. 104).

12. *The Spell, an Extravaganza,* ed. George Edwin McLean (Oxford: Oxford University Press, 1931), pp. 133 and 144. CB's knowledge of this tradition can be traced to her early reading of *Blackwood's Magazine* and its discussions of works by Hoffmann and Hogg. See, for instance, a review of Hoffmann's *The Devil's Elixir, Blackwood's* 16 (1824), 55–67.

13. "Narcissism and the Double," in *The Double: A Psychoanalytic Study,* trans. Harry Tucker (Chapel Hill: Univ. of North Carolina Press, 1971), pp. 69–86.

14. *Life,* p. 484.

The Reflecting Reader in *Villette*   Brenda R. Silver*

"Who *are* you, Miss Snowe?" Ginevra Fanshawe asks the narrator-protagonist of Charlotte Brontë's *Villette,* a question echoed by generations of readers and critics and encouraged by Lucy Snowe herself.[1] An orphan, an outsider, a woman without family or country, an "inoffensive shadow," and a ray so hot that at least one person shields his eyes from it — Lucy both courts and laments the roles assigned to her by others in what is rightfully read as her search for selfhood. Ultimately, however, *who* Lucy is is inseparable from *what* she is: a teller of tales unspeakable in the presence of either her comfortable and comforting godmother and the friends who surround her at La Terrasse, or the colder, more worldly, yet equally uncomprehending eavesdroppers at the pensionnat on the Rue Fossette. If, as has been argued, the "reality" of a narrative is a mutual creation of the text and its readers, and this act depends on the author's ability to stimulate the imagination in such a way as to make us think in terms different from our own,[2] then Lucy, as if aware of this relationship, has self-consciously structured her use of silence and revelation to immerse us in a world as complex and conflicted as that which she herself experienced. Knowing, however, that she cannot trust others to perceive her as she is — that even when she is not invisible she is more than likely to be misread — Lucy goes one step further: she projects her readers into the landscape of the novel, the text, and asks them to use their imaginations in a mutual act of creation which in turn validates her own emerging self. In this way her narrative both inscribes her evolving identity and establishes a community of readers whose recognition and acceptance provide the context necessary for an individual's growth to maturity — a context all too often denied to women.

Although several critics have recently explored the role of Lucy's narration in the discovery and creation of her identity, most have assumed that she is an "unreliable" narrator whose voice, according to Helene Moglen, is characterized by "indirection" and "neurotic rationalization,"

*Reprinted from *The Voyage In: Fictions of Female Development,* ed. Elizabeth Abel, Marianne Hirsch, and Elizabeth Langland (1983), 90–111, with the permission of the University Press of New England.

and whose form for the novel is "the form of [her] neurosis: a representation of the novel's subject."[3] Mary Jacobus is more direct: "Lucy lies to us. Her deliberate ruses, omissions and falsifications break the unwritten contract of first-person narrative (the confidence between reader and 'I') and unsettle our faith in the reliability of the text."[4] Gilbert and Gubar, on the other hand, accept Lucy's narrative reticence and evasions, her apparent attempts to mislead the reader, and attribute her "anxious and guilty" feelings about her narrative to the fact that her "life, her sense of herself, does not conform to the literary or social stereotypes provided by her culture to define and circumscribe female life." The result is nothing less than a "mythic undertaking — an attempt to create an adequate fiction of her own."[5]

But it can also be argued that Lucy is less evasive and even less unreliable than most critics have assumed — that she is, in fact, a self-consciously reliable narrator of unusual circumstances whose narrative choices ask her "readers" to perceive her on her own terms.[6] The difficulty may be that Lucy's terms are so different from the maxims and prejudices of the culture she inhabits and portrays that they are read by even sympathetic readers as perverse or implausible. Here I am borrowing the term and the concept of "implausibility" put forward by Nancy Miller in her essay "Emphasis Added: Plots and Plausibilities in Women's Fiction."[7] In this piece, Miller defines the persistent misreading of women's texts as extravagant, implausible, unmotivated, or unconvincing in terms of the reader's expectations of what a narrative should be, and illustrates how these expectations are in turn determined or judged according to the dominant cultural ideology. Taking Gérard Genette's analysis of "Vraisemblance et Motivation" as her starting point, Miller cites Genette's distinction between three different forms of narratives: the "plausible narrative," which implicitly and silently obeys the conventions of genre and the cultural maxims on which they rest; the "arbitrary narrative," which deliberately and silently destroys this collusion but refuses to justify itself; and the narrative with "a motivated and 'artificial plausibility.' " The last type, "exemplified by the 'endless chatting' of a Balzacian novel, we might call 'other-directed,' for here authorial commentary justifies its story to society by providing the missing maxims, or by inventing them" (pp. 38–39). As Miller points out, however, glossing Genette's analysis, what might seem to be silent or even absent in the arbitrary narrative — that is, an alternate set of maxims — "may simply be inaudible to the dominant mode of reception" (p. 39).

Within this framework, Lucy's tale employs characteristics of both the artificially plausible narrative and the seemingly arbitrary narrative that in fact inscribes an alternative ideology, and both these narrative modes are encoded in her dialogue with the reader. Her constant shifting between self-justification and "silence" thus becomes a plausible portrayal of the conflicting needs and desires she confronts and experiences without being able to count on either the ear or the understanding of those who dictate social behavior—and plots of novels. Rather than misleading or lying to us, or to herself, Lucy is deliberately creating not only a new form of fiction for women, but a new audience—part critic, part confidante, part sounding board—whose willingness to enter her world and interpret her text will provide the recognition denied to women who do not follow traditional paths of development.

In order to test this hypothesis, we must trace Lucy's relationship to the fictionalized reader in the text, the created recipient of her tale. There are, in fact, particularly in the beginning of the novel, at least two readers to whom Lucy reveals different aspects of her experience and herself, in order to justify them to her critics or to confide them to a sympathetic listener. Later, as the narrative and Lucy's sense of herself evolve, the reader develops into an audience so accustomed to and accepting of Lucy's "strange stammerings" (chap. 36), that the different readers are merged into one.

A similar development in the nature of the audience might also explain the ambiguity that informs our perception of the reader's gender. Although most readers today, I suspect, automatically think of the fictionalized reader addressed by Lucy as female, on the rare occasions that Lucy refers to her reader by pronoun, she uses the generic "he" and "his" (chaps. 8, 29, 30). In addition to following an accepted literary convention (and despite the fact that most novel readers were women), Lucy may deliberately be positing a male audience to emphasize that the power to pass both literary and moral judgments on her story belonged, in the public sphere, predominantly to men. Lucy's narrative choice here reflects her creator's experience in one such forum—critical reviews— where she had already suffered the pain of being labeled unconventional, unchristian, unfeminine, and unsexed. That the harshest judgments came from other women, writing anonymously, highlights the force that social maxims exert on women's self-perceptions and the complexity of gender identification for unconventional women—and women writers.[8]

In her presentation of herself to others, then, Lucy is trebly constrained: as woman, as heroine, and as storyteller. From this perspective, the split between the two readers in the early part of Lucy's narrative may well signify a split between those readers who accept the cultural maxims about women in a patriarchy and want to find them mirrored in novels— an audience that speaks with a male voice and male authority and might well condemn her actions—and those readers, similar to the female personifications who populate Lucy's psychic landscape, in whom she can confide.[9] If this distinction breaks down later in the novel when the different readers begin to merge, it may be owing to Lucy's sense that she has so shaped her audience to her own ends that gender becomes insignificant.

In the beginning of her narrative, however, the entity whom Lucy addresses explicitly as "reader" stands at a distance from Lucy herself in a potentially antagonistic posture. This reader first appears in her description of the eight years that intervene between the visit to Bretton described in the early chapters and the events that leave her on her own without family or support. "I will permit the reader," she writes, "to picture me . . . as a bark slumbering through halcyon weather, in a harbour still as glass—the steersman stretched on the little deck, his face up to heaven, his eyes closed: buried if you will in a long prayer"—the situation in which "a great many women and girls are supposed to pass their lives" (chap. 4). The identification of the reader here with the way things are supposed to be—with the conventional expectations for women's lives—makes this reader the exponent of truisms about women that Lucy knows from her own experience are not valid. The irony of her "permission" to her readers to deceive themselves emphasizes society's refusal to see or to admit the actual circumstances of her—and by implication other women's—existence. The result of this refusal is to invalidate Lucy's perception of her own reality, and to make Lucy herself invisible. From society's perspective, then, Lucy has no being, and her subsequent presentation of herself as a shadow, as well as other characters' misreading of her nature and her needs, mirrors her social reality.

Lucy's insight into the disparity between social expectations and reality for women, however, clashes throughout the novel with her simultaneous awareness that she has internalized the very maxims that restrict her development by their failure to recognize her existence. Not only does she lack a blueprint for her journey to selfhood—that is, a conventional plot—but she envisions and presents herself as a divided being whose strengths and weaknesses, as well as her economic and emotional needs, are continually at odds with each other. Forced by circumstances into self-reliance and exertion, denied the luxury of remaining in the prayerful sleep assumed of women, she struggles to compromise between her necessarily unconventional actions and her need to remain within the social structure. As Lucy herself tells us, early in life she developed "a staid manner of my own which ere now had been as good to me as cloak and hood of hodden grey; since under its favour I had been enabled to achieve with impunity, and even approbation, deeds that, if attempted with an excited and unsettled air, would in some minds have stamped me as a dreamer and zealot" (chap. 5).

Coming at the moment of her decision to go to London, this statement inscribes the parameters of Lucy's social and narrative stance: her realism and her rebellion. Her cloak of staidness ensures her the acceptance and help not only of Mrs. Barrett, her old nurse, but of the old waiter at the London inn who becomes the first of her many guides. Later, it secures her the approval of Madame Beck and the Count de Bassompierre, also enabling figures, and prevents others from detecting her love for Graham or Paul. But this cloak also masks her other self: the woman who chafes at her restrictions, even while apologizing for her pleasure in walking around London by herself or being rowed through the night to the boat that will carry her over the channel. And nowhere is this conflict clearer than in her dialogue with her two readers at the onset of her journey: the conventional or socialized reader, who embodies society's maxims about women and whom she creates to ask the implied questions and make the implied criticisms she anticipates in her relation with the world; and the rebellious or unsocialized reader, in whom she confides those perceptions and feelings so far removed from the social conventions as to have little or no plausibility if uttered aloud. If, in her justification of her actions to the socialized reader, she self-consciously creates an "artificially plausible" narrative, the dialogue with the rebellious reader assumes a shared perspective—an arbitrary narrative—that gradually dominates both readers and informs the text.

Before tracing the evolution of her two readers, however, we must examine the circumstances that force Lucy to create her own life. By the time we meet her at Bretton, all the seeds of the disaster that starts her upon her journey have already been sown, and she herself has begun to develop the social and narrative stances that become more pronounced later on. The most significant factor is, of course, her solitude. Residing with unidentified kinfolk, picturing her stay at Bretton as a period of calm in a pilgrim's progress, Lucy has already acquired a sense of herself as an outsider, an observer rather than an actor, who is capable of telling Polly that she must learn to hide her feelings and not expect too much from others. This restraint is particularly necessary, she implies, in the situation that prompts her remark: the unequal power relationship that exists between young men such as Graham, her god-brother, who go to school and visit friends, and the girls who sit at home reading and sewing and waiting for them.

Although Polly's role as Lucy's psychological double is well established, Kate Millett's cultural interpretation of this doubling is worth noting here: "Brontë keeps breaking people into two parts so we can see their divided and conflicting emotions; [Polly] is the worshipful sister, Lucy the envious one. Together they represent the situation of the girl in the family"[10]—the situation, we might add, of a younger sister in a family with an adored son. Under these circumstances, the sister/girl might, like Polly, choose to serve the idol; or she might resent the privilege and desire, however unconsciously, the power for herself. Lucy, even at this age, is divided between the two responses, but she does refuse to play Polly's role, and this choice inevitably increases her isolation. Instead, she adopts the protective facade of coolness, calm, and quiet that serves both to confine her conflicting desires and mask her rebellion.

Nowhere, perhaps, are the effects of Lucy's solitude more evident than in the loss of social status that accompanies her loss of family, a clear indication of the interconnected role of class and gender in determining a person's development—and worth. Denied the material support and visibility traditionally provided by father, husband, or kin, and denied the education that men of her class usually received, she had few if any options open to her that would not further her alienation from her class or prevent her from following the acceptable routes for female development: marriage or death. We have only to contrast the course of Graham's life after his family suffers a financial setback to Lucy's to see vividly the obstacles working against her growth. Both, as Lucy unequivocally states, began life in the same social station.[11] But whereas Graham enters his father's profession, medicine, and by virtue of it moves out into the world and up the social ladder—not to mention his support of his mother—Lucy withdraws into the two hot closed rooms of Miss Marchmont's house before crossing the channel to enter the conventual environment and enclosed garden of the Rue Fossette. The perils of her friendless and solitary state are graphically illustrated upon her arrival in Villette, when she not only has to ask the now lordly Graham to speak for her and suggest an inn, but, once separated from him, becomes the victim of male pursuit and harassment.

If these "respectable" men perceive Lucy, the solitary streetwalker, as a prostitute, they are only assigning to her the role often assumed by women left in her position—a role simultaneously recognized and out-lawed by society. Lucy chooses another path. In leaving England to seek work as a governess/teacher, she adopts one of the few means of support available to embarrassed gentlewomen, but this choice also forces her to "admit the realities of her status as a paid employee and resign herself to the loss of her place in English society."[12] However exhilarated Lucy may be walking around London or aboard ship, she realizes only too well that her loss of status will prevent her from achieving what women were expected to desire—marriage with an equal or superior and the protection that such a union would offer her. Denied the wealth, position, or beauty that would make her a desirable object of possession, she will be unable to overcome the inequality inherent in the relationship between supposedly passive women and successful young men such as Graham. Although Lucy is clear-sighted enough to perceive that she does not have the means to play the traditional female roles enacted by other women in the novel—Ginevra, Paulina, or Mrs. Bretton—the desires she represses haunt her still. They surface both in her poignant questions to Paul at the end of the novel: "Ah, I am not pleasant to look at—?" and "Do I displease your eyes *much*?" (chap. 41); and in her yearning to assume woman's most tradi-tional role by becoming, in her words, one of those who "lay down the whole burden of human egotism, and gloriously take up the nobler charge of labouring and living for others" (chap. 31).

The conflict between Lucy's acknowledgment of her social position and the emotional needs that she has internalized (a conflict that is reflected in her creation of the two readers) is further complicated by her unfeminine desire to be her own person—to achieve independence—and her knowledge of her powers: an active intellect and the ability to feel strongly and act decisively. When Ginevra, observant in her own worldly way, defines Lucy during their mirror scene after the play by declaring "Nobody in the world but you cares for cleverness" (chap. 14), she simultaneously acknowledges one of Lucy's strongest attributes and reflects its lack of value in the context of cultural expectations for women. Early in the novel, Lucy measures her pride of intellect (and it is great) against the transformation into a beautiful wife and mother she observes in a less intelligent woman who had been at school with her. Intelligence, she perceives, does not lead to social visibility or acceptance: she recognizes the older woman but is not in turn recognized by her. The language of this scene captures Lucy's conflicting self-definitions and her characteristic response: "Wifehood and maternity had changed her thus, as I have since seen them change others even less promising than she. Me she had forgotten [The "she" here is ambiguous: wifehood and motherhood, or the woman? Both, I would say.] I was changed, too, though not, I fear, for the better. I made no attempt to recall myself to her memory: why should I?" (chap. 5). Why indeed!

Lucy partly resolves the conflict between intelligence and womanhood by insisting throughout the novel that *others* perceive her as clever, or interested in learning, or quick, whereas in truth she was none of these things. In much the same way, she justifies to the reader her major decision to go forward into the classroom (rather than backward into the nursery) as a reaction to what she describes as Madame Beck's masculine challenge to her gifts. A closer look, however, reveals that through this "justification" she transforms what appears to be an arbitrary personal choice into an assertion of female selfhood broad enough to include intellectual ambition and achievement. She creates, that is, a plausible social and narrative context for her own self-development that in turn opens the way for other women to follow her. Later, goaded into intellectual activity by Paul, she declares: "Whatever my powers—feminine or the contrary—God had given them, and I felt resolute to be ashamed of no faculty of His bestowal" (chap. 30).

The power of conflicting cultural maxims revealed by Lucy's seeming denial of her own strengths manifests itself in linguistic as well as psychological evasions. Forced by her situation to speak as well as to act for herself, she adopts speech patterns that allow her simultaneously to justify her actions—both to society and to herself—and to mask their true import. The most striking of these is her well-documented presentation of herself as acted on, an object, rather than as actor, the subject or agent of the sentence or the deed. At every turning point in the novel, at every moment of decision, Lucy chooses instinctively to break free of social constraints and go forward to self-discovery and growth, even while denying that the decision or action is hers. "Fate," she writes, "took me in her strong hand" and directed her to knock at the door of the pensionnat; "a bold thought" — to go to London — "was sent to my mind; my mind was made strong to receive it" (chaps. 7, 5). Further complicating her self-presentation is her clear sense of what she is and is not, of what she will or will not do, a certainty that often masks itself in the grammatical construction, "it did not suit me." Later, however, as Lucy begins to gain confidence and a sympathetic audience, her assertions of herself as agent, "I," rather than object, "me," become more frequent; but she continues to the end to insist that other people or changed circumstances guide her and are responsible for her economic and social success.

While many critics have offered explanations for what Moglen calls Lucy's "language of passivity," they often fail to look at what I have been emphasizing: the reality of the codes that discourage women from actively pursuing their own ends except through marriage, and the limited models for development and access to material support once they are denied the protection of family and friends.[13] The problem of voice illustrated by Lucy's difficulty in saying "I" reflects her isolation within a culture that rejects her strengths for lack of a context in which to read them — the same isolation that forces her to create her own readers. In her conversation with Graham about the illness induced by her solitude, Graham's question " 'Who is in the wrong, then, Lucy?' " evokes the response. " 'Me — Dr. John — me; and a great abstraction . . . me and Fate' " (chap. 17). Fate here becomes the ironic embodiment of those circumstances that Lucy knows better than to speak aloud, even if she had the words to describe them, since they lack the social recognition or cultural context that would make her narration of them plausible. In fact, society itself is at a loss for words when describing Lucy's state, just as Dr. John is at a loss to prescribe anything to cure her. His suggestions for her future care — change of air and scene, cheerful society, exercise — may bear, as Lucy comments in one of her classic understatements, "the safe sanction of custom, and the well-worn stamp of use" (chap. 17), but they fail utterly to recognize how inimical "custom" and "use" are to women in Lucy's uncustomary situation. For custom and use are exactly those forces that move Lucy to justify her tremendous delight in walking around London alone, frown on her unaccompanied journey to Boue-Marine where she is the only woman in the hotel breakfast room, permit respectable men to pursue a solitary woman across town for their sport, and ultimately imprison her alone in the school during the vacation. Lucy's "bad grammar," then, her "me," accurately captures the way custom and use blind society to the reality of lives like Lucy's and reduce women to objects.

Yet another interpretation of Lucy's language of passivity is made possible by Miller's analysis of how psychology and fiction have supported the customary reading of women's ambitions and desires as erotic or romantic, thereby severely limiting their range of self-expression in either social discourse or daydreams. Quoting Freud's statement — " 'In young women erotic wishes dominate the phantasies almost exclusively, for their ambition is generally comprised in their erotic longings; in young men egoistic and ambitious wishes assert themselves plainly enough alongside their erotic desires' " (p. 40) — Miller finds in women's novels a challenge to this restrictive view, finds another economy: "In this economy, egoistic desires would assert themselves paratactically alongside erotic ones. The repressed content, I think, would be, not erotic impulses, but an impulse to power: a fantasy of power that would revise the social grammar in which women are never defined as subjects; a fantasy of power that disdains a sexual exchange in which women can participate only as objects of circulation" (p. 41). This power, however, will manifest itself as what it is — the power of the weak — and " 'the most essential form of accommodation for the weak is to conceal what power they do have.' "[14]

Lucy, then, must conceal in her discourse her supposedly masculine "ambitious wishes" as well as her erotic desires, both of which forcefully assert themselves on the one occasion when she is empowered by society to adopt the role of actor on the public stage. One of the most notable aspects of this scene, the school play, is its deliberate confusion of sex roles and gender identification. Cast as a man in a plot written by someone else, Lucy brilliantly enacts the initiative, the competitiveness, the courtship, the wit, and the power that in real life are denied her by her social status and her gender. As Graham says after the fact, she made "a very killing fine gentleman" (chap. 16), and her first act, once in the role, is to conquer the duplicitous Zélie St. Pierre by asserting the weakness of the latter's female sex.

Although Lucy does not want to *be* or to *win* the beautiful and self-confident Ginevra, the object of her desire within the fantasy/play, she clearly relishes the freedom to exercise her hidden powers. Her consciousness of this desire emerges in her acknowledged source of inspiration: the presence of Graham in the audience, the brother/rival who animated her to act "as if wishful and resolute to win and conquer" and in the process to "rival" and then "eclipse" him (chap. 14). What Lucy also recognizes, however, is that the roles men such as Graham play naturally by virtue of their gender, she can fill only by proxy, and her rejection of her faculty and relish for dramatic expression is in part a refusal to dissipate her energy on goals that she can achieve only by adding the tokens of manhood to her female self in the fantastic realm of the theater. The self-respect implicit in her refusal to dress completely as a man for the role — to deny her femaleness — demands that her search for identity and fulfillment occurs on a different stage. For her, the audience at the play did not number "personal friends and acquaintances"; "foreigners and strangers," the crowd could not provide the recognition necessary for her growth (chaps. 15, 14).

Although Lucy rejects living by proxy (Ginevra's way) and refuses to perform before an audience of strangers, the play does allow her to test her powers and find her voice, an experience that informs her ongoing dialogue with her chosen audience, the reader. "Who will lend me a tongue?" she asks near the end of her tale, knowing only too well that she can rely on no one but herself. Her struggle to take control of her narrative (as well as of her life) is mirrored in the creation of an audience whose presence and responsiveness increasingly provide her with the strength to be that comes from external recognition. The complexity of her relationship with her readers and the changing roles she assigns to them as the narrative progresses reflect in turn the difficulty of growing to selfhood amidst the contradictory needs and desires imposed upon her by the prevailing cultural codes.

Even before she explicitly projects and names her readers, however, while still at Bretton, Lucy's awareness of the social and emotional forces shaping her identity colors her narrative presentation of herself. Early in the second chapter, for example, we read, "I, Lucy Snowe, plead guiltless of that curse, an over-heated and discursive imagination," and we wonder to whom she is speaking and why she talks of herself in this way. The implied listener, depicted as judge and jury, is almost certainly a precursor of the conventional socialized reader before whom Lucy feels it necessary to disclaim the passionate expression of emotion enacted by Polly, even while implicitly admitting its power. Lucy names herself here by emphasizing the cold aspect of her name as well as the light, names herself as the plain, shy, dowerless girl who already perceives that emotions as strong as those displayed by Polly may find no outlet in the world created by her circumstances — and might well hinder her power to survive.

Throughout the first part of the novel, Lucy continues to preserve her self by distancing those emotions that threaten her precarious economic and psychic equilibrium, particularly her feelings for Graham. After a night of suffering, for example, caused by her bitter knowledge that the romance Madame Beck suspects between her and Dr. John does not exist, the "Next day," she tells us, she "was Lucy Snowe again" (chap. 13). A curious cross-over of roles between Polly and Lucy, however, occurs in the one scene where Lucy does act out her love for Graham — the night she loses his letter. " 'Oh! they have taken my letter!' cried the grovelling, groping monomaniac": this is Lucy's depiction of herself (chap. 22). The phrase "monomaniac" echoes her previous description of Polly's attachment to her father as "that monomaniac tendency I have ever thought the most unfortunate with which man or woman can be cursed" (chap. 2). The teasing response that Lucy's display of her feelings evokes in Graham makes us feel that her refusal to declare her love to him (she acknowledges it in a variety of ways to herself and her readers) is not neurotic, or evasive, or even mistaken. Graham may guide her in her explorations of her external environment from feelings of kindness or "camaraderie," but he will never perceive her inner life or fulfill her emotional needs. She observes him directly; he, as in the recognition scene in the nursery, sees her in the mirror of his own egotism and therefore fails to see her at all. It is not surprising, then, that she justifies to the reader her decision to conceal her identity from him by saying it would have made little difference had she "come forward and [announced], 'This is Lucy Snowe!' " (chap. 16).

Lucy's public silence and private dialogue with her reader are deliberate responses to what is perhaps the most potentially destructive aspect of her solitude: the isolation of vision that excludes her from the social discourse necessary for an ontological affirmation of self. However great her emotional self-discipline, Lucy realizes early on the need to acknowledge and share her perceptions of reality in order to continue to be. Thus, she reacts to her observation of Polly at the Bretton tea table by confiding, "Candidly speaking, I thought her a little busy body" (chap. 2). The as yet unnamed recipient of this confidence serves a crucial function both in the narrative and in Lucy's development, for no one actually present during that scene would have understood Lucy's rejection of Polly's exaggerated acting of the female role, just as no one at La Terrasse, including Mrs. Bretton, "could conceive" her suffering during the long vacation: "so the half-drowned life-boatman [Lucy] keeps his own counsel, and spins no yarns" (chap. 17). Continually a confidante herself, a mediator who interprets the infant Polly's unspoken need to say goodbye to her cherished Graham and who later smooths the way to their union by speaking for them to Mr. Home, Lucy, in her formative years, has no one to hear her unuttered words, or to speak in her place. The one exception is perhaps Miss Marchmont, who interprets Lucy's lack of words when confronted with an unorthodox question about suffering and salvation not as silence but encouragement (chap. 4). No wonder Lucy loves her, and after her death turns increasingly to the reader to fill the gap. Speak she must, though, for to remain silent would be to become the cretin who makes mouths instead of talking, and whose silence becomes a metaphor for Lucy's own potentially arrested development. To overcome this two-fold silence, Lucy evolves another reader, a nonjudgmental reader, a sharer of the insights that she cannot communicate to those more in tune with the accepted social codes.

When first left on her own, however, after the metaphoric shipwreck, Lucy's recognition of society's power to render her invisible and mute leads her initially to endow her newly created "reader" with the conventional assumptions about women and novels that she must challenge and change for her own life and tale to be plausible. The irony evident in her first direct address to this reader ("I will permit the reader to picture me . . . as a bark slumbering through halcyon weather . . .") allows her simultaneously to mock those who choose to remain locked within their traditional expectations and to offer them an alternate version of reality that would reflect and validate her existence. This same ironic stance informs Lucy's care to keep the reader abreast of the chronological "story" in her narrative, even as she manipulates the sequence and imagery to reveal a deeper stratum of her psychic life and the true meaning of her tale. "Has the reader forgotten Miss Ginevra Fanshawe?" (chap. 9), she asks after she is well established as a teacher and as a prelude to the introduction of Dr. John. The tinge of sarcasm in her question indicates that the perceptive reader will recognize the priorities implicit in the seemingly discontinuous narrative structure: the need for economic security—the effort of learning French and mastering a strange environment—far outweighed any other considerations in those early days. Later, the question "Does the reader, remembering what was said some pages back, care to ask how I answered [Graham's] letters . . . ?" (chap. 23) reminds both the curious reader and herself of her need to keep her emotions in check in the midst of the "new creed . . . a belief in happiness" that she has just described.

Often, Lucy's mode in dealing with the reader is a form of cooptation that transforms the reader into an accomplice in whatever observations she is about to make: "I need not explain, reader," or "The reader will not be surprised," or "My reader, I know, is one who would not thank me for an elaborate reproduction of poetic first impressions; and it is well, inasmuch as I had neither time nor mood to cherish such" (chap. 5). In this last address, she is undercutting romantic expectations as deliberately as she does when she rejects metaphors of buds and sylphs in describing the substantial young women of Villette (chap. 20) or tells us that "M. Paul stooped down and proceeded—as novel-writers say, and, as was literally true in his case—to 'hiss' into my ear some poignant words" (chap. 28). By mocking fictional and thereby social conventions, by challenging her readers to share her perceptions, she creates an audience who learns to read her narrative for what it is—the nontraditional story of a woman's life and a text in which she is not an invisible outsider but the informing presence.[15]

This dialogue, however, no matter how sarcastic it may be about conventions, also serves as self-protection and stems from Lucy's conflict between rebellious self-expression and survival. In this context, the reader becomes a foil whose role is to help her keep her own emotions in check. Thus, the irony in her early addresses is often directed as much toward herself as toward the social maxims she criticizes; she uses it to curb her own imagination and desires when she feels them destructive of her precariously held security, or to define herself within the limits she recognizes as realistic for someone in her position. When, after her romantic vision of Europe, she adds the postscript, "Cancel the whole of that, if you please, reader—or rather let it stand and draw thence a moral . . . *Day-dreams are delusions of the demon*" (chap. 6), she asserts the boundaries of what is possible in the battle she is then fighting for survival. When she makes comments such as "The reader must not think too hardly of Rosine" (chap. 13) for chattering to Dr. John, or "Think not, reader, that [Ginevra] thus bloomed and sparkled for the mere sake of M. Paul" (chap. 14), the sarcasm aimed at these two women is also a way of confronting her own potentially self-destructive frustration at the fact that her position and personality prevent her from acting as freely as Rosine and Ginevra do. In the first of these examples, she is also leveling an ironic eye on her own tendency to idolize Dr. John and the dangers of that idolization. One of the most painful of these exchanges occurs at the time she is fighting her disappointment at the loss of Graham's attention: "The reader will not too gravely regard the little circumstance that about this time" Madame Beck temporarily borrowed Graham's letters (chap. 26). The irony here is a self-protective reaction meant to distance the anger and pain that she is unable to allay except by containing them.

Rather than an attempt to deny the strength of her feelings or to deceive herself about them, as some critics have maintained, these passages speak to Lucy's recognition of the need to confront and control what she cannot realistically hope to gain or fulfill. To act out her emotional needs at this time might well threaten the economic and social security she achieves by ruthless, if painful, self-control. A revealing example of this struggle, and of her conscious involvement of the reader as a foil, occurs when Graham comes to take her to the theater: "And away I flew, never once checked, reader, by the thought which perhaps at this moment checks you: namely, that to go anywhere with Graham and without Mrs. Bretton could be objectionable" (chap. 23). The fact is that "society" might well look askance at this arrangement, except that society in the form of Mrs. Bretton, as Lucy tells us immediately, sees their relationship as that of brother and sister. In the face of society's blindness to any other possibility, Lucy reacts by saying that she would feel self-contempt and shame for suggesting an intimacy that did not exist. In this exchange, the reader, as society's voice, is reassured that all is conventional and well. By now, however, Lucy has also trained her reader to hear and approve what is not stated explicitly: the consciously chosen restraint that allows her to maintain the limited relationship offered her, and to benefit from it.

The dialogue with the reader, then, is both ironic and deadly serious, for Lucy's ability to retain her sense of her own integrity in spite of her invisibility and her conflicting needs is crucial for her growth. As the narrative (and with it Lucy's sense of selfhood) progresses, we can chart the nature of her development by the number and kind of addresses to her various readers. Not surprisingly, she appeals to her reader most often during times of intense self-conflict and when, owing to the lack of recognized context or precedent of her responses, she is least able to express herself openly. These moments occur both when she is alone and in social gatherings. Thus, left on her own, Lucy responds to the weight of her isolation ("To whom could I complain?") by deliberately rationalizing and justifying to the socialized reader what are by conventional standards her unorthodox actions and feelings: "In going to London, I ran less risk and evinced less enterprise than the reader may think" (chap. 5); "Before you pronounce on the rashness of the proceedings, reader [her decision to go to Villette], look back to the point whence I started" (chap. 7). By combining irony and defensiveness, these early explanations constitute a critique of the codes she recognizes as limiting even as they define her sense of self and her discourse. Although she gives the socialized reader permission to interpret her experience along traditional lines, she suffers from the potential misreading and its ability to control her life. The second address continues, "consider the desert I had left, note how little I perilled: mine was the game where the player cannot lose and may win"—a clear indication of a conscious choice aimed at physical as well as psychic survival, and part of Lucy's challenge to the fiction that women pass their lives in a long sleep.

The nature of her addresses to the reader begins to change once Lucy is accepted into the foreign world of the pensionnat at the Rue Fossette. After her introduction to Madame Beck, she appeals to the reader four times in quick succession to share her confused reaction of admiration and shock at discovering a woman so powerful, so independent, so successful, and, in many ways, so like her! Simultaneously observed and observing, she gains the strength to offer a compelling portrait of this fascinating woman to the "sensible reader" who will recognize that she did not gain "all the knowledge here condensed for his benefit in one month, or in one half-year" (chap. 8). With Madame Beck's power—and eye—to stimulate her, she educates the reader as she herself learns of her ability to control her environment—and her tale.

Once she enters the classroom and immerses herself in teaching and learning ("My time was now well and profitably filled up. . . . It was pleasant. I felt I was getting on" [chap. 9]), her rare addresses to the reader are limited to ironic observations about Ginevra and Rosine, who play more traditional female roles, with the exception of the crucial scene when she refuses to tell Dr. John—or the reader—why she is staring so intently at him: "I was confounded, as the reader may suppose, yet not with an irrecoverable confusion; being conscious that it was from no emotion of incautious admiration. . . . I might have cleared myself on the spot, but would not. I did not speak. I was not in the habit of speaking to him" (chap. 10). He, as she has already told us, barely notices her existence. Her decision not to reveal herself where she "can never be rightly known" has, not surprisingly, led to the strongest accusations of narrative unreliability, as well as accusations of lying, neurosis, and perversity—the words she herself uses during this scene: "There is a perverse mood of the mind which is rather soothed than irritated by misconstruction." But is it not possible that by this silence Lucy is creating a script other than that in which the lost god-brother/prince reappears and rescues her from her changeling role, the romantic or erotic fantasy that

Lucy finds it necessary to forgo while she makes an independent life for herself as a teacher? In terms of conventional fictions, she may be unreliable and her decision "implausible," but in terms of the subtext, her silence and refusal reflect the lack of a language or a plot by which women can communicate ambitions and desires outside of those encoded in the accepted social or literary conventions. I am reminded here of Miller's appropriation of Jakobson's observation about communication: " 'The verbal exchange, like every form of human relation, requires at least two interlocutors; an idiolect, in the final analysis, therefore can be only a *slightly perverse fiction*' " (p. 43). To transform Lucy's silence and refusal into a statement of alternative plausibility and action requires the participation of a reader willing to recognize and respond to her need for anonymity as part of her process of self-identification and growth.

Paradoxically, her silence initially gives Lucy power; under its protection she can observe and confront Graham's blindness toward Ginevra and plunge into the role of mediator in others' communications. She has begun the process that allows her, on the night of the play, to find her own voice. Left alone during the long vacation, however, she faces the "dumb future" with a despair she no longer tries to hide from even her socialized readers (the religious reader, moralist, cynic, epicure) or to justify herself except by saying, "perhaps, circumstanced like me, you [reader] would have been, like me, wrong" (chap. 15). The need for companionship, the need to speak, that drives her to the confessional at the height of her despair, becomes, once outside the church, a "confession" to a reader whose by now sympathetic hearing she relies on when she rejects Père Silas's tempting offer of religious community and chooses instead to live her life as a "heretic narrative" (chap. 15). In the scenes that follow this confession, she has ample opportunity to test the mettle of her now transformed reader/confessor, for her revelation to Graham that she is "Lucy Snowe" plunges her into a deeper stratum of isolation than that she had experienced before she was "known." During her stay at La Terrasse and the subsequent weeks, when her self-control and clarity of vision are most sorely tried, she turns to the reader more often than at any other time during the narrative.[16] Most of her addresses obsessively explain what she calls the "seeming inconsistency" of her portraits of Graham, an inconsistency that reflects her struggle to say honestly what she instinctively knows: that he is neither as perceptive nor sensitive nor selfless as he appears to others in public. Limited by his "masculine self-love" and conventionality, lacking the necessary sympathy, he will never replace the reader as the sharer of Lucy's inner life.

The battle against self-delusion that Lucy fights during this section of the narrative with the explicit help of the reader reaches its climax in the "Vashti" chapter. In fact, the five evocations of the reader during this chapter accurately inscribe the process of Lucy's self-recognition and growth. First, making use of an endearment that jars us coming from her usually more satiric pen, she shares with the "dear reader" both the initial ecstasy that Graham's letters brought her and the mellowing effect that time and self-knowledge had on their message. Next, she reminds the reader of her compromise in answering the letters – a struggle in which reason vanquishes imagination, but at a price: the painful confession to the reader of why it was acceptable for her to go out alone with her "brother" Graham. Immediately following this admission, she sees the light in the attic, indicative of the presence of the nun, which "the reader may believe . . . or not." Graham's disbelief, however, causes Lucy to comment negatively on his "dry, materialist views," views which color his subsequent "callous" reaction to Vashti, the passionate actress who enacts Lucy's own rebellion and self-mastery. Graham's "branding judgement" impresses upon Lucy once and for ever his inability to perceive who or what she is. The final vision of Graham that she offers to the reader that night mirrors her acceptance of his separateness: "Reader, I see him yet, with his look of comely courage and cordial calm" amidst the chaos released by Vashti's desires. He has become a statue, heroic perhaps, the ideal suitor for Polly, but not for Lucy a responsive human being.

After the period of solitary confinement and silence that follows this eventful night, Lucy returns to her dialogue with the reader stronger and calmer. She is now able to be warmly ironic and even humorous about the "perverseness" that leads her to "quarrel" with M. Paul (in contrast to her decision *not* to quarrel with Graham) and continues to define her distinctive emerging self. At least part of the change of tone – and the relative sparseness of the addresses to the reader she now speaks to without justification as a true companion – can be attributed to Paul, whose belief in her "fiery and rash nature" (chap. 26) gives her a warmer image of her self and whose own perverseness badgers her into speaking to him directly. One scene deserves note: the evening at the Hotel Crécy when her open anger and forgiveness wins from M. Paul a smile that she presents to the reader as her own accomplishment ("You should have seen him smile, Reader, . . ." [chap. 27]). Emphasizing his contrast to Graham, this smile transforms Paul from a mask or a statue into a human being.

Unable, however, to trust Paul completely, Lucy continues to share with the reader the difficulties of the unfolding relationship and of the man: "the reader is advised not to be in any hurry with his kindly conclusions" (chap. 30). Most significant, perhaps, she alludes again and again to the "perverse" aspect of her character that now prevents her from succumbing to Paul's "Est-ce là tout?" or remaining in the classroom when he seeks her on the evening after the country outing during which he had called her "sister" and encouraged her love (chaps. 29, 33). This behavior suggests that Lucy is experiencing a potentially irresolvable conflict between her long-concealed erotic desires and her supposedly masculine ambitious wishes. On the one hand, her greatest outburst of self-assertion—"I want to tell you [Paul] something . . . I want to tell you all" (chap. 41)—arises from erotic jealousy and wins her a proposal of marriage. On the other hand, her perverse silences reflect a highly developed instinct to protect the independence and power that she has achieved outside of erotic fulfillment, a power that continues to sustain her after Paul's death. Before this occurs, however, she makes good use of her own and her reader's accumulated strength to support her during the climactic, visionary night in the park when she believes she has lost Paul. Drugged and again alone, she repeatedly calls upon the reader during this scene to share her perception of what she terms the "TRUTH." Employing the words "we" and "us" in her appeals (chap. 39), she identifies her readers completely with her own perspective and includes them in a deliberate but psychologically necessary misreading of the scene.

At the end of her narrative, when Lucy asks the reader to "scout the paradox" of her three happiest years, she appeals for the last time to the community she herself has created to grant credence to the highly unconventional conclusion of her tale. She has by this time given us ample warning that "endings" for women are problematic, and traditional plots no help in assessing her own experience. She has explicitly shared with the reader her final words on the lives of the two more familiar fictional women after their marriages: Ginevra fails to come to the expected bad end, and, in fact, fails to develop at all; and Polly, she cannot help admitting to the reader, however blessed in the resolution of her tale, bears a distinct resemblance to a pampered and adoring spaniel (chaps. 40, 36).[17] Equally unexpected, perhaps, Lucy's life does not end with Paul's; the observant reader will have noted that the school clearly continues to prosper and that Lucy, by the time she begins her narrative, knows the West End of London as well as her beloved City (chap. 6). Rewriting the traditional novel to illustrate the limited plots available to women in literature, as in life, she has survived the destruction of the romantic fantasy and grown into another reality.

The path, however, to a maturity that is intellectually and financially fulfilling, and I would argue existentially fulfilling as well, involves more than just the telling of the tale; ultimately, Lucy's development resides in the mediation of the reader who grants her the recognition and the reality of her perceptions lacking in the external world. As readers ourselves, to the extent that we can enter into and accept Lucy's cryptic conclusion, we will join "in friendly company" with the "[p]ilgrims and brother mourners" (chap. 38) who acknowledge pain and hear, as Miss Marchmont did, the unspoken word of encouragement. Otherwise, we remain among those readers whose sunny imaginations still demand conventional endings, and who cannot conceive, as Lucy herself does, that while life for someone in her position is hard, in the reflections provided by the reader she has gained the power to grow and to speak, and with it the power to endure.

Notes

1. Charlotte Brontë, *Villette* (New York: Harper Colophon, 1972), chap. 27; all subsequent references are to this edition. Earlier versions of this paper were presented to the Pacific Coast Conference on British Studies and the University Seminar for Feminist Inquiry at Dartmouth College. I am grateful to the members of the University Seminar and to Marianne Hirsch, Paula Mayhew, and Thomas Vargish for extremely useful criticism and suggestions.

2. The wording here reflects that in Wolfgang Iser's *The Implied Reader* (Baltimore: Johns Hopkins University Press, 1974), pp. 274–94, although the idea is common to reader-response criticism. For a collection of the classic essays in this field, see *Reader-Response Criticism: From Formalism to Post-Structuralism*, ed. Jane P. Tompkins (Baltimore: Johns Hopkins University Press, 1980); for more recent speculations, see *The Reader in the Text: Essays on Audience and Interpretation*, ed. Susan R. Soleiman and Inge Crossman (Princeton: Princeton University Press, 1980).

3. *Charlotte Brontë: The Self Conceived* (New York: Norton, 1978), pp. 196, 199.

4. "The Buried Letter: Feminism and Romanticism in *Villette*" in *Women Writing and Writing about Women*, ed. Mary Jacobus (London: Croom Helm, 1979), p. 43.

5. Sandra M. Gilbert and Susan Gubar, *The Madwoman in the Attic: The Woman Writer and the Nineteenth-Century Literary Imagination* (New Haven: Yale University Press, 1979), pp. 418–19.

6. Tony Tanner shares this reading of the narrative. Lucy, he writes, "finds herself in 'bad' narrative in which she has effectively to create, or put together, her own ontology and value-system" ("Introduction," in Charlotte Brontë, *Villette* [New York: Penguin, 1979], p. 49).

7. *PMLA* 96, 1 (January 1981), 36–48. Hereafter, page references to Miller's essay appear in the text.

8. One need only recall Brontë's bitter comment in her explanation of why she and her sisters chose gender-ambiguous pseudonyms—"without at that time suspecting that our mode of writing and thinking was not what is called 'feminine' "—to measure the effect of criticism such as that in *The Christian Remembrancer*—"A book more unfeminine, both in its excellences and defects, it would be hard to find in the annals of female authorship"—and that of Elizabeth Rigby in the *Quarterly*: ". . . if we ascribe the book to a woman at all, we have no alternative but to ascribe it to one who has, for some sufficient reason, long forfeited the society of her own sex." (Charlotte Brontë's comment appears in the "Biographical Notice" to the 1850 edition of *Wuthering Heights* and *Agnes Grey*, quoted in Inga-Stina Ewbank, *Their Proper Sphere* [Cambridge, Mass.: Harvard University Press, 1968], p. 1; the reviews of *Jane Eyre* are quoted and discussed in Ewbank, pp. 43–46, and in Margot Peters, *Unquiet Soul: A Biography of Charlotte Brontë* [New York: Pocket Books, 1976], pp. 237–38.) Brontë was correct, moreover, to anticipate a similar response to *Villette*: Matthew Arnold, for example, found it "disagreeable . . . Because the writer's mind contains nothing but hunger, rebellion, and rage," and Thackeray criticized it as "rather vulgar—I don't make my *good women* ready to fall in love with two men at once" (quoted in Peters, p. 429). The most vicious attack, however, was Anne Mozley's anonymous review in *The Christian Remembrancer*. Although granting that the author of *Villette* had "gained both in amiability and propriety since she first presented herself to the world—soured, coarse, and grumbling; an alien, it might seem, from society, and amenable to none of its laws," her final judgment is severe. Brontë's "impersonations" are branded as "self-reliant" and "contemptuous of prescriptive decorum," and of Lucy she writes: "We will sympathise with Lucy Snowe as being fatherless and penniless . . . but we cannot offer even the affections of our fancy (the right and due of every legitimate heroine) to her unscrupulous and self-dependent intellect." Responding to this attack in a letter to the editor of the journal, Brontë consistently refers to

the reviewer as "he." (The extracts from Mozley's review [June 1853] and Brontë's response [July 1853] appear in Thomas James Wise and John Alexander Symington, eds., *The Brontës: Their Lives, Friendships, and Correspondence* [Oxford: Shakespeare Head Press, 1932], vol. 4, pp. 78–79, and in Peters, *Unquiet Soul*, p. 428).

For a discussion of nineteenth-century criticism of women's fiction, including Brontë's, see Elaine Showalter's chapter "The Double Critical Standard," in *A Literature of Their Own: British Women Novelists from Brontë to Lessing* (Princeton: Princeton University Press, 1977).

9. For another reading of the "oddly assorted female Powers who people the novel's cosmos," see Nina Auerbach's chapter on *Villette* in *Communities of Women* (Cambridge: Harvard University Press, 1978), p. 110.

10. *Sexual Politics* (New York: Avon, 1971), p. 193.

11. Speaking of Mrs. Bretton's "patronage" of her, Lucy remarks, "it was not founded on conventional grounds of superior wealth or station (in the last particular there had never been any inequality; her degree was mine)" (chap. 16). I stress this point as a corrective to Terry Eagleton's analysis of Lucy's class anger and its effect on her psychological life, an analysis which overlooks the role of gender in connection with class (*Myths of Power: A Marxist Study of the Brontës* [New York: Barnes and Noble, 1975]).

12. M. Jeanne Peterson, "The Victorian Governess: Status Incongruence in Family and Society," in *Suffer and Be Still: Women in the Victorian Age*, ed. Martha Vicinus (Bloomington: Indiana University Press, 1973), p. 16.

13. Moglen interprets this linguistic pattern as part of Lucy's anesthetized reaction to the guilt of being a survivor, a way of not having to participate in life, and labels it neurotic (see, for example, pp. 196, 203). Eagleton, looking at this same language, reads it as part of Lucy's (and Jane Eyre's) need to see herself as a "meek, unworldly victim unable to act purposively" in order not to be accused of self-interested enterprise and the desire for social advancement (pp. 62–63). The truth is, however, that no matter how strong Lucy's energy and will, she would not have acquired her own school nearly as soon without Paul's gift, nor could she have expanded it as rapidly without Miss Marchmont's legacy. These are economic realities.

14. Miller is here quoting from Barbara Bellow Watson, "On Power and the Literary Test," *Signs*, 1 (1975), 113.

15. Jacobus argues that "The novel's real oddity lies in perversely withholding its true subject, Lucy Snowe, by an act of repression which mimics hers," and that "Lucy's invisibility is a calculated deception—a blank screen on which others project their view of her" (pp. 43, 44). The nun, on the other hand, forces the reader to experience the "uncanny" aspect of Lucy's narrative and becomes the true mirror of the hidden self (p. 52). I would argue that rather than perversely withholding its true subject, Lucy's narrative deliberately illustrates why the true subject is invisible to those with conventional social and fictional expectations. Lucy's true fiction is there from the beginning, created in part through the dialogue with the reader.

16. See, for example, the four addresses to the reader in chapter 18, "We Quarrel."

17. Observations about Ginevra and Polly continue to be addressed directly to the reader throughout the narrative, for here Lucy's perceptions do perhaps differ most radically from those of a society that might well find her merely jealous. Toward Ginevra she is continually sarcastic, but her attitude toward Polly is more complex. Ultimately, however, she underlines the conventional quality in Polly which leads the younger woman to respond to Lucy's understanding that "solitude is sadness" but not death. " 'Lucy, I wonder if anybody will ever comprehend you altogether' " (chap. 37).

The Cypher: Disclosure and
Reticence in *Villette*   Karen Lawrence*

"It kills me to be forgotten, monsieur," Lucy Snowe tells M. Paul near the end of *Villette*.[1] Through much of the novel, however, Lucy cultivates the oblivion she here resists. "Unobserved I could observe," she tells us early on (p. 198). Lucy's first words in the novel are: "Of what are these things the signs and tokens?" (p. 7); indeed, she seems first and foremost a *decoder* of signs, an interpreter of *other* people and events. One can say that Lucy's development is marked by an increasing desire to signify, to mean something to someone.

And yet this notion of development as an increasing desire to signify is problematic, as is the idea, central to some feminist readings of Lucy, that Lucy's development is measured by her willingness to play a central role in her own story and to abandon her status as pure observer.[2] For throughout Lucy's story (the events of her life) and her narrative (the writing of her story), she displays dual impulses to be overlooked and to signify. She captures these dual impulses in the fascinating figure of herself she provides the reader late in the novel: she calls herself a "cypher," someone "to whom nature had denied the impromptu faculty; who, in public, was by nature a cypher" (p. 515). The word "cypher" can denote both meaning and absence of meaning. Among its definitions are, according to *Webster's New Twentieth Century Dictionary:* "a person or thing of no value or consequence, a nonentity"; "a secret or disguised manner of writing meant to be understood only by the persons who have the key to it"; "the key to such a code"; "an intricate weaving together of letters, as in the initial of a name, or a seal"; and in arithmetic, "a zero, which, standing by itself, expresses the absence of any quantity, but increases or diminishes the value of other figures, according to its position." Lucy chooses an ambiguous symbol that can suggest she is *less* significant than others (a nonentity), *secretly* significant (a code), *more* significant (a key), or significant *depending upon her relation to others* and possessing the power to make others variously significant as well.

What are we to make of the fundamental ambiguity of this self-articulation? Lucy's primary meaning in calling herself a cypher seems to be the first *figurative* definition—"a person or thing of no value or consequence, a nonentity." In *The Madwoman in the Attic*, Gilbert and Gubar use the word "cyher" in much the same way to demonstrate how women have been overlooked in literary history, particularly in the nineteenth century.[3] In using this figure, then, Lucy paradoxically articu-

*© 1988 by the Regents of the University of California. Reprinted from *Nineteenth-Century Literature* 42 no. 4 (March 1988), 488–66, by permission.

lates herself as a non-being; the cypher is a figure that refuses to "figure" Lucy, to give her a face or a body. Like her "cloak of hodden grey," the figure covers the person of Lucy. In assigning herself a figure like the cypher, Lucy deliberately obscures her intelligibility, her body, and her signature.

In calling herself a "cypher" in *public*, Lucy refers specifically to her insignificant presence in person. As plain a Jane as her literary predecessor, Jane Eyre, Lucy runs the risk of being overlooked, relegated to a place of nonsignificance. But in articulating herself with a figure that covers, Lucy causes us to wonder if invisibility is not also a strategy like the "cloak of hodden grey," specifically a strategy to avoid being "textualized" or read. Lucy's use of the word "cypher" refers to the only one of its meanings to shun associations with language or sign. All other meanings of the word besides "nonentity," Lucy's primary meaning, involve writing, signs, textuality. Lucy calls herself a cypher in public — an insignificant person, overlooked, that is to say, not one who becomes a sign or text to be read by someone else. Further, by saying she lacks the "impromptu faculty" in person, Lucy stresses that she does not articulate herself in person or speech extemporaneously and on demand. In diametric opposition to the "Juno" at the concert Lucy attends who is "a sort of mark for all eyes" (p. 299), Lucy as plain protagonist does not serve as an icon of beauty, a sign that automatically signifies "Woman" to be viewed, to be the center of attention. The representation of woman as image — i.e., as spectacle, object to be looked at, vision of beauty — is pervasive in our culture, and the history of the visual arts confirms the position of woman as object rather than subject, spectacle rather than spectator, "other" rather than constitutive consciousness.[4]

The history of the novel is different from that of the visual arts in the sense that woman as subject (consciousness) and spectator ("focalizer," to use Gérard Genette's term) has been depicted by both male and female writers. But one of the striking aspects of Lucy Snowe as protagonist is the degree to which she is primarily a viewer rather than viewed object, an interpreter rather than the erotic, mysterious "other" to obsess the male gaze and fantasy. Although she does become a character in plots of both ambition and love and begins to be a focus of attention in each,[5] it is worth noting that Lucy's "invisibility" is not wholly wished away in the course of the narrative, for it affords a sense of power related to her skills as narrator:

> It was not perhaps my business to observe the mystery of his bearing, or search out its origin or aim; but, placed as I was, I could hardly help it. He laid himself open to my observation, according to my presence in the room just that degree of notice and consequence a person of my exterior habitually expects: that is to say, about what is given to unobtrusive articles of furniture, chairs of ordinary joiner's work, and carpets of no striking pattern. (p. 135)

Two points are worth noting here: Lucy's plainness allows her to reverse the gaze, to observe the "mystery" of the male rather than provide the feminine mystique. Secondly, in the degree of her unobtrusiveness, she becomes a kind of fly-on-the-wall focalizer gaining access of vision by virtue of her insignificance. The power in these possibilities helps to qualify Mary Jacobus' statement that "Lucy's invisibility is an aspect of her oppression."[6] Gaining access to the dramas of others, developing her powers to observe and interpret, Lucy becomes an observer who often sees what others cannot. She witnesses "spectacles" where others see nothing, as when she sees a "full mournful and significant . . . spectacle" in the interaction of the King and Queen of Labassecour, a scene that "seemed to be wholly invisible" to others (p. 305).

Thus instead of being a mark to be deciphered, Lucy presents herself as nontextualized, resisting the male as viewer who would interpret her. Although, as critics have pointed out, Lucy represses her feelings unhealthily, particularly at the beginning of the story,[7] her emotional reticence does not eliminate the real power that develops by means of her "invisibility." Like the biblical Vashti who refused to display herself for the male gaze,[8] Lucy Snowe avoids the fate of spectacle and becomes spectator instead.

Another way to put it is to say that Lucy's resistance to being textualized stems partly from the sense that her person, failing to conform to the text that men view as significant enough to interpret, runs the risk of being misread.[9] Lucy begins to understand Graham's limitations as a "reader" of women and recognizes how he misapprehends her own character and nature: "he did not read my eyes, or face, or gestures; though, I doubt not, all spoke" (p. 455). Lucy guards herself against such misapprehension, biding her time until others learn to recognize her significance. Referring to her own physical plainness, Lucy describes herself all dressed for the fête: "We become oblivious of these deficiencies [i.e., physical plainness] in the uniform routine of daily drudgery, but they will force upon us their unwelcome blank on those bright occasions when beauty should shine" (p. 183). Lucy's self-deprecatory reference to the "unwelcome blank" ironically anticipates the responses of certain male critics who were loath to spend so much time with the "ugly" heroines of Brontë's books; but it also reinforces our sense of the process by which the cypher as blank becomes cypher as sign, only when her "public" is educated enough to read her. The elaboration of Lucy's meaning occurs with reluctance on the part of Lucy and with difficulty on the part of those who encounter her.

As an alternative to the perils of interpretation Lucy faces in person, she turns to writing, to self-articulation in her own autobiographical text. In calling herself "a cypher" in public, Lucy seeks to limit her insignificance to the realm of her person and to suggest an alternate world where her image might be better articulated and, hence, better understood. This alternative "Lucy" is alluded to earlier in the novel, in a kind of psychomachic dialogue between Lucy and her Reason over the possibility of writing to Graham to express her feelings. Lucy's Reason cautions against such a writing, and when Lucy objects that she has *talked* to Graham without incurring Reason's censure, Reason replies: " 'Talk for you is good discipline. You converse imperfectly. While you speak, there can be no oblivion of inferiority—no encouragement to delusion: pain, privation, penury stamp your language.' " Lucy rejects this self-image of impoverishment; she counters that "where the bodily presence is weak and the speech contemptible, surely there cannot be error in making written language the medium of better utterance than faltering lips can achieve?" (p. 327). Her writing, then, gives her access to power, a means of signifying herself in a different way. Her "heretic narrative" indeed offers an alternative to the inarticulateness of her speech, marked with privation, and the nun-like silence of her presence.[10]

In her narrative, she "textualizes" herself in her own way; she writes the script and therefore controls to a greater degree the circulation of her own sign. Just as in life Lucy schools the characters around her to interpret a female text different from those they have read before, so in writing she schools her readers to understand her significance. She does this partly, as Brenda Silver says, through covert strategies by which she encodes significance and provides clues for deciphering. Interestingly, then, the sign of Lucy Snowe and the text that elaborates that sign into narrative evoke "cypher" in some of its other definitions. In her narrative, Lucy constructs herself as a sign worth interpreting for readers able to see significance where others see only a blank. Silver's interpretation, among others, implies that a total revelation of Lucy is possible for the initiate who may find a "key" to the code of the text.[11] Indeed, Lucy's own opposition between speech and writing might seem to support the promise that Lucy will be revealed in her written text. But Lucy defers her own significance in writing as well as in person; her narrative, like her person, refuses to tell all. While Lucy's myth of binary oppositions suggests that the cypher applies primarily to her speech and presence, in fact the narrative, too, in its expressiveness and reticence, defers ultimate meaning.

The "myth" of full self-presence in writing as opposed to speech reverses the logocentrism that Derrida has traced in Western metaphysics—"lack" for Lucy is stamped on her face, on her person, but is presumably completed in her writing. Yet the text as a whole deconstructs this opposition, showing that no medium fully reveals presence or conceals significance. Lucy's cypher-like face ultimately cannot retreat from textuality; however much Lucy sometimes strives to remain out of circulation as a sign, at the very least her person and speech are "stamped" with deprivation, her presence bearing the mark of a lack. Analogously, her autograph, in the narrative of herself that she constructs *in writing*, is never fully revealed in the text.

In her study of Brontë, Karen Chase says, "both [*Jane Eyre* and *Villette*] seem to offer the transparency of a confession, until one thinks to ask who has confessed. The speaking voices are distinctive and memorable, but the speakers seem to disappear."[12] I would say, first, that it is not as "voice" but as autograph that we apprehend Lucy's text and that the "disappearance" of Lucy is not attributable wholly to the "passivity" and lack of desire Chase sees in her. As I have been trying to show, Lucy's cypher-like reticence derives partly from defensiveness and partly from a kind of feminist refusal to be viewed conventionally. But further, in turning the cypher into a narrative, Brontë shows that Lucy's "lack" is not the Lacanian "lack" which, as Luce Irigaray remarks, sees woman as unrepresentable, because lacking the phallus, the key to the symbolic.[13] Rather, Brontë presents the enigma of Lucy Snowe not from the male point of view, but as a complex, shifting nexus of meaning and deferral of meaning that, like the sign itself, never refers to an ultimate and stable identity. Lucy doesn't "disappear"; increasingly, we begin to understand that the cypher as blank is the cypher as a mysterious sign of meaning never fully disclosed in this text. Like the French language that remains untranslated, hence undomesticated in the text, Lucy remains, as Mary Jacobus says, a foreigner in her own text.[14] Lucy's autobiography does not fully divulge her essence; her meaning, like retrospective narrative itself, leaves only a trace, but an important trace nevertheless.[15]

Lucy's ambiguous sign contrasts with the myth of the fully adequate letter or autograph purveyed by Paulina in reference to her lover Graham. After receiving a letter from Graham containing a proposal of marriage, Paulina examines his seal and his autograph, his "cypher" as decorative signature. In telling Lucy about her love for Graham, Paulina goes on to say: "Graham's hand is like himself, Lucy, and so is his seal — all clear, firm, and rounded — no slovenly splash of wax — a full, solid, steady drop — a distinct impress: no pointed turns harshly pricking the optic nerve, but a clean, mellow, pleasant manuscript, that soothes you as you read. It is like his face — just like the chiselling of his features: do you know his autograph?" (p. 542). Lucy's extended signature in the form of her narrative is also a "distinct impress," but in its textualization of Lucy it does anything but provide "a clean, mellow, pleasant manuscript"; it is anything but a "full, solid, steady drop."

Implicit in my discussion of the cypher is an argument that although "specularity" and viewing are of major importance in this novel, they cannot be divorced from the activities of reading and writing, that is, from textuality. Spying, viewing, observation, and voyeurism are all central activities in this mysterious narrative, but they are integrally connected to the reading of significance and the *writing* or tracing of significance in the story and the narrative. Within the story, experience is seen as a marking of the self and is related to what Brontë calls "impressibility" — the ability to be marked or changed by one's experience, to be *impressed* in the sense not only of recognizing significance but in being *altered* by it, one's self engraved by the writing of experience. Of Dr. John, Lucy says, "*impressionable* he was as dimpling water, but, almost as water, *unimpressible:* the breeze, the sun, moved him — metal could not grave, nor fire brand" (p. 372). The imagery of impression suggests that experience is engraved on one's face (and thus is expressed as "character"). In contrast to Graham's, Lucy's face, by the end of the novel, displays to her lover Paul the undeniable impress of their relationship.

> "Well," said he, after some seconds' scrutiny, "there is no denying that signature: Constancy wrote it; her pen is of iron. Was the record painful?"
> "Severely painful," I said, with truth, "Withdraw her hand, monsieur; I can bear its inscribing force no more." (p. 698)

The "writing" of experience on one's "character" is painful, Lucy reminds us, a refrain that I will discuss later in the context of Lucy's resistance to the disturbance of story.[16] And when Lucy desires to see Paul after her visit to Rue des Mages, she feels his countenance will offer "a page more lucid, more interesting than ever; I felt a longing to trace in it the imprint of that primitive devotedness, the signs of that half-knightly, half-saintly chivalry which the priest's narrative imputed to his nature" (p. 577). As Lucy's description indicates, her reading of the signs impressed on Paul is also a writing or "tracing." Referring to the overwhelming effect on her of Vashti's performance, Lucy says it was "set down in characters of tint indelible" in what she calls the "book of [her] life" (p. 373). It is only a step from this idea of memory as trace to the writing of the narrative. Lucy writes her story with "white cap on white hair" — as with Lucy herself as sign, we sense an elsewhere of meaning, a sense that writing is a textual memory, never fully capturing any "subject."

It is from this overall consideration of impressibility and the link between character and writing that I would like to move to the narrative of *Villette* as a difficult process of transforming the blank page into a mark of significance, of elaborating the cypher into story.

I have been suggesting that from Lucy's point of view, to make the "unwelcome blank" a subject for narration can be painful and risky. *Villette* begins with a kind of resistance to its own story. In describing herself at the beginning of her story, Lucy tells us that she "liked peace so well, and sought stimulus so little, that when the latter came I almost felt it a disturbance" (p. 7). A comparable resistance to the disturbance necessary for narrative to begin marks the opening of the novel. Two useful terms from D. A. Miller will help to clarify the nature of the resistance I wish to describe. Miller is concerned with what he calls the "impulses" that underlie the structure of narrative; he seeks to focus on the "underlying impulsions in the narratable."[17] Miller's theory, like the Freudian theory of Peter Brooks,[18] is based on a metaphor of desire expressed in the narrative and its reading. For Miller and Brooks, a story is generated out of some kind of unfulfilled demand. For Miller, "narratable" instances are those of "disequilibrium, suspense, and general insufficiency from which a given narrative appears to arise" and the "nonnarratable" is the "state of quiescence assumed by a novel before the beginning and supposedly recovered by it at the end" (p. ix). The nonnarratable, then, is that which fails to generate a story.

According to Lucy Snowe, decorum has it that the face of the plain heroine, Lucy's "unwelcome blank," is not under ordinary circumstances made visible or legible. In other words, it is ordinarily an insufficient subject to generate a story. And *Villette* begins, as numerous critics have pointed out, with Lucy's saying very little about herself and much more about those around her. But the idea of the text's resisting its own story goes further. Lucy begins her narrative with a description of the kind of quiescence that Miller posits as preexisting the plot. She presents a general picture of an Edenic world of domesticity at Bretton. In this world Lucy is a favored child by virtue of her status as "one child in a household of grown people" (p. 5). Lucy figures this happy world as the "full river" of time, "gliding" through a plain (p. 6). It is as if events do not as yet make an impression on the page; no scene is yet imprinted in the narrative memory. The narrative memory is like Graham, as "unimpressible as water." As Peter Brooks says, time is "constitutive of the novel form"; meaning "unfolds through time" (p. 92). At the beginning of *Villette*, Lucy gives us a figure of time in which time fails to signify meaning, to be impressed, to be disturbed from quiescence. Like the "cypher" as a figure that refuses to figure the protagonist, this "full river" of time refuses to figure a plot.[19] It is as if the narrative liked "peace" and "feared disturbance" as much as Lucy Snowe.

Presumably, Lucy shows us an unfallen world from which the plot will depart, for the general picture gives way reluctantly to the specific scene of Polly Home's arrival. Polly's intrusion jostles Lucy into life and the text into plot. It is thus very self-consciously that the plot begins with an intruding *letter*, as if Brontë were enacting a very self-conscious inscription of the blank page. Lucy thinks the letter might be "from home" — an occurrence that would seem to return the story to the nonnarratable by sending Lucy back to the mysterious origins from which she came. As Peter Brooks puts it, narrative is always in danger of "short-circuit," of a "temptation to oversameness." His Freudian figure for this aborted process is incest — the plot of love would, of course, be short-circuited by the marriage to, as he puts it, "the annihilating bride" (p. 109). Lucy's "plot" is indeed in danger of short-circuit and, interestingly, for the woman protagonist omitted from Brooks's deliberately male-centered version of desire, the short-circuit threatens to deprive her of any fictional life at all—to send her back to the mysterious womb from which she came. Again, this novel deliberately, self-consciously shows us the attraction of quiescence and the inertia that narrative needs to overcome.

But instead of a letter "from home," Lucy receives a letter from "Home," that is Mr. Home, announcing the arrival of Polly, "a second guest": Polly is the second guest, reminding us that Lucy is the first. We realize that the tranquil river of time has been a figure that covers over the fact that home is strange for an orphan like Lucy. The tranquil river, the unimpressible medium of time, becomes complicated, for the events it fails to be impressed by are "nonnarratable" not because too insignificant but because too painful. The reader begins to see other disturbing details within the seemingly tranquil opening descriptions. Lucy's favored status as the "one child in a household of grown people" is called into question by her subsequent reference to Graham as "not yet full-grown." The "explanation" that Graham is away at school fails to erase the direct contradiction emphasized by the verbal repetition. Thus, right at the beginning of her story, Lucy is displaced from the secure center of the story by Graham, the young privileged male character most likely to generate a "story" in a novel, a story of both ambition and love, whereas Lucy Snowe is unlikely to generate either. There is no quiescent origin of Lucy Snowe. Her "origins" are clearly vexed from the beginning. Time's "full river" is a covering figure for a nonexistent utopian "origin." We begin to sense why both Lucy and her text resist story and how the idea of quiescence is more problematic than Miller suggests.[20]

As Gilbert and Gubar have pointed out, Lucy overcomes her resistance to telling her story by telling the story of certain female doubles,[21] beginning with Polly. But Polly's story is interesting not merely by virtue of its thematic or psychological doubling of Lucy, for it is Polly's arrival that stirs Lucy into participating in the watching and interpreting that becomes her hallmark. Although, as I have suggested, the opening expository paragraphs describe Bretton and Lucy's stay there in general terms, it is not until Polly's crib and chest of drawers are placed in Lucy's room that Lucy herself becomes situated for us in her story—at the sight of these intruding possessions, Lucy says, "*I stood still, gazed, and considered. 'Of what are these things the signs and tokens?'* " (p. 7; emphasis added). And thus begins Lucy's engagement in the semiotic system. Polly gives Lucy something to see and interpret: "During tea, the minute thing's movements and behavior gave, as usual, full occupation to the eye" (p. 19). As the alienated style of the above quotation suggests, Lucy at first defends herself against being truly "impressed" by Polly. Lucy cultivates her own cool detachment and represses any incipient feeling. But throughout the early scenes with Polly, Lucy develops her powers. Polly is interesting *with* and *for* Lucy. As Lucy puts it, Polly "lavishes" her "eccentricities" on Lucy; with Mrs. Bretton, instead, Polly is uninteresting, conforming to the expectation that she will be a perfect little lady. Lucy "ceased to watch her under such circumstances: she was not interesting" (p. 30).

Lucy watches as Polly is inducted further into the gendered world of little girls, but it is the dynamic between Graham and Polly that fascinates Lucy the most. Although Lucy describes Polly as a "neat" little girl who "fingered nothing, or rather soiled nothing she fingered" (p. 38), she does leave a trace on Lucy, a trace recorded as the first important scene in Lucy's story.[22] When Polly leaves Bretton, the story once again threatens to sink into the nonnarratable. Lucy marks the place of this nonsignificance with another metaphor, this time an image of herself gliding over smooth seas as a "bark." "Picture me," she indulges the reader, "as a bark slumbering through halcyon weather" just the way "a great many women and girls are supposed to pass their lives" (p. 46). Again, we encounter an image of the happy self of Lucy Snowe gliding over the seas of time; again, the self-portrait ("Picture me") refuses to picture. In fact, Lucy quickly revises this portrait, telling us of the "shipwreck" that more accurately, albeit still metaphorically, describes her lonely life. For Lucy the conventional pieties about women's lives are nonnarratable, as she lets us know by briefly toying with this picture and then erasing it. At this point, however, the true circumstances of her painful situation are impossible to narrate. The figure serves as a kind of bandage, marking the place of the pain, but covering it over.

Again, Lucy and the narrative retreat into a kind of blankness. After the narrative and Lucy are rescued by Miss Marchmont, and tempted to retreat into oblivion at her death, Lucy records her decision to journey to London in the following terms: she says she has "nothing to lose," because the past was a "desert" to her. In effect, this provides another beginning and turns the previous three chapters of the novel into a prologue, a dispensable section *before* the real story gets under way. The narrative past as well as Lucy's personal past is dismissed as "nothing," and the narrative is in search of the narratable, just as Lucy searches for some kind of significance in her life.[23] Lucy's journey to a foreign country is her attempt and the narrative's to enhance narratability — to heighten the mystery in the telling, as Lucy, the decoder of signs and enigmatic sign herself, encounters the foreign.

It is fitting that in crossing the threshold of a foreign country, Lucy should meet up with the third woman to provide her gaze with an object — the young English girl, Ginevra Fanshawe. For it is against Ginevra's beauty that Lucy's plainness begins to make itself visible, and against Ginevra's "incapacity to endure" that we recognize Lucy's particular genius for survival. People like Ginevra, Lucy says, "seem to sour in adversity, like small-beer in thunder" (p. 77). Suited to the romantic plot that propels the "mystery" of the nun in the narrative, Ginevra is less fit for the kinds of "shipwrecks" of events and emotions weathered by Lucy. If

Ginevra's beauty and "Englishness" in Labassecour seem to bring her a degree of freedom, she is, ultimately, bound by the kind of romantic role she plays. Although native shrewdness makes her a sometimes canny and refreshing observer of Lucy, Ginevra's narcissism and selfishness prevent her from being a truly convincing interpreter of character and events.[24] She heaps her hazy impressions of the world into her favorite catch-all French word, "*chose*," as opposed to Lucy's attempt to cope with the difficulties of language. Ultimately, although she seems to play a central role in Lucy's narrative as an actor in its main romantic mystery, in Lucy's heart Ginevra fails to carve "the outline of a place" (p. 202).

In Labassecour, Lucy's habitual sense of powerlessness and inarticulateness is intensified. As an English girl in Belgium, Lucy is literally deprived of her language. Her situation is emblematic: she is the image of the powerless female, without the keys to the culture or the power of its privileged discourse. After losing her luggage as well as her language, Lucy is forced to appeal to a young, good-looking Englishman who can converse both in French and, as Lucy puts it, in "the Fatherland accents" (p. 83). Later on Lucy reveals that the young Englishman is none other than Graham. When he speaks for her and guides her, Lucy's response is, "I should almost as soon have thought of distrusting the Bible" (p. 85).

However, travel for Lucy alters the terms of both Lucy's anonymity and ambiguity, her roles as both reader and text. On the one hand, her silence and anonymity are increased in this strange land as is the threat of annihilating loneliness; on the other hand, the semiotic stakes increase: Lucy as decoder *and* as sign becomes more active. Lucy, the foreigner, is likely to be scrutinized, to be "read" by others, and to impress them with her foreign "character." She quickly becomes an enigma to Mme Beck's watchful eyes, even a secret code. The spying, reading, decoding that are the major activities conducted at Mme Beck's in a sense give Lucy greater existence and power, both as interpreter and sign. From the moment M. Paul is called upon by Mme Beck to "read" Lucy's face upon her arrival (and finds "bien des choses"), Lucy is given greater existence (pp. 90–91). The foreign locale in a sense prolongs narrative, offering, as it does, hermeneutic mysteries far beyond the gothic mystery of the nun in the Rue Fossette. As I have said earlier, however, this increased focus on Lucy as sign to be interpreted is a mixed blessing, for, particularly in a foreign culture, Lucy is misread.

Yet, with all the energy generated by this foreign system of signs, the first volume of the novel ends with a chapter that poses the greatest threat to Lucy's narrative and narratability to be encountered. In despair after a terrifying dream in which she sees herself as totally unloved and insignificant, Lucy seeks out a priest. After speaking with Lucy, he enjoins her to return. Lucy describes her refusal as a choice of writing over silence, and heresy over an orthodoxy that would abort the story. It is in this section that she *names* her "heretic narrative," and, although her decision to write has *preceded* the first word of the narrative, this point in the text posits a crucial choice, as if it were occurring at the moment: "The probabilities are that had I visited Numéro 3, Rue des Mages, at the hour and day appointed, I might just now, instead of writing this heretic narrative, be counting my beads in the cell of a certain Carmelite convent on the Boulevard of Crécy in Villette" (p. 228).

This passage posits a very different destiny for Lucy and her text, for what is suggested is not only the return of Lucy to silence, but the *erasure of the entire narrative* as well. For a moment the intriguing mystery of the nun in the Rue Fossette threatens to be replaced by a nun whose story does not intrigue, whose privation is nonnarratable. It is here that Lucy defines narrative itself as *transgression*, a refusal to conform either to the conventional pieties of a young girl's life, or to the orthodox piety and self-denial of the convent.

The image of silence, however, is imagined as the outcome of a scene of confession to the priest. This once-and-for-all telling, this confession, would end all telling. As opposed to the audience for the "heretic narrative," this male authority would rob Lucy of her power to make and record impressions. This "father" is the kind of "blocking figure," to use Peter Brooks's term, that threatens to become an impediment to the protagonist's desire. It is worth quoting Brooks, however, to illustrate how gendered his "masterplot" is and how different the kind and outcome of the "blocking figure" in Brontë. Speaking of the hero's desire and ambition as the driving force of the narrative, Brooks says, "ambition provides . . . a dominant dynamic of plot, a force that drives the protagonist forward, assuming that no incident or action is final or closed in itself until such a moment as the ends of ambition have been clarified, through success or remuneration" (p. 39). Brooks speaks of the typical blocking figures in fiction, who provide the impediment upon which narrative thrives for the redoubling of its energy; he also speaks, elsewhere, of the kind of "annihilating bride" that threatens to halt the story for good. The priest to whom Lucy confesses threatens indeed to be a kind of "annihilating bride." It is not incest or taboo but orthodoxy and conformity that threaten to abort Lucy's narrative and whatever "ambition" she has. Similarly, Lucy later thinks of the priest as capable of erasing Paul's "fraternal communion with a heretic." "I seemed to hear Père Silas annulling the unholy pact," she writes (p. 600). Thus, orthodoxy and erasure are linked in the figure of "annulment"; the double plots of ambition and love are potentially threatened.

Although Brooks acknowledges the differences in "female plots," where the protagonist encounters a counterdynamic of "overt and isolating male plots of ambition" (p. 39), he fails to account for both the female protagonist's own attraction to silence, and the more complicated role that male figures can play.[25] If the Catholic father is a "blocking figure" who symbolizes the potential death of the heretic narrative, M. Paul is a more complex figure who combines blocking and enabling functions. As Lucy becomes intrigued by M. Paul's gruff attention, she comments to herself on the difference between "[her] own and [her] friends' impressions" and those of M. Paul. While Graham sees her as "a creature inoffensive as a shadow," Paul recognizes her passion and imagination (p. 482). He is the one male character who helps draw out the meaning of Lucy Snowe and, in turn, challenges her abilities in tracing his character. And yet, the very power of his presence as opposed to Lucy's threatens to overwhelm her. If she lacks the impromptu faculty, he "possessed it in perfection," a talent that makes Lucy marvel (p. 551). If it is Paul's presence that enables the love plot to continue, it is, as Karen Chase points out, Paul's absence that allows the plot of ambition to thrive—Lucy succeeds as a headmistress *and* writer, in the spaces provided by Paul's absence. The narrative energies that seem to be winding down with Lucy's outburst of passion and confession of love are revived for one last ambiguous chapter ("Finis") by his departure.

Three years pass, and Lucy tells us "Reader, they were the three happiest years of my life" (p. 711). Paradoxically, Lucy is nourished by his absence, for it is Paul's letters that provide "real food that nourished" (p. 713). Lucy's own body is *fed* by his letters in his absence; Paul's "full-handed, full-hearted plentitude," unlike Graham's more facile autograph, provides real sustenance for Lucy, but it is the distance between them that allows her writing to flourish. The "final evasion," as Mary Jacobus puts it,[26] the return to the covering figure, brings the reader to an ambiguous ending and the same "sunny" quiescence with which the narrative begins: "Here pause: pause at once. There is enough said. Trouble no quiet, kind heart; leave sunny imaginations hope. . . . Let them picture union and a happy succeeding life" (p. 715). Lucy returns us to herself as writer, "figuring" her story and its arbitrary ending ("enough said"). The space provided by Paul's absence has allowed for the writing of the "heretic narrative"; it allows a space for Lucy to record her experience with "resolute pen." Somewhere between disclosure and reticence, Lucy makes the cypher signify powerfully, although never completely, in a genre in which we are accustomed to seeing a different kind of beauty shine.

Notes

1. Charlotte Brontë, *Villette*, ed. Herbert Rosengarten and Margaret Smith, Clarendon Edition of the Novels of the Brontës (Oxford: Clarendon Press, 1984), p. 697. Subsequent references to *Villette* are to this edition and appear in the text.

2. See especially, "The Buried Life of Lucy Snowe," chapter 12 in Sandra M. Gilbert and Susan Gubar, *The Madwoman in the Attic: The Woman Writer and the Nineteenth-Century Literary Imagination* (New Haven: Yale Univ. Press, 1979), pp. 399–440, and Brenda R. Silver, "The Reflecting Reader in *Villette*" in *The Voyage In: Fictions of Female Development*, ed. Elizabeth Abel et al. (Hanover and London: Univ. Press of New England, 1983), pp. 90–111.

3. Interestingly, Gilbert and Gubar quote a line from a poem by Anne Finch that draws on two meanings of the word "cypher"—"nonentity" and arithmetical "zero" placed next to "male" integers: "Whilst we beside you but as Cyphers stand, / T'increase your Numbers and to swell th'account / Of your delights . . ." (p. 9).

4. On the history of the visual arts, see John Berger et al., *Ways of Seeing* (London: Penguin, 1972).

5. See Nancy K. Miller's discussion of the two "plots" in women's fiction and the way their inscriptions differ from those in fiction written by men ("Emphasis Added: Plots and Plausibilities in Women's Fiction," in *The New Feminist Criticism: Essays on Women, Literature and Theory*, ed. Elaine Showalter [New York: Pantheon, 1985], pp. 339–60). It is true that Lucy later wants Paul to find her attractive, but by this point he is able to read her character and see her face as expressively "beautiful."

6. "The Buried Letter: Feminism and Romanticism in *Villette*," in *Women Writing and Writing About Women*, ed. Mary Jacobus (London: Croom Helm, 1979), p. 45.

7. See Christina Crosby, "Charlotte Brontë's Haunted Text," *Studies in English Literature*, 24 (1984), 701; and Tony Tanner, Introduction to *Villette* (New York: Penguin, 1979), p. 20.

8. Vashti was the Queen of King Ahasuerus before Esther. Drunk with wine, Ahasuerus summoned Vashti to the banquet hall to display her beauty to his guests: when she refused, the King divorced her. The actress Vashti, who makes such an indelible impression on Lucy, does perform for the world's gaze, but Vashti is anything but passive object of that gaze. "She stood before her audience," we are told, "neither yielding to, nor enduring, nor in finite measure, resenting it: she stood locked in struggle, rigid in resistance" (p. 369). What Vashti embodies so completely and fully is female power, passion, and rage. The dynamic and potent meaning of Vashti on stage contrasts in Lucy's mind with the more static portraits of women, like Cleopatra, who are worshipped by the male gaze.

9. For an excellent discussion of the "gendered" reading of characters and texts, see Annette Kolodny, "A Map for Rereading: Gender and the Interpretation of Literary Texts," in *The New Feminist Criticism*, ed. Showalter, pp. 46–62.

10. In "The Laugh of the Medusa," Hélène Cixous speaks of woman's fear of speaking in public, of exposing her body in public: "Every woman has known the torment of getting up to speak. Her heart racing, at times entirely lost for words, ground and language slipping away—that's how daring a feat, how great a transgression it is for a woman to speak—even just open her mouth—in public" (trans. Keith Cohen and Paula Cohen, rpt. in *The "Signs" Reader: Women, Gender and Scholarship*, ed. Elizabeth Abel and Emily K. Abel [Chicago: Univ. of Chicago Press, 1983], p. 284).

11. Silver, "The Reflecting Reader in *Villette*," pp. 90–92, 104.

12. *Eros and Psyche: The Representation of Personality in Charlotte Brontë, Charles Dickens, and George Eliot* (New York and London: Methuen, 1984), p. 70.

13. *Speculum of the Other Woman*, trans. Gillian C. Gill (Ithaca: Cornell Univ. Press, 1985), p. 50.

14. "The Buried Letter," p. 43.

15. See "Charlotte Brontë's Haunted Text," Christina Crosby's fine discussion of Brontë's radical critique of consciousness in *Villette*. Crosby focuses on the specularity in the novel, showing how a series of mirrorings and doublings subverts the clear distinctions between the self and the other (p. 715).

16. In the above quotation, it is Paul to whom Lucy attributes the power to inscribe her "character." Although the complexity of the reciprocal process of inscription between Lucy and Paul qualifies the topos of the male writing on the blank page of the woman, Paul is the writing master who aggressively tries to leave his imprint on Lucy. The rhetoric of textuality applied to Lucy's and Paul's relationship is at times almost egalitarian, as when he tells her

they have similar "impressions" (I say "almost," because it is *he* who instructs *her* how to read their similar characters in the mirror.) On the other hand, Paul often tries to force Lucy to be written on or to write his way, even asking her at one point to be his amanuensis (p. 552). I will return to this crucial relationship later.

17. D. A. Miller, *Narrative and Its Discontents: Problems of Closure in the Traditional Novel* (Princeton: Princeton Univ. Press, 1981), p. ix.

18. *Reading for the Plot: Design and Intention in Narrative* (New York: Knopf, 1984). Further citations of this work appear parenthetically in the text.

19. Karen Chase in *Eros and Psyche* discusses the "narrative ataraxy" in the first part of the novel, primarily to comment on its relation to Lucy's passivity (p. 68). My own interest involves broader issues of representation and desire in the narrative.

20. Miller's book is excellent in discussing the playing out of narratable impulse, but I have some difficulty with his idea of "nonnarratable," which, for him, deliberately excludes the "unspoken." There seems a fine line between the quiescent and the repressed which Miller does not discuss.

21. *Madwoman in the Attic,* p. 404.

22. Later on in the novel, Lucy discovers these early scenes have left an indelible mark on "the book" of Polly's life as well. When Lucy encounters Polly years later, she supposes that the latter has "outgrown the impressions" of her youth. "The deep imprint must be softened away and effaced?" Lucy asks Polly (p. 396). But Polly tells Lucy she indeed remembers everything; Polly turns out to be a woman capable of impressibility, but one who lacks Lucy's own power to engrave these impressions in a text.

23. How different is Lucy's sense that she has nothing to lose from that of the typical heroine of the English novel, whose chastity is worth losing, and the preservation or loss of which is worth relating in a narrative. Of course, these early memories are not merely preamble in the narrative, for they leave a marked imprint on Lucy as well as Polly. If Lucy attempts to put Bretton behind her, tucked away only as a myth of origin, the plot will bring "Bretton" back in the uncanny scene of Lucy's awakening from her illness in the home of Mrs. Bretton.

24. Graham's final disenchantment with Ginevra occurs because she is incapable of truly reading the significance of Mrs. Bretton (pp. 310–12).

25. Nancy K. Miller's "Emphasis Added" provides a wonderful corrective to the androcentric model Brooks offers.

26. "The Buried Letter," p. 54.

INDEX